JOHN WESLEY
AND THE
RELIGIOUS SOCIETIES

JOHN WESLEY
AND THE
RELIGIOUS SOCIETIES

BY
JOHN S. SIMON, D.D.

AUTHOR OF
'A SUMMARY OF METHODIST LAW AND DISCIPLINE,'
'THE REVIVAL OF RELIGION IN ENGLAND IN THE EIGHTEENTH CENTURY,'
ETC.

WIPF & STOCK · Eugene, Oregon

Wipf and Stock Publishers
199 W 8th Ave, Suite 3
Eugene, OR 97401

John Wesley and the Religious Societies
By Simon, John S.
Copyright©1921 Methodist Publishing - Epworth Press
ISBN 13: 978-1-5326-3832-9
Publication date 7/27/2017
Previously published by Epworth Press, 1921

Every effort has been made to trace the current copyright owner
of this publication but without success. If you have any
information or interest in the copyright, please contact the publishers.

PREFACE

CANON OVERTON, in his *Life in the English Church*, 1660–1714, says that 'there is no doubt that John Wesley intended his Societies to be an exact repetition of what was done by Beveridge, Horneck, and Smythies sixty-two years before.' He continues: 'How it was that the Methodist Societies took a different course is a very interesting, and, to a churchman, a very sad question.' In this book I have given descriptions of the first Religious Societies, and have shown their development under the influence of Dr. Woodward and John Wesley. From those descriptions my readers will be able to judge the accuracy of Canon Overton's statement concerning John Wesley's intentions. There can be no doubt, however, that the relationship between the 'Religious Societies' and the 'United Societies of the People called Methodists' was so close that the latter cannot be understood without an intimate knowledge of the former.

In writing this book, I have kept the Methodist Church in view. My eyes have been fixed on John Wesley and the England in which his greatest work was done. We can never understand the revival of religion which glorified the eighteenth century until we see Wesley as he was, and get rid of the false impressions created by writers who have had an imperfect acquaintance with him and his evangelistic work.

It is impossible for me, in this place, to express my obligations to all those who have helped me to write this book. I am deeply in their debt. While acknowledging my indebtedness to those who have preceded me in the study of Methodist history, I must make special reference to the editor and the annotators of the Standard Edition of *The Journal of John Wesley*. That book has been my constant guide. I am also indebted to my fellow-workers of the Wesley Historical Society for the kindly light they have shed on many difficulties. The *Publications* and the *Proceedings* of the Society have been invaluable. To Mr. Arthur Wallington, who has read the proofs, and to the Rev. John Elsworth, who has compiled the Index, my special thanks are due. J. S. S.

August, 1921.

CONTENTS

CHAP.		PAGE.
I.	THE RELIGIOUS SOCIETIES	9
II.	WESTLEYS AND ANNESLEYS	28
III.	SAMUEL AND SUSANNA WESLEY	46
IV.	OXFORD IN THE EIGHTEENTH CENTURY	64
V.	JOHN AND CHARLES WESLEY AT OXFORD	75
VI.	'THE HOLY CLUB'	89
VII.	GEORGIA	106
VIII.	THE VOYAGE TO GEORGIA	115
IX.	FIRST DAYS IN GEORGIA	126
X.	WORK IN GEORGIA	140
XI.	LAST DAYS IN GEORGIA	157
XII.	THE GREAT CHANGE	174
XIII.	A NEW RELIGIOUS SOCIETY	194
XIV.	OXFORD AND GERMANY	201
XV.	CHARLES WESLEY	213
XVI.	CONFLICTS WITH THE LAW	223
XVII.	THE APPROACHING CRISIS	239
XVIII.	GEORGE WHITEFIELD	249
XIX.	BRISTOL IN 1739	264
XX.	JOHN WESLEY'S FIRST VISIT TO BRISTOL	280
XXI.	DECISIVE DAYS	296
XXII.	THE WEST OF ENGLAND	308
XXIII.	A NEW SOCIETY	322
	INDEX	335

I

THE RELIGIOUS SOCIETIES

IN the *London Magazine* for 1760 a letter from John Wesley appears. It was written in answer to an attack on him by one of his numerous literary antagonists, and its purpose was to give his assailant a clearer knowledge of the people whose proceedings had roused his anger. The letter contains sentences which shed light on the origin of the Methodist Church. Wesley says, 'About thirty years since I met with a book written in King William's time, called *The Country Parson's Advice to His Parishioners*. There I read these words : " If good men of the Church will unite together in the several parts of the kingdom, disposing themselves into friendly societies, and engaging each other, in their respective combinations, to be helpful to each other in all good Christian ways, it will be the most effectual means for restoring our decaying Christianity to its primitive life and vigour, and the supporting of our tottering and sinking Church." A few young gentlemen, then at Oxford, approved and followed the advice. They were all zealous Churchmen, and both orthodox and regular to the highest degree. For their exact regularity they were soon nicknamed Methodists. . . . Nine or ten years after many others " united together in the several parts of the kingdom, engaging, in like manner, to be helpful to each other in all good Christian ways." . . . Their one design was to forward each other in true Scriptural Christianity.'[1]

Wesley was mistaken in supposing that the book which had made so deep an impression on him was written ' in King William's time.' It was first published in 1680, in the reign of Charles II. It bears no author's name. In 1701, the year before King William died, a second edition was issued, and this was the book to which Wesley referred. It was carefully read and industriously distributed by the members of the 'Holy Club' at Oxford.

[1] Wesley's *Works*, xiii., 350, 351, 8vo ed.

THE RELIGIOUS SOCIETIES

The date of the first publication of the book is suggestive. About the year 1678, during the reign of Charles II,[1] through the influence of Dr. Anthony Horneck and Mr. Smithies, a number of young men in London who were seeking to lead a holy life began to meet together once a week in order that they might ' apply themselves to good discourse and to things wherein they might edify one another.'[2] Two years after the commencement of these Religious Societies *The Country Parson's Advice to his Parishioners* appeared, and it is natural to suppose that the idea contained in his book was suggested by his knowledge of the work the Societies were doing in Westminster and elsewhere. It is certain that Wesley was aware of the existence of these Societies, and was familiar with their organization. The origin, purpose, and character of the Methodist Societies can only be understood by bearing that fact in mind.

We are indebted to Dr. Josiah Woodward's *Account of the Rise and Progress of the Religious Societies in the City of London, &c.*, for the fullest information obtainable on the subject of the Religious Societies. The fourth edition, enlarged, is dated 1712, and from it much knowledge can be derived. As we wish to show the affinities between the Religious and the Methodist Societies we will avail ourselves of information not contained in Woodward's little book. It is necessary to understand the character of the first Societies, those formed under the direction of Dr. Horneck. We confine ourselves to one point. It is well known that he was chosen as the adviser of several of them. He drew up the following rules for the regulation of their meetings:

1. All that enter the Society shall resolve upon a holy and serious life.
2. No person shall be admitted into the Society until he has arrived at the age of sixteen, and has been first confirmed by the bishop, and solemnly taken upon himself his baptismal vow.
3. They shall choose a minister of the Church of England to direct them.
4. They shall not be allowed, in their meetings, to discourse of any controverted point of divinity.

---

[1] Care must be taken to distinguish between the first Religious Societies and the 'regulated Societies.' Overton's *Life in the English Church*, 1660–1714, contains some valuable information concerning the origin of the Societies. See 207–13.

[2] Woodward's *Account of the Rise and Progress of the Religious Societies*, 22.

5. Neither shall they discourse of the government of Church or State.

6. In their meetings they shall use no prayers but those of the Church, such as the Litany and Collects, and other prescribed prayers; but still they shall not use any that peculiarly belongs to the minister, as the Absolution.

7. The minister whom they choose shall direct what practical divinity shall be read at these meetings.

8. They may have liberty, after prayer and reading, to sing a psalm.

9. After all is done, if there be time left, they may discourse with each other about their spiritual concerns; but this shall not be a standing exercise which any shall be obliged to attend unto.

10. One day in the week shall be appointed for this meeting, for such as cannot come on the Lord's Day; and he that absents himself without cause shall pay threepence to the box.

11. Every time they meet, every one shall give sixpence to the box.

12. On a certain day in the year, viz. Whit-Tuesday, two stewards shall be chosen, and a moderate dinner provided, and a sermon preached, and the money distributed (necessary charges deducted) to the poor.

13. A book shall be bought, in which these orders shall be written.

14. None shall be admitted into this Society without the consent of the minister who presides over it; and no apprentice shall be capable of being chosen.

15. If any case of conscience shall arise, it shall be brought before the minister.

16. If any member think fit to leave the Society, he shall pay five shillings to the stock.

17. The major part of the Society shall conclude the rest.

18. The following rules are more especially recommended to the members of this Society, viz. To love one another. When reviled, not to revile again. To speak evil of no man. To wrong no man. To pray, if possible, seven times a day. To keep close to the Church of England. To transact all things peaceably and gently. To be helpful to each other. To use themselves to holy thoughts in their coming in and going out. To examine themselves every night. To give every one their due. To obey superiors, both spiritual and temporal.[1]

The rules drawn up by Dr. Horneck determined the main lines of organization and administration existing in the first Religious Societies. But the law of development worked and produced important changes. The effects of that law can be seen when we compare Dr. Horneck's rules with those which governed most of the 'regulated' Societies in Dr. Woodward's time. He says that 'though there be some little variations in

---

[1] Life of Anthony Horneck, D.D., Prebendary of Westminster and Preacher at the Savoy, in Hone's *Lives of Eminent Christians*, ii., 309, 310.

the orders of some of these Societies from others, yet the substance of them is generally one and the same.'[1] We will take the 'Specimen of the Orders of the Societies,' copied out of the Poplar book, as showing a Religious Society at its best. It must be remembered that Dr. Woodward was the 'minister of Poplar.' The orders, therefore, are of exceptional value. They are as follows:

I. That the sole design of this Society being to promote real holiness of heart and life, it is absolutely necessary that the persons who enter into it do seriously resolve, by the grace of God, to apply themselves to all means proper to accomplish these blessed ends. Trusting in the divine power and gracious conduct of the Holy Spirit, through our Lord Jesus Christ, to excite, advance, and perfect all good in us.

II. That in order to their being of one heart and one mind in this design, every member of this Society shall own and manifest himself to be of the Church of England, and frequent the Liturgy, and other public exercises of the same. And that they be careful withal to express due Christian charity, candour, and moderation towards all such Dissenters as are of good conversation.

III. That the members of this Society shall meet together one evening in the week at a convenient place, in order to encourage each other in practical holiness, by discoursing on such subjects as tend thereunto; observing the Holy Scriptures as their rule, and praying to God for His grace and blessing. And to this assembly any serious person, known to any of the Society, may be admitted upon request.

IV. That at such meetings they decline all disputes about controversial points, and all unnecessary discourse about State affairs, or the concerns of trade and worldly things; and that the whole bent of the discourse be to glorify God and edify one another in love.

V. That it be left to every person's discretion to contribute at every weekly meeting what he thinks fit towards a public stock for pious and charitable uses; especially for putting poor children to school. And the money thus collected shall be kept by the two stewards of the Society, who shall be chosen by majority of votes once a year, or oftener, to be disposed of by the consent of the major part of the Society for the uses above mentioned. And the said stewards shall keep a faithful register of what is thus collected and distributed, to be perused by any member of the Society at his request.

VI. That any respective member may recommend any object of charity to the stewards, who shall (with the consent of the rest) give out of the common stock according as the occasion requires. And in a case of extraordinary necessity every particular person shall be desired to contribute farther, as he shall think fit.

VII. That every one that absents himself four meetings together

---

[1] Woodward's *Account*, 118.

(without giving a satisfactory account to the stewards) shall be looked upon as disaffected to the Society.

VIII. That none shall be admitted into this Society without giving due notice thereof to the stewards, who shall acquaint the whole Society therewith. And after due inquiry into their religious purposes and manner of life, the stewards may admit them if the major part of the Society allows of it, and not otherwise. And with the like joint consent they may exclude any member proved guilty of any misbehaviour, after due admonition, unless he gives sufficient testimony of his repentance and amendment before the whole Society.

IX. It is hereby recommended to every person concerned in this Society to consider the dangerous snares of gaming, and the open scandal of being concerned in those games which are used in public-houses; and that it is the safest and most commendable way to decline them wholly, shunning all unnecessary resort to such houses and taverns, and wholly avoiding lewd play-houses.

X. That whereas the following duties have been too much neglected, to the scandal and reproach of our holy religion, they do resolve, by the grace of God, to make it their serious endeavour:

1. To be just in all their dealings, even to an exemplary strictness (as 1 Thess. iv. 6).

2. To pray many times every day; remembering our continual dependence upon God both for spiritual and temporal things (1 Thess. v. 17).

3. To partake of the Lord's Supper at least once a month, if not prevented by a reasonable impediment (1 Cor. xi. 26; Luke xxii. 19).

4. To practise the profoundest meekness and humility (Matt. xi. 29).

5. To watch against censuring others (Matt. vii. 1).

6. To accustom themselves to holy thoughts in all places (Ps. cxxxix. 23).

7. To be helpful one to another (1 Cor. xii. 25).

8. To exercise tenderness, patience, and compassion towards all men (Titus iii. 2).

9. To make reflection on themselves when they read the Holy Bible, or other good books, and when they hear sermons (1 Cor. x. 11).

10. To shun all foreseen occasions of evil, as evil company, known temptations, &c. (1 Thess. v. 22).

11. To think often on the different estates of the glorified and the damned in the unchangeable eternity to which we are hastening (Luke xvi. 25).

12. To examine themselves every night what good or evil they have done in the day past (2 Cor. xiii. 5).

13. To keep a private fast once a month (especially near their approach to the Lord's Table) if at their own disposal, or to fast from some meals when they may conveniently (Matt. vi. 16; Luke v. 35).

14. To mortify the flesh with its affections and lusts (Gal. v. 19, 24).

15. To advance in heavenly-mindedness, and in all grace (1 Pet. iii. 8).

16. To shun spiritual pride, and the effects of it; as railing, anger, peevishness, and impatience of contradiction, and the like.

17. To pray for the whole Society in their private prayers (Jas. v. 16).

18. To read pious books often for their edification, but especially the Holy Bible (John v. 39); and herein particularly Matt. v., vi., vii.; Luke xv., xvi.; Rom. xii., xiii.; Eph. v., vi.; 1 Thess. v.; Rev. i., ii., iii., xxi., xxii. And in the Old Testament Lev. xxvi.; Deut. xxviii.; Isa. liii.; Ezek. xxxvi.

19. To be continually mindful of the great obligation of this special profession of religion; and to walk circumspectly, that none may be offended or discouraged from it by what they see in them; nor occasion given to any to speak reproachfully of it.

20. To shun all manner of affectation and moroseness, and be of a civil and obliging deportment to all men.

XI. That they often consider (with an awful dread of God's wrath) the sad height to which the sins of many are advanced in this our nation; and the bleeding divisions thereof in Church and State. And that every member be ready to do what, upon consulting with each other, shall be thought advisable towards the punishment of public profaneness, according to the good laws of our land, required to be put in execution by the Queen's and the late King's[1] special order. And to do what befits them in their stations in order to the cementing of our divisions.

XII. That each member shall encourage the catechizing of young and ignorant people in their respective families, according to their stations and abilities; and shall observe all manner of religious family duties.

XIII. That the major part of the Society shall have power to make a new order to bind the whole, when need requires, if it be approved by three pious and learned ministers of the Church of England, nominated by the whole Society.

XIV. That these orders shall be read over at least four times in the year, by one of the stewards; and that with such deliberation that each member may have time to examine himself by them, or to speak his mind in anything relating to them.

XV. Lastly, that every member of this Society shall (after mature deliberation and due trial) express his approbation of these orders, and his resolution to endeavour to live up to them. In order to which, he shall constantly keep a copy of them by him.[2]

The 'Orders' of the Poplar Religious Society show the high Christian aim of those who drew them up, and those who consented to be governed by them. It is essential to note that

---

[1] The references are to Anne and William III.
[2] Woodward's *Account of the Rise and Progress of the Religious Societies*, 107–15.

THE RELIGIOUS SOCIETIES

the 'sole design' of the Societies was 'to promote real holiness of heart and life,' and it is clear that the pursuit of holiness was conducted with the intelligent enthusiasm of practical men, who were ready to adopt methods which had been proved effective by experience.

Our knowledge of the character and proceedings of the Religious Societies is increased by the information given by Dr. Woodward in his chapter entitled 'Directions for Religious Conference, with Prayers for the use of Religious Societies, and upon other Occasions.'[1] From this chapter we will select a few important points.

The relation of the Societies to the Church of England is affirmed in the 'Orders,' and taken for granted in the 'Directions.' In the latter Woodward says that it is very expedient that an 'orthodox and pious' minister should be chosen by each Society as its director and visitor, 'to preserve order, excite zeal, and resolve doubts.' He suggests that this director should be chosen every year by a majority of votes when the stewards were elected. He should receive no salary or reward. When present he led the devotions of the Society. It is possible for us to follow the course of proceedings in a Religious Society such as that at Poplar. A competent number of members having assembled, the director took charge of the meeting. When the minister was absent one of the stewards, or 'any other person desired,' occupied his place. The 'Directions' contain a form of service which was to be used. It is founded on the Liturgy of the Church of England, but contains several significant changes. It is, evidently, prepared for the use of laymen who were stewards. In its rubrics the word 'steward' takes the place of 'minister.' Its compilers saw that, owing to the lack of 'pious and orthodox' ministers, the conduct of the Societies, in some places, would fall into the hands of laymen. The Society whose proceedings we are watching is one in which no clergyman is present, and we have an opportunity of seeing the emergence of a Church of England layman into the prominent position of a conductor of the worship of the Society. After an opening exhortation the steward repeats three collects taken from the Book of Common Prayer. He then reads one of the chapters set down in the tenth 'Order.' The lesson is read slowly, the steward obeying

[1] *Account*, &c., 132–57.

the direction to pause so long at the end of every verse, that any one may have the opportunity to make any serious remark upon it. As an alternative, instead of this exercise ' some part of an approved exposition on the Holy Scriptures, or on the Catechism,' might be read. At this point a conference on ' one of the most important duties of our holy religion ' takes place, the subject having been proposed at the close of the previous weekly assembly. A list of forty appropriate subjects appears in the ' Directions.' It will be sufficient to indicate a few of them in order to understand the character of this important conference : The duty of self-examination ; Faith in our Lord Jesus Christ ; Evangelical repentance ; Effectual conversion to God ; Christian charity, including the love of God and the love of men ; Of endeavouring the conversion and salvation of others ; The sense of God's omnipresence; and Reading the Holy Scriptures. Woodward explains that he suggests forty subjects in order to assign one for every weekly ' conference ' in the year, reserving twelve weeks for discourses on the Lord's Supper, which, he says, ' every member is obliged, by the orders of the Society, to receive, where he may with conveniency, twelve times in the year.[1] By the selection of these topics it was intended that the chief parts of Christian duty should be considered and gone through every year, to the great increase of knowledge and practice. In the ' conversation ' no person was to speak above three or four sentences without a convenient pause, to give room to others to speak their mind ; in case of silence he might proceed, but with the same caution. In the absence of the clerical director, Woodward suggests that one of the stewards might propose the following questions when the duty to be spoken of was named : ' 1. Wherein consists the nature of this duty ? 2. What directions do you propose in order to make the practice of it more sure and more easy ? 3. What discouragements do any of you find in the practice of it ? 4. What motives may encourage our practice of this duty and our perseverance in it ? '

When the ' conference ' ended the devotional service was resumed. It consisted of the reading of certain sentences from the Scriptures, an admonition before prayer, the General Confession from the Liturgy, and ' a prayer for perfect remission and forgiveness,' which the steward alone was to say.

[1] *Account*, 138.

THE RELIGIOUS SOCIETIES

Before the singing of a psalm the steward read an 'Admonition to the praise of God.'

Singing in the Religious Societies was a special feature of their meetings. It is mentioned by Woodward with fervour. The singing accorded with the closing words of the 'Admonition': 'Let us, therefore, now strain up our affections to the highest pitch, and so sing the praises of God in heart and spirit, that angels and saints may join with us now, and we with them for evermore.' After the repetition of the Apostles' Creed prayers were read, one of them being a prayer for the Society, specially composed for such occasions. Then, all standing up, an exhortation to humility was read, another psalm was sung, and the meeting ended with the great sentences from the Communion Service, in which the communicants join with angels and archangels and with all the company of heaven in lauding and magnifying the glorious Name of God. The steward then dismissed the assembly with the Benediction.

The full service, as it appears in Woodward's *Account*, is long, but the conductor had liberty to shorten it at his discretion. When the clerical director was present he seems to have taken the service into his own hands and to have determined the course of its proceedings.

The progress of development is strongly marked in Dr. Woodward's 'Directions.' In Dr. Horneck's time the discourse about spiritual concerns among the members of the Societies was expressly said to be 'not a standing exercise which any shall be obliged to attend unto.' There can be no doubt that such discourses occurred in the earliest meetings. Speaking of the original society formed in the reign of Charles II, Dr. Woodward expressly says, 'These young men soon found the benefit of their conferences one with another, by which, as some of them have told me with joy, they better discovered their own corruptions, the devil's temptations, and how to countermine his subtle devices; as to which each person communicated his experiences to the rest.' These conversations with the veterans of the movement confirmed the conviction of the value of 'the discourses about spiritual concerns,' and we see that Dr. Woodward provided for them in the 'Directions.' It must be remembered that much had happened since Dr. Horneck's time. There had been a partial collapse of the Societies in the reign of James II. That collapse was arrested in the time of William and Mary. In the reign of Anne the Societies greatly prospered. It was during this period of prosperity that Dr. Woodward's book was written. It shows us the Societies at the height of their organization, and we do not wonder that a conversation about the spiritual experience of the members formed a distinct part of the proceedings. This fact intensifies their interest in the eyes of all who are acquainted with the history of the Churches of England.

Another fact possesses peculiar importance. We have shown that, in the opinion of Dr. Woodward, it was 'very expedient' that 'an orthodox and pious minister' should be chosen by each Society as its director. Dr. Horneck's rules were more explicit. A minister of the Church of England had to be chosen as the director, and no person could be admitted into the Society without his consent. The rapid multiplication of the Societies, and the difficulty of discovering a sufficient number of suitable ministers, in the reign of Queen Anne compelled a relaxation of the stringent rule. The force of circumstances prevailed. If a clergyman could not be secured to conduct the religious service in a Society a layman was permitted to take his place. He read the prayers and conducted the 'conversation.' If in the course of the 'conversation' questions concerning doctrine and the meaning of biblical statements arose, which the steward might not be competent to answer, a special arrangement was made. It was provided that in their reading of those practical portions of Holy Scripture to which their 'Orders' direct them they were to have recourse to Dr. Hammond's *Exposition*, or some other author recommended by their minister.[1] When a Society did not possess a clerical director we presume that this suggestion would lead to the adoption of some Commentary as a standard of appeal in cases of difficulty. These facts concerning the employment of laymen as conductors of the religious worship, and the guides of the spiritual conversations of the members of the Societies, possess prophetic value.

It was inevitable that some ecclesiastically-minded persons would watch the proceedings of the Religious Societies with suspicion. They suggested that ill and designing men might get into the Societies, as popish emissaries had into some others,

---

[1] Woodward's *Account*, 120.

and quite pervert their design to the prejudice of the Church; that there was a danger of schism and dissension in the weekly meetings; that by their reproving and admonishing those with whom they conversed, and by their visiting the sick, and sometimes praying with them, they invaded and intruded upon the minister's office; and, finally, that since a Church of Christ is a Society of Christian people, and these Societies were erected in a reformed Church, they were Societies within a Society, and 'a refining upon a reformed Church.'

Dr. Woodward's book contains short answers to these objections. It will suffice to quote his reply to the last. Speaking in behalf of the Societies, he says: ' 1. They have not yet learned that the reading of God's Word and conferring on the practical points of religion, in order to a more holy conversation, hath at any time, by good men, been thought prejudicial to the Church of Christ. On the contrary, our best Divines recommend these things both from the pulpit and the press as the best expedients to support and adorn our reformed Church and render it worthy of that venerable name. 2. They do not well understand what the objector means by refining upon our reformed Church. If it meant that they pretend to reform her doctrine, or quarrel with her government, they utterly disclaim any such practice. But if it be meant that they desire to refine and reform themselves and others so as to come nearer to her purity of doctrine in their practice than some others do who shelter their profane lives under the pretence of her Holy Communion, they own this, and must adhere to it, not doubting but they shall have the prayers of all good people that they may so do.'[1]

The dominant aim of the Religious Societies was the promotion of 'real holiness of heart and life.' Those who influenced them most profoundly had broad conceptions of holiness. In Dr. Horneck's sermons we find teaching on the subject anticipatory of the doctrines which became conspicuous in the eighteenth century. It was thoroughly 'evangelical.' As a preliminary to holiness he insisted on the necessity of the 'new birth.' For that great change he says 'baptism prepares us.' Then he continues, ' The Word of God convinces us, the Holy Ghost changes us, the merits of Jesus Christ recommend us, our good works testify of us, and at last heaven

[1] Woodward's *Account*, 121-25

receives us.' He declares that to make a person 'a child of God' more is required than 'bare nature or natural gifts.' Grace is 'the chief ingredient ; grace manifested not only in discourses and speeches and answers, but in works and actions, divine, spiritual, and edifying, and, in the eye of the world, unreasonable and contrary to good manners.' In his sermon on ' Be ye therefore perfect, even as your Father which is in heaven is perfect,' he gives directions for approaching perfection. He urges the necessity of 'a fervent love of the Lord Jesus ; such a love as we find in St. Paul, in St. John, in Mary the sister of Martha, and others ; a love which must rise from the strong impresses made upon the soul by the sufferings of Christ and His love in descending from heaven and dying for us.' With a steady hand he points to the path of perfect love as the way to Christian perfection. When he preached before King William and Queen Mary, at Whitehall, on November 17, 1689, the theme of his sermon was ' The Nature of true Christian Righteousness,' and his sermon contains solemn and fervent appeals to his hearers to aim at ' consistent and holy living.'[1] The ' Rules ' he drew up for the earliest Religious Societies, and the ' Orders ' of the Poplar Society, sufficiently prove that, with him and Dr. Woodward, ' holiness was the main thing.'

The principal promoters of the Religious Societies had a broad and practical view of the meaning of holiness. The love of God was united with the love of man. The latter was shown by the care for the poor which, from the beginning of the movement, was manifested by the members of the Societies. Out of the ' public stock ' they relieved the individual necessities of the poor of the parish and put their children to school. They visited the poor at their homes, maintained orphan children, fixed some poor persons in a way of trade, set sundry prisoners for debt at liberty, assisted poor scholars at the University, and were greatly instrumental in establishing nearly one hundred charity schools in London, as well as others in the country.[2] Like John Howard, they ' trod an open but unfrequented path to immortality in the ardent and unintermitted exercise of Christian charity.'

The influence of the Societies spread beyond the solemn boundaries of English poverty, ignorance, and misery. Overton has given prominence to a fact which has not been sufficiently

[1] Hone's *Lives of Eminent Christians*, ii., 287-90. [2] Woodward's *Account*, 22.

emphasized. The Society for Promoting Christian Knowledge is declared by him to be ' the daughter of the Religious Societies, inasmuch as it was the spirit awakened by these Societies which, more than anything else, called her into existence, and, moreover, these Societies interested themselves largely in procuring subscriptions for her.'[1] The Society for Promoting Christian Knowledge, formed on March 8, 1699, had a wide outlook. It aimed at erecting catechetical schools in and about London ; it supported Dr. Bray's scheme for promoting religion in the plantations ; it arranged for the printing of good books to be circulated among the poor, steps having been previously taken for founding lending libraries in America. In 1701 it sent books for distribution in the Army and Navy ; and in 1705 the Society agreed to set apart a portion of its funds to furnish the poor of the country with Bibles and Prayer Books at a cheap rate. The statement concerning the primary objects of the Society reveals the broad designs of its founders. It was the forerunner of those great organizations which, at a later period, arose to add distinction to the Church life of England.[2]

The present Society for the Propagation of the Gospel in Foreign Parts is, according to Overton, ' simply an offshoot of the Society for Promoting Christian Knowledge.' An earlier Society for the Propagation of the Gospel in New England had been established by an Act passed by the Long Parliament in 1649, but the later Society was distinct from it. When Dr. Bray returned from Maryland in 1701 he found that the various designs of the newly formed Society for Promoting Christian Knowledge were too extensive for any one association. He therefore proposed the establishment of a separate Society, whose object should be to propagate the gospel throughout the foreign possessions of the British Empire. In association with Archbishop Tenison and Bishop Compton, he procured a Royal charter for constituting the new Society a body corporate, and on June 27, 1701, its first meeting was held, under the direction of the Archbishop at Lambeth. Speaking of the relation of the two Societies, Overton says, ' The selfsame men were the supporters of both ; the older Society deputed

---

[1] Overton's *Life in the English Church*, 216.
[2] It is interesting to note the name of Samuel Wesley, the father of John Wesley, among those of the men who were ' the earliest and warmest supporters of the Society for Promoting Christian Knowledge.'

some of its functions to a separate corporation; that was all.'[1] The Society for Promoting Christian Knowledge and the Society for the Propagation of the Gospel in Foreign Parts are enduring monuments of the early Religious Societies.

The philanthropic work of the Religious Societies among the poor, and in connexion with the spread of Christian knowledge at home and abroad, kindles admiration. One branch of its numerous activities, however, has not escaped considerable criticism. The Societies were closely connected with an attempt to secure the purification of the social life of England. The origin of that attempt has not been always understood, but Dr. Woodward's statements enable us to see it in a clear light. He tells us that about the year 1690 four or five gentlemen of the Church of England consulted together on the subject of the iniquity of the times, and resolved that they would do all that they possibly could, by the authority of our laws, to chastise and suppress those impudent vices and impieties which they saw very provoking in the sight of God and very grievous to the spirits of all good men.[2] As some of them had made a special study of law they collected an abstract of our penal laws against vice and profaneness, and drew up such prudential rules as are fit for the legal conviction and prosecution of such as offend against them. In 1691 they induced Queen Anne, through the medium of Bishop Stillingfleet, to issue royal letters admonishing the magistrates to do their duty. Archbishop Tillotson took the matter up warmly, and so did his successor, Archbishop Tenison, who issued a circular letter to his suffragans begging them to urge their clergy to help on the good work.[3]

In 1692 a Society was formed for the purpose of checking the prevalent immorality by bringing offenders under the arm of the civil power. It was called the Society for the Reformation of Manners. It consisted of Churchmen and Dissenters, and that fact differentiates it from the Religious Societies. It undoubtedly effected much good. As it proceeded by the prosecution of offenders before the magistrates it was necessary to gather reliable evidence, and it was at this point that many of the members of the Religious Societies came into close association with the new organization. Dr. Woodward says

---

[1] *Life in the English Church*, 218, 219.   [2] Woodward's *Account*, 54.
[3] See Overton's *Life in the English Church*, 213, 214.

that 'the Societies formed themselves into two considerable bodies for information against public enormities, the one in London, the other in Westminster, according to their respective places of abode.'[1] These 'Societies for giving of Information,' as they were called, organized themselves for their special work, and allied themselves with the men who had originated the Society for the Reformation of Manners. The work of these Vigilance Committees was done with great zeal, and many prosecutions before the magistrates were successful. Some persons will be conscious of a feeling of incongruity when they see the members of the Religious Societies acting as 'informers.' The word has a sinister sound. It was often heard in the seventeenth and eighteenth centuries, when plots and persecutions abounded. Dr. Woodward was conscious of the incongruity. He takes pains to draw a sharp distinction between the Societies that acted as Societies for Reformation and the forty Religious Societies in London and its suburbs. He says, ' Though all agree in the promotion of virtue and opposition to vice, yet their first and more direct design of association seems to be distinguished thus: In that the Societies for Reformation bent their utmost endeavours from the first to suppress public vice; whilst the Religious Societies endeavoured chiefly to promote a due sense of religion in their own breasts, though they have since been eminently instrumental in the public reformation. The former endeavoured to take away the reproach of our religion by curbing the exorbitancies of its professors; the latter attempted to retrieve that holy vigour in the practice of religion which becomes Christians.'[2] The judicial mind recognizes the difference indicated by Dr. Woodward, but we doubt if it would be apparent to those who were convicted on the evidence of the members of the Religious Societies. The hurry and stress of life are often fatal to fine distinctions. The prejudice against the Reformation Society extended to the Religious Societies, and injured them in public esteem.

A brighter page in the history of the Religious Societies contains the record of the spiritual influence they exerted in the Church of England, the nation at large, and in other countries. In the perilous times of James II, when they were threatened, danger evoked the best qualities of courageous

[1] Woodward's *Account*, 55. [2] *Ibid.*, 65.

and faithful men. At this crisis 'the remnant' manifested an unconquerable spirit. Although their numbers were much diminished, they entered heartily into the contest against Popery. Seeing that 'the Mass' was publicly celebrated, not only at the Royal Chapel, but in other places, they set up at their own expense public prayers every evening, at eight o'clock, at St. Clement Danes, in the Strand. Not long after they established an evening monthly lecture in the same church, 'to confirm communicants in their holy purposes and vows which they made at the Lord's Table.' When the days of storm and stress passed, and were succeeded by the sunshine of the 'glorious revolution,' the Societies emerged into the light. For a time they had abandoned their original name, styling themselves Clubs, but they resumed it, and with the old name they began new work in the old spirit. Once more the members bound themselves together to assist each other to live in all respects as it becometh the gospel. Their renewed activity caused them to be summoned to appear before Compton, the Bishop of London, to justify their undertakings. Their 'apology' was so complete that the Bishop dismissed their representatives with the words, 'God forbid that I should be against such excellent designs.'[1] Fortified by the good opinion of the Bishop, and of many of the leading clergymen in London, the Societies commenced a career of renewed activity. The members appeared in large numbers at the churches as monthly, or still more frequent, communicants; and they arranged that in some church in the City a sermon should be preached every Lord's Day in the evening on the subject of 'the due preparation for the Lord's Table, and a meet deportment after it.' After a time the number of churches in which these sermons were preached was increased. In addition, daily public prayers were provided in some churches at the cost of the Societies, and this part of the movement was strikingly successful. The declaration of Tindal, in his *Continuation of Rapin*, is quoted by Overton with approval. Tindal says, ' Prayers were set up in so many places and hours that devout persons might have that comfort every hour of the day, and there were greater numbers and greater appearance of devotion at prayers and sacraments than had been observed in the memory of man.'[2]

[1] Woodward's *Account*, 36.   [2] Overton's *Life in the English Church*, 1660-1714, 211.

THE RELIGIOUS SOCIETIES

The reigns of King William and Mary and of Queen Anne were the times when the Religious Societies reached the height of their prosperity. Some of the dignitaries and many of the clergy of the Established Church encouraged them. Among the latter Overton makes special mention of Samuel Wesley. He says, ' Among their warmest supporters was the rector of Epworth, Mr. Wesley. A " Letter concerning Religious Societies " (1699) and a " Sermon preached to one of the Religious Societies " (1698), full of most seasonable advice to its members, are still extant. There is no doubt that the father handed down his sentiments on the subject to his more famous son.'[1]

It must not be supposed that the Religious Societies only existed in London and Westminster. Dr. Woodward tells us that it had come to his knowledge that, in some places, Societies having the same scope and design ' had been formed by persons who knew nothing of the London Societies, nor had so much as heard any report of them. In one town some persons, considering the great benefit of a strict observance of the Lord's Day, came to a resolution to meet together on the evening before it, ' to enliven each other's affections towards spiritual things as a meet preparation for the duties of the sacred day following ' ; and finding the great advantages of this practice they continued it for the space of three years before they heard of what had been done in London.[2]

No one acquainted with the history of Christian fellowship from the days of the apostles will have any difficulty in understanding the formation of these unrelated Societies in different parts of the country. Dr. Woodward was the son and nephew of ministers who were ejected from the Church of England in 1662. He would be familiar with the stories of the Nonconformist fellowship meetings held, often in secret, when Christian people craved for spiritual communion with each other, and would not be surprised at his discovery that the old Puritan practice still persisted among members of the Church of England in country towns and villages. In this connexion it is important to note that among the places in which the revived spirit of fellowship was being revealed were the Universities of Oxford and Cambridge. Recording this fact, Dr. Woodward says : ' There can be no doubt but that the efforts of these

[1] Overton's *Life in the English Church*, 212.   [2] Woodward's *Account*, 4.

famous Universities to retrieve the primitive vigour of our religion would excel all that has been already done of the like tendency by others.'¹

The publication of Dr. Woodward's book gave an impetus to the formation of Religious Societies within the Church of England. Its influence was more widely extended. The book was translated into German, and a letter from Francke, of Halle, encouraged the author by showing him that the Religious Societies movement was making considerable progress on the Continent. At Nuremberg, Augsburg, Ratisbon, and Schaffhausen, Societies had been formed, and at Altorf Dr. Lange had begun to use religious exercises with his pupils in imitation of those at Halle, as Dr. Spener had long since done at Frankfort. The letter containing this information concludes with words which sound like an echo of the ' Country Parson's ' prophecy : ' I look upon these things as comfortable signs that the Spirit of God is now about a great work to put a new face on the whole Christian Church.'²

It is well known that the promise of these days of high prosperity was not fulfilled. As the years went by the Religious Societies gradually lost their efficiency, declined in numbers, and disappointed the hopes of those who had looked upon them as the agents of a national revival of religion. Overton, whose description of the Societies is written with much sympathy and appreciation, advances several reasons for their collapse. He reminds us that when the Hanoverian kings began to reign a strong party in England favoured the claims of the representatives of the Stuarts. The Societies came to be suspected of Jacobite tendencies. They were especially charged with using their influence over the charity schools for political purposes. The charges against them on this score were very vague, but they were quite sufficient, in the sensitive state of men's minds, to cast discredit upon them. Overton, on this, remarks that the mixing up of politics with religion is ' the old, old trouble, which has so often interfered with the progress of Church life.' He adds two other causes in his description of the collapse of the Societies. He says that as it was of the essence of the Societies to take their tone entirely from the clergy who had the exclusive direction of them, and as the clergymen of the second generation of the Societies' existence

¹ Woodward's *Account*, 48, 49.   ² *Ibid.*, 9.

THE RELIGIOUS SOCIETIES

were not men of so high a type spiritually as their predecessors, this told sadly to their disadvantage. But he considers that the chief cause of their collapse was that people confused them with the Society for the Reformation of Manners; and we have seen that the methods adopted by that Society excited much hostile criticism.[1] Whatever may have been the reasons for their decline, the fact of their failure during the opening years of the eighteenth century must be admitted. It became apparent that if a Society was to be used as the instrument of the Holy Spirit to bring about a great and permanent reformation it must differ in several respects from the existing Religious Societies. While preserving their best characteristics, it must add to them. Especially it must extend the boundaries of its sphere of work beyond the limits of a particular Church; it must be filled with the spirit of a fervent evangelism; it must be restless until it achieves the salvation of mankind.

[1] Overton's *Life in the English Church*, 212-13.

II

WESTLEYS AND ANNESLEYS

IN attempting to explain the origin and to trace the growth of the Methodist Church in its earlier stages, it is essential that we should understand the character and spirit of the men who were used by the divine hand to effect the great religious reformation that has given the eighteenth century its chief distinction. We must know much about the Wesleys. We must become familiar with the facts concerning their ancestry, their home training, their education; we must discern the influences that moulded them during the years when they made their great decisions, and commenced and carried on their work. Those who have studied the history of the Methodist Church have recognized the broad, deep, and permanent impression that John and Charles Wesley made upon it. To this hour they inspire, control, and guide it. The secret of their influence was the use that God made of them; but we reverently ask why they were selected for their task. A complete answer to that question is beyond us, but it is impossible to ignore the fact that they possessed inherited and personal qualities that made them eminently fitted for the work assigned to them. We will in this and the following chapter turn our attention to their rich inheritance.

The Wesleys were Englishmen whose original settlement, in Saxon times, was in Sussex. An exceptionally well-informed writer, in a paper contributed to the *Proceedings of the Wesley Historical Society*,[1] traces their pedigree, and shows that, at the battle of Senlac, all the male members of the family over sixteen years of age perished. The widow, with her young children, fled into Somersetshire, where they settled on an estate known as Welswe, or Welslegh. About the end of 1420 that estate, by the marriage of Elizabeth de Wellesleigh, the only child and heiress of Sir Philip de Wellesleigh, passed into

[1] *W.H.S. Proceedings*, ix., 113-16.

another family. A brother of Sir Philip continued to live in the neighbourhood, and from him the Wesleys descend. The spelling of the name passed through various changes. It assumed the form of Welsly; this quickly passed into Wesley; then, owing to mispronunciation, it became Westley. In 1620 Westley had nearly supplanted the old spellings in the English branch of the family, though Wesley continued to persist, sometimes alternately with Wellesley, in the Irish branch down to 1805, when a return to what may be called the original spelling, Wellesley, was decided on by the Duke of Wellington and his brothers.[1] The first known instance of the use of Wesley for Wellesley occurred in or about 1539, when Walter Wellesley so used and signed his name. Anthony Wood, in *Athenae Oxoniensis*, describes him as Walter Wellesley, commonly called Wesley, Prior of the Mitred Abbey and Bishop of Kildare.

Leaving the Irish branch of the Wesley family out of consideration, we turn to the West of England for traces of John Wesley's ancestors on his father's side. Diligent search has recovered the names of a John Westley, Prebendary and Vicar of Sturminster Newton, and of John Westley, Rector of Langton Matravers. In 1655 Jasper Westley resided at Weymouth; and, in 1691, James Westley was one of the Bailiffs of Bridport. These names and places cause us to direct our attention to Dorset in our search for the immediate ancestors of the Wesleys.

We strike the direct line of the Wesley pedigree when we come on the name of Bartholomew Westley. He was born about 1600, and his earlier years were spent in Bridport and its neighbourhood. He was the son of Sir Herbert Wesley, and of Elizabeth de Wellesley, of Dangan, co. Meath, Ireland. At the University, supposed to be Oxford, he studied physic as well as divinity. In 1619 he married the daughter of Sir Henry Colley, of Kildare. About 1645 he became the Vicar of Charmouth and Catherston, in Dorset. Residing in Charmouth, he obtained considerable notoriety by attempting to

[1] The Duke of Wellington was not a Wesley. His grandfather, Richard Colley, assumed the arms and name on succeeding to the Wesley estates in Ireland in accordance with the will of his maternal cousin, Garrett Wesley, of Dangan—a succession which was, at one time, designed for Charles Wesley, who declined the honour. The Duke of Wellington nevertheless had Wellesley blood in his veins, through the female line. He was also closely related to the family by frequent intermarriages between the Wellesleys and the Colleys, the Fitzgeralds, the Plunketts, and the Cusacks. See *W.H.S. Proceedings*, ix., 115.

prevent the escape of Charles II to France from Lyme Regis, after the battle of Worcester.[1] One fact emerges from the clouds of misrepresentation which obscured the reports of Bartholomew Westley's action. He was loyal to the Commonwealth and prompt in its defence. He paid the penalty at the Restoration, being ejected from his livings. After his ejectment it is supposed that he resided in Bridport, and subsequently in Lyme Regis. His first wife died before his ejectment, and he married again. He lived for a few years in comparative retirement, preaching when he had opportunity, but having much more employment as a physician than as a minister. His popularity as a preacher was hindered by his use of ' a peculiar plainness of speech.' His last days were saddened by the frequent tidings of the persecutions of his beloved son, John Westley. The broken-hearted father died at Lyme Regis. Mr. Broadley tells us that he was buried there, on February 15, 1671, in the beautiful sea-girt churchyard, almost within sight of the Whitechapel Rocks, and of the secluded dell where he and his persecuted and proscribed parishioners had been wont to meet during the troublous times which followed the Restoration. Five months afterwards his wife was interred in the same churchyard.[2]

The facts concerning Bartholomew Westley that have escaped the ravages of time are few; the years have been kinder in their treatment of the records concerning his son, John Westley. We are chiefly indebted to Dr. Calamy for a knowledge of the more striking episodes of his career. He had the advantage of using a diary which John Westley kept for many years. It has disappeared, and the historian mourns its loss. In addition to the facts contained in Calamy's well-known *Account of the Ministers ejected after the Restoration*, others have been discovered which cast a strong light on the character and career of a remarkable man.

In attempting to see John Westley with ' the inward eye ' we are assisted by the portrait which has survived. His face impresses us. It is firm, but its resoluteness is tempered by the wistful look of the eyes. The figure is clothed in the habit of a clergyman of the period. If it were not for the cassock

---

[1] Descriptions of the adventures of Charles II in Charmouth, taken from Royalist sources, are contained in Mr. A. M. Broadley's *The Royal Miracle*.

[2] *W.H.S. Proceedings*, iv., 90.

and bands we might think the painter had depicted a soldier who had fought in some fierce battle, and had brought from it an incurable wound. His bearing is that of a man fit to ride in the crashing charges of Cromwell's Ironsides. But the pathos of the eyes appeals to us, and turns our thoughts away to other battlefields. The weapons of his warfare are not carnal. He is a fighter against the rulers of this world's darkness. He assails them with the arms of righteousness, truth, faith, and with 'the sword of the Spirit.' Doubtless he is also equipped with 'the hope of salvation,' but the tranquil light which irradiates the men who possess that hope does not relieve the solemnity of this Christian warrior's face. The portrait speaks to us of faithfulness unto death rather than unto conscious victory. The heroic face haunts us. It bears the marks which ennoble the men who dare to follow the Son of God when He goes forth to war.

John Westley was born in, or about, the year 1636. The place of his birth is supposed to have been Bridport, or its suburb Allington. He matriculated at Oxford on April 23, 1651, entering New Inn Hall. At the University he displayed the Wesley hunger for knowledge, and distinguished himself by his study of Oriental languages. He attracted the attention of Dr. John Owen, who at that time was the Vice-Chancellor of the University, who highly esteemed him. He took his Bachelor's degree on January 23, 1655, and the degree of Master of Arts on July 4, 1657. Going down from Oxford, he spent some time at Melcombe Regis, in Dorset, now better known as a part of Weymouth. There he struck his life-path. He became a member of Mr. Janeway's 'particular Church,' and was sent to preach in the villages of the neighbourhood. His preaching was of the evangelistic type, which distinguished many of the Presbyterian ministers of the period. He aimed at, and secured, the conversion of his hearers. John Westley, in his well-known interview with Gilbert Ironside, the Bishop of Bristol, stated what he meant by conversion. He said that some of his hearers had been 'converted to the power of godliness from ignorance and profaneness.' The Bishop was puzzled by the definition, and Westley, asking him to lay down any evidences of godliness agreeing with the Scripture, said if such evidences were not found in the persons to whom he had alluded he was content to be discharged from his ministry; adding, 'I will stand or fall on the issue thereof.'[1]

In 1658 the parishioners of the secluded village of Winterbourne Whitchurch, in Dorset, lost their vicar by death, and John Westley succeeded him. The village lies among smoothly rolling hills and spreading chalk downs, about eleven miles from Dorchester. Those who know the hidden villages and hamlets of England are delivered from the delusion that they have no history. The well-informed wayfarer often pauses in yew-shadowed graveyards, or in silent country churches, and muses on the men whose influence has gone out from these rural solitudes not only through the nation but sometimes through the world. We can imagine such a wanderer poring over the old registers, still preserved in Winterbourne Whitchurch, and kindling at the sight of John Westley's signature.[2] The historical imagination is quick to reconstruct the picture of the condition of the village when these entries were made. They were written during the period in the seventeenth century when many of the villages of England were in an excited and troubled condition. They were stirred by the events of the Civil War, the temporary establishment of the Commonwealth, and the crisis caused by the substitution of Presbyterianism for Episcopalianism as the national form of Church government. Keen controversies raged in hall and cottage, and knights and peasants discussed, after their own fashions, high points of politics and religion. The removal of many of the Episcopal clergymen from their livings caused much heart-burning in some places, and embittered the struggles of the time. In Winterbourne Whitchurch most of the villagers loyally supported the new vicar, but there were some men, occupying influential positions, who eyed him askance, and held him to be a Presbyterian intruder and an enemy of the king. They longed for the coming of the day when Charles II would return, and the vicar would be cast out from church and manse. The antagonism of the victorious and the vanquished parties in the Civil War disturbed the placidity of the Dorset village. It was one of the many symptoms of the approaching storm.

[1] Calamy's *Continuation of the Account*, &c., i., 442, First ed.; John Wesley's *Journal*, v., 123.
[2] See Mr. Broadley's article on the Dorset Wesleys in the *Proceedings of the W.H.S.*, vi., 1–4. A photographed page of the register is prefixed to the article. It shows the signature of John Westley, who writes his name 'John Wesly.'

A few months after John Westley became the Vicar of Winterbourne Whitchurch he married. His wife was the orphan daughter of John White, ' the patriarch of Dorchester,' who was born in 1575, and became the Rector of Holy Trinity, Dorchester, in 1606. In him we find another illustration of a man, dwelling in a quiet country town, whose influence has affected the world. The founding of ' a Commonwealth in Massachusetts,' which has resulted in the creation of the State of Massachusetts, in America, must be attributed to his sagacious and indomitable efforts.[1] John White married the sister of Dr. Cornelius Burges, whose name is conspicuous in the religious history of the time. Dr. Thomas Fuller married another sister. The thought of Dr. Fuller warms the heart. We picture him with his light flaxen hair, bright blue and laughing eyes, his frank and open face, as he talks with his niece, who was destined to share the checkered life of John Westley. During the Civil War he adhered to the Royal cause, but he maintained his cordial relations with the friends from whom he differed in opinion. He died on August 16, 1661, a year before the tragic St. Bartholomew's Day. The Civil War brought its special calamity to John White. In 1642 a party of Prince Rupert's horse broke into his house in Dorchester and stole his books. He fled to London, where he became Rector of Lambeth. When peace was restored he returned to Dorchester. He was chosen as a member of the Westminster Assembly of Divines, his name appearing in the list, together with that of Dr. Cornelius Burges, as an Assessor. On July 21, 1648, he died suddenly in Dorchester, and was buried in the porch of the south doorway of St. Peter's Church. A mural tablet in the porch records his connexion with the Massachusetts settlement.

John Westley's brief stay in Winterbourne Whitchurch was disturbed by storms. They broke upon him immediately after the Restoration, and continued until the passing of the Act of Uniformity. The ostensible cause was his refusal to use the Book of Common Prayer in the services of the church, but his well-known sympathy with the principles of Presbyterianism and the Commonwealth made him objectionable to the triumphant Royalists. He was summoned to appear

---

[1] For the story of the initiation of the scheme and its realization see Dr. John Brown's *Pilgrim Fathers of New England*, 261-265. *W.H.S. Proceedings*, x., 117-19.

before the Bishop of Bristol, who, after hearing his explanations, dismissed him with courtesy, and promised not to meddle with him. His lay antagonists were of a sterner mood. In the beginning of 1662—that is some months before St. Bartholomew's Day—they caused him to be arrested, and he was committed to Blandford jail. He was bailed out, in a fit of remorse, by one of his adversaries, but had to appear at the Assizes. His appearance had a remarkable effect on the judge, who though ' a very cholerick man spake not an angry word.'

John Westley gives an account of the trial in his diary. It takes but little legal knowledge to see that the charge brought against him was vexatious. Its chief count concerns his refusal to read the Book of Common Prayer, but that charge did not lie until the arrival of St. Bartholomew's Day. The judge perceived the flaw in the indictment, and contented himself with binding him over to appear at the next Assizes. He returned to his church, and preached there as formerly. His last service was held on August 17, 1662, when he bade his weeping flock farewell.

Calamy records a fact which ought to be preserved. It reflects honour on the parishioners of Winterbourne Whitchurch. The living was not declared vacant until October, 1662, when the profits were sequestered; but they paid John Westley his ' dues.' There is great significance in the fact. The Bill for the ' Uniformity of Public Prayers,' when sent up to the House of Lords, contained the date of Michaelmas Day as the time when the ministers had to decide their acceptance of the new Book. On that day their payment for the year would be due; and the arrangement as to the date was just. Their lordships amended that part of the Bill. Dr. Robert Vaughan says, ' The change of St. Bartholomew's Day for Michaelmas Day was a fraudulent and cruel innovation, inasmuch as it would rob the ejected, who had done the service of their cures through the current year, of the income of that year.'[1] But, in some parishes, Englishmen refused to defraud the ministers who had served them; and, as in Winterbourne Whitchurch, this device of the Act failed.

We cannot be surprised that a high-minded and conscientious man like John Westley surrendered his vicarage. The Act of Uniformity was so constructed that no other course was open

[1] *English Nonconformity*, 331.

to him. The declaration that all ministers, if they would retain their livings, were obliged to make, was extraordinary. When the Bill went up to the House of Lords that declaration contained a sentence concerning the Book of Common Prayer which many Presbyterian ministers might have accepted. It expressed their consent to use the Book. But the House of Lords, not being satisfied with such an expression, amended it. It was changed into a declaration of ' unfeigned assent and consent to all and everything contained and prescribed in and by the book.' The declaration covered not only the liturgical services, but also the forms for the administration of the sacraments and other rites and ceremonies of the Church; and also another form for making, ordaining, and consecrating bishops, priests, and deacons; in fact it involved assent and consent to all the contents of the Book of Common Prayer. Cardwell, whose sympathies were almost entirely with the Church of England, admits that this declaration was the more certain to occasion separation from the Church as the minds of men had long been employed on the question of the contents of the Prayer Book, and ' the strong currents of the times had compelled them to make direct and public avowal of their opinions.'[1] It must also be noted that the Book of Common Prayer had been revised by the Convocation of 1662, and the revision had been ratified by the Act of Uniformity. Dr. Tenison computed that about six hundred alterations had been made. Many of these alterations were of minor importance, but some were in direct antagonism to the convictions and contentions of the Presbyterian ministers. The difficulties of ' assent and consent ' were increased by the delay which occurred in the publication of the revised book. It was not published before August 6, 1662, and only a few days were allowed for its distribution through the country. In those times of slow transit the ministers in remote villages ran the risk of not receiving the new book before St. Bartholomew's Day. Those who did receive it had little time to study its contents. Dr. Robert Vaughan says : ' Some of the ejected pastors complained of being called upon to give their assent *ex animo* to the contents of a volume which they had not read, and could not procure.

[1] *History of Conferences connected with the Revision of the Book of Common Prayer*, 379.

Many gave their assent without seeing it—assenting, in fact, to they knew not what.'[1] The Lords' amendment of the declaration answered its purpose. It secured the ejection of the most conscientious Presbyterian ministers from the Church of England. It is a singular fact that the declaration survived the criticism of two hundred years. In 1865 a new canon was framed by the Convocations of Canterbury and York which presented the old declaration in a chastened form.[2]

The Act of Uniformity contained another obstacle which prevented John Westley's retention of his living. Cardwell states the case clearly. 'Lord Clarendon says that the provision requiring reordination from all ministers who had not been episcopally ordained, and which, though enjoined by the governors of the Church, had not hitherto been made imperative by the legislature, was introduced by the Lords and adopted after much earnest debate. The practical result was that " very many of those who had received Presbyterian orders " submitted ; but the clause was doubtless very offensive to the more rigid Nonconformists, as it not only involved an acknowledgement of many errors, but also compelled them to forgo the feeling they entertained against Episcopacy, a feeling the more difficult to surrender as it was a combination of argument and of hatred.'[3] In his interview with Bishop Gilbert Ironside John Westley explained his views on the subject of ordination. Hatred certainly did not influence them. They were the result of argument. He was convinced of the sufficiency of Presbyterian orders ; and, in our judgement, he would never have submitted to Episcopal reordination. If we place the events of St. Bartholomew's Day in their historical setting, and view them through the atmosphere of that distant time, John Westley's decision commands our respect. He listened to the voice of his conscience, made the great surrender, and took up the heavy cross, the weight of which gradually exhausted his strength. He did not immediately leave Winterbourne Whitchurch. His people were devoted to him and would shelter him. We know that a son was born to him who was baptized in the village church on December 17, 1662. The entry of the baptism is in his handwriting, and we infer from the fact that his successor showed him consideration.

---

[1] *English Nonconformity*, 377.   [2] Blunt's *Book of Church Law*, 389.
[3] Cardwell's *History of Conferences, etc.*, 378-79.

On February 22, 1663, John Westley removed with his family to Melcombe Regis. In March he had to leave the town. The Corporation made an order against his settlement there, imposing a fine of £20 on his landlady and of five shillings a week on himself. He turned his face towards Somerset. At Bridgwater, Ilminster, and Taunton he found temporary resting-places, and met with great kindness from all the three denominations of Dissenters. He preached among them, and enjoyed a brief respite from his troubles. When the spirit of the spring was awaking the beauty of the apple-lawns and meadows of Somerset his fortunes suddenly improved. The owner of a house at Preston, a little village that lies in a fold of the hills about three miles from Weymouth, offered him the house free of rent. Thither he went. In his seclusion he brooded over the critical condition of public affairs, and had great debating in his mind as to whether he would remain in England. He thought of going to Surinam, where, under the Dutch, religious liberty was to be enjoyed, or to the British colony of Maryland. But he determined to abide in the land of his nativity and to bear the stress of the gathering storm. He attended the services of the church after some controversy with his conscience. He also preached frequently in private to small companies at Preston, Weymouth, and other places in the neighbourhood. After a time he was called by a number of Christian people to be their pastor at Poole, in Dorset; and, says Calamy, ' in that relation he continued to the day of his death, administering all ordinances to them as opportunity offered.'

But the storm broke. In 1664 and 1665 the Conventicle Act and the Five Mile Act were passed. The latter drove John Westley from his retreat in Preston. Notwithstanding all his prudence in the management of his private meetings he was often disturbed. Several times he was apprehended, and four times he was imprisoned. He was confined in Poole jail for six months, and for three months in the jail at Dorchester, the other commitments being for shorter periods. When released he recommenced his itinerant life, being intent on finishing the ministry which he had received of the Lord Jesus. He preached ' the gospel of the grace of God ' with the fervour of an apostle. But his strength waned. His soldierly spirit sustained him for some years; then it began to give way under the burden of his loneliness, his imprisonments, his sufferings, and his fears for the future of the kingdom of God. The change in him was manifest. He had not reached the prime of life, but he had lived much without living long. Calamy's words sound solemnly as we watch the gathering of the shadows around this warrior of 'the noble army of martyrs.' 'Having filled up his part of what is behind of the afflictions of Christ in his flesh for his body's sake which is the Church, and finished the work given him to do, he was taken out of this vale of tears into the invisible world, where the wicked cease from troubling and the weary are at rest, when he had not been much longer an inhabitant here below than his blessed Master, whom he served with his whole heart, according to the best of his light.'[1] The date of his death and the place of his sepulchre are not definitely known. It is probable that he died in 1670; if so, he was then only thirty-four years old. It is a tradition that a request was made that he might be buried in Preston Church, and that the vicar would not comply with it. Many years afterwards it was discovered that some one had been interred in the garden attached to the house in which John Westley had lived at Preston. It was concluded that he had found a resting-place close to his old home.

In tracing the ancestry of John Wesley it will be convenient, at this point, to turn from the paternal to the maternal family line. Those who form their conceptions of the character and appearance of the Nonconformist ministers of the seventeenth century from the caricatures of 'Puritans' and 'Dissenters' which disfigure some modern novels would be startled if they could clearly see Dr. Samuel Annesley, surrounded by his family, in his house in Spital Yard, Bishopsgate, London. Mrs. Clarke, in her brightly written sketch of Susanna Wesley in the *Eminent Women Series*, has displayed the insight that comes from knowledge and sympathy. With a few strokes of her pencil she makes Dr. Annesley stand before us. We see a remarkably handsome man, tall and robust, with wavy brown hair, an aquiline nose, short upper lip, and eyes that long years have failed to dim. He has an air of unconscious dignity. If we could rescue 'the grand old name of gentleman' from its common use we should instantly apply it to him. In spirit and bearing he reminds us of the best type of the British nobleman.

[1] *Continuation of the Account*, &c., 451.

Dr. Annesley's great-grandfather was Robert Annesley, a man of good position, who lived at Newport Pagnell, in Buckinghamshire. His son Francis was closely connected with the English administration in Ireland. He received knighthood and baronetcy from James I. Charles I created him Baron Mountnorris and Viscount Valentia. Lord Mountnorris was outrageously ill-treated by Sir Thomas Wentworth, afterwards Earl of Strafford, when the latter was Lord Deputy of Ireland. When Strafford was tried for his life in 1641 Mountnorris appeared as a witness against him, and his testimony did much to determine the fatal result of the trial. Hallam says that the conduct of Strafford towards Mountnorris was such ' as to prevent any good man from honouring his memory.'

Lord Mountnorris died in 1660, leaving two sons, Arthur and John. The former succeeded to his father's titles as an Irish peer. In 1645 he was sent by Parliament as a commissioner to Ulster. Afterwards he aided Monk in the restoration of Charles II. He was admitted to the Privy Council in 1661 ; and the next year he was created Baron Annesley, of Newport Pagnell, and Earl of Anglesey, in the English peerage. He became Lord Privy Seal about the year 1679, and died in 1686.[1] The name of the Earl of Anglesey is familiar to students of the history of the seventeenth century. He took a prominent part in the discussions in Parliament which accompanied the progress and passing of the Act of Uniformity. He was one of the principal members of the Committee of the House of Lords that recommended that the following proviso shall be inserted in the Act : ' That such persons as are put out of their livings by virtue of the Act of Uniformity may have such allowances out of their livings, for their subsistence, as His Majesty shall think fit.' After making a few verbal alterations the House of Lords adopted the proviso, but it was withdrawn in consequence of the strong opposition of the House of Commons. In the collection of documents relating to the settlement of the Church of England by the Act of Uniformity of 1662, issued at the time of the bi-centenary celebration, and edited by the Rev. George Gould, copious extracts from the journals of Parliament relating to the passing of the Act are included. The document is of the greatest value. By consulting it we

---

[1] The writer is indebted to the Rev. T. E. Brigden for several particulars concerning the Annesley pedigree.

get light upon the more obscure incidents that occurred in connexion with the passing of the fateful measure. It is a pleasure to rescue from unmerited oblivion the record of the generous suggestion of the House of Lords.

Lord Mountnorris's younger son, John Annesley, went on his way unadorned by titles of nobility. He left the ancestral home and settled in Warwickshire. He had a son, an only child, Samuel Annesley. The boy was born at Kenilworth, and baptized in Haseley Church on March 27, 1620. In the register of the church he is described as 'Samuell the son of John Anslye and Judith his wife.' We know that John and Judith Annesley were godly people. The boy was dedicated to the work of the ministry from his birth. When he was four years old his father died, and for some years afterwards he was trained by his devout mother. His mind was set on entering the ministry, and the influences of his home confirmed his resolution. When he was fifteen he entered Queen's College, Oxford, and, at the usual times, took his degrees. He was ordained, in 1644, on his appointment as chaplain to the *Globe*, under the Earl of Warwick, at that time Lord High Admiral of England. The copy of his ordination certificate, printed in Calamy's *Continuation of the Account of the Ejected Ministers*, shows that his ordination took place on December 18, 1644, when he was set apart ' to the office of a Presbyter and work of the ministry of the gospel by laying on of hands.' The ordaining ministers declare him to be ' a lawful and sufficiently authorized minister of Jesus Christ.' He seems to have held the office of chaplain for some years, discharging his duties on shipboard when the fleet put out to sea. He was also the Rector of Cliffe, near Gravesend. The time of his residence at Cliffe is uncertain. The old registers of the church contain his signature in November, 1645, and in 1646.[1] The story of his persecution in his Kent parish is well known to the readers of Calamy. Some of the more violent of his parishioners, excited to fury by the ejection of the clergyman who preceded him, and by Dr. Annesley's opposition to their evil ways, assailed him ' with spits, forks, and stones ' in their attempts to get rid of him. But he was a strong and courageous man. He determined that he would stay until he had improved the character and manners of his opponents. His work for their

---

[1] *Proceedings* W.H.S. ii., 53.

benefit was unwearied, his kindness was irresistible. The belligerents were subdued, and when he left the place his people bade him farewell with loud cries and tears. The date of his departure is not known.

During Dr. Annesley's residence in Cliffe he lost his first wife. The register shows that her Christian name was Mary. She was buried in the chancel of the church on December 2, 1646. Later her son Samuel was buried in the same place.

In 1652 Dr. Annesley was chosen as the minister of the Church of St. John the Evangelist, in Friday Street, London. In 1655 he preached two sermons in St. Paul's Cathedral, which were published ; and on July 8, 1657, he was appointed lecturer there in succession to Dr. Cornelius Burges. On October 20, 1658, he was 'admitted' to the vicarage of St. Giles's Church, Cripplegate, on the presentation of Richard Cromwell, the Lord Protector of the Commonwealth of England.[1]

The church of St. Giles still stands as one of the most venerable of the ecclesiastical monuments of London. In 1666 it escaped destruction at the time of the Great Fire. Sir John Baddeley, in his *Account of the Church and Parish of St. Giles, Cripplegate*, attributes its escape to the intervention of the City wall, and to the width of the churchyard. But it was in great peril. There is an entry in the parish accounts of nearly £30 for reglazing part of the windows probably broken by the heat of the fire. Oliver Cromwell and Elizabeth Bourchier, the daughter of Sir James Bourchier, one of the many country gentlemen who made Cripplegate their London home, were married in the church on August 22, 1620. Wandering in this building the eye rests on monuments that suggest great episodes in English history. John Milton greets us. Sir Martin Frobisher, that Doncaster man who was one of the first to explore the Arctic regions and the West Indies, and who fought stoutly against the Spanish Armada, seems to live again ; John Foxe, the martyrologist, reminds us of the dark days when the Protestantism of England was in peril, and was saved by the courage of men and women who did not count their lives dear unto themselves. Pacing slowly from monument to monument, the mind looks down the dim vistas of the past,

---

[1] For copy of the Certificate of Admission see Calamy's *Continuation of the Account*, 69.

and the heart is solemnized as we think of vanished times and heroic men.

During Dr. Annesley's incumbency St. Giles's was the only church standing in a wide district extending to Shoreditch, Islington, and Pentonville. It was in the neighbourhood of green fields, in which a few houses clustered at intervals. Little groups of worshippers came along the meadow-paths on Sunday in answer to the sound of the bells. The congregations were large. Calamy says that at St. Paul's and at Cripplegate Dr. Annesley had two of the largest audiences in the City. It is clear that, for a time, he exercised much influence in London. But his fortunes changed. About 1660 he was removed from his lectureship at St. Paul's, and his position at St. Giles's became insecure. However, he worked on steadily, establishing a 'Morning Exercise' in his church, and toiling in his parish. Then, in 1662, the testing-time came. He had special opportunities of knowing the intentions of the Parliament in the matter of the Act of Uniformity, for he was in touch with his relative, the Earl of Anglesey. He knew that the choice had to be made between conformity and the surrender of his church. The financial consideration did not trouble him, for he was possessed of a considerable private estate inherited from his father, but the thought of sacrificing St. Giles's Church and his work in the parish oppressed him. The Earl of Anglesey offered to help him to considerable preferment in the Church of England if he would conform, but that temptation had little strength. He reached his decision by the light of intellect and conscience. Refusing all compromises, he was ejected from his living on St. Bartholomew's Day.

It is difficult to trace Dr. Annesley's course during the years that immediately followed his ejection from the Church of St. Giles. Obscurity was then a friendly shield to Nonconformist ministers. But we get a glimpse of him in a return of the number of 'conventicles' in London in 1669. In it we find his name associated with a 'conventicle' in Spitalfields, 'at a new house for that purpose, with pulpit and seats.' The attendance was estimated at eight hundred persons—the largest congregation mentioned in the list. The publication of the list alarmed the High Church party. The old Conventicle Act had lapsed through efflux of time, and a new Bill was introduced which, after considerable discussion, became an Act. Its career in the Upper House was marked by an incident worthy of lasting remembrance. Dr. Stoughton has recorded the fact that Dr. Wilkins, the Bishop of Chester, opposed the measure, although the King used his influence with him to prevent him from taking any part in the business. The Bishop insisted upon his right as a peer, and declined to withhold either his vote or his voice. With the passing of the Act of 1670 the respite following the lapse of the Act of 1664 came to an end.

During the period covered by the first Conventicle Act Dr. Annesley was a constant preacher, and felt the weight of the hand of the law. Neal, in the *History of the Puritans*, says that he had his goods distrained for a 'latent' conviction; that is, a conviction on the oaths of persons he never saw, and on a summons to answer for himself before a justice of the peace he never received.[1] On one occasion he escaped apprehension and imprisonment because the justice who was signing the warrant died in the act. During these dark days his meeting-house was a rallying-place for the Nonconformist ministers of London, who often gathered there for secret conference and worship.

In 1672 the rigour of the Conventicle Act was lessened by the 'Indulgence' which was granted, unconstitutionally, by the King. It was intended to favour the Roman Catholics, but many Dissenters availed themselves of it. About the time of the 'Indulgence' a meeting-house was erected in Little St. Helen's, which adjoins Great St. Helen's, on the east side of Bishopsgate Street. It is described by Wilson as 'a moderate-sized building, with three good galleries.' It was conveniently situated, and became a centre for lectures and other public services among the Dissenters.[2] Dr. Annesley was the minister of this meeting-house until the year of his death. For more than thirty years he exercised a remarkable influence among the Dissenters. The estate he had inherited from his father enabled him to give great assistance in the work of the churches. Wilson says, 'When he heard of any minister oppressed with poverty, he immediately employed himself for his relief. He was also very useful in filling vacant churches.

---
[1] iii., p. 236.
[2] Wilson's *History of Dissenting Churches*, i., 363.

and was the means of introducing the gospel into many dark and benighted villages. The poor looked upon him as their common father; and he spent much in distributing Bibles, catechisms, and other useful books. His assiduous labours and extensive beneficence were accompanied with many other amiable qualities, which rendered his character truly estimable.'[1] Dr. Daniel Williams, the founder of the well-known library in London which bears his name, preached his funeral sermon. He pronounced a high eulogium on him as a faithful preacher, a helper of the poor, and a public benefactor.[2]

In connexion with the Little St. Helen's meeting-house an event occurred which requires special mention. It is clear that by the Act of Uniformity the Government intended to stop the practice of ordaining Presbyterian ministers in England. Several of the more influential Presbyterian ministers yielded implicit obedience to the law on this question, but others, Dr. Annesley among them, took a different course. They determined to continue such ordinations. Until the Revolution the ordinations were conducted in private. So late as October, 1688, the month before William of Orange landed at Torbay, Joseph Hussey was ordained in Dr. Annesley's house in Spitalfields in an upper chamber. On June 22, 1694, the first public ordination among the Dissenters in London took place in Dr. Annesley's meeting-house in Little St. Helen's.[3] Dr. Annesley was one of the ordaining ministers, and among the seven who were ordained was Edward Calamy. It must be noted that there were some eminent Presbyterian ministers who objected to this public service. Wilson informs us that ' the great Mr. Howe ' absolutely refused to take part in this service through fear of offending the Government, and Dr. Bates urged some other reasons to excuse himself; but Dr. Annesley, Daniel Williams, and four other presbyters set the men apart for the work of the ministry. It is important to notice that the objection of John Howe had nothing to do with the validity of Presbyterian ' orders.' In reference to his own ordination he was accustomed to say that ' there were few men whose ordination had been so truly primitive as his, having been devoted to the sacred office by a primitive bishop and his officiating presbytery.' In his interview with Seth Ward,

---
[1] *History of Dissenting Churches*, i., 369.
[2] Dr. Williams's sermon was republished in the *Arminian Magazine* for 1792.
[3] Wilson's *History of Dissenting Churches*, iv., 72–73.

the jovial prelate and fiercely persecuting Bishop of Exeter, the question of reordination was raised. ' Pray, sir,' said the Bishop, ' what hurt is there in being twice ordained ? ' ' Hurt, my lord ? ' rejoined Howe. ' It hurts my understanding ; the thought is shocking ; it is an absurdity, since nothing can have two beginnings. I am sure I am a minister of Christ, and am ready to debate that matter with your lordship, if your lordship pleases ; but I cannot begin again to be a minister.'[1] Howe's objection to the public ordination of Presbyterian ministers, in 1694, was its inexpediency. ' Comprehension ' was at that time in the air. It is true that the preliminary efforts to bring it about had failed, but in the opinion of Howe and others it was far from being a lost cause.

We cannot conclude this sketch of Dr. Annesley without referring to his religious experience. He used to say that he did not remember the time when he was not converted. Recalling his mother's influence, we can understand his meaning. His heart was gently opened to receive the truths which lead a child into the paths of peace. But a decisive change took place in his experience. For a considerable time during his ministerial life he ' walked in heaviness.' Then about forty years before his death there came a crisis, and he obtained clear and abiding assurance of personal salvation. After that he had ' no darkness, no fear, no doubt at all of his being accepted in the Beloved.' In his last illness he often said, ' I have no doubt, nor shadow of doubt ; all is clear between God and my soul. He chains up Satan, he cannot trouble me.' His latest words are memorable, ' I shall be satisfied with Thy likeness. Satisfied ! Satisfied ! ' He passed away on December 31, 1696, in the seventy-seventh year of his age.

[1] Henry Rogers's *Life of Howe*, 31, 152.

III

SAMUEL AND SUSANNA WESLEY

JOHN WESTLEY of Winterbourne Whitchurch had a numerous family, but it is only necessary to follow the fortunes of one of his sons. In the old register of the village church there is this entry of baptism, ' Samuel Wesley, the son of John Wesley.' The boy was baptized there on December 17, 1662. The entry is in John Westley's handwriting. This is our first glimpse of Samuel Wesley, and after his baptism, we lose sight of him for a time. It is probable that he grew up as a child in the cottage at Preston, sharing the poverty of his father and mother, and listening to stories of the persecutions assailing the Nonconformists of the county. He was sent to the Free School at Dorchester, where he was educated until he was a little more than fifteen years of age. The original school in South Street had been burnt down in 1613. It was rebuilt in 1618. It has disappeared, and the present Grammar School stands in its place. Samuel Wesley's master was Henry Dolling, of Wadham College, Oxford, who translated into Latin *The Whole Duty of Man*. Wesley held him in high esteem, and when he himself became an author, he dedicated to him the first book he published. When Samuel Wesley left the Free School he was considered ' almost fit for the University,' but his mother was too poor to send him there. Another solution of the educational problem had to be reached. Mrs. Westley's Nonconformist friends came to her help. A fund raised by a Dissenting congregation for assisting similar cases provided an exhibition of £30 a year, and Samuel Wesley was sent to London, to a Dissenters' Academy. Its principal was Edward Veal, who had been at Christ Church, Oxford, and afterwards entered Trinity College, Dublin. Samuel Wesley's stay at this academy was short. The magistrates succeeded in breaking it up, and Wesley migrated to another academy at Newington Green, the principal of which was Charles Morton, of Wadham College, Oxford. He remained there until the summer of 1683. Two years after Wesley left Morton was obliged to abandon the academy. He went to America, was chosen pastor of a church at Charleston, and became Vice-President of Harvard College. The Stoke Newington Academy contained some notable students. Daniel Defoe, whose parents were members of Dr. Annesley's congregation when he was at St. Giles's, Cripplegate, and who followed him to his meeting-house after his ejection, was one of Wesley's fellow students. Defoe, who had an abnormal eye for the interesting, must have been attracted by the name of another fellow student, Timothy Cruso, who became known as ' the golden preacher,' and occupied a distinguished position among the Dissenters of London.

The Dissenters' academies were regarded with suspicion by the magistrates. In some cases that suspicion was excusable. We do not know how far we may trust the description which Samuel Wesley gives of these academies in the pamphlet he wrote twenty years after he left Stoke Newington. At the time of writing it he had changed his ecclesiastical views, and had abandoned his old comrades. His criticisms were resented and his statements were sharply contested. There can be little doubt that a virulent spirit possessed many of the men in these academies, which was roused whenever a question concerning the Church of England, or the Government, was raised. If we place ourselves in the circumstances of the time we can scarcely wonder that such was the case. While Wesley is unsparing in his denunciations of the opinions and conduct of the students, he always speaks of Charles Morton with respect. He possessed a well-balanced, judicial mind, and a generous temper. He was not an extreme militant Dissenter. Wesley says of him : ' I must and ever will do my tutor the justice to assert that whenever the young men had any discourse of the Government, and talked disaffectedly or disloyally, he never failed to rebuke and admonish them to the contrary, telling us expressly, more than once, that it was none of our business to censure such as God has set over us ; that small miscarriages ought not to be magnified, nor severely reflected on. . . . He also cautioned us against writing lampoons and scandalous libels concerning our superiors, and that not only because it was dangerous so to do, but likewise immoral.'[1] We think that Mr. Morton must have glanced at Samuel Wesley when he uttered his warning against the writing of lampoons. In that unsavoury department of controversial literature Wesley was exercising himself with great vigour at the time when his tutor's words fell on his ears.

Samuel Wesley is an illustration of the fact that an extreme Dissenter is sometimes a High Churchman in a stage of transition. Several reasons have been given for the change of his ecclesiastical views. We will content ourselves by quoting one of them. John Wesley says: 'Some severe invectives being written against the Dissenters, Mr. S. Wesley, being a young man of considerable talents, was pitched upon to answer them. This set him on a course of reading which soon produced an effect different from what had been intended. Instead of writing the wished-for answer, he himself conceived he saw reason to change his opinions, and actually formed a resolution to renounce the Dissenters and attach himself to the Established Church. He lived at that time with his mother and an old aunt, both of whom were too strongly attached to the Dissenting doctrines to have borne, with any patience, the disclosure of his design. He, therefore, got up one morning at a very early hour, and, without acquainting any one with his purpose, set out on foot to Oxford and entered Exeter College.'[2] It was a bold step to take, and it brought much obloquy on him from his Dissenting acquaintances. They did not fail to remind him of the sufferings of his grandfather and father, and of his obligations to Dissenters for his education. But the invective of controversy had its usual result—it widened the breach between him and his former friends. He became an enthusiastic Churchman, and an irreconcilable antagonist of Dissent.

There was a debt he owed to Dissenters that Samuel Wesley had no wish to repudiate. Rejecting their views of Church government, he clung to their evangelical doctrines. When he was a resident in London he frequently attended the ministry of Stephen Charnock, John Bunyan, and many of the most popular Dissenting preachers of the day. He 'took down' many hundreds of their discourses. Tyerman says: 'It would be folly to deny that these Dissenting sermons greatly

---

[1] Tyerman's *Life and Times of the Rev. Samuel Wesley*, 72.
[2] *Ibid*, 77.

enriched his mind and helped him to mould his moral character.'
'The evangelical note' was distinctly and constantly sounded by the men to whom he listened. It was afterwards prolonged by himself.

During his walk to Oxford, Samuel Wesley must have been perplexed concerning the financial problem that confronted him. He had enough cash to pay his 'caution money.' The entry in the books does not lack pathos: 'Samuel Westley, paup. schol. de Dorchester, £3.' When that claim was discharged he had only a few shillings left. He entered Exeter College as a servitor, and during the five years of his residence in Oxford he frequently sounded the deeps of poverty. But he practised the art of the saver. He so managed the moneys he received as a servitor that, when he quitted the University, he found, to his surprise, that he was richer than when he entered it. It would have been well for himself and others if he had retained the saver's skill.

It is not necessary to describe in detail Samuel Wesley's experiences at Oxford. We may say, in passing, that during his residence he devoted some of his time to visiting the prisoners at the Castle. In after years, when reviewing the events of his stormy life, he reflected on this work with much satisfaction. He took his Bachelor's degree on June 19, 1688, being the only Exeter man who did so that year. The subject which claims our special attention is the influence of Oxford on his ecclesiastical views and position. He became a High Churchman, and it is essential that we should attempt to determine the meaning of that name at the close of the seventeenth century. It is not easy to detect its origin. Hallam says that it first appeared in a pamphlet published in the reign of Charles II. Swift, writing in the *Examiner*, tells us that the party-names High Church and Low Church came into use soon after the Revolution. Leaving the origin of these names to the historical explorer, let us try to discover what was meant by a High Churchman at the time of which we are writing. Hallam describes him as a man who was distinguished by great pretensions to sacerdotal power, both spiritual and temporal, by a repugnance to toleration, and by a firm adherence to the Tory principle in the State.[1] This description may be accepted as accurately defining the general body of High

---

[1] *Constitutional History of England*, iii., 242, eighth ed.

Churchmen in the reigns of William and Mary and Queen Anne. But, outside the circle of the men who were chiefly distinguished by political animus and activity were other High Churchmen who are not covered by Hallam's definition. We catch sight of them in a pamphlet, published in 1705, under the title *The Distinction of High Church and Low Church*. It was written anonymously, but Dr. Daniel Waterland, in the copy we possess, has marked it ' Norris.' We have only to read a few sentences at the commencement of the pamphlet to discern a gentle figure with which some of us are familiar. Apologizing for entering upon his undertaking, the writer says : ' Indeed my natural inclination does not much lead me to things of this nature. The quiet and serene contemplation of those necessary and eternal truths which are the steady and immutable subjects of philosophick theory and science, is the delight of my heart, and the proper entertainment of my spirit, the dayly *manna* that I feed upon, and the very life and nourishment of my soul.' These are not the words of a fiery politician, who delights to live in the dust of conflict. In the long years ago they were traced by the hand of John Norris, the Cambridge Platonist, as he sat in his calm retreat in Bemerton, in Wiltshire. He was the rector of the little church there, and was one of the worthiest successors of George Herbert.

The descriptions of the Churchman and the High Churchman contained in John Norris's pamphlet exhibit the strength of his idealism ; but we are convinced that, in many parts of the country, men were to be found in whom they were realized. He first sketches the Churchman, and describes him as one that is truly and sincerely for the Church of England, as established by the laws of England, and a cordial friend to it in all its interests. He is a Churchman, ' not only as to external communion, so as not to make any open or downright schism or separation from it, but as to inward principle, sentiment, and affection, and loves it not in word and in tongue, but in deed and in truth, as St. John describes the brotherly love which Christians should have toward one another.' He allows and consents to her doctrine, reverences her order and discipline, heartily likes and approves her worship, that beauty of holiness, that reasonable service, that appears in all her offices and ministrations. In one word, he is a man ' that wishes well to, and has a zealous concern for, her whole constitution, which indeed is truly Christian and primitive.' He then answers the question, ' What does a High Churchman add to all this ? ' He replies, ' Though High Churchman may perhaps, in the formality of the expression, signify something more than mere Churchman, yet those whom they are pleased to call High Churchmen are really no more, at least for the generality of them. I deny not but that even among those who are all of them real friends to the Church, some may be more zealously affected towards her than others, and may espouse her interests with a more quick and sensible concern ; and these comparatively to the others may, if you please, in this respect be called High Churchmen. But, alas! this is not according to the use of that word in this distinction. For as the word is now generally used and applied, if a man appears to have a hearty zeal for the Church, is at all strict in the observation of its rules and orders, expresses any concern for its safety, or is found to be in those measures which are necessary for its security and preservation (without which he cannot be so much as a Churchman), he is presently dignified and distinguished with the not honourable, as intended, but odious character of a High Churchman, as I doubt not but that I myself shall be for writing this treatise.'[1]

Norris's pamphlet gives us much insight into the meaning of the term High Churchman as used at the opening of the eighteenth century. His definition, at its close, seems to suggest a fact which requires fuller expression. It must be remembered that among the schools of thought which then existed in the Church of England there was one which had a remarkable history. It may be said to have been founded by Bishop Andrewes. He died in 1626. It is well known that he aimed at the recovery of a more liberal and catholic theology, and at the restoration of decency and order in public worship. As to the latter, Mr. Frere intimates that his standard of external ceremonial and ornament was that set up at the beginning of Elizabeth's reign.[2] His lineal successor was Laud, a man unlike him in spirit and in the manner in which he thrust his ritualistic reforms upon unwilling congregations. The influence of Andrewes and Laud was great, and, in the eighteenth century, its effect was seen in the existence of a

[1] *The Distinction of High Church and Low Church*, 22-25.
[2] *History of the English Church*, v., 386.

group of High Churchmen that will demand our attention at a subsequent stage.

From the descriptions of High Churchmen given by Norris and Hallam it will be seen that, in the eighteenth century, the term was often used without precision. It was sometimes recklessly applied, and still needs to be used carefully. We may say at once that, in Samuel Wesley's case, extreme ideas of its meaning must be discarded. He was evangelical in doctrine, and loyal to the discipline of the reformed Church of England. But when we note that Hallam's definition of a High Churchman includes his ' repugnance to toleration ' we feel that we are in sight of Wesley's position. He looked upon Dissent as a standing danger to the State Church, and he steadily opposed it. His ' repugnance ' was, doubtless, modified by the remembrance of his mother's piety and his father's sufferings. But the spirit of intolerance is so subtle and masterful that he yielded to its influence. The High Churchman in him at last prevailed. During his later days we do not suppose that he would have personally assisted in the persecution of Dissenters, but we think that he would have been relieved if there had been no Dissenters in the country to persecute.

Samuel Wesley's High Churchmanship was displayed most clearly in the realm of politics. The controversies that followed the landing of William of Orange split up the people of England into fiercely contending parties. The King on the throne and the King ' over the water ' became rallying centres ; fidelity to the one or the other was supposed to reveal the character of a man's Churchmanship. The Nonjurors who refused to take the oath of allegiance to William III were considered by their numerous admirers to be High Churchmen of the finest type. The Jacobite clergy, who abounded in the country, belonged to the same party. When the Stuart cause became hopeless, at the time of the accession of the Hanoverian line of kings, a large number of the clergy yielded to the inevitable. The Nonjurors gradually disappeared ; the Jacobites sank into obscurity, but there were many of those who had gone over to George I who still retained their ' high ' doctrines concerning the person and the privileges of a king.

Samuel Wesley's residence in Oxford influenced, if it did not determine, the political character of his Churchmanship. It is alleged that he was, at one time, a Jacobite. If so, his loyalty to James II must have received a rude shock when he witnessed the boisterous interview between the King and the Fellows of Magdalen. He then discovered that James was 'a tyrant,' and his enthusiasm was chilled. During the reign of William III he was certainly 'a King William's man'; he was a hearty supporter of Queen Anne, and loyal to George I and George II. We may safely dismiss the legend of his Jacobitism, but it is indubitable that he was a strong politician, and threw his energies into the propagation and defence of Tory principles. On two special occasions he stepped into the political arena and fought for the triumph of his party. In the election of a member for Lincolnshire, in 1705, he was active in attempting to secure the return of the Tory candidate. He laboured in vain, but his interference in the election brought upon him the resentment of some of his parishioners. One of them showed his displeasure by demanding immediate payment of a debt owing to him. As Wesley was unable to pay it he was committed to Lincoln prison, where he stayed for three months. Later in life he made a more important appearance in the world of politics. In 1710 the Sacheverell riots and triumphal processions disturbed the country. Their originating cause was a sermon preached by Sacheverell in St. Paul's Cathedral on November 5, 1709, in which he laid down and enforced the High Church doctrine of 'absolute and unconditional obedience to kings in all things lawful,' attacked Archbishop Tillotson's 'Comprehension' scheme, and assailed Dissenters with foul-mouthed abuse.[1] Instead of allowing the sermon to hasten to oblivion Parliament secured its inglorious immortality by ordering its author to attend at the bar and answer for it. He was impeached, and a prolonged trial before the two Houses took place, which lasted from February 27 to March 23, 1710. After his counsel had concluded the speech for the defence, Sacheverell answered for himself. His speech displayed an intellectual force and a literary style that was indiscernible in his St. Paul's harangue. Sudden touches of pathos stirred the emotions of the audience. All men wondered. Cool critics came to the conclusion that the speech had been composed for him, and they were right. It was thought, for

---

[1] Extracts from the sermon are given by Tyerman in his *Life and Times of Samuel Wesley*, 335-37.

a time, that Smalridge and Atterbury had assisted him, but the secret of authorship was revealed, in after years, by John Wesley. He emphatically declares that the speech was written by his father, Samuel Wesley.[1] Tyerman, deploring the fact of authorship, says that it proves that Wesley, who began his ministerial life as a moderate Churchman, and an admirer of Archbishop Tillotson, had become a member of the High Church clique, and was allied with men who regarded the Dissenters with the bitterest hostility.[2] The authorship of the speech, although a mystery in London, was recognized in Lincolnshire. The High Churchmen in that county were delighted, and the clergy of the diocese once more chose Wesley as their representative in Convocation; and, for seven successive years, they showed their confidence in him in the same way.

Those who are familiar with the history of Nonconformity in England will note the collaboration of Samuel Wesley and Sacheverell with special interest. They were both closely related to ministers who had quitted their livings in 1662. Sacheverell was the grandson of John Sacheverell, of Wincanton. After being silenced, he retired to Stalbridge. For attending a meeting in Shaftesbury, with other ministers, he and they were sent together to Dorchester jail, where he remained for three years. Calamy tells us that, in this imprisonment, Sacheverell and his companions took it by turns to preach out of a window to a considerable number of people that stood to hear on the other side of the river. His imprisonment sapped his strength. Before it he was a cheerful, active man, but, after his release, he became very melancholy. He died in his chair, ' speaking to those about him, with great vehemence and affection, of the great work of the redemption of sinners.'[3] We have no information showing that Samuel Wesley's father and Dr. Sacheverell's grandfather met as fellow prisoners in Dorchester jail, but they both suffered there for their nonconformity. It may be safely said that neither of them, in his prison musings, ever dreamed of the High Church outbreak in which Samuel Wesley and Henry Sacheverell were to play so conspicuous a part.

We have attempted to define Samuel Wesley's High Churchmanship, and must now return to the course of his history.

---

[1] John Wesley's *History of England*, iv., 75.
[2] *Life and Times of Samuel Wesley*, 340.   [3] Calamy's *Account*, 599.

He was ordained deacon by Dr. Thomas Sprat, the Bishop of Rochester, at his palace at Bromley, in Kent, on August 7, 1688. On February 24. 1689, he was ordained priest by Dr. Compton, the Bishop of London, in St. Andrew's Church, Holborn. After his ordination his friendly relations with Nonconformists began to change, but they continued long enough to lead to a decisive event. When he was a student at the Stepney Academy he attacked some Greek verses which appeared in a volume published by John Dunton, rightly described as 'the eccentric bookseller.' Dunton was attracted to Wesley by his poetical criticism, and the two men formed an intimate friendship. On August 3, 1682, Dunton married Elizabeth Annesley, and Samuel Wesley, then a Nonconformist, was at the wedding. He became acquainted with the Annesley family. Coming under the influence of the Annesley girls, he was especially attracted by the youngest of them. Mrs. Clarke describes her as slim and very pretty, and says that she retained her good looks and symmetry of figure to old age.[1]

Susanna Annesley possessed an indefinable charm of character. The spirit of her father was strong in her, but we also perceive an intellectual force and breadth of view, and a judicial habit of mind, which distinguish her from most of the women of her day. We know little of her mother, but it is sufficient to remember that she was the daughter of John White, an eminent lawyer, who, for several years, was the well-known member for Southwark. He possessed the confidence of the House of Commons, and was appointed the chairman of the Grand Committee, consisting of the whole House, that had to inquire into ' the scandalous immoralities of the clergy.' This committee and its sub-committees had difficult work to perform, and their decisions raised up a host of Royalist assailants. John White was asked by the House of Commons to defend its actions, and he published his well-known pamphlet *The Century of Scandalous Priests*. By this publication he attracted the lightnings that were flashing on Parliament. They concentrated on him; and he had to bear the blame of any injustices that might have been perpetrated by sub-committees and the Grand Committee of the whole House. But, notwithstanding virulent attack, he retained the confidence and esteem of those who knew him.

[1] *Susanna Wesley*, 7–8, Eminent Women Series.

That fact is shown by his appointment as one of the lay-assessors of the Westminister Assembly of Divines. He was associated with John White, 'the patriarch of Dorchester,' and with other ministers in the office of assessor. John White, Dr. Annesley's father-in-law, died on January 29, 1645, soon after the Assembly commenced its work. He was buried in the Temple Church, London, ' with great funeral solemnity.'[1]

When we think of John White as the grandfather of Susanna Annesley we are conscious of the sharpness of the contrast between the grave lawyer and the sprightly and beautiful girl ; but when we remember her letters, her clear-sighted and carefully expressed expositions of profound Christian doctrines, her mature judgements on points of casuistry, her management of complicated business affairs, her wisdom as a counsellor on the conduct of life, that contrast seems less glaring. She proved herself to be a cultured and strong woman, possessing a well-trained, acute, judicial mind. Long before this country dreamed of the higher education of women she was an enthusiast for learning, rejoicing in the light of knowledge as flowers revel in sunshine.

The friendship of Samuel Wesley and Susanna Annesley deepened into love. When Wesley abandoned the Nonconformists we can imagine that Dr. Annesley's fears for the future were excited. He saw the progress of his daughter's affection and watched her growing estrangement from his own Church. He knew that she was studying the points in dispute between Episcopalians and Presbyterians, and was coming to conclusions antagonistic to his own opinions. We cannot accept the theory that those decisions were of the heart rather than the head. She was an independent thinker. Much as she loved Wesley, she did not agree with him on all points. For instance, she was a Jacobite. But she did, in the main, accept the Church of England position, and her father's hopes were disappointed. Samuel Wesley and Susanna Annesley were married on November 12, 1688 ; the place of their marriage has not been determined.

Samuel Wesley began his married life in a state of poverty. He fought his debts with his pen, and made little impression on them. His writing, however, made him known in political circles. The Marquis of Normanby, who was afterwards the

[1] Neal's *History of the Puritans*, ii., 354.

Duke of Buckingham, befriended him. He used his influence with the Massingberds, who were lords of the manor and patrons of the living of South Ormsby, in Lincolnshire, and Wesley became the rector of that little parish. While there, the Marquis made a strong attempt to secure for him an Irish bishopric, but failed. In 1697, the year after Dr. Annesley's death, he obtained the living of Epworth, in Lincolnshire, with a stipend of £50 a year. It is understood that the living was presented to him in consequence of a wish expressed by Queen Mary shortly before her last illness.

The Epworth Rectory occupies a distinguished position among English parsonages, and its distinction arises from the fact that it was the home of Susanna Wesley and her sons.

Life in the Epworth Rectory was like that in many parsonages scattered through the small towns and villages of England. With the ordinary details of a country clergyman's life we are not now concerned, but there are certain facts about the Wesley home which must be recorded in order that we may detect the influences which told on and determined the character of the children. Susanna Wesley had nineteen children, several of whom survived their birth only for a short time. A threatening cloud of poverty constantly hung over the home. The boys and girls were brought up on plain fare, and sometimes had little to eat. In the dismal days when Samuel Wesley was imprisoned in Lincoln jail, Dr. Sharp, the Archbishop of York, showed Mrs. Wesley much kindness. In his interview with her he ventured to say to her, ' Tell me whether you ever really wanted bread?' She answered, ' My lord, I will freely own to your grace that, strictly speaking, I never did want bread. But then I had so much care to get it before it was ate, and to pay for it after, as has often made it very unpleasant to me. And I think to have bread on such terms is the next degree of wretchedness to having none at all.' ' You are certainly in the right,' he replied ; and, says Susanna Wesley, ' he seemed for a while very thoughtful.'[1] At this distance of time Mrs. Wesley's answer touches us deeply. Into it was compressed the suffering of many weary years. There can be little doubt that the scarcity of food in the house injured the health of mother and children. Even John

[1] Adam Clarke's *Wesley Family*, i., 391.

Wesley, that emblem of virility, suffered from delicacy in the earlier part of his life.

The management of the house, the glebe, the children, was in the hands of Mrs. Wesley. Her husband toiled in his study, writing poetry and prose which ought to have increased his income and relieved the strain on his family. As a Convocation man he was away from home for long periods and at considerable expense. In London he pushed his literary and political fortunes without much financial success. He was doomed to be a poor country clergyman all the days of his life, and he accepted his fate with surprising cheerfulness.

Mrs. Wesley, being in command of the family, soon revealed her extraordinary qualifications for the position thrust upon her. She had her own scheme of discipline and education. Her discipline was strict, methodical, gentle, and successful. She trained her daughters admirably. Several of them became cultured women, one of them attaining to unusual scholarship. The girl was assisted in classics and mathematics by her father, but she owed most of her education to her mother. Mrs. Wesley bore her part in preparing John Wesley for the Charterhouse, and Charles Wesley for Westminster. She reduced her theory of education to practice, and proved its efficiency by her own efforts. She inspired her children with a life-long love of knowledge, and to her John Wesley owed that insatiable zest for reading which gave him a unique position among the educated men of his century.

In a letter written by Susanna Wesley to John Wesley, in 1732, she speaks with her habitual modesty of her way of education. She admits that no one could observe her method without renouncing the world in the most literal sense. But in a memorable sentence she reveals the secret of her self-sacrificing toil. She says, ' There are few, if any, that would entirely devote above twenty years of the prime of life in hopes to save the souls of their children, which they think may be saved without so much ado ; for that was my principal intention, however unskilfully and unsuccessfully managed.'[1] When we examine her ' way of education ' we, now and again, venture to demur to some of her proceedings, but when we regard them in the light of her ' principal intention ' we can understand the reason of their adoption. Much as she desired

---

[1] Mrs. Clarke's *Susanna Wesley*, 30, 31.

that her children should acquire knowledge, her mind was set on the training of their character and the salvation of their souls. She never relinquished this noble enterprise. When her sons left their home, and were flung into the temptations of great schools, she sympathized with them in their work and applauded their successses, but ever reminded them of the higher wisdom which they must pursue. In her letters to Samuel, her son, when he was at Westminster, we catch the tones of her solicitude. She urges him, as one that has 'the greatest concern imaginable' for his soul, to aim at the possession of the mind of a Christian, that mind which should be 'always composed, temperate, free from all extremes of mirth or sadness, and always disposed to hear the still small voice of God's Holy Spirit which will direct him what and how to act in all the occurrences of life, if in all his ways he acknowledge Him and depend on His assistance.'[1] In addition she sent him, from time to time, letters intended to guard him against the assaults on Revelation which were excited by the writings of the Deists. She was aware that some parts of her letters were beyond his comprehension at that time, but she told him to keep them till he was older and better able to understand them. In the same spirit she wrote to her daughter Susanna, in 1710, when she went to London to stay with her Uncle Annesley, after the fire at the Epworth Rectory. She says, 'My tenderest regard is for your immortal soul, and for its spiritual happiness, which regard I cannot better express than by endeavouring to instil into your mind those principles of knowledge that are absolutely necessary in order to your leading a good life here, which is the only thing that can infallibly secure your happiness hereafter.'[2] One of the most striking illustrations of her efforts to convince her children of the truth of the Christian religion is to be found in a *Religious Conference*, written in 1712. It has been printed from the original in the collection of Wesley MSS. at Headingley College, Leeds, and published by the Wesley Historical Society. It is in the form of a dialogue between a mother and daughter, the daughter being the scholarly Emilia, afterwards Mrs. Harper, but its title shows that it was written for the use of all her children. The *Conference* concerns the great truths of religion, religion being defined as 'such a firm persuasion of

[1] Mrs. Clarke's *Susanna Wesley*, 49. [2] *Ibid.*, 84.

the being and perfection of God as influences our practice; that is, as makes us very serious in studying His nature and will, and very careful to perform all the duties He requires of us, to the end we may honour and please Him, so as to enjoy His favour, the consequence of which favour is eternal happiness.'[1] As Emilia has laid down the condition 'that things may be clearly and plainly proved before you demand my assent to the truth of them,' the mother proceeds to comply with it. The arguments proving the Being and Perfection of God are strong, clear, and convincing. They are urged with the calmness which indicates wide and accurate knowledge, deep meditation, the keen insight of a cultured mind, and the habitual 'practice of the presence of God.' This *Conference* does not stand alone. Another possessing the same characteristics is printed in Dr. Adam Clarke's *Wesley Family*.[2] These treatises were written by Mrs. Wesley for the training of her children because she could not find books on the subjects which satisfied her requirements.

On February 9, 1709, the Epworth Rectory was burnt down, John Wesley being rescued from the flames. A new house was built. Samuel Wesley left his new home and went up to London in November, 1710 to attend Convocation. In his absence his daughter Emilia found a book in his study and read it to her mother. It contained the account of the Danish Mission to Tranquebar, written by the two devoted men who had worked in it. The Mission was founded soon after the commencement of the eighteenth century, the missionaries sailing for Tranquebar in November, 1705. Protestant Foreign Missions were then uncommon, and as Emilia read the account of the Danish Mission to her mother Mrs. Wesley's heart was deeply stirred by the story. For some days she could think and speak of little else. Her desire for the salvation of souls was intensified, and she resolved to live in a more exemplary manner, to pray more for the people of the parish, and to speak with more warmth to those with whom she had opportunity of conversing. She determined to begin with her own children, and she made and carried out a plan for conversing with them, each child by itself, once a week. The recent rescue of their son John from the fire had caused her to think

---

[1] *Publications of W.H.S.*, No. 3, 6.
[2] *Works*, ii., 38-72.

that God had spared him for a special purpose, and to him she paid exceptional attention. His evening was Thursday, and so well did he respond to her motherly care that his father allowed him to become a communicant when he was eight years old.[1]

The fire which had been kindled in Susanna Wesley's heart burned with a steady flame. She began to hold a service every Sunday evening in the rectory kitchen for her children and servants. A serving-man told his parents, and they asked permission to attend. Others made the same request. The congregation grew rapidly, until by the end of January, 1711, two hundred were present, and many were obliged to go away because there was not even standing room. Speaking of the first services Mrs. Wesley says, ' With those few neighbours who then came to me I discoursed more freely and affectionately than before. I chose the best and most awakening sermons we had, and I spent more time with them in such exercises. Since then our company has increased every night, for I dare deny none that asks admission. . . . We meet not on any worldly design. We banish all temporal concerns from our Society; none is suffered to mingle any discourse about them with our reading or singing; we keep close to the business of the day, and as soon as it is over they all go home.'[2] The Society remained for the family prayers, and this caused Mrs. Wesley some disquiet of mind. That disquiet did not arise barely because so many were present, for she was convinced that ' those who have the honour of speaking to the great and holy God need not be ashamed to speak before the whole world '; but she doubted whether it was proper for a woman to present the prayers of the people to God. She would fain have dismissed them before prayers; but they begged so earnestly to stay that she durst not deny them. The effect of her meetings on the attendance at church and on the character of her neighbours was decisive. By the meetings more people were brought to church; some families, who seldom went there, became constant in their attendance; and one person, who had not been there for seven years, was prevailed upon to go with the rest. A moral reform began in Epworth, and the spirit of the people towards the Wesleys changed, and Mrs.

---

[1] Benson's *Apology for the Methodists*, 1.
[2] Mrs. Clarke's *Susanna Wesley*, 105.

Wesley was able to say 'now we live in the greatest amity imaginable.'[1]

The description of the proceedings of the Society showed that it was conducted, with certain variations, on the lines of the Religious Societies of which Samuel Wesley was a strong supporter. In his *Letter Concerning the Religious Societies*, published in 1699, he argues that so far from being any injury to the Church of England they would greatly promote its interests, and he expresses a wish that such Societies might be formed in all considerable towns, and even in populous villages; and he urged the necessity of their formation on the ground that, without them, the members of the Church have no opportunity for that 'delightful employment of all good Christians,' pious conversation.[2] These were his excellent sentiments, but he was alarmed by his wife's proceedings, and she had to defend herself against his objections. Her proceedings certainly did not conform, in all respects, to the 'Orders' of the Religious Societies. In them we find no arrangement for the management of a Society by a woman. Mrs. Wesley was conscious of the irregularity in her own case, but was so convinced of the usefulness of her meetings that she would not discontinue them unless her husband sent his positive command, in such full and express terms as might absolve her from all guilt and punishment for neglecting this opportunity of doing good 'when you and I shall appear before the great and awful tribunal of our Lord Jesus Christ.' Her husband did not send his 'positive command'; so the Society continued to meet until he returned from London, when it was dissolved.

We may be inclined to blame Samuel Wesley for his reluctance to allow the meeting of the Society in his rectory; but we must remember the circumstances of the time. It was asserted in Epworth that these meetings were conventicles. The curate-in-charge so styled them, and no one who is acquainted with the provisions of the Conventicle Act can doubt that he could have proved his case. We have shown that the Religious Societies in London had some cause to suspect that their proceedings were not in harmony with the provisions of statute law. Samuel Wesley had reason to know

---

[1] Mrs. Clarke's *Susanna Wesley*, 106–107.
[2] Tyerman's *Life and Times of Samuel Wesley*, 227–228.

that the full rigour of the law had been exercised on the Nonconformists who had held meetings similar to those his wife was conducting, and he was alarmed when he heard that the ugly word 'conventicle' was being whispered in the streets of Epworth. Mrs. Wesley, however, was not to be frightened. The curate and another opponent might call her meeting a conventicle, but she says, 'We hear no outcry here, nor has any one said a word against it to me. And what does their calling it a conventicle signify? Does it alter the nature of the thing? Or do you think that what they say is a sufficient reason to forbear a thing that has already done much good, and may, by the blessing of God, do much more?'[1]

The years went on their way, bringing strange and sorrowful experiences to the inmates of the Epworth Rectory. The boys left the well-guarded home, and had to face the experiences of the great schools on their way to the University. The mother followed their course with deep solicitude. The varied and often painful experiences of the Wesley girls do not come within the scope of our inquiry; but no one can read their record without profound sympathy with the mother who watched over them with the love that beareth all things, believeth all things, hopeth all things, endureth all things—the love that never fails.

[1] Mrs. Clarke's *Susanna Wesley*, 107.

IV

OXFORD IN THE EIGHTEENTH CENTURY

OXFORD in the eighteenth century was a grey city lying in the midst of far-spreading meadowlands. It possessed the irresistible charm of association and beauty. The years have brought changes in its aspect; but 'the sweet city, with her dreaming spires,' still stirs the heart with indescribable emotion.

What was the appearance of Oxford in the opening years of the eighteenth century? Some answer may be given if we consult Hollar's map of the city, dated 1643, inserted in Boase's *Oxford*, in the Historic Towns Series. It is founded on Ralph Agas's earlier map, which gives a bird's-eye view of Oxford in 1578. The fifty years that followed the publication of Hollar's map did not essentially change the general aspect of the city.

Glancing at the map, we see that the University, unlike that of Cambridge, has taken possession of the town. Most of the colleges lie within the circle of the ancient walls. At the present time fragments of those walls still remain, and their lines can be traced. The hand of time and the zeal of the 'improver' have borne heavily on the old defences; walls and gates have been destroyed. In the early years of the eighteenth century a traveller, approaching Oxford from the north, would enter the city by a gate that would arrest his attention. Its appearance is well represented in an illustration in Godley's *Oxford in the Eighteenth Century*. Over the gate he would notice a prison. He would soon be reminded of the poverty of the prisoners by seeing a hat, dangling from a string, let down from a window, and by the cry, 'Pity the Bocardo Birds.' Bocardo was the old gate-house used at that time as the town prison. Its name is supposed to be derived from the form of syllogism called Bocardo, out of which the reasoner could not 'bring himself back into his first figure without the use of special processes.' By the side of the prison there was a church, the tower of which is exceptionally interesting to the antiquary. Its style denotes that it belongs, at latest, to the early Norman period. Some think it was erected in the reign of Edward the Confessor. It seems to have been built, at first, for military purposes, and for a time stood alone. A church was built near it which afterwards, by enlargement, was brought up to it. Such is supposed to be the early history of St. Michael's, at the north gate. It carries our thoughts far beyond the beginnings of academic Oxford.

Many are the scenes of misery associated with Bocardo. One of its most pathetic memories belongs to the sixteenth century. On October 16, 1555, a procession passed through the gate on its way to the bank of the town ditch. In that procession Latimer and Ridley walked to their doom. As they approached Bocardo they looked up to one of the windows, hoping to get a farewell from Cranmer, who had been confined in the Bishop's Hole for nearly three years. But his attention at the moment was engrossed by a Spanish friar who was endeavouring to effect his perversion. The procession passed on. 'Without the city,' probably immediately opposite the gateway of Balliol College, the martyrs were burned. As they suffered, Cranmer, standing on the tower of St. Michael's Church, witnessed with great compassion the torture of his friends. He knelt down and prayed for them, complaining of the mismanagement that prolonged the sufferings of Ridley. It was from St. Michael's tower that he looked his farewell, conscious of the approach of the day when he would share the same fate. It was on March 21, 1556, that he was led out of Bocardo, and in the front of Balliol died in the flames. Looking at the map that lies before us, these vanished scenes re-appear. We listen to a voice saying, 'Be of good comfort, Master Ridley, and play the man. We shall this day light such a candle, by God's grace, in England, as I trust shall never be put out!'

If the traveller, having seen Bocardo, determines not to enter the town by the north gate, but to turn his face westward and skirt the walls, he would after a time come to the castle. The mound was raised probably about the year 913. In 1071 Robert D'Oilly[1] began to build the castle. One 'stern, rude, but picturesque' tower remains as a memorial of the Norman

[1] The name is spelt in several ways.

stronghold. In 1074 Robert D'Oilly, with his wife and his friend, Roger Ivry, began the foundation of the Church of St. George, which stood near the tower in the castle, and which continued to exist until 1805. Within the castle walls there was a prison given by Henry III ' to the peculiar jurisdiction of the Chancellor of the University as a place of confinement for rebellious clerks.' By a statute of the same king it was appointed as the common jail of the county. After the destruction of Bocardo, in 1771, the city prisoners were confined within the castle walls, the tower still remaining being for some time used as the prison.[1]

What was the condition of the county jail in the eighteenth century? In 1782 John Howard, in his ' circumnavigation of charity,' came to Oxford. It must be remembered that the prison was used for debtors as well as for criminals. In his report he says that ' the debtors had no free ward, and for lodging, even in the tower on their own beds, they had to pay 1s. 6d. per week. The felons' day-room for men and women, down five steps, was 23ft. by 11, the men's dungeon, down five more, was $18\frac{1}{2}$ by $16\frac{1}{2}$, with only small apertures, and swarming with vermin; the women's night-room, $6\frac{1}{2}$ by $4\frac{1}{3}$; the court common to both, 29 by 23. . . . There was no infirmary, no bath, no straw; the prisoners lay in their clothes on mats.' He continues, ' It is very probable that the rooms in this castle are the same as the prisoners occupied at the time of the Black Assize. The wards, passages, and staircases are close and offensive, so that, if crowded, I should not greatly wonder to hear of another fatal assize at Oxford. In 1773 eleven died of the small-pox.'[2] Howard's reference to the Black Assize has an ominous sound. It was held in 1577, when ' a most pernicious infection, caused by the smell of the jail when prisoners have been long and close nastily kept,' spread among the people assembled in the Session House, which then stood within the castle precincts. The infection was carried into the city and the neighbouring villages. In five weeks five hundred and ten persons, including one hundred ' scholars,' died. John Howard's report, which refers to the condition of the castle jail in 1782, may be taken as fairly representing its condition in the earlier years of the eighteenth century. Like

---

[1] Timbs's *Abbeys, Castles, and Ancient Halls of England and Wales*, ii., 80.
[2] Boase's *Oxford*, 201, 202.

most of the prisons in that day it was a repulsive place, the home of disorder, disease, and death.

If the traveller, after leaving the castle, entered the city by the west gate, he would strike a street leading to Christ Church. This college stands conspicuous in the University. It owes its origin to Cardinal Wolsey, who commenced it, erected some of its buildings, and intended that it should be known as Cardinal College. But his ambitions were not fulfilled. Henry VIII interfered, and refounded the college in 1532. After bearing the name of the King for a time, it finally was called Christ Church. The college makes a strong appeal to the lover of architectural design, but it has a deeper voice. If we stand before the west front our attention is arrested by the tower, commenced by Wolsey and finished by Wren, who added to it the octagonal cupola. In the tower there hangs the great bell once belonging to Osney Abbey, and recast in 1680. The name of the vanished abbey evokes many memories, and the tolling of the bell brings back the solemn past. The old abbey also speaks to us, in even clearer tones, when we listen to the music of 'the bonny Christ Church bells.' They also were transferred from Osney. During the eighteenth century Christ Church occupied, in one respect, almost a unique position. Godley says, 'Intellectually, there is no doubt that it may pass for the show college of the century.'[1] He adds that Nicholas Amherst, who has a hard word for most of his contemporaries, has no graver charge against Christ Church men, in 1733, than that of 'undue pride—whether based on superiority of birth or intellect.' Before 1733 such a verdict could not have been delivered. In that year John Conybeare, whose name is familiar to the students of the Deistic controversy, was transferred from Exeter College and became the Dean of Christ Church. He was not only a theologian but a ruler. He had effected great reforms in Exeter College and was translated to Christ Church to cleanse that 'Augean stable.' The reforms needed were moral rather than intellectual. In the barren years of the eighteenth century Christ Church men were noted for their attainments in 'pure' scholarship. The college realized more completely than almost any other the intellectual ideals of a University.

In order to find the other college which might be considered

[1] Godley's *Oxford in the Eighteenth Century*, 62.

the chief, if not the only, competitor of Christ Church in scholarship, the traveller would turn his face to the north of the city, and make his way to Lincoln. There, from 1730 to 1740, learning flourished, and the college chronicler speaks of the period as 'a golden age.' From 1719 to 1731 John Morley was rector. It was during his time that the tone of the college began to rise. He was succeeded by Euseby Isham, who was Vice-Chancellor of the University in 1744, and his successor at Lincoln was Richard Hutchins. 'Two excellent rectors' is their enviable record. They continued the good work commenced by Morley. It is pleasant to read these testimonies concerning the rectors of Lincoln at a time when the annals of Oxford are not bright with the names of moral reformers. The early history of Lincoln is closely connected with the progress of religion in England. It carries us back to the fourteenth century, when Wiclif's influence was pervading the country. Wiclif, in 1361, was the Master of Balliol Hall. He is acknowledged to have been the greatest schoolman of his day. But the pursuit of scholarship did not satisfy him. He was moved by a passionate desire to make the gospel known to all ranks of Englishmen. It was the time when the mendicant friars had passed their zenith as travelling preachers, and were beginning to darken their testimony with gross superstitions. Wiclif saw the danger, organized a body of 'poor preachers,' and sent them out as messengers, to show how the Scripture might be preached without mendicity. Boase says, 'The two forces that had built up the mediaeval system, the subtlety of the schoolman and the enthusiasm of the penniless preacher, were now arrayed against it. Besides his followers in the University, Wiclif was supported by the artisans of the towns. The upper classes in England, too, were at first favourable to him, but they were frightened by the outbreak of the villains in 1381 and Wiclifism lost its chance.'[1] At first Oxford sided with the new views, partly from attachment to Wiclif himself; but later a reaction set in which was strong and almost complete. In the fifteenth century an incident occurred which illustrated that reaction. In 1427 Richard Fleming was Bishop of Lincoln. At one time he had been inclined to accept the 'new views,' but he changed his mind. In 1427 he founded Lincoln College expressly as

[1] Boase's *Oxford*, 93.

'a little college of theologians to help in ruining heresy.' Lollardism was then fighting for its life, and Lincoln was founded to assist in its extermination. It was fortunate for Bishop Fleming's peace of mind that the future was hidden from his eyes. He was unable to see that a Fellow of Lincoln, in another century, would stir the hearts of the people of England by proclaiming the evangelical doctrines of the Scriptures, and that by means of his preachers he would spread the knowledge of those doctrines throughout the world.

Our wanderings in and about Oxford have brought us into the presence of four buildings which have attracted special attention—Christ Church, Lincoln, Bocardo, and the castle; and it is essential that we should see them as they appeared towards the beginning of the eighteenth century and perceive their significance. But we must do more. We shall not see the Oxford of that distant day aright unless we also watch the crowds that move along the streets; and, above all, attempt to discern the spirit of the place.

Walking along the streets, we soon come in contact with the 'scholars.' They impress us by their youthfulness. Some uncertainty exists as to the minimum age of matriculation at that time. Godley, judging by Dr. Macray's register of Magdalen College, thinks that through most of the century matriculation was commonest at sixteen or seventeen. At the close of the century there are instances of matriculation at the age of fourteen, or even thirteen. Christopher Wordsworth affirms that a precocious boy could enter at an age at which nowadays he would be not only discouraged, but practically inadmissible. As the century went on its way matters improved in this respect, but so late as 1752 Gibbon matriculated when he was only fourteen. As we are chiefly concerned with the Oxford of the first half of the century it will be enough to say that many of the 'scholars' were little more than boys. Youth has the defects of its qualities, and those defects were conspicuous in Oxford. Released from the strictness of the schools from which they came up, the 'men' found themselves 'cursed with an excess of liberty.' It is impossible to contend against the evidence which proves the weakness of the discipline that existed. It was in a state of torpor. In the sixteenth or even the seventeenth century, when boys arrived at Oxford or Cambridge, they found that they had not said farewell to the birch. But in the eighteenth century that instrument had disappeared. The comparative juvenility of Oxford undergraduates must be borne in mind when we are tempted to accept their opinions on great religious movements, and on men conspicuous for their moral strictness and high religious character.

The condition of morals in Oxford in the eighteenth century is a question that cannot be hastily decided. Burke declared that ' he did not know the method of drawing up an indictment against a whole people.' A remembrance of that sagacious saying should always check our tendency to broad generalization. We think it certain that the moral condition of Oxford in the eighteenth when contrasted with the previous century shows signs of distinct improvement. Still, there was much that needed reform in the University and the town. It must not be forgotten that Oxford had been subjected, during the seventeenth century, to influences that had disastrously affected its morals. The genesis of evil in the University is not hard to trace. At the beginning of the century James I, with his court, came to reside there for a time. Anthony Wood dates the outbreak of drunkenness in the University from this visit. The vice had not been previously conspicuous. Wood affirms that ' the court left such impressions of debauchery on the students that by a little practice they improved themselves so much that they became more excellent than their masters, and that also without scandal because it became a laudable fashion.'[1] In 1610 the statutes against drunkenness had to be revived. In Laud's Chancellorship an attempt was made to reduce the number of the three hundred ale-houses that existed in the city. From 1621-25 Lord Clarendon was at Magdalen Hall, and in his *Life* he speaks strongly against the drunkenness of Oxford. Boase, referring to Clarendon's protest, says that he made it with cause, for his eldest brother was ruined by the vice. The evil effects of the visit of James I were repeated and aggravated during the Civil War. Charles I made the city the Royalist capital, and it became for a long time the camp and court of the King. The ' call to arms ' roused the University, and the men flocked to the colours. The quads rang with the tramp of soldiers. Fortifications were thrown up in the fields, and the city was put into a state of

[1] Boase's *Oxford*, 136.

OXFORD IN THE EIGHTEENTH CENTURY 71

defence. The military excitement was rivalled by an unrestrained enthusiasm for pleasure. 'The groves and walks of the colleges, and especially Christ Church meadow, and the grove at Trinity, were the resort of a brilliant throng of gay courtiers and gayer ladies; the woods were vocal with song and music; love and gallantry sported themselves along the pleasant river banks.'[1] Distracted by military exercises and the allurements of pleasure, the Oxford man had little time or inclination for steady work. The example of his academical guides did not increase his intellectual industry in that time when 'wit, learning, and religion joined hand in hand as in some grotesque and brilliant masque.' The beaten paths of humdrum life were forsaken, and new ways of pleasantness were haunted by the unwary 'scholar.' Under the influence of the King, the court, and the army, Oxford became a gay and joyous city. Then came a change. The hope of victory over the forces of the Parliament perished. The clouds gathered over Oxford. On October 29, 1642, Charles I had entered with his army through the north gate into the city. On April 27, 1646, he stole over Magdalen Bridge, disguised as a servant in attendance on two other travellers; and soon after his escape Oxford was surrendered to Fairfax.

The triumph of the Parliament was followed by a period which left a deep and ineffaceable mark on the memory of Oxford. The 'reign of the saints' began. A strong hand was laid on the University. The colleges were brought under an iron discipline, which daunted the more riotous spirits and checked conspicuous vices. But the old ways were not altogether forsaken. In the eyes of many of the Oxford men of that day the new reforms were hateful. They hoped that a time would soon come when reforms and reformers would trouble them no more. That time lingered; but, while they waited for it, a bitterness against 'puritans and precisians' grew up which afterwards manifested itself in a remarkable manner. At last the Restoration came, and Oxford once more was a joyous city. In 1665 Charles II and his court were driven out of London by the plague, and again gay cavaliers filled Christ Church College. The loose manners of the court were introduced into the college precincts. Those who know

[1] Headlam's *The Story of Oxford*, Mediaeval Towns Series, 362-67.

the condition of the King's court will recognize the perils to the morals of Oxford which accompanied the Restoration. When we duly estimate the influence of the Stuarts on the University we gain some idea of its condition from the time of James I to that of Charles II. In the years following improvement set in ; but much of the influence of the age of licence persisted through the opening years of the eighteenth century.

Turning from the disheartening problem of the moral condition of Oxford in the eighteenth century we must face the question of its intellectual and scholastic condition. We have seen that some of the colleges were answering their purpose as places for the advancement of learning. But such a verdict cannot be pronounced on the whole University. Godley, who is a genial critic, declares that in Oxford the period of least academical efficiency coincides with the reign of the first two Georges—that is, from 1714 to 1760.[1] He styles this period ' the dark age for most colleges.' It was a time of incapable teaching and ridiculous examinations. Oxford owes its Honour Schools to the years immediately preceding 1800 ; through the greater part of the eighteenth century there was little to stimulate the student to aim at scholastic distinction. The condition of things is well described by Godley. He says : ' The eighteenth century had but little adventitious stimulus to learning. It was a period of conventions. Oxford gave her degrees really for residence, on the basis of the plausible and pleasing convention that Universities, being places of study, are inhabited by students, and that residence implied the habit of serious study. No doubt this attractive theory was at variance with the obvious facts of life ; still, those who entertained it may at least have the credit of maintaining a theory which is nothing if not respectable, and the few who did actually try to verify it must be the more laudable for the lack of incentive. In the absence of honour examinations and even of pass examinations other than merely farcical, they did nevertheless teach and learn.'[2] The lack of ambition to learn in the undergraduate corresponded with the lack of ambition to teach in most of the tutors. Amid the records of tutorial inertness there were exceptions, the brightness of such exceptions being intensified

---

[1] Godley's *Oxford in the Eighteenth Century*, 17.
[2] *Ibid.*, 39–40.

by the prevailing darkness. But speaking generally, it may be said that a tutor's determination to teach caused him to be regarded with 'a wondering eye.' Two persons excited the suspicion of the University at that time—the enthusiastic tutor, and the undergraduate who showed signs of moral strictness and religious 'seriousness.'

It is only necessary to note one other fact in order to enable us to discern the spirit and temper of the University during the eighteenth century. Oxford was strong for the King and the Church. When the tumult of the Civil War and the Restoration subsided, and quieter times came with the accession of William and Mary, Oxford gradually accepted the new settlement, and transferred its loyalty to the King and Queen. But the old devotion to the House of Stuart still burned in the breasts of many Oxford men. That devotion had been put under a tremendous strain by James II. The election of the President of Magdalen gave him several opportunities for exercising his fatal facility in making mistakes. He nominated a disreputable Cantab of notoriously bad character, who had migrated to Oxford and was reputed to be a Roman Catholic, and insisted upon his being elected as President. The Fellows of Magdalen were firm in their refusal to accept him. Their firmness was strengthened when James in his fury roared at them, 'Get you gone! I am King! I will be obeyed!' He little knew the weight of the blow he then struck at the loyalty of the whole University. The eyes of many were opened. They saw that he was a tyrant and abandoned him. When the Hanoverian Kings began to reign there were great searchings of heart at Oxford. Prudent men saw that the Stuart rule in England was doomed. Some clung to the 'lost cause.' Political discussions were keen. They were so frequent and prolonged that little time was left for other work. Some of the colleges took a strong stand in favour of the new dynasty, Christ Church being conspicuous among them. With three others it 'voted solid for the Whigs' in 1750. But time brought its usual remedy, and fierce passions were controlled. The Jacobites, Hearne's 'honest men,' still existed as a party, but their influence slowly declined until it ceased to be a source of serious danger in the University.

The loyalty of the University to the Church was fervent and

absolute. The incidents of the reign of James II had made its Protestantism more pronounced and confirmed its prejudices against Roman Catholics. Oxford was a staunch supporter of the Church of England, its system of government, its doctrines, rites, and ceremonies. Oxford men were convinced that the Church displayed, in the superlative degree, religion, moderation, and common sense. They were enamoured with its moderation, and listened eagerly to warnings against the danger of being 'righteous overmuch.' Like the great mass of their co-religionists, they had a strong dislike of 'enthusiasm,' and were ready to suppress it as soon as it showed itself in a University man. 'The reign of the saints' created traditions that kept alive a horror of excessive religious zeal. Puritans and Dissenters were utterly out of favour. At the beginning of the eighteenth century it would have been difficult to find any place more completely devoted to the Church of England than the University of Oxford.

V

JOHN AND CHARLES WESLEY AT OXFORD

ON January 28, 1714, John Wesley was admitted to the Charterhouse as a foundation scholar on the nomination of the Duke of Buckingham. The foundation scholars were limited in number, wore a distinctive dress, and were exempted from fees and charges. Dr. Walker was the head master. He was attracted by Wesley's brightness and earnestness. The boy was of a gay and sprightly temper, with a turn for wit and humour ; but he was a hard worker, and soon won a reputation for scholarship, especially as a writer of Latin verse. The younger boys in the great public schools are generally ruled with an iron hand by the elder boys, and at Charterhouse that rule was severe. However, Wesley submitted to it without much complaint. Notwithstanding his hardships he was ever a loyal and enthusiastic Carthusian. In after times he was accustomed to visit the old school at least once a year, walking through the grounds, and thinking again 'the long, long thoughts of youth.'

In 1720, the time having come when it was usual for the 'foundation' boys of highest repute and longest standing in the school to go to Oxford, John Wesley left Charterhouse with an exhibition of £40. He was entered at Christ Church on June 24, 1720. That college is closely associated with the names of the Wesleys. Samuel, John, and Charles, the sons of Samuel and Susanna Wesley, were all Christ Church men. John Wesley had an intense love for places rich in historic associations, and he was captured by the charm of Oxford. As he walked about the streets, wandered through the 'quads,' lingered in the chapels, strolled in the meadows, and looked at the city from the heights of Cumnor, there came to him a longing to spend all the days of his life in Oxford. This was no transient feeling. Time deepened his affection. In the stormy days that were before him he often paused in his lonely pilgrimage to recall the scenes of the past, and when he did so he longed to rest in academic shades once more. Towards the close of his life his admiration for Oxford diminished, but in certain moods the old love returned and burned in his heart.

The materials for reconstructing the scenes of John Wesley's life as an undergraduate are slight. We must think of him as he moved about in the Oxford of the eighteenth century. He responded to the influences of the University, and for a time it was a question as to the stream which would bear him away. But the law of heredity acted, his previous training played its part, and his mother's letters and his visits to his home assisted to keep him true to his 'better self.' He resisted the temptation to indulge in the special vices of the place, he sowed no 'wild oats,' he was a hard worker. He occasionally got into debt, to the dismay of his father, but there is no evidence that he spent any part of his scanty resources on forbidden 'pleasures.' As to religion, he went through the experiences of some of the better sort of young men who have been brought up strictly at home. He used his liberty, relaxed some of his religious observances, and waited for the coming of the crisis when a man sees truth and duty for himself and not through the eyes of another person. As an undergraduate he easily reached the standard of 'religion' that had been tacitly fixed in the University. Mr. Curnock, the editor of the standard edition of *The Journal of John Wesley*, has given us an appreciation of Wesley as an undergraduate which possesses exceptional value. He describes him as winning the reputation of an industrious, keen-witted, and successful student, and of a thoughtful, versatile, and lively comrade. He held his own in the tennis court, could swim, ride, hunt, and walk long distances. He had a great love of company, read all kinds of books, was sprightly in conversation, victorious in debate, and covetous of knowledge. Mr. Curnock thinks that Wesley's frail health while he was at Oxford 'compelled him to indulge in a disproportionate amount of rest and recreation,' and he suggests that his occasional 'idleness' consisted more frequently than not in excursions into by-paths of literature and knowledge, and in visits to the Coffee House to read the news.[1]

[1] *John Wesley's Journal*, i., 20–21, Standard ed. The quotations from the *Journal* are taken from this edition.

JOHN AND CHARLES WESLEY AT OXFORD

Every glimpse we get of him in his undergraduate days confirms the correctness of Mr. Badcock's estimate of him in the *Westminster Magazine*. In his eyes he appeared ' the very sensible and acute collegian—a young fellow of the finest classical taste, of the most liberal and manly sentiments.'[1] He had many friends in the University. In his *Diary*, under the date March 10, 1725, he sets out their names with affection. They belonged to Christ Church, Corpus, Merton, Magdalen, Wadham, Exeter, New College, and Lincoln. We can picture the joyous fellowship of these early days in which high debate, relieved by the gleam of humour and the sparkle of wit, was heard in college rooms. The voices of that bright company have long been silenced, but we can imagine the gladness of the hours which Wesley spent in the company of his friends.

John Wesley entered heartily into the ordinary life of the Oxford undergraduate. Then a change came. Mr. Curnock, searching the pages of the little note-book in which Wesley's first Oxford *Diary* is contained,[2] found an entry which seemed to indicate that at the close of 1721, when Wesley was in his nineteenth year, something occurred which induced him to take a more serious view of life. The moving cause cannot be discovered, but it is clear he then formed and carried out a plan for the regulation of his work. He knew that he was wasting his time, and determined to squander his hours no longer. He adopted a methodical system of study, and wrote out a scheme on the inner cover of the note-book. It includes a time-table for each day of the week, studies for 1722, and an order of correspondence with his father, mother, sisters, and brother. Such was the beginning of Wesley's attempts to economize time and methodize work. The scheme was subsequently elaborated, and his after-life testifies to the wisdom of the plan adopted.

The attempt to stop a prodigal waste of time was only a first stroke in Wesley's battle for self-mastery. He was compelled to face the future, and he had to learn the hard lesson that the things which we ought to do are often the things we most dislike to do. What was to be his career when his pleasant

---

[1] Henry Moore's *Life of Wesley*, i., 117.
[2] Mr. Curnock suggests that this note-book originally belonged to John Westley, of Winterbourne Whitchurch ; that it passed into the possession of his son Samuel Wesley, and so came into John Wesley's hands. The evidence produced favours the conjecture.

undergraduate days were over ? The outlines of a scheme of his life were traced in his mind. The spell of Oxford was on him. He would remain there after he had taken his degrees. Hope whispered to him that he might become a tutor, or a Fellow of a college ! But in Oxford he was, and there he intended to remain. The world outside had few attractions for him. Its roar and the cry of its pain and need came to him at intervals ; but, usually, the sounds were deadened by distance and made no imperative appeal to his sympathy. His regardlessness did not arise from lack of heart ; it was the result of the absorbing interest of his University life. His tastes and inclinations had found a sphere in which they were satisfied. It might have been supposed that with ancestral examples before him the ministry would have attracted him ; but ancestral examples do not always excite in young men a passion for imitation. It is certain that, at the outset of his University career, he had no intention of becoming a clergyman.

It is impossible to understand John Wesley's life if we refuse to recognize that it was under the control of God. He had to carry out a divine scheme, not to realize a pleasant dream of his own concerning idyllic days in academic groves. He had to learn that God had determined to give him an almost unexampled opportunity of reforming the nation and the Church, and of spreading the influence of the gospel throughout the world. It was possible for him to make ' the great refusal,' and surrender the enduring glory of the man who does God's will on earth as it is done in heaven. Those who watch him in the days of hesitation in Oxford are aware of the peril of his reluctance. It is with intense interest they see him slowly turning his feet into the hard path he had to travel.

Many of the incidents which led to Wesley's determination to surrender his own life-design are hidden. He was utterly unconscious of the remarkable work that he was destined to do. Several years had to elapse before the divine plan of his life began to glimmer through the haze. He followed the course of events, and some of those events are difficult to discern. It is generally supposed that his father put pressure on him to induce him to be his successor in Epworth. Whatever may have been the immediate cause, it is certain that towards the end of 1724, a change in his views concerning his future career took place. He determined to enter into holy orders, and he communicated the fact to his father and mother. His decision caused great joy in the rectory. On January 26, 1725, his father wrote to him in his characteristic fashion, and urged him to the study of the languages that would enable him thoroughly to understand the original text of the Scriptures. His mother's advice was that he should read practical divinity, which she considered the best study for candidates for orders ; adding, ' Mr. Wesley differs from me, and would engage you, I believe, in critical learning, which, though accidentally of use, is in no wise preferable to the other.'[1] Without neglecting ' critical learning,' John Wesley began to pay special attention to ' practical divinity.' He had previously seen Thomas à Kempis's *Imitatio Christi*, and had turned over its pages without being much attracted by them. His critical faculty was generally wide awake, and Thomas à Kempis provoked its exercise. But he took up the book again, and, judging it by its best side, he was much impressed by it. In addition he carefully read Jeremy Taylor's *Holy Living and Dying*. As a consequence he became fascinated by the thought of holiness, and he entered on its pursuit. It was at this stage that he lacked the guidance of a friend with whom he might have free and intimate conversation concerning the subjects that were stirring strange thoughts in his heart. His University companions could not assist him, so he had to take counsel with himself. On April 5, 1725, he began to speak to himself in a *Diary* now famous. He did not intend that its contents should be seen by any other eye than his own. He wrote the entries in longhand, shorthand, and in a cipher which for many years baffled all investigators.[2] The transliteration of the *Diary* reveals the sharpness of the watch Wesley kept over himself, not only in respect of the economizing of his time, but of the discharge of his religious duties. We seem to be reading a book of battles in which there are records of many defeats, but in which there is also a tone suggestive of ultimate victory. Wesley's communings with himself in his *Diary* assisted him in his pursuit of holiness, but something more was needed. On April 14, 1725, he met for the first time ' a religious friend,'

---

[1] Tyerman's *Life of Samuel Wesley*, 391–92.
[2] By the patient skill and ingenuity of Mr. Curnock the entries in the *Diary* have been interpreted. It is an interesting fact that Wesley's aunt, Elizabeth Annesley, who married John Dunton, kept a similar diary for nearly twenty years. Dunton says that much of what she wrote in it was ' in a shorthand of her own invention.' Dunton's *Life and Errors*, i., 277.

who subsequently gave him most valuable help in his spiritual conflicts. Mr. Curnock has produced strong evidence to show that this religious friend was Miss Betty Kirkham, the daughter of the Rector of Stanton, in Gloucestershire. The friendship continued for several years, and brought Wesley into intimate association with a charming circle of cultured women who resided in the villages of Broadway, near Evesham, and Buckland, in Gloucestershire. Mrs. Pendarves, a young widow who afterwards married Dr. Delany, the Dean of Down, is the best-known member of this circle. Dr. Rigg describes her as 'a woman of high accomplishments and of almost unequalled charms and attractions, who moved in the best society of the country, and was honoured for half a century and more with the intimate friendship and confidence of King George III and his Queen.'[1] In conversation and correspondence with Mrs. Pendarves and her friends Wesley spent some of the happiest moments of his life, and the light of those brilliant days never faded. But, as we have suggested, there was one member of the group by whom he was specially attracted. When he describes her as 'the first religious friend' he ever had it is evident he uses the phrase in a special sense, as denoting some one of his own age, with whom he could converse with absolute freedom on religious questions. It is true that his mother was his usual confidante; but she spoke with an authority that Wesley recognized so long as she lived. In facing his mental difficulties he needed the assistance of some one to whom he could speak on equal terms, and tell out the story of his perplexities without any fear of being suspected of dangerous declinings from orthodoxy and the religion of his youth. It was fortunate for him that Miss Betty Kirkham knew the books he was then reading, and was aware of their defects. It was also well that she was not a theologian. If she had been, Wesley would have argued with her and exercised his exceptional skill in the discovery of fallacies, and wasted his time in attacking the weak side of very strong books. She had the intelligent woman's original way of looking at things which so often helps us to see old truths in a fresh light. Above all, she had interpreted by experience the meaning of Thomas à Kempis and Jeremy Taylor and was able to distinguish between the teaching that

[1] *The Living Wesley*, 1st edition, 56.

was vital and that which was questionable. Emphasizing the vital, she abandoned the questionable to Wesley's destructive dialectic. As a result the practical view of holiness prevailed, and his determination to seek it was confirmed.

Wesley now devoted much of his time to the reading of practical divinity. He read with keenness, but encountered many difficulties. Some of them were solved by conversation with Miss Betty Kirkham; others he submitted to his mother. In a letter written to his mother, dated June 18, 1725, we see the working of his sane and sober mind. Quoting Jeremy Taylor's affirmations concerning humility, in the fourth section of the second chapter of his *Holy Living*, he says that he hesitates to accept such statements as the following: ' We must be sure, in some sense or other, to think ourselves the worst in every company where we come.' ' Give God thanks for every weakness, deformity, or imperfection, and accept it as a favour and grace to resist pride.' It is no wonder that Wesley, who was in search of a reasonable view of Christianity, challenged the wisdom of these directions, especially as Taylor seemed to insist that they must be obeyed if the humility essential to salvation is to be possessed. In his letter, lately in the collection of Mr. George Stampe, of Grimsby, this note is inserted in Mrs. Wesley's firm, clear handwriting : ' Weakness, deformity, or imperfection of body are not evil in themselves, but accidentally become good or evil according as they affect us and make us good or bad,' a qualification of Taylor's assertion that somewhat reduces its sternness. But the most important part of Wesley's letter is a criticism of Taylor's statement on the supreme subject of the forgiveness of sins. Taylor's statement is first set out : ' Repentance contains in it all the parts of a holy life from our return to our death. A man can have but one proper repentance, viz. when the rite of baptism is verified by God's grace coming upon us, and our obedience. If after this change, if we ever fall into the contrary state, there is no place left for any more repentance. A true penitent must all the days of his life pray for pardon, and never think the work complete till he dies. Whether God has forgiven us or no we know not, therefore still be sorrowful for ever having sinned.' John Wesley's remarks on this statement, viewed in the light of after-events, are of the utmost importance, and should be closely studied. He says :

I take the more notice of this last sentence, because it seems to contradict his own words in the next section where he says that by the Lord's Supper all the members are united to one another and to Christ the Head ; the Holy Ghost confers on us the graces we pray for, and our souls receive into them the seeds of an immortal nature. Now surely these graces are not of so little force as that we can't perceive whether we have them or no ; and if we dwell in Christ and Christ in us, which He will not do till we are regenerate, certainly we must be sensible of it. If his opinion be true, I must own I have always been in a great error, for I imagined when I communicated worthily, i.e. with faith, humility, and thankfulness, my preceding sins were *ipso facto* forgiven me ; I mean so forgiven that unless I fell into them again I might be secure of their ever rising in judgement against me, at least in the other world. But if we can never have any certainty of our being in a state of salvation, good reason it is that every moment should be spent, not in joy, but fear and trembling ; and then undoubtedly in this life we are of all men most miserable. God deliver us from such a fearful expectation as this. Humility is undoubtedly necessary to salvation, and if all these things are essential to humility, who can be humble, who can be saved ?[1]

Having determined to seek holy orders, Wesley prepared himself not only by reading, conversation, and correspondence, but by habitual attendance at the Lord's Supper. His view of the benefits to be derived from that solemn ordinance, by a worthy communicant, is contained in his letter to his mother, and it is no wonder that he approached the table once a week. Exercising a care over himself which was rare at that period, he prepared himself for the office of deacon. He had some scruples about the Athanasian creed, but these seem to have been removed. He subscribed the Articles, and on September 19, 1725, he was ordained deacon by Bishop Potter. The state of mind induced by his careful preparation for his ordination persisted. He continued to keep vigilant watch over himself. Towards the close of 1725 he resolved to fast every Wednesday, and, at some time during the following year, he began the practice of holding, on every Saturday evening, an inquisition on himself regarding his religious experiences during the week.[2]

On March 17, 1726, John Wesley, chiefly through the influence of Dr. Morley, was elected Fellow of Lincoln. By his election he was released from the condition of chronic poverty in which he had spent his undergraduate days. His

---

[1] Our quotations are from the original letter.
[2] *Journal*, i., 51.

harsh experiences had made him proficient in the art of economizing. Speaking of his financial position, Dr. Rigg says: 'Exercising economy as rigid over his personal expenses afterwards as in his greatest poverty before, he was able to assist his brother Samuel in helping their father, and to be, to the end of his life, a benefactor to his family. He never saved to enrich himself.'[1] The new honour, however, brought its disadvantages. In the eighteenth century the holding of a Fellowship without residence, except under certain specified conditions, was considered a scandal. The majority of the Fellows, finding that there was little employment for them in Oxford, and that they were forbidden to seek it elsewhere on pain of losing their Fellowships, gave themselves up to a comfortable, leisurely life, enjoying the benefits of their Founders until it was possible for them to take a living and a wife.[2] Sometimes, when a Fellow was invited to act as a tutor or chaplain to ' a person of quality ' he received permission to be non-resident. To a man of Wesley's abnormal activity the prospect of the life of the drowsy don was unbearable. His father wanted him to act as his curate in his two parishes of Epworth and Wroot, and he was wishful to help him. He was relieved when the precedent in the case of chaplains was stretched in his favour, and he received permission to absent himself from the University. He was away from April to September, 1726. In the latter month he returned to Oxford, and found that his life was not to be consumed in idleness. On November 7 he was elected Greek lecturer, and Moderator of the Classes, and also became a tutor of Lincoln College. He was little more than twenty-three years of age. His time was well occupied. In addition to his other work, he read for his Master's degree, which he took on February 14, 1727, acquiring considerable reputation by his ' disputation.' In August he resumed his work as his father's curate. In September, 1728, he was in Oxford, and was ordained priest by Bishop Potter, but the next month he returned to Lincolnshire, and did not take up his residence in Oxford again until November 22, 1729.

During three years the residence of John Wesley in Oxford was intermittent, but all the time he was advancing in his quest after holiness. He read Law's *Serious Call to a Devout*

[1] *The Living Wesley,* 51.   [2] Godley's *Oxford,* 71, 81, 82, 108.

and Holy Life, and his treatise on *Christian Perfection*. These books convinced him more than ever of the absolute impossibility of being 'half a Christian.'[1] The perception of the difference between the 'half' and the 'whole' Christian had come to him so early as the middle of 1725. In a letter to his mother he describes an interview with a friend in St. Mary's Church, Oxford, and in it the phrase 'a whole Christian' occurs. Its use suggests that he had begun to see that there was a deeper meaning in the name Christian than he had supposed, and that it was his duty to discover it.

In order to understand the importance of the years 1726–1729 we must leave John Wesley for a time, and fix our attention on his youngest brother. Charles Wesley entered Westminster School in 1716. His eldest brother Samuel, who was the head usher there, had married the daughter of the Rev. John Berry, who kept a boarding-house for Westminster boys, and his marriage and position enabled him to offer Charles Wesley a home and an education. Charles lived with his brother from 1716 to 1721. In the latter year he became a King's scholar, and as such his board and education were free. In 1725 he was captain of the school, and in 1726 he was elected to Christ Church, Oxford. His nine years at Westminster laid the foundation of his scholarship, and his close association with his brother Samuel, who was a scholar, a poet, and a Christian, left enduring marks on his character. Samuel Wesley was the friend of Bishop Sprat and Bishop Atterbury, and the acquaintance of Alexander Pope. He was a High Churchman, and 'extremely rigid in his principles.'[2] His warm affection for Atterbury, and his readiness to defend him, brought him under grave suspicion of being a Jacobite. When Atterbury was banished for being implicated in the great Jacobite plot he expressed his admiration for him in a poem overflowing with eulogy. Samuel Wesley was not a Jacobite, but his advocacy of his friend was so ardent that he often seemed to be one. As a consequence he raised a prejudice against himself which was shown when he was passed over at the time of the appointment of the second master of the school. He left Westminster, and for several years was the head master of the famous Blundell's School, Tiverton. Remembering his close association with his brother Samuel, it is not

[1] Benson's *Apology for the Methodists*, 6.   [2] Dr. Whitehead's *Life of Wesley*, i., 90.

surprising that throughout his life Charles Wesley was a political and ecclesiastical High Churchman.[1]

John Wesley owed many of his intellectual and moral qualities to his mother; in Charles Wesley we often recognize his father. He possessed that perilous dower, the artistic temperament, so capable of giving pleasure and pain. Henry Moore, who knew him well, describes him, in his younger days, as exceedingly sprightly and active, very apt to learn, but arch and unlucky, though not ill-natured.[2] His sprightliness was soon displayed in Oxford. He entered with zest into the pleasures of University life. He frankly confesses that he lost his first year 'in diversions.' That statement needs some qualification. John Wesley's testimony is, ' He pursued his studies diligently, and led a regular, harmless life; but if I spoke to him about religion he would warmly answer, " What! Would you have me be a saint all at once?" and would hear no more.'

In 1728 a change came over Charles Wesley. We do not know the cause, but he began to apply himself steadily to work, and became more serious. In January, 1729, he wrote to his brother John and consulted him on the question of beginning to keep a Diary, asking what cipher he should use. In his letter he says: ' God has thought fit, it may be to increase my wariness, to deny me at present your company and assistance. It is through Him strengthening me I trust to maintain my ground till we meet; and I hope that neither before nor after that time I shall relapse into my former state of insensibility. It is through your means, I firmly believe, that God will establish what He has begun in me; and there is no one person I would so willingly have to be the instrument of good to me as you. It is owing, in great measure, to somebody's prayers, my mother's most likely, that I am come to think as I do; for I cannot tell myself how or when I awoke out of my lethargy—only it was not long after you went away.'[3]

The change in Charles Wesley occurred at a critical time in the history of the University. The discussion of the questions raised in the course of the Deistic controversy had disturbed the minds of the undergraduates. The attacks on Revelation had produced their inevitable result. Religious conviction

[1] For important information concerning Samuel Wesley see articles by Rev. T. E. Brigden in *W.H.S. Proceedings*, xi.
[2] *Life of Wesley*, i., 151.   [3] *Ibid.*, i., 153–54.

was weakened, and that led to carelessness in religious observance. The condition of morals was lowered, and those who were responsible for the men began to be alarmed. The Vice-Chancellor, with the consent of the heads of houses and proctors, issued a *programma* which was fixed up in most of the halls of the University. In this document the tutors of each college and hall were directed to discharge their duty ' by a double diligence, in informing their respective pupils in their Christian duty, as also in explaining to them the Articles of Religion which they profess, and are often called upon to subscribe, and in recommending to them the frequent and careful reading of the Scriptures, and such other books as may serve more effectually to promote Christianity, sound principles, and orthodox faith.'[1] The action of the Vice-Chancellor was not universally approved. The Dean of Christ Church, who was at the same time the Bishop of Bristol, would not allow the notice to be put up in the hall of his college. His action made him conspicuous. The note of alarm sounded by the Vice-Chancellor roused attention, and stirred some of the tutors into greater activity.

One ' Christian duty ' notoriously neglected in the University was the duty of attending the Sacrament of the Lord's Supper. The habitual neglect of the Sacrament was in defiance of law. If canons and rubrics had been obeyed the Communion Services held in the cathedral and the colleges would have been well attended. If we turn to the twenty-third of the *Constitutions and Canons Ecclesiastical* which govern the Church of England we see a suggestion of a solemn assembly at the Sacrament in the University.

> In all colleges and halls within both the Universities, the masters and fellows, such especially as have any pupils, shall be careful that all their said pupils, and the rest that remain amongst them, be well brought up, and thoroughly instructed in points of religion, and that they do diligently frequent public service and sermons, and receive the Holy Communion; which we ordain to be administered in all such colleges and halls the first or second Sunday of every month, requiring all the said masters, fellows, and scholars, and all the rest of the students, officers, and all the other servants there, so to be ordered, that every one of them shall communicate four times in the year at least, kneeling reverently and decently upon their knees, according to the order of the Communion Book prescribed in that behalf.

[1] Moore's *Life of Wesley*, i., 154-55.

JOHN AND CHARLES WESLEY AT OXFORD 87

In addition to the canon the rubric at the end of the Communion Service in the Book of Common Prayer directs that ' in cathedral and collegiate churches and colleges, where there are many priests and deacons, they shall all receive the Communion with the priest every Sunday at the least, except they have a reasonable cause to the contrary.' Notwithstanding canon and rubric, religion had fallen so low in Oxford that frequent attendance at the Lord's Supper exposed a man to remark and ridicule.

Charles Wesley, being roused from his religious lethargy, began to consider the duty of communicating more frequently. He was compelled by canon to receive the Lord's Supper at least four times in the year, but after thinking over the matter he decided that he needed spiritual help so much that it would be better to attend more frequently. On May 29, 1729, he wrote to his brother John on the subject, and his resolution was fixed. He was a man born for companionship, and among his friends he found three or four men who shared his view as to regular attendance at the Sacrament. They went to the Communion weekly in the cathedral, which was the Christ Church College Chapel. Some writers have described the march of the little company through the streets of Oxford to the cathedral, but all who know Christ Church are aware that it can be reached through the quad without going outside the precincts of the college. Charles Wesley and his friends made no parade, but simply attended the Sacrament week by week. Such attendance was certain to excite astonishment. In addition they had attracted attention by the exact regularity of their lives, their devotion to work, and their observance of the statutes of the University. It was not long before a Christ Church man, watching them on their way to the cathedral, jocosely cried, ' Here is a new set of Methodists sprung up!' The genesis of a joke is hard to trace, and the original joker seldom gets his rights. It is affirmed that the name of Methodists was first applied to Charles Wesley and his companions by a tutor of Merton. It was supposed to have been suggested by the name given to a set of physicians who, in ancient times, declined to treat their patients in a haphazard fashion, and insisted on curing them methodically; a course which must have been to the advantage of suffering humanity. The diligent research of the ecclesiastical philologist has led to the discovery of the word as descriptive of parties of religious men in years preceding the eighteenth century; but we content ourselves by recording the circumstances of its application to the little group who attended the Sacrament with conspicuous regularity in Oxford in 1729. John Wesley, in after years, rarely used the nickname without careful qualification, such as ' the people in derision called Methodists,' or ' the people vulgarly called Methodists,' or ' the people called Methodists '; but at the time of its invention he admits that it was new and quaint, that it took immediately, and that the ' Methodists ' were known by it all over the University.[1]

[1] *A Short History of Methodism.* See *Works*, viii., 348, 8vo ed.

VI

'THE HOLY CLUB'

On October 21, 1729, Dr. Morley, the rector of Lincoln College, wrote a letter to John Wesley. In it he told him that at a meeting which had been held to consider the proper method to preserve discipline and good government, among several things agreed on, in the opinion of all present it was necessary that the Junior Fellows, who should be chosen moderators, should in person attend the duties of their office if they did not prevail with some of the Fellows to officiate for them. Dr. Morley said that he had tried to get some one to take Wesley's place, but had failed. The letter concluded as follows: 'We hope it may be as much for your advantage to reside at college as where you are, if you take pupils, or can get a curacy in the neighbourhood of Oxon. Your father may certainly have another curate, though not so much to his satisfaction; yet we are persuaded that this will not move him to hinder your return to college, since the interest of college and obligation to statute require it.' Wesley complied with the rector's request. On November 22 he resumed his residence in Oxford.

The time had come when the heads of houses felt that a strong effort must be made to preserve discipline and good government and to improve the moral and religious tone of the University. Wesley threw himself into the work with the 'double diligence' which had been commended by the Vice-Chancellor, and he met with some success. Outside Lincoln he also made his influence felt. The study of Greek was gradually reviving in the University. At one time it was so neglected that it was rare to meet a man who took any interest in it.[1] But better days had come. The work of Walton, Fell, Mill, and others had roused the enthusiasm of a select band of scholars, who devoted themselves to the study of New Testament Greek. John and Charles Wesley belonged

[1] Godley's *Oxford*, 44.

to this company.¹ It was natural that when an undergraduate felt the fervour of a desire to understand his Greek Testament he should turn his eyes towards the Lincoln Greek lecturer. We are not surprised to find that in November, 1729, John Wesley, Charles Wesley, William Morgan, a Commoner of Christ Church, and Robert Kirkham, of Merton, began to meet together, and agreed to spend three or four evenings in a week in reading the Latin and Greek classics, and especially the Greek Testament. In addition, they determined to meet on Sunday evenings for the special consideration of divinity. This little group of ardent scholars arrests attention. Some of them were 'Methodists.' We can imagine the topics on which they conversed on Sunday evenings. John Wesley was in complete sympathy with them in their practice of frequent Communion. Apart from legal obligation he was convinced of the benefit to be derived from steady rather than desultory attendance at the Table of the Lord. As the year ran to a close the little meetings, deepening in tone, ministered consolation to those who, by reason of their greater religious earnestness, were beginning to be isolated from the mass of Oxford men.

In 1730 the small group increased in number. Acting in harmony with the Vice-Chancellor's instructions, John Wesley made the religious condition of his pupils his special care. Charles Wesley, who had begun to take pupils, followed his example. As a consequence three or four of them asked permission to attend the meetings of the company. In March John Gambold, of Christ Church, became acquainted with Charles Wesley, and afterwards was introduced to John Wesley. We are indebted to Gambold for a sketch of the brothers at this time. He says: 'Could I describe one of them, I should describe both. And therefore I shall say no more of Charles, but that he was a man made for friendship; who, by his cheerfulness and vivacity, would refresh his friend's heart; with attentive consideration would enter into and settle all his concerns; so far as he was able, would do anything for him, great or small; and, by a habit of openness and freedom, leave no room for misunderstandings.'² Gambold joined the

---

¹ Charles Wesley's Greek Testament was in the possession of Mr. George Stampe. It is a 12mo. of the Plantin Press of Leyden, dated 1591; the text is that of Stephens, revised by Beza. See article by Rev. A. W. Harrison in *W.H.S. Proceedings*, ix., 107.
² Tyerman's *Oxford Methodists*, 157.

company, and brought with him much zeal in the study of the Greek New Testament, as well as the influence of a fine character.[1]

In the summer of 1730 William Morgan, moved by curiosity, called at the castle to see a man who had been condemned for killing his wife. He was struck by the strange spectacle of criminals and debtors herded together. He talked with one of the debtors, and was convinced that if a sober person, now and then, would converse with the prisoners, much good would be done among them. Being urgent about the matter, he induced John and Charles Wesley to accompany him to the castle. They saw the need of the work Morgan suggested to them, and agreed to visit the prisoners once or twice a week. Soon afterwards Morgan desired John Wesley to go with him to visit a poor woman in the town who was ill. They went together, and finding their advice well received, they determined, now and then, to pass an hour in such charitable visits. It occurred to them that their visitation of the poor might give offence to the parish ministers, and so they waited on those whose parishes they entered and obtained their consent. In addition, they applied to Mr. Gerard, the bishop's chaplain, who had the care of prisoners under condemnation, for permission to visit them. They also asked him to allow John Wesley to preach to the prisoners once a month, if the bishop would consent. Mr. Gerard approved of the suggestion, and soon afterwards intimated that the bishop had given his permission, and had sent his hearty good wishes for the success of the attempt. This work, therefore, was done with the express approval of the ecclesiastical authorities.

Gambold in his description of the proceedings of the company expresses the opinion that though some of the practices of the first 'Methodists,' such as their fasting on Wednesday and Friday, and their communicating at Christ Church on those Sundays when there was no Sacrament at their own colleges, were much blamed, yet nothing was so much disliked as their charitable work. It is a surprising statement; but Gambold was in a position to know the facts, and his testimony may be accepted. At this point it will be convenient to anticipate the course of events and give a brief description of that work. The

---

[1] In 1742 Gambold published a Greek text of the New Testament. It followed Mill in the readings he preferred, and adopted Bengel's punctuation and divisions into paragraphs. See *W.H.S. Proceedings*, ix., 113.

visitation of the prisoners in the castle and in Bocardo was constant. At the castle the prisoners who cared to attend assembled in the chapel. A book was read to them, such as the *Christian Monitor* and the *Country Parson's Advice to his Parishioners*, and conversation followed. Particular attention was paid to prisoners condemned to death. As to the debtors, in order to release those who were confined for small debts and ' were bettered by their affliction, and likewise to purchase books, physic, and other necessaries,' the members of the company raised a small fund, to which many of their acquaintances contributed quarterly. John Wesley and those associated with him had prayers at the castle, as a rule, on Wednesdays and Fridays, a sermon was preached there on Sundays, and the Sacrament was administered once a month. When the case of a poor family was taken up, some of the ' Methodists ' saw them at least once a week ; sometimes gave them money, admonished them of their vices, read to them, and instructed the children.

A school was set up. Gambold thinks that John Wesley commenced it. He paid the mistress, and clothed some, if not all, of the children. When the school was visited inquiries were made as to the behaviour of each child ; their knitting and spinning were inspected ; their reading was heard, so was their catechism, the latter being explained to them. In the same manner the children in the workhouse were taught, and the old people had books read to them.[1] In these modern days, when the work of the University settlements in our large towns is so generally applauded, it is difficult to understand the opposition of Oxford to the ' charitable employments ' of the ' Methodists.' But they had to endure the hardships of the men who cut ' wilderness roads ' over the mountains, and to suffer the fate of philanthropic pioneers.

It must have been in 1729 or early in 1730 that the Methodist company received a new name. At one of their meetings, when the Methodists numbered five persons, Robert Kirkham, of Merton, told them that he had been much rallied the day before for being a member of ' The Holy Club,' and that it was become a topic of mirth at his college, where they had found out several of their customs. The phrase coined by the merry wits of Merton became current in the University, and increased

[1] Tyerman's *Oxford Methodists*, 158-59.

its gaiety, but John Wesley's keen sense of humour was sufficient for him. He went on his way, applying this rule to all misrepresentations of the proceedings of the 'company;' 'We do indeed use all the lawful means we know to prevent the good which is in us from being evil spoken of; but, if the neglect of known duties be the one condition of securing our reputation, why, fare it well! We know whom we have believed, and what we thus lay out He will pay us again.'[1]

It soon became evident that weapons sharper than raillery were needed to crush the Methodists. They were employed. A man, described as 'a gentleman, eminent for learning and well esteemed for piety,' had a nephew who had formed the habit of going to weekly Communion. He was told by his uncle that if he did so any longer he would turn him out of doors. As he persisted in the practice, this gentleman 'well esteemed for piety,' took him by the throat, and shook him violently. The argument failed. Changing his tactics, the uncle tried the effect of 'a soft and obliging manner,' and succeeded in inducing his nephew to absent himself five Sundays out of six from the Sacrament. The success of the experiment was noised abroad. In its gentler form, we presume, it was tried on two other frequent communicants, who promised they would only communicate three times a year. The domestic pressure on the Methodists was supplemented by the action of some of the authorities of the University. At the beginning of 1731 a meeting of several of the officers and seniors of one of the colleges was held to consult on the speediest way of stopping the progress of 'enthusiasm.' The result of the consultation was not disclosed, but it was soon publicly reported that 'Dr. —— and the censors were going to blow up the Godly Club.' John Wesley was not terrified by this rumour. He possessed a valiant spirit. Although a man of extraordinary strength of character, he rarely acted at critical moments without taking counsel with people whose judgement he valued. After the college meeting he wrote to his brother Samuel at Westminster, who answered him in April.

I designed [he says] to have written by Mr. Bateman, to whom I read part of your last letter, concerning the execrable consultation, in order to stop the progress of religion by giving it a false name. He

[1] Benson's *Apology*, 17, 29.

lifted up his eyes and hands, and protested he could not have believed such a thing. He gave Mr. Morgan a very good character, and said he should always think himself obliged to him for the pains he took in reclaiming a young pupil of his who was just got into ill company, and upon the brink of destruction. I do not like your being called *a club* ; that name is really calculated to do mischief. But the other charge of *enthusiasm* can weigh with none, but such as drink away their senses, or never had any. For surely activity in social duties, and a strict attendance on the ordained means of grace, are the strongest guards imaginable against it.[1]

John Wesley also wrote to Mr. Hoole, an aged clergyman with whom he had formed a strong friendship when in Lincolnshire. Mr. Hoole replied :

As to my own sense of the matter, I confess I cannot but heartily approve of that serious and religious turn of mind that prompts you and your associates to those pious and charitable offices ; and can have no notion of that man's religion, or concern for the honour of the University, that opposes you, as far as your design respects the colleges. I should be loth to send a son of mine to any seminary where his conversation with virtuous young men, whose professed design of meeting together at proper times was to assist each other in forming good resolutions, and encouraging one another to execute them with constancy and steadiness, was inconsistent with any received maxims or rules of life among the members.[2]

To these contemporary opinions on the conduct of 'the Methodists' we will add the testimony of one modern, unprejudiced observer. Dr. Godley, speaking of them, says :

The means they employed were what most ages would have called purely beneficent; never, one might have supposed, did any revival lay itself so little open to adverse criticism. There was no vulgarity, no sensational appeal to the emotions of large and excitable audiences —in Oxford, at any rate. All that the Methodists did was to encourage each other to virtuous living and good works. They were diligent in religious observance ; they fasted with the over-asceticism of a new enthusiasm ; they started schools for the poor, they relieved the sick, they visited prisoners in jail. And they were consistently and uninterruptedly derided, abused, even punished. The mass of undergraduate opinion would have none of Methodism. . . . Perhaps we should not judge a learned University by its foolish youth. But the attitude of the authorities towards a wholly blameless and virtuous movement is really not explainable ; it seems to justify all the hard

---

[1] Moore's *Life of Wesley*, i., 169-70, 175-76.
[2] Moore's *Life of Wesley*, i., 176-77.

things that have been said of the century. . . . The hostility of Oxford to the Wesleyan movement, in its fully developed activity, is easy enough to understand. It is less easy at first sight to account for the intolerance of 1730; yet it was not out of keeping with the narrow formalism and party bitterness of that rather inexcusable period.[1]

John Wesley's father had given him the wise counsel 'Bear no more sail than is necessary, but steer steady,' and he adopted it. He stood on the same course, and guided his ship through the troubled waters. The year 1731 brought its special difficulties. In April John and Charles Wesley visited Epworth, walking there and back, for, says Moore, 'now they saved every penny they could to give it to the poor.' On their return to Oxford in May they found that the 'Holy Club' was threatened with extinction. The little company that used to meet on a Sunday evening was 'shrunk into almost none at all.' Morgan, whose health was frail, had gone to Holt; Boyce was at his father's house at Barton; Kirkham was on the point of leaving Oxford to be his uncle's curate, and, says Wesley, 'a young gentleman of Christ Church, who used to make a fourth, either afraid or ashamed, or both, is returned to the ways of the world, and studiously shuns our company.' It appeared as if the attrition of time would accomplish more than the assaults of Oxford opponents. Their opposition, however, was maintained, and John Wesley had often cause to admit the truth of a saying of Dr. Hayward's when he examined him for priest's orders : 'Do you know what you are about ? You are bidding defiance to all mankind. He that would live a Christian priest ought to know that, whether his hand be against every man or no, he must expect every man's hand should be against him.' Towards the close of the year the sorely tried brothers were encouraged by a visit from their father, who saw the work they were doing, and in a letter to his wife told her of 'the shining piety' of their two sons.

In 1732 a change came over the fortunes of the 'little company.' The decline in numbers was arrested, and several notable men were added to its membership. Thomas Broughton, of Exeter College, who was for thirty years the secretary of the Society for Promoting Christian Knowledge, was one of them ; Benjamin Ingham, of Queen's, another ; and, from our point of view, the most noteworthy of all, John Clayton,

Oxford in the Eighteenth Century, 266–69.

of Brasenose. Clayton also brought with him two or three of his pupils. He was a Manchester Grammar School boy. His father was a bookseller in Manchester, well known to the literary and religious men of that town, who came to his shop, turned over the books, and conversed on the topics of the day. He was acquainted with the Nonjurors of Manchester, such as Dr. Thomas Deacon and John Byrom, and sympathized with their religious if not with their political views. His business brought him into relation with the Rivingtons, the London publishers. One day, when John and Charles Wesley were in London, they visited the Rivingtons' shop. Mr. Rivington, finding out they were from Oxford, asked if they knew Mr. Clayton, of Christ Church. At that time they did not; but when John Wesley was walking in the street at Oxford on April 20, 1732, he met Clayton, who spoke to him and delivered a message from Mr. Rivington. That was a sufficient introduction. Wesley invited him to his room at Lincoln, and an acquaintance began which ripened into friendship. Clayton had been in Oxford since 1726, and at the time of his interview with Wesley he was a college tutor. At the first opportunity Wesley explained to him the design of the 'Club,' and he immediately joined it. Describing the result of the coming of Clayton, Wesley says: 'The two points whereunto, by the blessing of God, we had before attained, we endeavoured to hold fast: I mean, the doing what good we can; and in order thereto, communicating as often as we have opportunity. To these, by the advice of Mr. Clayton, we added a third—the observing the fasts of the Church, the general neglect of which we can by no means apprehend to be a lawful excuse for neglecting them.'[1] Conversation with Clayton excited Wesley's interest in the questions concerning the constitution and practices of the Early Church. He does not seem to have paid close attention to them previously, but soon he became absorbed in the study of the history of primitive Christianity.

The year was shadowed by the death of William Morgan. His health had been frail for some time. He went to Holt for rest; then he returned to Oxford. But on June 5, 1732, he left the University, and on August 26, he died in Dublin. His father believed that his health had been undermined by the austerities he practised as a 'Methodist.' It is more likely

[1] Wesley's *Journal*, i., 101.

that his prison work was the cause. Morgan's death was a
'calamity to the company.' In Wesley's *Journal*[1] there is a
letter addressed to Morgan's father. It contains a calm statement of the facts of the case, and throws light on the design
and proceedings of the 'Society.' Mr. Morgan was convinced
that Wesley was not to blame for the death of his son, and
afterwards showed his confidence by placing William Morgan's
younger brother under his care.

The death of William Morgan had another result. On
December 9, 1732, *Fog's Journal* contained a letter severely
criticizing Wesley and his associates. As the 'Methodists'
were almost universally derided and despised in Oxford, the
public discussion of their peculiarities was welcomed, and the
charges made against them were greedily believed. The
attack, however, had one good result. John Wesley, in July,
had made his way to the house of William Law, in Putney,
and had been welcomed by the famous Nonjuror and mystic,
to whom he owed so much. A copy of *Fog's Journal* being
sent to Law by a friend, who in a letter asked for some information concerning the 'Methodists,' he determined to go to
Oxford and make investigation on the spot. He questioned
several University men, but could not find one who was friendly
to the Methodists. As he was determined to hear both sides
before forming his judgement he was compelled to interview
the 'Methodists' themselves. From them he heard the
story of the origin and design of their proceedings. He
gathered up the facts he had ascertained by observation and
conversation, and stated them in a pamphlet he published
anonymously.[2] He sums up as follows: 'That this society
think themselves obliged in all particulars to live up to the
law of the gospel. That the *Rule* they have set themselves
is not that of their own inventions but the Holy Scriptures,
and the orders and injunctions of the Church, and that not as
they perversely construe and misinterpret them, but as they
find them in the holy canon. That, pursuant to these, they
have resolved to observe with strictness not only all the duties
of the Christian religion according to their baptismal engage-
ments, but the fasts, the prayers, and sacraments of the
Church; to receive the blessed Communion as often as there

---
[1] i., 87-102.
[2] Three editions were published; the first in February, 1733, the second in 1737, and the third, ' with very great alterations and improvements,' in 1738.

is opportunity; and to do all the good they can, in visiting the sick, the poor, the prisoners, &c., knowing these to be the great articles on which they are to be tried at the last day; and in all things to keep themselves unspotted from the world. It would be found that, if they rise earlier than ordinary, if they are sparing in eating and drinking or any expensive diversions, 'tis to save time and money for improving those glorious ends[1]; and not, as is unfairly insinuated, that they make such things to be essentials in religion, much less out of a gloomy and Pharisaical spirit, to shun the company or upbraid the practice of others. These are the *Rules*, this the *Method*, they have chosen to live by.'[2]

On January 1, 1733, John Wesley preached before the University in St. Mary's on 'The Circumcision of the Heart.' His theme was holiness, and his sermon was strongly tinctured by the teaching of Jeremy Taylor. Those who are interested in the development of Wesley's doctrinal views will examine with interest the paragraphs which concern faith. He defines it as 'an unshaken assent to all that God hath revealed in Scripture, and, in particular, to those important truths, " Jesus Christ came into the world to save sinners "; " He bare our sins in His own body on the tree "; " He is the propitiation for our sins, and not for ours only, but also for the sins of the whole world."' He had to travel a weary path before he learned to put the right emphasis on the words, 'He loved me and gave Himself for me'; but when his University sermon was published, in 1748, the defect in his definition of faith was amended.

The year 1733 brought great anxiety to John Wesley. His father's strength was waning and the end of his life's journey was in sight. John Wesley rode to Epworth, and there was much talk in the rectory concerning the future. His father wished him to be his successor in the living, and he had to determine whether it was his duty to surrender his position at Oxford, and abandon the religious work he was doing there. Having acted as his father's curate, he knew the condition of the Lincolnshire parish and was able to compare the two spheres of usefulness. He would not have

---

[1] It was a direction of the Early Church that the money saved by fasting was to be given to the poor.
[2] *The Oxford Methodists, Being some account of a Society of Young Gentlemen in that City, so denominated*, 30-31, first ed.

hesitated for a moment to decide in favour of Oxford had it not been for the fact that by yielding to his father's wish a home would be secured for his mother. He returned to Oxford full of perplexing thoughts.

In May he visited Epworth once more. He varied his accustomed route; and, in going and returning, he stayed at Manchester. At the beginning of the year Clayton had left the University and settled in Manchester. Wesley had been strongly influenced by him during their short acquaintance, and had formed a high estimate of his judgement. Arriving in Manchester on June 2, he stayed with Clayton, and the next day he preached in the 'old church,' now the cathedral, and also at Salford, and in St. Anne's. It was during this visit that he came into completer contact with men who greatly impressed him, and altered, for a time, his ecclesiastical standpoint. We have already mentioned the Manchester Nonjurors, and it is now necessary that we should deal more fully with the question of their influence on John Wesley.

The Nonjurors, for our purposes, may be divided into three classes. The first consists of the men who, although they would not take the oaths to William and Mary, were loyal to the Church of England as by law established. While refusing to pray for the King by name, they accepted heartily the Book of Common Prayer. When Ken voluntarily surrendered the diocese of Bath and Wells into the hands of a successor, and Lloyd, the last of the original Nonjuring bishops, died, the schism was considered to have lost its *raison d'être*. A large number of Nonjurors, comprised in the first class, returned to their allegiance and resumed their orderly attendance at their parish churches. But there was a second class. It consisted of those who were not so easily reconciled. Believing that their separation from the State Church was to be permanent, they had organized themselves as a Church, and had consecrated bishops, and ordained priests and deacons. They had their own service book and used it. In general it followed the lines of the Book of Common Prayer, but there was one striking exception. Instead of the Communion Service used in the State Church they adopted the form contained in the well-known 'First Prayer Book of Edward VI.' That book, at the time of its compilation, was hurriedly prepared and adopted. It was intended to supply a temporary need, and it was subsequently revised and brought into harmony with the convictions of the Protestant Reformers. The Communion Service contained in it differed little from the Roman Mass. When the 'Second Prayer Book of Edward VI' received the authority of Parliament on April 14, 1552, it was ordered that the 'First Book' should be called in and destroyed.[1] Some copies escaped destruction, and, although the use of the 'First Book' was illegal, the Nonjurors of the second class used the form of 'Mass' contained therein. For several years this action on the part of the 'advanced' section of the Nonjurors caused much controversy. It raged especially round the question of the 'usages' which had been adopted by the compilers of the new service book. The 'usages' were: mixing water with the wine at the Sacrament; prayer for the dead; the prayer for the descent of the Holy Spirit on the sacramental elements; and the oblatory prayer, which implied that the Eucharist is 'the Christian sacrifice.' These 'usages' were countenanced by the 'First Prayer Book.' The Nonjurors of the first class strongly opposed them, and defended the Protestant view of the Sacrament set forth in the Book of Common Prayer.

The third class of Nonjurors claim our close attention. It consisted of a small number of men who formed themselves into a separate Church. One of its bishops was Thomas Deacon. He was not only a bishop, but practised as a physician in Manchester. The Nonjurors of the other classes held that his consecration was irregular because only one bishop took part in it, and he, and those associated with him, were deemed 'separatists,' and were ostracized by the other Nonjurors. Dr. Deacon was the friend of Clayton, and the friendship brought him into close association with John Wesley. Their acquaintance produced remarkable results. In 1733 Deacon was busily engaged in compiling a new service book for the use of the 'separatists.' It was published in 1734, and from it we learn much concerning Deacon's ecclesiastical and sacramentarian views. The book professes to be 'a complete collection of devotions,' both public and private, taken from the apostolical constitutions, the ancient liturgies, and the

---

[1] See *The Prayer Book, Articles, and Homilies*, by J. T. Tomlinson, 17-33; also Cardwell's *The two Liturgies of Edward VI Compared.*

Common Prayer Book of the Church of England. It consists of two parts. The first comprehends the public offices of the Church. It is humbly offered to the consideration of the present Churches of Christendom, Greek, Roman, English, and all others. The second part contains a Primitive method of Daily Private Prayer; Hymns and Thanksgivings for the Lord's Day and Sabbath[1]; Prayers for Fasting Days; Devotions for the Altar; and Graces before and after meat. In the supplement to the book there is an essay the object of which is 'to procure Catholic Communion upon Catholic principles.'

Keeping our eyes on what is essential to our inquiry we gather the following particulars of Deacon's new service book from Lathbury's *History of the Nonjurors*. To the Orders for Morning and Evening Prayer, which were altogether different in structure from the Book of Common Prayer, Deacon adds Prayers for the Catechumens, Energumens, the Candidates for Baptism, and the Penitents. The Energumens were persons supposed to be possessed by evil spirits, and certain prayers were appointed to be used by the priest when he acted as exorcist. The next 'Form' is called the Penitential Office, and it was appointed to be used on Wednesdays and Fridays, and on other specified occasions. After it comes the Communion office. It is entitled 'The Holy Liturgy: or the Form of Offering the Sacrifice, and of Administering the Sacrifice of the Eucharist.' In addition to the mixture of water with the wine, the priest is directed to sign his forehead with the sign of the cross. He also is directed to administer the elements to infants. Among the other orders in the book is one for 'The Communion at the Burial of the Dead,' which, in substance, is taken from the First Prayer Book of Edward VI. Public baptism is only allowed between Easter and Pentecost. The sign of the cross, a form of exorcism, the anointing with oil, and trine immersion are enjoined. A portion of consecrated milk and honey, and white garments, as an emblem of innocency, are to be given to each child. A form for consecrating the milk and honey is appended to the office. In the Burial Service prayers for the departed are added to the form in the Book of Common Prayer. The last of the public offices, the

---

[1] In the Early Church, especially in congregations in which there were many Christian Jews, Saturday was recognized as Sabbath as well as the Lord's Day.

Service for Ordinations and Consecrations, contains a form for the ordination of deaconesses which is nearly similar to that for the ordination of deacons. The second part of the book, which relates to private devotions, contains devotions for the morning, the evening, for the ancient hours of prayer, to be used in the church and at the altar. There are also offices for daily Private Communion, and for the Commemoration of the Dead. The office for Private Communion contains a form for a sick person to administer the Sacrament to himself, the elements being reserved from the public administration.[1]

Lathbury, describing the new service book, says that Deacon, 'though a man of considerable learning, was evidently fond of novelties.' Those who are familiar with *The Apostolical Constitutions* and *Canons* will not hastily endorse the latter clause of the sentence. Much that wears an air of novelty in the service book is derived from these documents. In Deacon's time, and during the closing years of the seventeenth century, attention was directed to the question of their authorship and contents, and some were convinced that they were genuine products of the apostolic age. In his *Primitive Christianity Revived* Whitson declared that 'these sacred Christian laws or constitutions were delivered at Jerusalem, and in Mount Sion, by our Saviour to the eleven apostles there assembled after His resurrection,' an opinion that has been justly characterized as 'peculiar.' Cave's *Primitive Christianity* is much more sane, and in his Preface he assigns them, in their completed form, to a later period. He absolutely rejects the theory of apostolic authorship, but he also cannot consent to their being relegated to the sixth century or a little before, his conclusion being 'the truth doubtless lies between these two.' At present we have not got much beyond Cave's position, so far as dating the documents is concerned, but it is clear that Dr. Deacon considered that the *Constitutions* and *Canons* occupied a supreme place as authorities on the organization and worship of the Church in the apostolic age, and he succeeded in persuading some other people that his views were correct. The other Nonjurors, outside the little circle of the 'Separatists,' rejected his service book.

John Wesley's visits to Clayton brought him under the influence of Dr. Deacon. By his advice he began to study the

[1] Lathbury's *History of the Nonjurors*, 497–501.

Apostolical Constitutions and *Ecclesiastical Canons*. Charles Wesley joined him in his researches. His lively imagination was excited by the visions of Church life in primitive times. For a time the two brothers sat down at the feet of Dr. Deacon and received his instructions with surprising humility. In watching John Wesley at this interesting stage of his religious development we must guard ourselves against the notion that, in 1733, he became a 'Ritualist' in the modern acceptation of the term. He certainly considered it to be his duty to practise some of the rites of the Ancient Church, but he was at all times true to the doctrine of the Sacrament contained in the Book of Common Prayer. He rejected the Roman doctrine of transubstantiation. In justice to the Nonjurors it is necessary to remember that the negotiations for union between themselves and the Greek Church, which were carried on by some of the more extreme men amongst them during the years 1716-1725, broke down because the Nonjurors refused to accept the teaching of the Oriental Church on transubstantiation and the invocation of saints. Lathbury, who gives a full description of the negotiations in the eighth chapter of his *History*, is justified in saying that the correspondence he reproduces is a sufficient refutation of the malignant charge of Popery so frequently alleged against the Nonjurors. He admits that some of them held peculiar opinions on the 'usages,' but asserts that even they were not inclined towards Rome.[1] As to John Wesley, we may ascertain his views of the Sacrament from a discourse he wrote about the year 1733 for the use of his pupils at Oxford. He published it as a sermon in 1788, and asserts that he had not seen cause to alter his sentiments in any point therein contained. The sermon is entitled 'The Duty of Constant Communion.'[2] There are slight traces of Wesley's patristic studies in a few places in it. Once he uses the phrase 'the Christian sacrifice,' and once he quotes an ancient canon. Otherwise his teaching is that of the Church of England. It may be expressed in his own words: 'The design of this Sacrament is, the continual remembrance of the death of Christ, by eating bread and drinking wine, which are the outward signs of the inward grace, the body and blood of Christ.'[3]

---

[1] *History of the Nonjurors*, 360.
[2] See *Works*, vii., 147-57, 8vo ed.
[3] p. 149.

When John Wesley returned to Oxford he found that the condition of the Holy Club was not satisfactory. On June 13, 1733, he makes this entry : ' Our seven and twenty communicants at St. Mary's were on Monday shrunk to five ; and the day before the last of Mr. Clayton's pupils who continued with us informed me that he did not design to meet us any more.' It must be noted that John Wesley was not able to attend to the affairs of the club so closely as he had been accustomed to do. He made many excursions to distant places, walking, in the last two years of his residence in Oxford, upwards of two thousand miles, and constantly preaching on Sundays. There can be no doubt that, although he repudiated the title of ' President ' of the club, he was its principal manager, and that the loosely organized association was knit together by his influence. Once more he put his hand to the task, and in spite of the ridicule of his enemies, and the desertion of some of his friends, he calmly resumed his work among his pupils and in the Holy Club, trusting that a brighter day would dawn. The better organization of the club occupied his thoughts. He wrote to Clayton on the subject, who replied : ' I was at Dr. Deacon's when your letter came to hand, and we had a deal of talk about your scheme of avowing yourselves a Society, and fixing upon a set of rules. The doctor seemed to think you had better let it alone ; for to what end would it serve ? It would be an additional tie upon yourselves, and perhaps a snare for the consciences of those weak brethren that might chance to come among you. Observing the stations[1] and weekly communion are duties which stand upon a much higher footing than a rule of a Society ; and they who can set aside the command of God and the authority of His Church will hardly, I doubt, be tied by the rules of a private Society.' Wesley accepted the counsel contained in Clayton's letter, and the little company at Oxford, so far as organization was concerned, continued unaltered. The religious condition of his pupils also weighed on Wesley's mind. We have mentioned the instructions he gave them on the subject of ' constant communion.' He did more. With the aid of Clayton he compiled a collection of forms of prayer for every day in the week. It was printed in 1733, and was Wesley's

---

[1] The stations are the fasts of the fourth and sixth days of the week, Wednesday and Friday, in memory of our Lord's condemnation by the Council and of His passion.

first publication. It is probable that, in addition to prayers, the original edition contained a series of questions for self-examination.[1]

In July, 1734, the success of John Wesley's work in Oxford was imperilled by the serious failure of his health. His mother wrote him two or three letters in which she blamed him for his neglect of himself. By proper care and a prudent management of his daily exercise he gradually recovered his strength. It was fortunate that he did so, for the closing months of the year brought much to harass him. In November his father wrote him on the subject of the succession at Epworth. He had written to his eldest son, but had failed to persuade him to apply for the living. Once more he turned to John Wesley, and his son Samuel supported his appeal by endeavouring to convince his brother that he was not at liberty to resolve against undertaking a cure of souls. He asserted that at his ordination he had solemnly engaged to do so ' before God, and His high-priest, and His Church.' As the ' high-priest ' who had ordained him was Bishop Potter, John Wesley wrote him asking whether he had, at his ordination, engaged himself to undertake the cure of a parish. The Bishop replied, ' It doth not seem to me that, at your ordination, you engaged yourself to take the cure of any parish, provided you can, as a clergyman, better serve God and His Church in your present or some other station.' This answer satisfied him, and he determined to remain at Oxford. The controversy about Epworth continued ; but, on April 25, 1735, his father died, and in May the living was given away and the controversy ended.

It is not necessary, at this point, to recount the history of the Holy Club any farther. At the beginning of 1735 its fortunes were at a low ebb. There is one fact, however, that must be recorded. At the time of its declension George Whitefield, of Pembroke College, joined its membership. But in spite of Wesley's efforts its disintegration as an organization proceeded rapidly ; and events which speedily happened led to its dissolution.

[1] *W.H.S. Proceedings*, iii., 202 ; Green's *Bibliography*, 9.

VII

GEORGIA

In 1728 a military officer might have been seen entering the Fleet prison in London. A friend of his, an architect named Castel, was confined there for debt. His health was fast failing under the hardships he endured, and the frequent visits of his soldier friend consoled him. They talked together, and the visitor learned much about the treatment of prisoners that filled him with burning indignation. We have no difficulty in recognizing the soldier. He is James Edward Oglethorpe, an officer who has distinguished himself in campaigns in Germany and Hungary. Quitting active military service for a time, and returning to England, he has been elected Member of Parliament for the borough of Haslemere. He is a man whom we must watch, as he is destined deeply to influence the career of John and Charles Wesley.

Oglethorpe, believing that Castel's case was not exceptional, moved in the House of Commons for a committee to inquire into the state of the jails in England. A large committee was appointed, of which he was the chairman. The investigations of this committee brought to light the tragedies of prison life. The country was shocked by the disclosures. The late and the acting wardens of the Fleet were ordered to be prosecuted, and a Bill was brought in for the better regulation of the prison, and for more effectually preventing and punishing arbitrary and illegal practices in the place. As a consequence of the committee's investigations many prisoners were set at liberty, and their forlorn condition strongly appealed to Oglethorpe's sympathies. Brooding over the problem of their future, he struck out a scheme for their benefit. That scheme included their removal to America to a colony that might be founded there if the Government would make a grant of land for their settlement. Oglethorpe was a practical man. He saw that something more would be needed than the mere removal of men who had failed in business from one continent to another. He, and those associated with him, were convinced that the success of the colonists would depend on their being brought under strong religious influences, and a discipline that would improve their character. His advocacy of the scheme was successful. The Government granted a tract of land that lay to the south of the Savannah river and spread to the northern boundaries of the Spanish settlements in Florida. A corporation was formed called 'The Trustees for the Colonization of Georgia.' The corporation received full powers of administration for twenty-six years, at the expiration of which term all privileges were to pass to the Crown.[1] Parliament granted £10,000 towards the founding of the colony, and congregational collections and private subscriptions largely supplemented that amount.

During the time when the arrangements for the creation of the colony in Georgia were being made, events occurred on the Continent of Europe which deeply stirred the emotions of the Protestants of England. A fierce outburst of Roman Catholic intolerance drove many exiles to the English shores. Fixing our attention, for the moment, on Salzburg, in Bavaria, we note that the Archbishop of that city, who was the Legate of the Holy See Apostolical and Primate of Germany, issued an edict on October 31, 1731, by which 20,678 men, women, and children were driven out of Salzburg for the sole reason of their Protestantism. They were expelled when the land was covered with snow, and they endured keen and bitter sufferings. They found refuge in some of the German towns, but many wandered through the country seeking in vain for a place of rest. The news of their pitiful plight was brought to England, and at once excited that compassion for the persecuted which is characteristic of the British people. A fund amounting to £33,000 was raised for their relief. Oglethorpe not only mentioned their case in Parliament, but also proposed to his co-trustees of the projected colony that a general invitation should be given to the expatriated Salzburgers to cross the Atlantic and find a home in Georgia. The invitation was sent, considered, and, after a time, accepted by several of the persecuted people.

In the autumn of 1732 Oglethorpe began to colonize Georgia.

[1] *The Thirteen Colonies of North America*, by R. W. Jeffery, 156–57.

He gathered together nearly one hundred and twenty settlers, most of whom were of the debtor class, and embarked for America. Some who watched the beginning of his experiment prophesied the failure of the colony. If its success had depended on the first party of emigrants it is probable that the prophecy would have been fulfilled. Mr. Jeffery is right when he says, ' The men who had so hopelessly failed in England had not that grit and sturdy endurance necessary for founders of new homes in the West.' We presume that Oglethorpe was aware of the risks he was running, but he accepted them in the cause of philanthropy. On January 13, 1733, the ship arrived at Charlestown, the port of Carolina; the settlers landed and went down to the tract of country assigned to them by the Government. They built a cluster of rude huts about twenty miles from the mouth of the Savannah river, and found shelter from the winter storms. A plan of the new town was prepared,[1] and the settlers had lots assigned to them. The selection of the site of Savannah was, in part, governed by military considerations. The town was guarded on the water side by high banks, and on the land side impenetrable swamps served as a barrier against incursions of French, Spaniards, and Indians. The perils of attack were reduced by Oglethorpe's wise management of the Indians in the neighbourhood. He secured their friendship, and many of them pitched their camps near the little town.

It was not long before Oglethorpe learned by painful experience that his chief difficulties were to be found inside Savannah. The colonists soon displayed their worst characteristics. They grumbled, quarrelled, disputed, and revelled in grievances. It was evident that the Cave of Adullam had been reproduced in Georgia. But help was at hand. During Oglethorpe's absence from England the trustees of the colony took active measures for the relief of the persecuted Salzburgers. A ship was sent to Rotterdam to receive such of them as were willing to embark for the American wilderness. Those who accepted the offer were first conveyed to Dover, from whence they sailed, on January 8, 1734, to Charlestown, where Oglethorpe met them and accompanied them to Savannah. The choice of a situation for their settlement was offered them, and they chose a spot the scenery of which bore some resemblance to that of their own

[1] See John Wesley's *Journal*, . 177.

country. They were accompanied by two of their own pastors and by Baron von Reck, who acted as commissary. Having selected a site for their new home, they held a service and determined to name the town, when built, Ebenezer.[1]

When the Salzburgers arrived, Oglethorpe, after making arrangements for the government of the colony during his absence, left for England, landing there on May 7, 1734. He brought with him several Indians, who made a deep impression on the religious public by declaring their desire that both they and their people should be instructed in the Christian religion. When the visit of the Indians came to an end they returned to Georgia, accompanied by many Salzburgers, and by a number of Scotch Presbyterian Highlanders. The Highlanders settled at a place called New Inverness. The coming of the Scotchmen and the Salzburgers strengthened the moral and religious element in the colony.

The original colonists, settled at Savannah, were under the spiritual care of Samuel Quincy, a clergyman who was a native of Massachusetts but educated in England. He was appointed to an unenviable position by the Georgia trustees. We get some insight into the state of the town in 1735 from an *Account* published in the *Collections* of the Massachusetts Historical Society.[2] Mr. Quincy says: 'Affairs here are but in an evil condition through the discouragements attending the settlement. . . . The magistrate, to whom the government of the colony was left, proves a most insolent and tyrannical fellow. Several just complaints have been sent home against him which do not meet with a proper regard, and this has made people very uneasy. . . . In short, Georgia, which was seemingly intended to be the asylum of the distressed, unless things are greatly altered is likely to be itself a mere scene of distress. . . . Notwithstanding the place has been settled nigh three years, I believe I may venture to say there is not one family which can subsist without further assistance.' Mr. Jeffery thinks that Mr. Quincy's statement is exaggerated. It certainly bears traces of a depressed mind. He was about to give up his charge, and may have let loose some of his pent-up irritation with his parishioners; but, with the possible exception of the closing sentence, his description seems fairly accurate.

[1] Charles Wesley's *Journal*, Intro., i., xxix.   [2] See Jeffery's *Thirteen Colonies*, 158.

The trustees of the colony were aware of its unsatisfactory condition. Their consultations with each other during the summer of 1735 were grave. Oglethorpe, who was at home, shared them and assisted in the solution of the problems that had arisen. The discussions concerned, among other things, the case of Savannah and the mission to the Indians, and important conclusions were reached on these subjects. They saw that a stronger religious force was needed in the colony, and that the time had come for selecting men who would carry out their original design of extending Christianity and establishing good discipline among the colonists. In addition, they believed that it was possible to begin the mission to the natives. They knew that its success would depend on the character of the missionaries chosen for this arduous and perilous work. It was natural and necessary that they should act, in both these matters, in association with the Society for the Propagation of the Gospel in Foreign Parts. The design of that Society was stated by Dean Willis in the sermon he preached at its first anniversary in 1702. He said it was, ' in the first place, to settle the state of religion, as well as may be, among our own people in the foreign plantations; and then to proceed, in the best methods they can, towards the conversion of the natives.'[1] The case of Georgia fulfilled the conditions that governed the operations of the Society, and the trustees wisely sought its aid.

One of the most influential of the Georgia trustees was Dr. John Burton, of Corpus Christi College, Oxford, one of John Wesley's closest friends when they were both undergraduates. He did not join the Holy Club, but he admired the character and work of its members. During the deliberations of the trustees his mind turned towards the club. He was convinced that if he could secure its members for the Georgia enterprise the designs of the trustees regarding the religious work among colonists and natives could be accomplished. The transfer of all the members of the club to Georgia, much as he desired it, was out of the question, and so he fixed his eyes on the Wesleys as the men most capable of facing and conquering the difficulties of the mission. He knew that if he could bring about a meeting between them, Oglethorpe, and the other trustees, his opinions would be approved. Events favoured

[1] Overton's *Life in the English Church*, 221.

him. In August, 1735, John Wesley came to London to fulfil his father's dying request concerning the publication of Samuel Wesley's book on *Job*, and its dedication to Queen Caroline. On August 28 Dr. Burton met him; and on the next day he was introduced to Oglethorpe. Oglethorpe knew some of the Wesleys. The Rector of Epworth was one of the earliest and most enthusiastic supporters of the Georgia scheme; and Samuel Wesley, his eldest son, had eulogized Oglethorpe's prison reforms and philanthropic work in flowing verse. In one of his letters the Rector of Epworth declared his willingness to attempt the mission to Georgia; but his age prevented such an adventure. The negotiations between Oglethorpe and John Wesley initiated a scheme which slowly matured. Before Wesley's final decision was given, he followed his usual practice of consulting his trusted friends. He asked the advice of his brother Samuel and of William Law. Then he went to Manchester, and saw Clayton, Dr. Byrom, and several others. Afterwards he visited his mother and laid the case before her. Her answer was: ' Had I twenty sons, I should rejoice that they were all so employed, though I should never see them more.'[1]

Dr. Burton returned to Oxford. He there waited for Wesley's decision. Knowing that he had gone to Manchester, he sent him a letter, dated September 8, 1735, addressed to him at Clayton's house.[2] But Wesley had left Manchester, and Clayton readdressed the letter to Lincoln College, where it awaited his return. In this letter, which seems to have exercised a determining effect on Wesley's career, there are some sentences which reveal the writer's estimate of the clergy of the period. Dr. Burton says: ' That state of ease, luxury, levity, and inadvertency, observable in most of the plausible and popular doctors, are disqualifications in a Christian teacher, and would lead us to look for a different set of people. The more men are inured to contempt of ornaments and conveniences of life, to serious thoughts and bodily austerities, the fitter they are for a state which more properly represents our Christian pilgrimage.' Further conversation with Dr. Burton and the members of the club led Wesley to decide to abandon Oxford and go to Georgia. On September 18 Dr.

---
[1] Moore's *Life of Wesley*, i., 234.
[2] The letter was in Mr. George Stampe's collection.

Burton wrote him expressing his great satisfaction at his decision. The arrangement finally made was that John Wesley and Benjamin Ingham should go to Savannah as missionaries to the Indians; and that Charles Wesley, in addition to being Oglethorpe's private secretary, should be Secretary for Indian Affairs. When the arrangement concerning Charles Wesley was made he was not in holy orders. Dr. Burton suggested that he should be ordained. He yielded to persuasion, and was ordained deacon by Dr. Potter, on Sunday, September 21, 1735, and priest by Dr. Gibson, the Bishop of London, on Monday, September 29.[1]

In October the Wesleys went up to London to embark for Georgia. Their former home had been with their brother Samuel, in Great College Street, Westminster, but he had removed to Tiverton. Next to Samuel Wesley's old house there resided a clergyman, the Rev. John Hutton,[2] and with him they stayed. Those who are quick to observe the incidents which bring people into association with each other will mark this acquaintance with the Huttons. It began casually, but had important results. Mr. Hutton's son, James, was educated at Westminster School, but did not proceed to the University. He was apprenticed to a well-known bookseller in London, whose shop stood at the west end of St. Paul's Churchyard. Visiting Oxford to see some of his old Westminster friends, he met Charles Wesley, who introduced him to his brother, John Wesley. He gave them an invitation to stay at his father's house when they next came to London. The invitation was accepted when the Wesleys were on their way to Georgia, and Mr. and Mrs. Hutton heartily welcomed them to their home. Mr. Hutton was a Nonjuror. He was much interested in the Religious Societies, several of which existed in Westminster, and was in charge of one of them, which met at his house. He asked John Wesley to speak to the members. He consented, and preached to them on 'One thing is needful.' The sermon made a deep impression. It led to the quickening of the Society. Benham, in his *Memoirs of James Hutton*, expresses the opinion that this quickening of the College Street Society 'was a sort of preparation for the general

---

[1] The original certificates are in the safe of the Wesleyan Conference Office, City Road, London.

[2] In an article by Mr. Brigden in the *W.H.S. Proceedings* several interesting facts concerning Mr. Hutton are mentioned. See xi., 99–100.

awakening that afterwards took place.' James Hutton and his sister were much affected. Speaking of the former, Benham says, ' As he had lived very wildly in the world his awakening became the more earnest ; and so great was his affection towards the Wesleys, who had thus been instrumental in arousing him to a sense of his condition as a sinner, that he felt a great desire to accompany them to Georgia.'

In the journal of the Georgia trustees there is a record of the appointment of John Wesley to his work, under date October 10, 1735. He was afterwards presented to the Society for the Propagation of the Gospel with a request for his appointment. The request was granted, the formal sanction of the committee being given at a meeting held on January 16, 1736, after Wesley had sailed for America. The form of the committee's resolution is significant. ' A memorial of the trustees for establishing the colony of Georgia, in America, was read, setting forth that the Rev. Mr. Samuel Quincy, to whom the Society had been pleased, upon their recommendation, to allow a salary of fifty pounds per annum, has by letter certified to the said trustees that he is desirous of leaving the said colony of Georgia, and returning home to England in the month of March next, to which they have agreed ; and the said trust also recommends the Rev. Mr. John Wesley to the Society, to allow him the said fifty pounds per annum from the time Mr. Quincy shall leave the said Colony, in the same manner Mr. Quincy had it. Agreed that the Society do approve of Mr. Wesley as a proper person to be a missionary at Georgia, and that fifty pounds per annum be allowed to Mr. Wesley from the time Mr. Quincy's salary shall cease.'[1] This resolution implies that the appointment of Wesley was similar to that of Mr. Quincy, nothing being said of the projected mission to the Indians. There can be no doubt, however, that the mission was in the minds of the Georgia trustees, and that it was Wesley's ' main design ' in consenting to Dr. Burton's request.

As Wesley, on his arrival at Savannah, was to be the paid agent of the S.P.G., he had to act in accordance with the ' Instructions ' given to the missionaries of the Society. Mr. Butterworth has rendered a great service to the memory

[1] See Mr. Butterworth's article in *W.H.S. Proceedings*, vii., 99-100.

of Wesley by stating the principal contents of those 'Instructions.'[1]

We turn with interest to the sections which relate to the conduct of missionaries ' upon their going on board the ship designed for their passage ' ; and ' upon their arrival in the country whither they shall be sent.' As to their conduct on shipboard, they were instructed to demean themselves not only inoffensively and prudently, but so as to become remarkable examples of piety and virtue to the ship's company. They were ' to prevail with the captain or commander to have morning and evening prayer said daily ; as also preaching and catechizing every Lord's day,' and ' to instruct, exhort, admonish, and reprove as they have occasion and opportunity, with such seriousness and prudence as may gain them reputation and authority.' On arrival in the country whither they had been sent, among other things they were to be careful concerning their studies, and as to their manner of living. The Society directed them to ' acquaint themselves thoroughly with the doctrine of the Church of England, as contained in the articles and homilies ; its worship and discipline, and rules for the behaviour of the clergy as contained in the liturgy and canons,' &c. They were also instructed ' not to be nice about meats and drinks . . . but contented with what health requires, and the place easily affords.' Other rules had to be observed. They concerned the distributing of books, setting up of schools, visiting out-stations, and concern about heathen and infidels. The missionaries were also expressly directed to ' duly consider the qualifications of those adult persons to whom they administer baptism, and of those likewise whom they admit to the Lord's Supper, according to the directions of the rubrics in our liturgy.' These ' Instructions ' Wesley studied, and they ruled his conduct on shipboard and in Georgia. We shall see that his zeal in carrying them out brought him into great difficulties ; but, having received a charge, he kept it with unfaltering faithfulness.

[1] *W.H.S. Proceedings*, vii., 100-102.

VIII

THE VOYAGE TO GEORGIA

THE Georgia trustees had chartered two ships for the voyage to America, the *Simmonds* and the *London Merchant*. The Lords Commissioners of the Admiralty had also given directions to the commander of H.M. sloop *Hawk* to proceed to Spithead to convoy the emigrant ships and afterwards to survey the coast of Georgia. John Wesley, accompanied by his brother Charles, Benjamin Ingham, and Charles Delamotte, one of their friends, went on board the *Simmonds* on October 14, 1735. The ships were lying off Gravesend, and there they were detained for a week. Wesley, looking on the ships as his parish, made himself acquainted with his parishioners. He found among them a company of Moravians from Herrnhut, numbering twenty-six persons, whose bearing and spirit made a deep impression on him. They were the second group of Moravians who had migrated to Georgia. The first had been led there by the well-known Moravian elder, August Gottlieb Spangenberg, and they were awaiting the arrival of the second contingent conducted by David Nitschmann, one of their bishops, in order that their Church might be fully organized in Georgia. The motive of the migration of the Moravians is a little difficult to discover. They were not driven out of Herrnhut by persecution. Dr. Stoughton says that the conversion of the heathen was the principal object contemplated, and that their settlement in Georgia had been opposed on the ground that the trustees of the colony wished to receive real exiles oppressed at home, 'not those who were living at peace under Zinzendorf's wing.' The opposition was formidable, but, fortunately, it was borne down by the influence of Oglethorpe, who strongly favoured the Moravian strangers. It is probable that a desire to settle in America, and to carry on mission work there, explains the migration from Herrnhut.[1] In order that he might converse a little with these Moravians, John Wesley at once began to learn German. His teacher was Ambrosius Tackner, and it is characteristic of Wesley that, finding that Tackner had only received 'lay baptism,' he proceeded at once to baptize him.

Sunday, October 19, 1735, was a day which Wesley long remembered. He recalls its events in after years, and dwells on them with satisfaction. The *Simmonds* lay off Gravesend. The weather was fair. On such a day, 'most calm, most bright,' the thought of a service in a crowded cabin was not to be entertained; so, in the morning, we see a numerous and serious congregation assembled on the quarter deck listening to John Wesley, who, in this quiet way, began that wonderful campaign of open-air services which was destined to awaken the conscience of England. He tells us that on this occasion, for the first time, he preached extempore. His surroundings inspired him, and out of his heart he spoke living words. The service being over, the crew and passengers dispersed. Then Wesley and his 'company' retired and celebrated the Holy Eucharist. Ambrosius Tackner and two others communicated with them. In the evening he joined the Moravians at their service, singing with them the deeply spiritual hymns, the meaning of which he was soon to understand and to express in words that are now sung by thousands of Christian people throughout the world.

The presence of Ambrosius Tackner at the Sacrament throws some light on his rebaptism by Wesley. The expert in the laws of the English Church will feel some surprise at Wesley's action, and we admit that it was unjustifiable. But it must be remembered that his knowledge of ecclesiastical law was imperfect, and that the clarity of his mind had been disturbed by his contact with Dr. Deacon and the Manchester Nonjurors. He certainly had spent much time in studying rubrics and canons, and had a larger acquaintance with them than most clergymen possessed, but there were considerable tracts of Church law which he had not explored, and, at the outset, he had to pay the penalties of half-knowledge. It was not long before he became conscious of some of his mistakes, and he frankly confessed them.[2]

[1] Stoughton's *History of Religion in England*, vi., 102.
[2] The validity of lay baptism is unquestionable. The decisions of the Arches Court in the case of Kemp v. Wickes in 1809, and of Mastin v. Escott in 1841, were

John Wesley, under Deacon's influence, was gradually being persuaded to accept the views of the more advanced Nonjurors concerning the Sacraments. He had reached the conclusion that a person who had been baptized by a man not episcopally ordained was worthless. It is to be regretted that he did not submit the point to his own diocesan, Dr. Edmund Gibson, the Bishop of London. The ship had not left Gravesend, and it did not leave England for several weeks after the sailing from the Thames. Gibson was the most powerful prelate in the Church of England at that time, and he was its greatest expert in ecclesiastical law. His *Codex Juris Ecclesiastici Anglicani* was a work of supreme authority, which Wesley might have consulted with great advantage. If he had done so, he would have avoided many serious mistakes. Gibson's *Codex* presents the view of the law concerning lay baptism, which was afterwards confirmed by the Privy Council; and, in addition, it condemns the 'ignorance' of the 'priests' who insist on re-baptizing persons who have been baptized by laymen.[1]

The case of Tackner raises another interesting question. Wesley was directed by the S.P.G. duly to consider the qualifications of those adult persons to whom he administered baptism, and of those whom he admitted to the Lord's Supper, according to the directions of the rubrics in the liturgy. Studying the rubrics at the close of the office for 'the ministration of baptism to such as are of riper years' his eye would fall on the words, 'It is expedient that every person, thus baptized, should be confirmed by the Bishop so soon after his Baptism as conveniently may be; that so he may be admitted to the Holy Communion.' If he turned to the rubric at the end of the Confirmation office he would find that no one was to be admitted to the Holy Communion 'until such time as he be confirmed, or be ready and desirous to be confirmed.' The absence of confirmation in Tackner's case must have induced some hesitation in the mind of a man who, almost instinctively,

---

both in favour of the validity of lay baptism. In the latter Sir H. Jenner said, 'It seems to me, upon the whole of the case, that the law of the Church is beyond all doubt, that a child baptized by a layman is validly baptized.' The decision in Mastin v. Escott was confirmed by the Queen in Council, on appeal, in 1842, the judgement of the Privy Council being delivered by Lord Brougham. These decisions did not make new law; they declared the law of the Church as it then stood in the authoritative legal standards. See *The Book of Church Law*, by the late Rev. John Henry Blunt, revised by Sir Walter G. F. Phillimore, 43-48, sixth ed.

[1] Gibson's *Codex*, 368, second ed.

submitted to rubrics, but such hesitation was only temporary, and without any consultation with his bishop Wesley almost immediately admitted Tackner to the Sacrament. We presume that he would have pleaded the practice of the day. It is undoubted that the neglect of the rite of confirmation throughout England at that time was general. In addition, he would be aware that it would be impossible to obey the rubrics concerning confirmation in Georgia, as there was no English bishop in the American colonies; and so he disregarded one of the plainest directions of the Book of Common Prayer before he had left this country. His strictness in the matter of lay baptism contrasts with his generous interpretation of the law governing admission to the Sacrament of the Lord's Supper. He had yet to learn that laws consist of letter and spirit, and that apart from spirit a law is lifeless.

The emigrant ships left Gravesend on October 21. Ten days afterwards they sailed out of the Downs, and reached Cowes Roads on November 2, where, after one attempt to leave, which was stopped by baffling winds, they lay until December 10. The delay was caused in part by the condition of the weather, but chiefly by the necessity of fitting out the *Hawk* for the survey of the coast of Georgia. The tedium of waiting was relieved, if not banished, by the activities of Wesley and his companions. The association with the Moravians became more intimate. Bishop Nitschmann and other Germans began to learn English, and conversation with them became easier and more enlightening. The 'Instructions' of the S.P.G. concerning pastoral work were carried out. In addition to preaching and catechizing and holding daily services, the passengers were frequently 'instructed, exhorted, admonished, and reproved.' The zeal of the members of the 'company' was so ardent that it caused considerable irritation. The admonitions and reproofs were delivered with 'seriousness,' but it is impossible to say that in every case they were urged with 'prudence.' In addition, a compact was made which knit together Wesley and his companions. It was founded on the Oxford rules; and, in effect, it created a section of the 'Holy Club' on board the *Simmonds*. During the long stay in the Roads Charles Wesley went ashore and preached his first sermon in Cowes Church.

THE VOYAGE TO GEORGIA

The voyage to Georgia may be said to have begun on December 10, 1735, and it lasted until February 6, 1736. In the pages of the standard edition of his *Journal*, during the whole of this time John Wesley lives as under a microscope. What is lacking in his ' Account ' of the voyage is supplied by extracts from his private diary, and by Mr. Curnock's illuminating comments. We must allow the *Journal* to speak for itself on minor incidents and turn towards some of the facts which enable us to watch the processes of development which were affecting Wesley's mind and character.

Large benefactions of books had been made for Georgia direct to the trustees, or through ' Dr. Bray's Associates,' and on one occasion we find that Wesley spent four hours in sorting them, and even then had not completed his task. A man is known not so much by his collection of books as by his select library, and in the *Journal* we see the titles of the books Wesley studied and used during his voyage. Noting them, we shall be able to detect the standpoint from which he viewed certain supremely important religious and ecclesiastical questions.

Arranged within easy hand-reach in his cabin we see the volumes which influenced Wesley during his Atlantic voyage. Thomas à Kempis and William Law were still his guides. In 1735 his friend, Mr. C. Rivington, had published for him *The Christian's Pattern : or a Treatise of the Imitation of Christ*. Wesley had compared it with the original, corrected it throughout, and written a preface containing an account of the usefulness of the treatise, with directions for reading it with advantage. In the same year a beautiful little pocket edition was also published, with a new preface.[1] But the circle of his literary friendships was being continually enlarged. As a missionary he was profoundly interested in the *Life of Francis Xavier*, and we see it among his chosen cabin-books. His quest of holiness had led him to study the *Life of Gregory Lopez*. Throughout the coming years the example of the Spanish saint influenced him. He longed for such an open intercourse with God, such a close, uninterrupted communion with Him, as Lopez enjoyed.[2] So late as 1789 he says : ' For many years I despaired of finding any inhabitant of Great

---
[1] *A Bibliography of the Works of John and Charles Wesley*, by the Rev. Richard Green, 10.
[2] *Wesley's Works*, xii., 429, 8vo ed.

Britain that could stand in any degree of comparison with Gregory Lopez, or Monsieur de Renty.' It was only when he met John Fletcher that he found their peer. Like all great men, he had a high admiration for a great man; but he was not blind to Lopez's limitations. He calls him a good and wise but much mistaken man. Notwithstanding his defects, the heart of Wesley clave to him.

John Wesley says that, before he began his voyage, he had said farewell to the mystic writers. If so, that farewell was spoken with many a lingering look behind. He and his brother were mystics in the best sense of the term. We are not surprised to see them poring over the pages of the *Theologia Germanica*. It is true that, in 1741, John Wesley laid the book aside; but on board the *Simmonds* he read it with avidity. Looking over the cabin library we see a volume which immediately arrests attention. It was written by a man whose name summons up the members of the school of Cambridge Platonists who have endeared themselves to all who desire to 'live in the spirit.' He was the last of the group, and we have already mentioned him. John Wesley greatly valued Norris's treatise concerning *Christian Prudence*. In 1734 he had published extracts from it. It was a wise proceeding. Overton, describing Norris's literary style, says that, like all the Platonists, his thoughts were too subtle and his language too refined for the multitude, but Wesley possessed remarkable skill in extracting from abstruse books the paragraphs which could be ' understanded of the people,' and his skill befriended the readers of Norris. We also note in the select library Francke's *Pietas Hallensis*, and his *Nicodemus, or Treatise on the Fear of Man*.

Turning from the devotional and practical books, we are impressed by the number of volumes in the cabin library which reveal the influence of the Nonjurors, and especially of those who held extreme views of the Sacraments. Near Robert Nelson's *Festivals and Fasts* we see John Johnson's book *The Unbloody Sacrifice and Altar Unveiled and Supported*. It was published in 1714, and was much approved by Nelson and by Dr. Thomas Brett, who was a bishop among the Nonjurors. Johnson, who was the Vicar of Cranford, in Kent, held a special view of the Christian sacrifice. He affirmed that the sacrifice in the Eucharist was not the body and blood of

Christ, but the elements of bread and wine. It was the ' pure offering ' predicted by Malachi. The sacrifice of Christ was of His sacramental body. The same sacrifice was repeated in the Eucharist. He further affirmed that as Christ made a sacrifice for sin, so the priesthood makes the same sacrifice in the Church. The efficacy of the sacrifice offered by the priest is derived from the sacrifice on the cross, but the priest's offering is for the sins committed since Christ was crucified, inasmuch as sins cannot be forgiven before they are committed. By and in the Eucharistic oblation the application of the benefits of Christ's atonement is received.[1] This view fascinated Wesley, and, for a time, he seems to have held it. It was opposed to the doctrine of the Church of England, as was clearly shown by Dr. Waterland, who wrote against the teaching of Johnson and Brett; but, under the influences controlling him at the time Wesley was tempted to accept a doctrine which could not be harmonized with the statements of the Book of Common Prayer. The entries in his *Diary* show that he read Johnson's book with eagerness, and expounded its theories to his companions. Another volume in the library may be considered an antidote to Johnson's book. It was written by Dr. Daniel Brevint, the Dean of Lincoln, and is entitled *The Christian Sacrament and Sacrifice*. It made a deep impression on John and Charles Wesley. Brevint's treatise, which should be read in conjunction with his *Depth and Mystery of Roman Mass laid open and explained*, has been much misunderstood. The word ' sacrifice ' has caught the eye, and conclusions have been hastily reached which cannot be justified. Dr. Waterland, who so strongly opposed Johnson and Brett, declares that Brevint stood upon the ancient ground, looked upon evangelical duties as the true oblation and sacrifices, and resolved the sacrifice of the Eucharist, actively considered, solely into them. He continues, ' It is worth the noticing how acutely Dr. Brevint distinguished between the sacramental sacrifice of Christ and the real and actual sacrifice of ourselves. We cannot properly sacrifice Christ; we can only do it by signs and figures, that is, improperly and commemoratively; but we may properly offer ourselves to God, and that is, in strict propriety of speech, our sacrifice, our spiritual sacrifice. Dr. Brevint rejected with disdain any thought of a material

[1] See Hunt's *Religious Thought in England*, iii., 57–58.

sacrifice, a bread-offering, or a wine-offering, tartly ridiculing the pretences commonly made for it.'[1]

We often see in Wesley's hands, during his voyage to Georgia, Jeremy Collier's *Reasons* for restoring some prayers and directions contained in the First Prayer Book of Edward VI. The object of the book is easily divined. It aimed at the restoration of the 'Usages,' such as mixing water with the wine at the Sacrament, and other practices that found no place in the King's Second Book.[2] The last volume in Wesley's library that claims our attention is Hickes's *Reformed Devotions*. Dr. Hickes was a prominent Nonjuror who was removed from the Deanery of Worcester because of his refusal to take the oaths to William and Mary. In 1693 he became a bishop among the Nonjurors. Strictly speaking, the *Reformed Devotions* should not bear his name. The original book was written by John Austin, a Roman Catholic. It was revised, 'reformed,' and adapted to the English Church by Mrs. Susannah Hopton, for whose edition Dr. Hickes wrote a preface.[3] A distinguished feature of Mrs. Hopton's book was the introduction of a number of hymns intended to be used in devotional services. It is well known that Dr. Hickes fought a good fight against the tyranny of Sternhold and Hopkins. He was an early advocate of the singing of hymns in the services of the Church of England. Wesley supported his advocacy, and used some of the hymns in *Reformed Devotions* in his meetings in Georgia.

On board the *Simmonds* Wesley secured much time for reading; but he also found work to do in which he afterwards excelled. He had many opportunities of studying the art of managing men. He was assisted in his task by an incident that occurred in Oglethorpe's cabin. Several officers and other invited guests were present, and some of them treated the Wesleys with great discourtesy. Oglethorpe was indignant, and cried out, 'What do you mean, sirs? Do you take these gentlemen for tithe-pig parsons? They are gentlemen of learning and respectability. They are my friends, and whoever offers any affront to them insults me.' The news of this outburst got abroad, and from that time the Wesleys were treated with great respect by all the passengers. The incident confirms

[1] *Works*, viii., 167. [2] See p. 99 *ante*.
[3] Green's *Bibliography*, 93.

the abundant testimony concerning the low opinion of the clergy which obtained in certain classes during the eighteenth century, and Oglethorpe's protest was necessary, and assisted in the creation of a respect for the Wesleys that helped their work. The brothers and their companions toiled incessantly to effect the religious reformation of their fellow passengers, and their work was not altogether in vain. That work taught them many lessons, which they learned more perfectly in after years.

In the management of the men on board the *Simmonds* John Wesley had a certain amount of success, but so much cannot be said of his attempts to manage women. His failures arose from defects in his character to which the compassionate critic will be ' a little blind.' In the management of women he often acted like an incurable optimist. He perceived in them intellectual powers and spiritual graces unseen by less sympathetic observers. His misreading of them stirred the wonder and the temper of his brother Charles, and led to several regrettable incidents. There is a touch of pathos in the spectacle of John Wesley seated in the cabin of the ship, in which one of Oglethorpe's women-servants lay sick, reading to her long passages from the Cambridge Platonist's treatise on *Christian Prudence*. The maid recovered with startling rapidity, and the readings ended. His over-estimate of some of the women on board was especially shown in the case of the wife of the ship's surgeon. He detected in her signs of the beginning of spiritual earnestness, and deemed her fit for admission to Holy Communion. His companions of the Holy Club saw through her simulated seriousness, and when the question of her admission to the Sacrament was mooted they strongly condemned the proposal. The controversy was so keen that the relations of the members of the club became strained. When John Wesley got to Georgia he had to revise his estimate of the surgeon's wife. On the voyage, however, he toiled to effect her improvement. Observing the directions in the Book of Common Prayer, he sought to bring quarrelsome women into love and charity with their neighbours, and to reconcile those betwixt whom he perceived malice and hatred to reign. Most men would have shunned this delicate task, but he was driven to it by a sense of duty. His failures were numerous, but they did not diminish his courage. His estimate of women in general remained to the end as high as ever.

Books and men and women were not the only subjects studied by John Wesley on his voyage. He became better acquainted with himself and saw certain points in his own character which caused him anxious thought. The supreme discovery he made concerned his personal religious experience. He was led to suspect that his method of pursuing holiness might be defective, and he became conscious that some other Christian people enjoyed a peace in the midst of danger which passed his understanding. So early as October 31, 1735, when the *Simmonds* sailed out of the Downs, a storm broke on the ship, and he was awakened by a great noise. There was no danger, ' but,' he says, ' the bare apprehension of it gave me a lively conviction what manner of men ought those to be who are every moment on the brink of eternity.' The conviction was so keen that he resolved to amend, and read a resolution to that effect to his brother and friends. On November 23, when the *Simmonds* had been forced back to Cowes, he was awakened once more by the tossing of the ship, and the roaring of the wind. Thinking about himself, he came to the conclusion that he was unfit, because unwilling, to die. Between January 17 and 19, 1736, a succession of storms assailed the little fleet that was staggering across the open Atlantic. The wind was blowing a hurricane. One of the worst days was Sunday, January 25. It seemed as if the doom of the ship was sealed. The winds roared and wailed. The *Simmonds* rocked to and fro. Every ten minutes came a wave-shock that threatened to dash the planks into a thousand pieces. It was almost impossible to creep along the deck, but Wesley, who possessed extraordinary natural courage, contrived to make his way to the evening service held by the Moravians. He says, ' In the midst of the psalm wherewith their service began the sea broke over, split the mainsail in pieces, and poured in between the decks as if the great deep had already swallowed us up. A terrible screaming began among the English. The Germans looked up, and, without intermission, calmly sang on. I asked one of them afterwards, " Was you not afraid ? " He answered, " I thank God, no." I asked, " But were not your women and children afraid ? " He replied mildly, " No ; our women and children are not afraid to die." ' These answers went to the heart of the problem that Wesley was pondering. Writing them in his ' Account,' he says, ' This was the most glorious day which I have hitherto seen.' When calmer weather came he declares, ' I can conceive no difference comparable to that between a smooth and a rough sea, except that which is between a mind calmed by the love of God and one torn up by the storms of earthly passions.' Out of the darkness of the tempest a light began to dawn, a ' kindly light ' that was to lead him to his desired haven.

On Wednesday, February 4, the cry of ' Land ' came from the masthead ; and, in the afternoon, the trees of Georgia were visible from the main deck. We can imagine the joy of Wesley and his friends when they saw ' the long, low line where the wilderness of waves met the wilderness of woods.'

IX

FIRST DAYS IN GEORGIA

As the *Simmonds* stood on her course towards the mouth of the Savannah river it is probable that Wesley once more examined the motive which had led him to undertake his mission to Georgia. He frankly tells us that he went there hoping ' to save his own soul.' At first sight the motive seems inadequate, and it is open to the criticism that has assailed it. But everything depends on our understanding of what Wesley meant by the salvation of his own soul. We know that he was a sincere seeker after a righteousness which was to come to him through self-denial, hard work, scrupulous obedience to the laws of the Church, incessant attendance at services and sacraments, and by a constant cultivation of the religious spirit by a strict introspection, an absolute submission to the commands of conscience, and a rigorous fulfilment of everything which he knew to be his duty. The sternness of the pursuit of righteousness was relieved by light which had come to him from some of the mystical writers. He knew that the salvation of the soul came not only by the accurate discharge of the requirements of the law, but also by deep and habitual communion with God. He imagined that among the woodlands of Georgia time would be found for contemplation of the Divine Presence, and that amidst their stillness he would acquire the power to worship God in spirit and in truth. In after years he must have wondered at his dreams of Georgia as a favourable sphere for realizing his visions of righteousness. He then discovered that he had been led to America by a will not his own, and for a purpose of which he had been ignorant. He found that he had gone there that he might endure ' a temptation in the wilderness.'

Wesley's motive in undertaking his work in Georgia was ' the salvation of his own soul '; but that end was not to be achieved by musing and contemplation merely, but through the influence of austere and dangerous work. His 'main design' was to forsake the beaten path of ordinary clerical life in an English colony, and to strike and follow the trail which led through forests to the Indian hunting-camps and towns. He believed that the way of righteousness could be best found apart from the white man's settlements, and he welcomed the prospect of work that would make him endure hardness, and might even imperil his life. At that time a considerable number of Creeks, Choctaws, Chickasaws, Uchees, and Cherokees dwelt in the country lying between the thin strip of white settlements on the Atlantic and Gulf coast and the Mississippi river.[1] Some of them had been brought into contact with white men, and impulsive writers had sketched their character and manners with the pen of the idealist. The possibility of their conversion to Christianity was proclaimed, and the prospect roused the zeal of generous men. With a valour which still excites our admiration missionaries of various Churches had set out on their perilous task. Some of them, after suffering horrible torture, laid down their lives in their attempt to win the red men for the Church of Christ. The Church of Rome paid a heavy tribute of missionary martyrs in the period preceding the years of which we are writing. We cannot read Francis Parkman's descriptions of the first Jesuit mission to the Indians without being deeply moved. In its subsequent stages that mission lowered and lost its spiritual aims and became, in great part, a political and commercial agency, but that fact must not make us blind to the moral grandeur of the men who were its pioneer workers. As to Protestant missions, the name of John Eliot, the minister of Roxbury, in New England, is enshrined in many hearts. When we think of him, surrounded by his 'praying Indians,' the words he wrote at the end of his Indian grammar come to our mind: 'Prayers and pains through faith in Christ Jesus will do anything.'

It must be confessed that the writers of the romantic school have beguiled us by their descriptions of 'the dark Americans' who roamed through the woods and over the prairies in the seventeenth and eighteenth centuries. In these later days Parkman has disillusioned us; but before his time Wesley had written that calm description of their manners and customs

[1] McTyeire's *History of Methodism*, 95.

which appears in his masterly sketch of Georgia.[1] No one can study that statement without injury to the dreams of his youth. It convinces us of the almost insuperable difficulties confronting a man whose 'main design' in coming to America was to convert the Indians. The time of success came later; and, among the more modern workers, John Wesley's successors marched in the van. As Wesley never carried out his 'main design,' it will not be necessary to refer, save incidentally, to his contact with the Indians.

On February 5, 1736, the *Simmonds* anchored in the Savannah river, near Tybee. The next morning Wesley 'first set foot on American ground,' landing on an island now known as Cockspur Island, on which Fort Pulaski has since been built.[2] At that time Cockspur Island was uninhabited. It was of small extent, but possessed natural beauty. Oglethorpe led a party through the marshy land near the shore to a rising ground, and the little company knelt down, gave thanks to God, and pleaded for the continuance of His Fatherly protection. Oglethorpe then took boat for Savannah, and left the emigrants under the charge of John Wesley and John Brownfield. They were soon joined by 'the rest of the people,' and Wesley held a service in an open place surrounded with myrtles, bays, and cedars, which sheltered the worshippers from the sun and wind. The open-air services, which had been discontinued on the *Simmonds*, were now resumed, and became of frequent occurrence in Wesley's life in Georgia.

Wesley soon found that Oglethorpe's action in making him a manager of the emigrants at the mouth of the Savannah river involved him in difficulties. He was at once brought into contact with rough work. The crews of the ships, together with some of the passengers, celebrated the end of the voyage by getting drunk. Wesley first interviewed the captains, and then he registered a vow of personal abstinence from flesh and wine. After that he staved in the rum casks that had been brought from England. His action as a temperance reformer probably hastened the destruction of any popularity he might have acquired on the voyage.

Finding it hard to serve God without distraction in the midst of secular business, John Wesley gradually approached one of the crises of his life. While the new emigrants were

---

[1] *Journal*, i. 406–409.   [2] *The Wesley Bi-centenary in Savannah*, 5.

FIRST DAYS IN GEORGIA

waiting at the mouth of the river August Gottlieb Spangenberg came from Savannah to welcome the new arrivals. He stands out conspicuously in the story of Wesley's life. He had been a scholar of Jena, and a lecturer at the University of Halle. He was a Moravian who had the enviable gift of introducing men to the living Christ. On the evening of his arrival he had a conversation with Wesley, who was eager to acquire further knowledge of the Moravians. Referring to this conversation, Wesley says, ' He told me several particulars relating to their faith and practice and discipline, all of which were agreeable to the plan of the first ages, and seemed to show that it was their one care, without desire of pleasing or fear of displeasing any, to retain inviolate the whole deposit once delivered to the saints.' The interview with a cultured man like Spangenberg was most refreshing to Wesley's spirit. They became friends ' at first sight.' On Sunday, February 8, 1736, Wesley proceeded to take counsel with his new friend on the course of conduct he ought to pursue when he began his work in Savannah. Such a consultation was in harmony with his custom when he was conscious of his need of advice, and was in the company of men whose judgement he respected. The custom was in accordance with the spirit of the rules of the Holy Club, but its origin is to be sought in Wesley's mental constitution. He habitually declined to enter on an important course of action until he had debated it not only with himself, but with competent counsellors. When he departed from this custom, and acted on his own impulses and emotions, as he did sometimes in Georgia and elsewhere, he had reason to rue the consequences of his impetuosity.

Spangenberg listened sympathetically to Wesley's questions concerning his public conduct, but all the time he was watching him with quiet eyes. He saw how intent he was on the religious reformation of his new parishioners, and admired his zeal and sincerity, but he came to the conclusion that this ardent reformer was on the verge of severe disappointments. As the first work of a reformer is to reform himself, Spangenberg put a few piercing personal questions. ' Do you know yourself ? ' That abrupt and seemingly irrelevant question changed the current of Wesley's thinking, and turned it into a familiar channel. He had practised introspection until he had reduced the examination of self into a fine art ; but he was haunted by a suspicion that he did not yet know himself. Overcome by surprise at the suddenness of the question, he was silent. Perceiving his embarrassment, Spangenberg asked, 'Do you know Jesus Christ?' Wesley paused, as well he might. He was confronted by two of the greatest questions that can be put to a thoughtful man: 'Do you know yourself? Do you know Jesus Christ?' After a few moments of solemn thought Wesley replied, 'I know He is the Saviour of the world.' 'True,' Spangenberg rejoined, 'but do you know He has saved you?' Wesley could only say, 'I hope He has died to save me.' But that answer did not satisfy his questioner. His ear caught the accent on the word hope, and he believed, with St. Paul, that 'if in this life only we have hoped in Christ, we are of all men most pitiable.' Swift as light came the question from the lips of Spangenberg, 'Do you *know* yourself?' Wesley, little suspecting that in the distinction between 'hoping' and 'knowing' that Christ died to save us one of the great secrets of the coming reformation lay hidden from his eyes, replied, 'I do'; but, in recording the incident he adds, 'I fear they were vain words.' The answer lacked the emphasis of true knowledge and conviction, and Spangenberg was too deeply versed in the processes of personal salvation to misread the position in which Wesley stood.

Listening to this momentous conversation on the banks of the Savannah river we are reminded of an interview which had taken place, some time previously, between Spangenberg and a young man at the University of Jena. His visitor was in anguish of mind because of the intolerable burden of his sins, which weighed on him and made him miserable. Spangenberg then said a few words to him about the way of salvation and the Saviour's power to free from sin, which brought relief to the mind of the penitent, who said, 'I have tried everything in the world except this, but this I will try.' The young man's name was Peter Böhler. Wesley, however, had not reached Böhler's spiritual position. His mind was fatally equipped with preconceived ideas concerning the way in which salvation is to be sought, and preconceived ideas are often an invincible shield against the arms of light. Noticing the tone of Wesley's 'vain words,' Spangenberg turned to other topics, and gave him the benefit of his own experience in the management of men. Although the inquisition had been sharp, Wesley's esteem for his questioner was increased. He cultivated his friendship and asked his advice on many topics, but the coming of the moment of illumination on the problem of personal and conscious salvation was delayed.

For nearly three weeks Wesley was detained at the mouth of the river, paying a flying visit to Savannah but returning the next day. When in the little town he called at the parsonage, still in the occupation of Mr. Quincy, who did not vacate it until the middle of March. One of the most interesting incidents that occurred during his long tarrying on the seaboard was an interview with Tomo-chachi, a Creek chief, and some men of his tribe. It is also noticeable that Wesley baptized an infant, aged eleven days, by trine immersion, ' according to the custom of the first Church and the rule of the Church of England.'

In the evening of February 26 Wesley went to Savannah in company with Spangenberg, Nitschmann, Andrew Döber, and Charles Delamotte, in order that he might begin to discharge his duties as the minister of the place. Instead of staying at the parsonage with Mr. Quincy, he and Delamotte lodged with the Germans. Wesley's residence with the Germans brought him under wholesome and formative influences. An event was about to occur in connexion with the Savannah Moravians which was to produce a lasting impression on his mind. We have seen his deep interest in the study of Church organization. He had read widely on the subject, and knew much more about it than the great majority of the clergymen of his day. His attention had been directed to books dealing with the condition of the Christian Church in the first three centuries. Though the materials for constructing mental pictures of the Church in primitive times were scanty in comparison with those we now possess, by diligent research he had become acquainted with many of the principles and facts which determined the government and proceedings of the Church in the apostolic and sub-apostolic ages, and his studies had led him to see visions of those remote days which fascinated him. On his arrival in Savannah he found that the company of the Moravians was to be organized into a Church by the ordination of a bishop, and he looked forward to the event with great expectation. So far as we know he did not question the validity of such an ordination.[1] Wesley had a conversation on the matter with Spangenberg, and was surprised to find that while he approved of the episcopal form of Church government he denied the fact of the apostolical succession of bishops. Wesley's own judgement was in suspense on that vital question. His conviction was that the uninterrupted succession of the Roman bishops from the apostles had not been proved. At a subsequent period he declared, ' I never could see it proved, and I am persuaded I never shall.'[2] Free from blinding prejudice, he attended the ordination service when Bishop Nitschmann consecrated Anton Seifart a bishop of the Moravian Church. His description of the ceremony is memorable. Speaking of the Germans, he says : ' After several hours spent in conference and prayer they proceeded to the election and ordination of a bishop. The great simplicity, as well as solemnity, of the whole almost made me forget the seventeen hundred years between, and imagine myself in one of those assemblies where form and state were not, but Paul the tentmaker or Peter the fisherman presided, yet with the demonstration of the Spirit and of power.' The following day Wesley went down to the coast. The scene he had witnessed had time to engrave itself on his memory, and the impression produced was ineffaceable. His feelings had been deeply stirred. His heart was touched once more when, at the river's mouth, he bade Spangenberg farewell.

The departure of Spangenberg for Pennsylvania was a serious matter for Wesley. He was a counsellor whose advice was invaluable, and Wesley was bereft of him when he most needed to be directed. In addition, Oglethorpe had his mind set on securing the defence of Georgia against the attacks of the Spaniards, and was about to go to the south. A pioneer party of fifty unmarried emigrants had preceded him, and had begun to build huts at Frederica for the accommodation of themselves and the married people who were to follow them. These pioneers had taken Benjamin Ingham with them as their minister. On March 3, four boats containing married emigrants set out for Frederica ; among them we note Mrs.

---

[1] Archbishop Potter considered all the objections to the Moravian succession trivial, and declared that only those who were ignorant of Church history could doubt its validity. Wesley's *Journal*, i., 170 *n*.
[2] *Journal*, iv., 438.

Hawkins, the surgeon's wife; Charles Wesley, the Indian Secretary, also sailed with them. John Wesley was thus deprived of his old companions, with the exception of Charles Delamotte. Oglethorpe left for Frederica the next day. From February 29 to March 3 Wesley had been in constant consultation with Oglethorpe concerning the management of affairs in Savannah. He received the General's 'orders and instructions' relating to business, and then, on March 6, he returned to the town. Mr. Quincy was still at the parsonage, but Wesley began to prepare it for his own occupation. He was there during the day; in the evening he returned to his old quarters with the Germans.

The aspect of Savannah during Wesley's residence there may be imagined from the plan of the town which appears in his *Journal*. It was laid out in rectangular form, its streets and avenues being a minor prophecy of the shape of a modern American city. In the foreground of the little town ran the river. Then came a semicircular gap in the forest in which there was a group of wooden huts, three of them being of considerable size—the court-house, the store-house, and the parsonage. The last stood in a broad clearing close to the wood, near a plot of land reserved for the erection of a church. The population was small. On July 30, 1737, Wesley, who had great skill in 'numbering the people,' took an accurate list of the inhabitants. He tells us that there were in the town five hundred and eighteen souls, one hundred and forty-nine of whom were under sixteen years of age. He adds that about one hundred and eighty of the adults were, or were called, of the Church of England. We have already mentioned the extraordinary character of the population. It was a strange mixture of men who had been released from debtors' prisons, vagrants rescued from the London streets, sturdy Scots who were strong Presbyterians, Germans, and Indian traders who spent most of their time in the backwoods but returned at least once a year to get their licences renewed by Oglethorpe or his representative. It is difficult to get a clear idea of the form of government under which the town was placed. We presume that until the time arrived when the colony had to be handed over to the King, the trustees, in all civil matters, formed a kind of high court of appeal, the final court being the King in council. The trustees acted through the governor whom they appointed, or through his representatives when he was absent from the colony. Ecclesiastically, Georgia was in the diocese of London. This awkward arrangement necessitated the appointment of commissaries. The commissary who was nearest to Savannah was Dr. Garden, who lived in Charlestown, in South Carolina. He does not seem to have exercised any jurisdiction over Georgia, but as a man well versed in Church law he was often consulted by Wesley. It was unfortunate that there was no ecclesiastical official in immediate contact with the colony whose judgement on controverted questions might have been respected in case disputes arose. The civil control of Savannah was also defective. During Wesley's residence the greater part of Oglethorpe's time was taken up with military affairs, and he was compelled to govern by deputy. We have seen him handing over the charge of the emigrants to John Wesley when the *Simmonds* had disembarked her passengers, and afterwards charging him with ' orders and instructions.' Oglethorpe soon discovered Wesley's aptitude for business and availed himself of his secretarial help. He listened to his advice, was influenced by it, but, so far as we know, he left Wesley's position in reference to civil matters undefined. In connexion with subsequent events, we see that a chief magistrate, a recorder, and a bailiff had been appointed in Savannah. They dispensed justice in the court-house, had power to punish criminals, and were considered persons of importance in the town. But Oglethorpe, under whom his deputies acted, had slight connexion with the place during Wesley's residence there. He paid it a few short visits; but Frederica and the southern frontier received his chief attention. Then he returned to England to consult the trustees about matters which affected the colony, and the controlling force of his presence in Savannah was lost when it was urgently needed. It is no wonder that surprising events occurred. Most of the crudities of the amateur administration of the town may be left under the veil of a kindly oblivion; but they cannot all be dismissed, and, in their place, they will have to be mentioned.

It would help us to understand the events of John Wesley's life in Georgia if we could erase from our minds the impressions produced by most of his portraits. The only painter who

FIRST DAYS IN GEORGIA

possessed adequate insight into Wesley's character, in his earlier years, was John Michael Williams, R.A. An admirable description of Williams' portrait of Wesley, written by the Rev. Richard Green, appears in the fourth volume of the *Proceedings of the Wesley Historical Society.* We do not wonder that when Dr. Alexander McLaren visited Didsbury College, Manchester, and saw the portrait, he exclaimed, ' Now I can understand the Methodist reformation.' The portrait was painted in 1743, five years after Wesley left Georgia, but, making that time allowance, we may accept it as a faithful representation of the firm, strong, graceful, intense man whose fortunes we are following. As he is busy in the parsonage, sorting and arranging his books, we look at him. He is in the prime of life, being thirty-three years of age ; he is small in stature, standing five feet three inches high. He is no worn and wasted ascetic, but possesses ' an iron constitution,' and his abstemious habits keep him constantly fit for sustained exertion. To walk a hundred miles in a few days is to him an exhilarating form of exercise. He lives in the open air. As we follow him in Georgia we find him in the forest clearings, swinging his axe for hours against the trees. He is ready to put his hand to any kind of work, whether it is the building of a hut or an arbour. He loves his garden exceedingly ; at all opportunities he works in it, and joyfully lingers among its flowers. He is a strong, alert, cheerful man In the early days at Oxford, during his country walks, he and his brother Charles beguiled the way with song, and on the forest trails of Georgia his melodious voice is often heard. He has a deep and calm enjoyment of natural scenery. The woodlands soothe him as he wanders through them, they rouse him as they shake in the shock of storms. He loves solitude, but he is no recluse, husbanding a little religion by avoiding the world ; on the contrary, he is a most companionable man. He evokes antagonism, but he also makes friendships that withstand the tests of time and misfortune. On Sundays and for public religious services he is dressed in cassock and gown, but at other times his dress is adapted to his work. In his forest journeys, at nightfall he rolls his cloak around him and stretches himself at the bivouac fire ; as he travels by sea his friendly cloak defends him from the splashing waves. He moves among the rough settlers with an air of distinction of which he is unconscious, but which constantly reminds us of his mother, Dr. Annesley's beautiful daughter.

On Sunday, March 7, John Wesley commenced his public ministry in Savannah. There was no church in the town, and a small hut was used for the service. He had been informed by a gentlewoman that he would see ' as well-dressed a congregation as most he had seen in London.' The prediction was fulfilled, and the minister made a quiet note of the fact. He had carefully prepared for the service by once more studying the ' Instructions ' of the S.P.G. concerning the conduct of missionaries on their arrival in the country whither they shall be sent, and had been impressed with the Society's direction duly to consider the qualifications of those adult persons whom he admitted to the Lord's Supper. He preached from the Epistle for the day, 1 Cor. xiii., and at the close of the service he read a paper which contained a list of the duties which he had to discharge. He told his hearers that he must admonish every one of them, not only in public but from house to house ; that he could admit none to the Holy Communion without previous notice ; that he should divide the morning service on Sundays in compliance with the first design of the Church ; that he must obey the rubric by dipping all children who were able to endure it ; that he could accept none who were not communicants to be sureties in baptism ; and that, in general, though he had all the ecclesiastical authority which was entrusted to any within that province, yet he was only a servant of the Church of England, not a judge, and therefore obliged to keep to her regulations in all things.[1] The people listened to this frank declaration, and were at once acquainted with Wesley's intended course of procedure. This preliminary notice does not seem to have weakened Wesley's influence with his congregation. The strength of that influence may be judged by the fact that he succeeded in curbing the passion for display which was exhibited at his first service. He tells us that soon after he took occasion to expound those Scriptures which relate to dress, and adds, ' All the time that I afterward ministered at Savannah, I saw neither gold in the church, nor costly apparel, but the congregation in general was almost constantly clothed in plain clean linen or woollen.'

[1] *Journal*, i., 393.

On March 15, Mr. Quincy left for Carolina, and Wesley moved into the parsonage. He worked in it by day, making it ready for his own occupation, and spent the night with the Germans, whose company refreshed and strengthened him. His knowledge of their language steadily increased, and with them he sang those deep-toned and profoundly spiritual hymns to which he had listened in sunshine and in storm during his voyage across the Atlantic. The Germans lent him their tune-books, and in the parsonage he practised the melodies on his flute. Other books they lent him. We find him studying Tauler, that writer who still continues to fascinate Christian seekers after truth who are gifted with delicate spiritual discernment.

The month of March was probably the happiest period of Wesley's residence in Georgia. He was securing a hold on his people, and brightening prospects shone before his eyes. But we know that even then the clouds were gathering. We see a suggestion of coming disturbance in his action in the case of a man whom he considered to be unjustly detained in prison. His sympathy with the oppressed was keen, and had been shown at Oxford. At the castle and Bocardo the members of the Holy Club had met with many cases of hardship, and had interfered successfully in some of them. It was natural that he should interest himself in a man whom he considered to be unjustly treated by the Savannah local authorities; but, by taking up his case, he created a strong prejudice against himself which had a serious effect on his fortunes.

Among the books in Wesley's library was *The Country Parson's Advice to his Parishioners*. It had made a deep impression on his mind at Oxford, and the little volume was highly prized and widely distributed by the members of the Holy Club. Its well-known suggestion as to the formation of ' Societies ' had been accepted by many earnest men, and a striking example of the wisdom of the suggestion had been furnished by the founding of the ' Religious Societies,' whose character and work we have described. The formation of Societies became one of Wesley's fixed ideas; he was not committed to the precise form they should assume, but he was convinced that, apart from the ordinary public services of the Church, it was expedient that opportunities should be provided for the more serious parishioners to assemble in private and informal meetings in which they might pray, sing, search the Scriptures, and help each other by religious conversation. He lost no time in forming such a Society in Savannah. He tells us, in his *Journal*, that it began in April, 1736. If so, it must have been formed at the beginning of the month, for he was absent from the town from April 4 to April 19, and we know that Benjamin Ingham, who was supplying his place, met the Society on April 11. Wesley's account of the formation of the Society is as follows : ' Not finding, as yet, any door open for the pursuing of our main design '—that is, the mission to the Indians—' we considered in what manner we might be most useful to the little flock at Savannah. And we agreed (1) to advise the more serious among them to form themselves into a sort of little Society, and to meet once or twice a week, in order to reprove, instruct, and exhort one another ; (2) to select out of these a smaller number for a more intimate union with each other, which might be forwarded, partly by our conversing singly with each and partly by inviting them all together to our house ; and this, accordingly, we determined to do every Sunday in the afternoon.'[1] The editor of the standard edition of the *Journal* says, in a footnote, that the arrangement was that the Society, as a whole, was to meet once or twice a week, i.e. on one or both of the fast-days of the Holy Club ; an inner circle was to meet on Sunday afternoon ; and he adds, ' The *Diary* clearly points to a hitherto unsuspected fact, namely, that the membership of this little Society, was largely German.'[2] These facts show that while the Society had much in common with the Religious Societies, its arrangements were made to conform to special existing circumstances. It will be seen that within a month after his settlement as the minister of Savannah Wesley was led to adopt methods that were prophetic of the future of Methodism.

John Wesley watched with high expectations the progress and promise of his work in Savannah. He must have seen that if he could give himself wholly to it he might realize his ideal of a Church that would be true, not only to the standards of the Church of England, but to the spirit of the Church of the apostolic age. That ideal was constantly before his eyes.

[1] *Journal*, i., 197-205.
[2] *Journal*, i., 198.

But, suddenly, his schemes were interrupted, and he was compelled to abandon Savannah at the moment when his presence there seemed indispensable. On March 30 Ingham brought heavy tidings from Frederica, and it was imperative that John Wesley should go south to assist his brother Charles, who stood in sore need of his counsel. Taking Delamotte with him, he left Ingham in charge of Savannah.

X

WORK IN GEORGIA

WE have watched the boats setting out for Frederica, and have caught sight of familiar figures in them. Charles Wesley is there, and so is Mrs. Hawkins, and we know that between them there is strong antipathy. Charles Wesley read the woman's character aright, and he was irritated with the blindness of his brother. With her, in the boats, was Mrs. Welch, who had also raised John Wesley's hopes. These two women had been treated with exceptional indulgence by Oglethorpe. When the emigrants arrived at Frederica, and were settled there, the Governor still continued his friendly relations with them, and soon had cause to repent his indiscretions. We have no intention to enter minutely into the details of the squalid story that may be read in the *Journals* of John and of Charles Wesley. It is enough to say that the two women, by insinuations and confessions, admitted to the Wesleys that the relations between Oglethorpe and themselves were immoral. This false accusation became known among the settlers; the rumour reached the ears of Oglethorpe, who was justly indignant. The women laid the blame of the disclosure on Charles Wesley, and Oglethorpe, without making sufficient inquiries, changed his attitude towards his secretary, and treated him with inexcusable roughness and cruelty. At this unfortunate crisis Charles Wesley's health broke down, an attack of dysentery, accompanied by racking fever and pain, bringing him to the point of death. When Oglethorpe's wild passion had cooled, and he began to listen to reason, he received explanations which must have made him ashamed of his heartless conduct. The good relations between the two men were restored; but Charles Wesley's health had received a severe blow, and his stay in Georgia soon came to an end.

Charles Wesley's experiences in Georgia evoke our pity. His mercurial spirit fretted his body. He was unlike his brother in many respects. He had not John Wesley's physical constitution, nor had he the same power of enduring the temporary loss of the good opinion of those who surrounded him. At Oxford the charm of his character had secured the admiration of troops of friends. He missed their genial and exhilarating society. He was placed, in the ends of the earth, among men and women with whom he had little intellectual and emotional sympathy. His work as Indian Secretary was distasteful. Those who have some understanding of the artistic temperament will appreciate the entry in his journal on March 16, 1736. He says, ' I was wholly spent in writing letters for Mr. Oglethorpe. I would not spend six days more in the same manner for all Georgia.' That note is vibrant with sincerity. He, like his brother, had left England 'to save his own soul' by practising the presence of God in the solitudes of the American wilderness, and had made the unwelcome discovery that the turmoil of life is not confined to busy cities. His expectations of abundant leisure for calm reflection were disappointed. He had not the happy faculty which enables a disappointed man to submit to the ruin of his hopes, and to strike out another scheme of life more promising because more practicable. His thoughts turned to England and 'the line of festal light in Christ Church hall,' and the poet's pensiveness darkened the deeps of his soul.

Discontented as Charles Wesley was with his surroundings and especially with his position as Oglethorpe's secretary, he found comfort in his work as a clergyman. He and Ingham ministered to the unsympathetic people of Frederica, and, although their success was small, the work itself sustained them. The services were sometimes held in the hut which was used as the store-house, but they also went into the open air. We note that Charles Wesley read evening prayers in the open air on the day of his landing on St. Simon's Island; we see him again between five and six o'clock the next morning, reading short prayers to a few people gathered around the fire before Oglethorpe's tent in a hard shower of rain; and, at a later date, we find him standing under a great tree with his hearers clustering near him. Like his brother, he was 'an open-air preacher' in Georgia. In the midst of innumerable distractions he carried on his work as a clergyman, holding daily services, and governing his ministerial conduct by the rubrics and canons of the

Church. He had an exalted idea of his position and power as a minister. He found comfort in Bishop Hall's assurance that a clergyman is raised up by God to supply His place and to be a representation of Himself. This view was in harmony with George Herbert's assertion in the opening sentences of *A Priest to the Temple*, a book well known to the Wesleys, and highly prized by them. Herbert says : ' The country parson is in God's stead to his parish, and dischargeth God what he can of His promises. Wherefore there is nothing done, either well or ill, whereof he is not the rewarder or punisher.' This declaration might have impressed the people of Bemerton ; it found little acceptance among the squatters of Frederica.

Charles Wesley's view of his powers as a clergyman was influenced by the contents of Deacon's service book. The administration of the Lord's Supper was to him ' the offering up of the Christian sacrifice.' It is difficult to discover the meaning he attached to the phrase, but it is clear that he often used it, and continued to use it long after he left America. It may, however, be safely said that he never accepted the doctrine of transubstantiation. We doubt if he approved of George Herbert's unguarded words in his chapter on ' The Parson in Sacraments ' in *A Priest to the Temple*. Herbert says, ' At Communion times he is in great confusion, as being not only to receive God, but to break and administer Him ; ' words which easily lend themselves to misconstruction. How far Charles Wesley went in the direction suggested by Herbert we cannot say, but it is on record that the people of Frederica strongly doubted his Protestantism. The influence of Deacon's book was further illustrated by his proceedings at Savannah at a later date. He visited a girl of fifteen, ' who lay a-dying of an incurable disease.' Believing her to be possessed of a devil, he read over her ' the prayers for the energumens,' contained in Deacon's book. He thought they had some good effect, for the girl made signs for him to come again. A man holding these views of his position and powers was sure to prove a storm-centre in such a place as Frederica. It is no wonder that difficulties arose, and that John Wesley's influence was needed to moderate the conflict.

John Wesley's visit to Frederica was brief. During his stay he gained some insight into the character of the two women whom he had tried to influence on board the *Simmonds*,

WORK IN GEORGIA

but it needed a still sharper experience before his eyes were fully opened. The quarrel between Charles Wesley and Oglethorpe was 'composed,' and, with Delamotte, he returned to Savannah, reaching it on April 20, 1736. He was delighted to be at home once more. In his letter to Oglethorpe announcing his arrival he says, ' Savannah was never so dear to me as now. I found so little either of the form or power of godliness at Frederica that I am sincerely glad I am removed from it.'

When John Wesley returned to Savannah he resumed his interrupted work. On his landing in Georgia he had commenced morning services at five o'clock, and when he became resident in Savannah such early services were the rule. Prayers were read and a brief exposition was given. He says, ' All the prayers usually read morning and evening at Frederica and here put together do not last seven minutes.' On Sunday, May 9, an important change was made in the place of meeting. The small hut which had been used became inadequate to the requirements of the growing congregation. An adjournment was made to the larger wooden building known as the court-house, where, with some slight interruptions, the subsequent services were held. Acting ' according to the original appointment of the Church,' Wesley, on Sundays, divided the public prayers. He arranged that at five o'clock the ' morning service' should be read; the ' Communion office' was read at eleven o'clock, and a sermon was preached; and in the afternoon at three o'clock the evening service was read. No public service was held afterwards on Sundays, and so time was afforded for the meeting of the ' inner circle ' of the Society which had been formed. It met in the parsonage, and Wesley's spirit was refreshed by his fellowship with the more earnest and spiritual people living in the town.

The meeting of the Society must have fed the flame of Wesley's devotion, and quickened the hope which he never abandoned, the hope that even in the eighteenth century it was possible to reproduce the experiences and practices of the Christians of the earliest ages. The books over which he pored in the hours of his seclusion suggest his keen pursuit of the lost ideals of the Church. These books were not skimmed; their contents were absorbed. He had formed the habits of the reflective reader, and often paused for quiet meditation. He went farther. Having discovered a good idea, or a nobly expressed sentiment, he carefully ' collected ' it—that is, he wrote it out in his book of extracts, and so fixed it in his memory. The *Diary* bears witness to the persistence of his habit of ' collecting.' After his return from Frederica he devoted much time to the study of Fleury's *Manners of the Christians*, in which special descriptions are given of their habits, prayers, reading of the Scriptures, fasting, their general demeanour, their marriages, public assemblies, care for the poor and sick, and their hospitality. The book was a seed-plot out of which he raised a harvest. He was not content with ' collecting,' he commenced a practice which profoundly influenced his future work. He abridged Fleury's book ; and, on his return to England, he published the abridgement as a pamphlet.[1] His study of Fleury must have reminded him of the Holy Club, and must have convinced him that he had entered on a way that would lead to his goal. Whilst he could not have perceived much to encourage his hope of the resurgence of the Primitive Church among the general population of Savannah, he fixed his eyes on the ' inner circle ' of the Society, and read a promise of the return of the best days of Christian life.

The organization and proceedings of the Savannah Society remind us of the constitution and character of the Religious Societies. It is only necessary to indicate two points of resemblance. In the first place, the division of the larger Society was sure in process of time to lead to the appointment of persons, other than clergymen, to take care of the sectional meetings. We have shown that in England laymen presided over the meetings in places where it was not possible to secure the help of a clergyman. In Georgia the sectional meetings held on the week-days were put under the care of men and women of established piety, integrity, and wisdom. In the next place, we know that ' psalm-singing ' was a special feature of the meetings of the Religious Societies, and we judge that the term includes the singing of hymns. The singing of hymns was more common in the private worship of the English Church than is generally supposed. Hickes's *Book of Devotions* and other manuals bear witness to the fact. Under the influence of Wesley the singing of hymns was sure to become a part of the

---

[1] Six editions were published ; the last, in 1798, after Wesley's death.

worship of the Societies. The soul of the singer was in him and in his brother. He listened with intense interest to the singing of the Moravians on board the *Simmonds*, and constantly joined in their services. The German hymns fascinated him. As he acquired a fuller knowledge of the language he caught sight of their strength and beauty; as his spiritual apprehension was quickened he was arrested by the revelation of truths which he welcomed, although he stood afar off from the realization of their profoundest meaning. He yielded to the lure of the light and followed it. He began to translate some of the hymns with a skill in poetical composition that was innate, and had been exercised and developed at the Charterhouse and Christ Church. Inspiration did not fail him. He set free from their imprisonment some of the greatest hymns in German psalmody, and made them the perpetual possession of the English Churches. It was in the wilderness of Georgia that some of his translations were first sung.

John Wesley's promising work was soon interrupted. On Sunday, May 16, his brother arrived unexpectedly. He had come on secretarial business, which included the issuing of licences to the Indian traders who were assembling in Savannah. That work was, in a sense, vital to the well-being of the colony. The experience of the French in Canada, as described by Francis Parkman, had revealed the danger of allowing hunters and trappers to carry on unrestricted trade with the Indians. The *coureur de bois* is a picturesque figure in a romance, but, in reality, he often was a lawless vagabond.[1] It was necessary that the Indian Secretary should come to Savannah, but his absence from Frederica meant that some other clergyman would have to supply his place. After a conversation it was agreed that his brother and Benjamin Ingham should supply Frederica alternately; and, on May 18, John Wesley quitted the parsonage and set his face towards the south.

Charles Wesley's residence in Georgia speedily came to an end. For a few weeks he took charge of his brother's work in Savannah, finding that the hardest duty imposed on him was the expounding of the lesson morning and evening to one hundred hearers, the size of the congregation being another

[1] Parkman's *The Old Régime in Canada*, 309-15.

indication of John Wesley's ministerial success. Oglethorpe arrived on May 31, and secular affairs demanded attention. A week afterwards Charles Wesley made up his mind to resign his post. He stayed in Savannah for some weeks longer ; but in August he sailed for England. His mission to Georgia lasted for about six months. It was impossible for him to look back upon it with pleasure. The pressure of uncongenial work had worn out his strength, his high spirits had been subdued by constant contact with ' a gainsaying people,' his health had broken down under the burdens he had to bear. As we read the details of his experiences in his *Journal* our sympathy is excited, and we share his sense of relief when, on December 3, 1736, he knelt down on the English shore and blessed the Hand that had conducted him ' through such inextricable mazes.'

John Wesley, accompanied by Delamotte, arrived in Frederica on Sunday, May 23. He conducted the public service at nine o'clock, the congregation being small. During the day he saw Mr. Dison, a chaplain of the Independent Company which had a settlement a short distance from Frederica. He also met Mr. Horton, who, with Major Richards, had been captured by the Spaniards under a flag of truce and had been rescued, without bloodshed, by Oglethorpe's resourcefulness and courage. He dined with Oglethorpe, and their conversation lasted far into the night. Mrs. Hawkins and Mrs. Welch occupied their thoughts, and were the subject of part of their discussions.

Wesley's account of his visit to Frederica, as his brother's ' supply,' brings out some important facts. He found that the religious condition of the settlers was very unsatisfactory ; but, with indomitable hopefulness, he determined to improve it. There were a few of his old shipmates who had benefited by his pastoral care on board the *Simmonds* who formed a kind of ' remnant ' among their careless and godless fellow settlers, and he began with them. On June 10 he and Delamotte made an attempt to gather them together. He proceeded along the lines adopted at Savannah, and says, ' Our design was, on Sundays, in the afternoon, and every evening after public service, to spend some time with the most serious of the communicants in singing, reading, and conversation. This evening we had only Mark Hird. But on Sunday Mr. Hird and two more desired to be admitted. After a psalm and a little conversation I read Mr. Law's *Christian Perfection*, and concluded with another psalm.' Subsequently the arrangements as to hours of meeting were modified. At that time there was no place in which such a Society could meet in privacy, the storehouse being used as the church. Wesley secured the erection of a hut for public services. He had considerable skill in carpentry, and assisted in putting up the building. Mark Hird was a man on whom he strongly relied, and he looked to him to care for the little Society during the time when no minister was present in Frederica.

It is interesting to note that when Wesley was forming Religious Societies in America other members of the Holy Club were rendering assistance to similar Societies in England. Tyerman publishes several letters received by Wesley which prove the fact. Richard Morgan, who was still at Oxford, told him that he read every Sunday night to 'a cheerful number of Christians at Mr. Fox's.' Apart from the letter we know that a Religious Society was accustomed to meet at Mr. Fox's house. Morgan adds the interesting news that he had undertaken the care of Bocardo, and went there three days in the week and Broughton a fourth. At a later date, when Broughton had become curate at the Tower of London, he read prayers every night to a Society meeting in Wapping Chapel. William Chapman, a student of Pembroke College, also informed him that he read five times a week to a Religious Society in St. Ebbs' parish.[1]

During his visit to Frederica John Wesley had an illuminating talk with Mr. Horton, who acted as magistrate during Oglethorpe's absence. He learned from him something as to the state of public opinion concerning himself and his brother. Mr. Horton, after stating that the settlers considered themselves Protestants, continued: 'As for you, they cannot tell what religion you are of. They never heard of such religion before. They do not know what to make of it.' There can be little doubt that, in Georgia, both John and Charles Wesley came under the suspicion of being Roman Catholics in disguise. Tyerman, quoting from *A True and Historical Narrative of the Colony of Georgia*, published in 1741, gives the following reasons for this suspicion so far as John Wesley was concerned:

[1] Tyerman's *Life of Wesley*, i., 131-33.

1. Because he rigidly excluded all Dissenters from the Holy Communion until they first gave up their faith and principles, and, like Richard Turner and his sons, submitted to be re-baptized by him. 2. Because Roman Catholics were received by him as saints. 3. Because he endeavoured to establish and enforce confession, penance, and mortification; mixed wine with water at the Sacrament; and appointed deaconesses in accordance with what he called the apostolical constitutions.[1] Those who can read between the lines of this accusation can understand the reasons for the suspicions that had been excited. Wesley's obedience to the 'Instructions' of the S.P.G., his acceptance of Deacon's views concerning the First Prayer Book of Edward VI, and the formation of Religious Societies that met in private, led him into courses of conduct which made him a strongly suspected man. If the people had possessed sufficient knowledge and acuteness they might have added another article to their indictment. In later years Wesley would have been the first to acknowledge that his strong belief that righteousness was to be secured by 'the works of the law,' made him, fundamentally, a Roman Catholic; but that point escaped the vision of the critics of Georgia.

On Saturday, June 26, John Wesley returned to Savannah. On his journey he looked forward to resuming his services in the court-house, but a large party of Creeks had come to the town, and the court-house and the parsonage were required for their accommodation. The Germans lent him their house of meeting for his services, and he gave up the parsonage to the Indians and slept in the garden. The sight of the Indians rekindled the fire of his zeal for their conversion. He found that among the Choctaws there was an opportunity of achieving success, and he resolved to make an attempt to reach them. As usual, he sought the advice of those whose opinion he valued before undertaking the new enterprise; but Oglethorpe and the Moravians considered that his duty was to stand by his work as the minister of Savannah.

Several Spanish Jews were among Wesley's parishioners. In order that he might converse with them he commenced to study Spanish. He made such progress in the language that by July 2 he had translated that hymn which gives expression to the passionate longing of the lonely soul for the presence of

---

[1] *Life of Wesley*, i., 147; cf. *Journal*, viii. 304.

God. When we read it we think of the nights Wesley spent in the garden of the parsonage in that ' desert land.'

> O God, my God, my all Thou art!
> Ere shines the dawn of rising day
> Thy sovereign light within my heart,
> Thy all-enlivening power display.

The name of the original writer is not known. It has been suggested that its author was Miguel Molinos, the Quietist, who wrote that treasury of golden thoughts, *The Spiritual Guide*. The suggestion may be right. All that can now be said with certainty is that we owe to John Wesley the English translation of ' one of the most melodious and perfect hymns for public worship we possess.'[1]

It was at this time that Wesley's mind was filled with a project he afterwards accomplished. He was bent on preparing a collection of hymns that could be used by English Churchmen in Georgia. From his Oxford days he had been familiar with the hymns of Watts, and it is probable that he made a selection from them for use in the devotional meetings of the Holy Club. In Savannah George Herbert's *The Temple : or Sacred Poems and Private Ejaculations*, was often in his hands ; he studied the books of Norris and Hickes which contained devout songs for Christian singers ; his association with the Germans made him acquainted with the Herrnhut collection and Freylinghausen's *Gesang-Buch*, and his knowledge of French and Spanish still further increased his store of hymns. From these and other sources he commenced to gather together much material for his enterprise. The editor of his *Journal* says, ' He seems to have tested every hymn he selected, altered, translated, or composed, by singing it repeatedly—by himself, with his friends, in public or " society " worship, or in his visitation of the sick ' ; and justly adds, ' It was John Wesley, not Charles, who led the way in the hymnological transformation which within a few years was to revolutionize the worship of praise in the English Church and throughout Christendom.'

June and July, 1736, were critical months in the life of John Wesley. The gathering of the Indians to meet Oglethorpe in Savannah raised a number of important questions, but there were other matters stirring and inflaming the minds of the

---

[1] Bishop Bickersteth, quoted in Telford's *Methodist Hymn-Book Illustrated*, 269.

colonists which required attention. Wesley was not satisfied with the way in which justice was administered by the magistrates in the intervals between Oglethorpe's visits to the place. He insisted on an aggrieved person's right of appeal to the Governor from the action of his subordinates. He conversed on the subject with Oglethorpe, who accepted his advice. In a meeting at the court-house the Governor addressed the people to the following effect : ' If any one here has been abused or oppressed by any man, in or out of employment, he has full liberty of complaining. Let him deliver in his complaints in writing at my house. I will read all over by myself and do every particular man justice.' The magistrates were in consternation, and told him that they hoped ' he would not discourage government ' ; by which, the editor of the *Journal* says, ' they meant the power to imprison people without trial, or proof, or indeed hearing.' Charles Wesley, who records the incident, says that Oglethorpe told him that he feared ' his following my brother's advice in hearing all complaints would ruin the people, and he should never have any to serve him. I replied, I thought the contrary ; and that such liberty was the happiest thing that could happen to the colony, and much to be desired by all good men.'[1] John Wesley's defence of the rights of the people raised up prejudice against him in certain quarters, and strongly influenced subsequent events.

In Savannah at this time disputes between the people gave constant occupation to peacemakers, but graver matters occupied the thoughts of Oglethorpe. In his perplexities he often turned to John Wesley for counsel. Wesley was ready to help him. He had become convinced from what he had seen in Georgia that he had been long under a great mistake in thinking ' no circumstances could make it the duty of a Christian priest to do anything else but preach the gospel.' He believed that questions had arisen in connexion with the colony which, though not directly belonging to his ministry, yet were, by consequence, of the highest concern to its success. The first related to the Indian traders. The trustees of Georgia had submitted to the King in Council a law which required that none should trade with the Indians within the province of Georgia until he was licensed by the specified authorities of

[1] John Wesley's *Journal*, i., 241 *n*.

WORK IN GEORGIA

that province, and the law had been ratified by the King. In spite of this law Carolina had passed an ordinance which asserted that it was lawful for any one not so licensed to trade with the Creeks, Cherokees, or Chickasaws. The upshot was that traders and men, licensed in Carolina but not in Georgia, had been sent among the Creek and Chickasaw Indians. This defiance of the act of the King in Council could not be tolerated, and Oglethorpe strenuously opposed the invasion of the Carolina traders. John Wesley mastered the legal points involved in the dispute. He puts them tersely and clearly in his letter to Mr. Hutcheson, and his assistance was of great value to the Governor.[1]

If the Indian trader controversy had been the only matter of colonial dispute in which Wesley interfered he would have carried the people of Georgia with him, and would have increased his popularity. But there were two other subjects of vital importance which cried aloud for settlement, and were clearly within his sphere of influence as a clergyman. The trustees had refused to sanction the introduction of the slave trade into their colony. It existed in South Carolina, and the settlers in Georgia clamoured for the right to import negroes to labour in their plantations. The trustees would not alter their decision, and Oglethorpe and Wesley supported them. Slavery at all times was hateful to the soul of Wesley, and his opposition was unyielding. As the planters could not shake the resolution of the trustees they introduced what was then known as 'white slavery' into the colony, and against this iniquitous subterfuge Wesley raised powerful and indignant protests. There was another mischief he fought with all his might. The trustees had forbidden the ordinary sale of spirituous liquors in Georgia; their action provoked much resentment, but Oglethorpe determined that their commands should be obeyed. His loyalty to the directions of the trustees impaired his popularity, and Wesley knew it was hazardous to support him. He did not hesitate for a moment; everywhere he went he opposed the trade in spirituous liquors. His action in the matters of the slave trade and the sale of spirituous liquors had its inevitable result. A strong opposition arose against him in a powerful section of the population. In Savannah and Frederica he became the subject of suspicion

[1] *Works*, xii., 43-44, 8vo ed.

and enmity, and men and women watched for an opportunity to drive him out of Georgia.[1]

At the end of July, 1736, Charles Wesley, having provisionally resigned his secretaryship, set sail for England. He carried dispatches from Oglethorpe to the trustees, the Board of Trade, and, probably, to the Government. John Wesley went with him to Charlestown, and there bade him farewell. During his visit to the place he met Dr. Garden, the Bishop of London's Commissary for South Carolina. He preached in the church to a congregation numbering about three hundred, and tells us that there were nearly fifty persons present at Holy Communion. The visit to Charlestown is noteworthy, as it is probable that during it he called on Lewis Timothy, the printer, and made preliminary arrangements for the publication of a collection of hymns he had compiled.

On August 8 Wesley returned to Savannah. Finding that Oglethorpe had gone back to Frederica, he followed him and delivered to him the letters he had brought from Carolina. His reception by the people was unfriendly. He says, 'From that time I had less and less prospect of doing good at Frederica, many there being extremely zealous and indefatigably diligent to prevent it, and few of the rest daring to show themselves of another mind for fear of their displeasure.' Notwithstanding his discouragement he discharged his duty as a clergyman. He also took up Charles Wesley's work as Oglethorpe's secretary, and so connecting himself with the government of the place he increased the dislike of the discontented settlers. The Frederica climate, which had wrecked his brother's health, told on his 'iron constitution.' He suffered from intermittent fever, attacks of which recurred during many years of his life. It was during this time of misery that the mask fell from the face of Mrs. Hawkins. Wesley was obstinately persuaded of the good that was in the woman. She had shown her dislike of him, but he attributed her sudden change to the influence of some one who was poisoning her mind against him. But when he visited her, and she committed a violent assault on him with pistol, scissors, and teeth, his good opinion of her changed, and the Hawkins episode ran to its close. In spite of his exciting adventures he found time to pursue his studies. He commenced to read Cave's *Primitive Christianity ; or, the*

[1] *Journal*, i., 244 *n*.

WORK IN GEORGIA 153

Religion of the Ancient Christians in the First Ages of the Gospel. It arrested his special attention and made an ineffaceable impression on his mind. The book describes vividly the organization and experiences of the primitive Church, and as Wesley read it in the wilds of Frederica the old ideals glowed once more in those days of gloom.[1]

Wesley left Frederica on September 2 and returned to Savannah. As Ingham had taken up his residence at Cowpen, near Savannah, in order to prepare himself for a mission to the Indians, before leaving Frederica Wesley obtained a promise from Mr. Reed to conduct the public evening prayers in his absence. Five or six persons also agreed to spend an hour together every day in singing, reading, and exhorting one another. The employment of a layman to read the evening service reminds us of the arrangement existing in the Religious Societies described in Dr. Woodward's book. It was prophetic of the action of Wesley in the years that were rapidly approaching.

Wesley's stay in Savannah lasted for about a month, and during it a few incidents occurred which must be noted. We have mentioned Mr. Dison, the chaplain of the ' Independent Company.' Charles Wesley had a low estimate of his moral character, and we know nothing which proves that the estimate was wrong. This unsatisfactory man had been in Savannah for several weeks, and his proceedings in town and country had done much to overturn the discipline Wesley had tried to establish. He went to Dison's lodgings and taxed him with baptizing several strong, healthy children in private houses, and with marrying several couples without first publishing the banns, a custom which he knew was contrary to both rubric and canon. In addition, Wesley charged him with endeavouring to make a division between himself and his parishioners by speaking against him before them as to his life and preaching. Dison denied the second and third charges, but owned that he had baptized in private houses. He promised Wesley never to do it again, and did the same thing the next day. His denial of the second charge—marrying people without first publishing the banns—must be borne in mind. Wesley's record of his interview with Dison closes with the words, ' O Discipline, where art thou to be found? Not in England, nor (as yet) in America.'

[1] Wesley published an abridged edition of Dr. William Cave's book in 1753.

Sickness was rife in Savannah, and Wesley was assiduous in his visitation of the homes of the people. The pressure of his work was heavy, and he began to feel that it was getting beyond his strength. In addition to Savannah and Frederica he had the pastoral care of outlying stations such as Thunderbolt, Skidoway, Irene, and Cowpen. Little settlements had grown up in the woods and demanded attention. His pastoral visitation was thoroughly done. He studied the chapter on ' The Parson in Circuit ' in Herbert's *A Priest to the Temple*, and it is easy to perceive the effect it had on his work. Wesley doubtless received help from the members of the ' Societies,' and especially from those who were in charge of their different sections, among whom we may mention Miss Bovey, of Savannah, who was looked upon as a ' deaconess ' by the more captious parishioners; but he longed for the coming of some one from England to share his toils, and wrote to members of the Holy Club and asked them to come out to Georgia. The mortality among his parishioners increased the number of orphan children in Savannah. He received some of them into the parsonage, but felt that an organized effort should be made to meet their case. One object of Charles Wesley's visit to England was to lay this matter before the trustees and to secure the erection of an orphanage in Georgia,[1] but John Wesley had to leave the colony without seeing the realization of that benevolent scheme.

John Wesley's *Journal* of this period contains abundant evidence of his care for the children of his parish. He catechized them in accordance with the directions of the Church ; he also continued the custom of the Holy Club at Oxford, and, in connexion with Delamotte, he set up a school for them in which they received, on week-days, an elementary education. It was in this school in Savannah that an incident occurred which relieves the grimness of the story of Wesley's experiences in Georgia. It reveals his active sense of humour, and casts light on the obtuseness of some of his modern critics. In the school a number of poor children were taught in company with boys whose parents were in fairly prosperous circumstances. The poor children came to the school with bare feet, and the young Savannah aristocrats laughed them to scorn and persecuted them after the manner of wayward

---

[1] Charles Wesley's *Journal*, i., 79.

boys. Delamotte was unable to suppress the tyrants, and spoke to Wesley about the matter. Wesley listened, and then asked Delamotte to let him teach in the school for a time. The next day he appeared barefooted, and the boys stared at him and muttered their surprise. The persecution died down, and, after a few days, ceased. It was impossible to harry lads for being like their master, and Wesley's method prevailed. The critics point solemnly to Wesley's bare feet as a sign of his monkish austerity in Georgia.

The principal events of the remainder of the year 1736 affecting the life and work of Wesley may be briefly stated. He went to Frederica on October 13 and spent a few days there. The condition of the place was deplorable, and the change back to Savannah was welcome. He brought back with him Miss Hopkey, the niece of Causton, the chief magistrate of Savannah. She was a young girl of eighteen of whom we shall have something to say at a later stage. In November Oglethorpe arrived in Savannah on his way to England. Wesley assisted him in his investigation of a serious case, wrote letters for him, and was in close consultation with him concerning the affairs of the colony. On November 23 Oglethorpe sailed for England, and Wesley was thus left without a counsellor, and Georgia was deprived of the presence of its Governor. Oglethorpe's place as the administrator of the civil affairs of Savannah was, we presume, taken by the magistrates; but the absence of the trustees' representative soon brought confusion. On December 28 Wesley, accompanied by Delamotte, set out on his last visit to Frederica. He stayed there about a month. In taking leave of that unfortunate settlement, he says, in his *Journal*: ' It was not any apprehension of my own danger, though my life had been threatened many times, but an utter despair of doing good there which made me content with the thought of seeing it no more.'[1]

When Oglethorpe left Georgia he told Wesley that he expected strong opposition in respect of his management of the colony. If a letter subsequently received in Savannah can be trusted his expectation was realized. In this letter it was declared that Sir Robert Walpole had turned against

---

[1] Frederica, from the first, was doomed to failure as a settlement. When the writer visited Georgia, in 1910, he was told that it was still only a small collection of houses and a place that had never risen much above its original condition.

him, that Parliament was resolved to make a severe scrutiny into all that had been transacted in the colony, and that even the trustees were so far from acknowledging his services that they had protested his bills, and had charged him with misapplying the moneys he had received and with gross mismanagement of the power wherewith he was entrusted. Wesley wrote to Oglethorpe communicating the rumours which were being circulated among the settlers, and expressing his high admiration of him and his confidence in his integrity. We can understand how the mere news of such allegations would serve to weaken the Governor's influence. The cloud of coming calamities was gathering, and its shadow crept over the life of Wesley. He found that the whispering gossips were not inclined to spare him. It was suggested that he was guilty of embezzling the goods of the trustees, and that an accusation to that effect had been forwarded to England. Wesley, on hearing the rumour, wrote at once to the trustees. Their secretary, in their behalf, replied that no complaint of any kind had been laid before them relating to him. The letter expressed the hope that, for the future, he would not believe or listen to any private informations or insinuations such as would make him uneasy and might lead him to distrust the justice of the trustees and the regard they had for him.[1]

On the day Wesley wrote to Oglethorpe Benjamin Ingham left Georgia and commenced his voyage to England. It had been determined, after consultation, that he should go there to stir up interest in the religious condition of the colony, and try to persuade some clergyman to come out to assist those who were working there. Wesley wrote on the same topic to his friend Dr. Burton, of Corpus Christi College. Having done all that was possible, he and Delamotte continued to toil on, longing for the coming of better days.

[1] Tyerman's *Life of Wesley*, i., 136 ; cf. *Journal*, viii. 312.

XI

LAST DAYS IN GEORGIA

THE opening months of 1737 were of critical importance to Wesley. It was unfortunate that he had to face exceptionally difficult circumstances without the aid of counsellors, especially of men equipped with more worldly wisdom than he possessed. During this fateful year he was deprived of the advice of Oglethorpe, Charles Wesley, Ingham, and Spangenberg. Delamotte remained; but although he was a faithful friend, he was young and inexperienced. His judgement in some matters was sound, but we can understand that he would hesitate to interfere too persistently with Wesley's course of action.

Pursuing his lonely way, Wesley was sustained by the visions that had previously inspired him. He was an idealist. His optimism was invincible. He had to admit the failure of his work in Frederica and of his attempt to reach the Indians, but the programme of his life was not exhausted. He was convinced that in Savannah he could form a Church that would answer the descriptions contained in books that had caused his imagination to kindle. He found his ideal, in part, in the Church of England as it was intended to be, and as it would be if its ministers were true to its spirit and doctrine, and would firmly administer its discipline as it was expressed in rubrics, canons, and the Book of Common Prayer. But even the Church of England did not express his full conception of the Church as it existed in apostolic times. Its formularies did not sufficiently provide for the fellowship of Christian people. They recognized communion in worship and at the Sacrament of the Lord's Supper, but he saw that they were defective in provision for that spiritual personal fellowship between individual Christians which was a distinguishing mark of the Church at the beginning of its history. It was enjoyed by the members of the best kind of the Religious Societies in

England, but he was aware that such Societies had arisen from individual initiative rather than any ecclesiastical direction or command. He could not deny that, in many instances, such meetings had been opposed by persons in authority as illegal and mischievous, and that the justification of this form of Christian fellowship was to be found in the pages of the New Testament rather than in the ecclesiastical law books of the Church of England. The discovery he made was important. He was a strong Churchman, but the spirit of his Nonconformist ancestors lived in him and unconsciously influenced some of his proceedings. He found it was impossible to realize his vision unless he enlarged that conception of the Church which satisfied most of the members of the Church of England.

Following his convictions, Wesley pursued his course. In reading the story of his mission in Georgia we are conscious of the increasing loftiness of his aims. We find that his ideal of the Church was not completely expressed in common worship and the close association of its members in Religious Societies. He was intent on gathering together not only a congregation and a Society but also a distinctively religious household, zealous of good works. The parsonage was not only the gathering-place of the select Society on Sunday evening, but, during the week, it became a guest-house for the traveller, an orphanage, an almshouse for widows, a school, and a scene of varied benevolence. Its activities were carried on with constant prayer and Christian song. Work was worship, and worship was the supreme work of those who lived with Wesley in his wilderness home. In watching the daily life of the people who dwelt in the parsonage we often wonder as to the source from which he derived his ideal of ' the Christian family.' We suggest that in his *Life of Mr. Fletcher*, published in 1786, he reveals the secret. He says, ' When I was young, I was exceedingly affected with a relation in Mr. Herbert's *Life*—an account of Mr. Ferrar's family at Little Gidding, in Huntingdonshire, a very particular description of which is given in the *Arminian Magazine*. I longed to see such another family in any part of the three kingdoms.'[1] The *Life* of George Herbert to which he alludes was evidently written by Izaak Walton. It is probable that the book was

[1] *Works*, xi., 332-33, 8vo ed.

in the library in the Epworth Rectory. Izaak Walton's description of the 'happy society' at Gidding Hall is well known to those who are familiar with the quiet by-ways of seventeenth-century religious literature. We do not wonder that the picture of the Little Gidding home 'exceedingly affected' Wesley, and we know that it left an enduring impression on his mind. Looking across the seas into 'the forest primeval' we note the beginning of an attempt to form a Christian 'family' within the wooden walls of the parsonage at Savannah.

Never losing sight of his ideal, Wesley went on his way. But his work was increasingly difficult, and circumstances conspired to make success impossible. It was his fate throughout his life to excite feelings of intense loyalty in his friends and of bitter antagonism in his enemies. In Savannah the little group of those who were devoted to him was encompassed by a hostile majority. Such a result was inevitable. In the absence of Oglethorpe he took a prominent part in the civil affairs of the town, and was generally on the unpopular side. He championed the cause of those whom he deemed wrongly accused and unjustly treated by the magistrates; he opposed licentiousness, blasphemy, drunkenness, slavery, and every violation of the laws of God and man. He was a social reformer of an advanced type, and his attempts to raise the moral tone and conduct of the community were strongly resented. An unappeasable irritation was excited in his adversaries, who waited for an opportunity to drive him out of the colony.

It was not long before Wesley gave his opponents their chance. They were too prudent to select, as their main line of attack, the support he had given to the trustees, so they determined to bring charges against him concerning his ecclesiastical proceedings and other matters, and arranged that they would hear the charges themselves. Their knowledge of Church law was small, and the shrewder men among them doubted the soundness of their strategy. The arguments of lawyers on technical points seldom arouse popular interest. In order to endow them with vivacity it is necessary to show that they have a bearing on the rights and liberties of the subject. In Wesley's case a discussion of fine points of ecclesiasticism by a group of Savannah magistrates would not have lacked grotesqueness ; but if it could be shown that he, as an intolerant clergyman, had inflicted harsh punishment on an innocent person, then the temper of the colonists would be roused, and the contemplated end would be secured. After waiting for a time, this powerful weapon was placed in the hands of Wesley's adversaries.

It is not our intention to tell, once more, the story of Wesley's love-affair in Georgia. He has told it himself with an astonishing minuteness. The amplitude of his narrative illustrates the fact that in him the organ of secretiveness was not fully developed. When his proceedings in the matter were challenged and misrepresented in England he felt it his duty, in self-defence, to state everything that had occurred during his acquaintance with Miss Sophia Christiana Hopkey. His statement may be found at length in the standard edition of his *Journal*, and to it we refer all who desire to read an exciting romance of the American backwoods. There are certain facts in that romance, however, which it is essential that we should note.

Miss Sophy Hopkey, who was about eighteen years of age, was the niece of Mrs. Causton, the wife of Thomas Causton, the storekeeper and chief magistrate of Savannah. He had come to Georgia in the first batch of emigrants. He had been in trouble concerning a fraud he had practised on the revenue. Getting into Oglethorpe's favour, he was put in charge of the stores sent by the trustees for the use of the colonists. He continued in that position for some time. In September, 1737, however, charges were made against him of grossly abusing his power as storekeeper, and of hindering people from settling on lands allotted to them by the trustees. His accounts excited suspicion. After the charges had been investigated by a ' grand jury ' in Savannah they were forwarded to England, and the trustees dismissed him from all his offices, refusing at the same time to accept his accounts as correct.[1] These facts cast light on Causton's career, and enable us to understand incidents which otherwise would be obscure. Oglethorpe's confidence in him, and Wesley's intimacy with him, show that he possessed the power to make a good impression on men who had not perfected themselves in the art of reading character.

Miss Sophy Hopkey, according to Wesley's description, must have possessed great attractiveness. Before he met her

---

[1] Tyerman's *Life of Wesley*, i., 145.

she had excited the admiration of a man who had publicly declared that if she did not marry him no one else should have her. The threat had a disturbing effect on her mind; but, inasmuch as her lover had fallen into the clutches of the law and was in prison, its accomplishment was postponed. Wesley met her on March 13, 1736, and marked the event in his *Diary*. He seems to have been immediately impressed with her. She became his pupil, and visited the parsonage constantly. On one occasion, when he was ill, she nursed him day and night. If rumour may be trusted, Oglethorpe, who watched the trend of events with a favouring eye, advised her to wear a white linen dress because he knew that her patient admired such simplicity. And so events moved on. Miss Hopkey learned much from her conversations with Wesley. She was of a devout disposition, and soon enthusiastically accepted his views concerning Church services, and especially about the duty of constant communion. She attended the early morning services with conspicuous regularity, and became one of the most hopeful members of the Savannah Society and Church. Oglethorpe strongly desired that Wesley should marry her. He wanted to retain him in the colony, as he highly valued his influence and work, and everything pointed to the fulfilment of his desire. There can be no doubt that Wesley was deeply in love with the girl, although he hesitated to declare his love to her and ask her to marry him. His hesitation may have arisen from the opposition of Delamotte and the Moravians, whom he consulted, and who disapproved of the match; but he declined to give their counsel weight and continued on his way. Finally, after much conflict with himself, he decided to put the idea of marriage out of his mind. It was a stunning blow to him when, in March, 1737, he was asked to publish the banns of marriage between Miss Hopkey and William Williamson, a young adventurer who had come to Georgia after Wesley had landed there, and whose future career showed he was utterly unworthy of the girl he married. The blow staggered Wesley for a time, but the news soon reached him that, without waiting for the publication of banns, Williamson and Miss Hopkey had gone to Purrysburg and had been married there by a clergyman notorious for his irregular proceedings. Wesley was sore at heart, and also indignant at the contempt which had been shown for the laws of the Church.

On Sunday, March 20, a week after her marriage, Mrs. Williamson presented herself at the communion, and Wesley administered the Sacrament to her. He spoke to her afterwards in the street, and before they parted she informed him that her husband desired that she should not speak to him again. Williamson's wish that the acquaintance between Wesley and Mrs. Williamson should cease raised a serious question. Wesley was the clergyman of the Church in Savannah, and it was his duty to ascertain the fitness of communicants for admission to the Lord's Table. The rules of the S.P.G. required its missionaries to be careful as to such admissions, and the rubrics prefixed to the Order of the Administration of the Lord's Supper in the Book of Common Prayer emphasized the obligation of interviews and conversations between clergymen and communicants. As the weeks went by Wesley was pained to see the change that was evident in Mrs. Williamson. She gave up fasting and neglected all the morning prayers, although she still acknowledged her obligation to observe both of these duties, 'which,' says Wesley, 'made a wide difference between her neglect and that of others.'[1] He consulted Delamotte, and after much consideration determined to take his advice, which was that 'he should bear with her until he had spoken with her once more.' For nearly five months he left the question in suspense and refrained from decisive action. During that time Mrs. Williamson's attendance at the Sacrament became irregular, in spite of her conviction that it was her duty to communicate constantly. We can imagine the effect produced on the Society and Church of Savannah by her changed behaviour. The legality of her marriage was questionable, and would certainly be discussed in the town, and her neglect of the things which she confessed she ought to do would deepen the uneasiness of those who remembered her former conduct. Still, from March to August Wesley waited hoping that the instincts of her better self would prevail.

During the interval of waiting Wesley's work went on, and it is necessary to note some of the events which happened. In April he made an attempt to stop the proceedings of the clergyman who was notorious for celebrating irregular marriages. He found that he had undertaken a difficult task.

[1] *Journal*, i., 356.

LAST DAYS IN GEORGIA

The condition of the Church of England in America was chaotic. The colonies, as we have previously said, were presumed to be in the diocese of London ; at any rate they were supposed to be under the care of the Bishop of London. Bishop Samuel Wilberforce, in his *History of the Protestant Episcopal Church in America*, has shed light on the origin of this supposition. He traces it to the fact that when the earliest schemes of the Virginian Company for establishing the Church amongst their settlers were announced the then Bishop of London gave his hearty concurrence to the proposals. In consequence of his sympathy he was asked to find and appoint the first Virginian clergy, and from this practice there gradually grew up a notion that they were in some way in his diocese. When Bishop Edmund Gibson was appointed to the see of London in 1723 he faced a question which had never been thoroughly investigated. He determined to discover the source of his authority. Pursuing his inquiries, he was told that, though no strict ecclesiastical title could be found, yet by an order in council in the reign of Charles II, the colonies were made a part of the see of London. Diligent search was made for this order, with the result that he discovered that none such existed. Finding that he had no jurisdiction over the colonies he declined even to appoint a commissary, and for a time the colonies were separated from all episcopal control. This was, in the eyes of English ecclesiastical statesmen, an intolerable condition of affairs, and, finally, as Wilberforce says, ' Having obtained a special commission from the Crown, committing this charge to him, and thinking it better, under all the circumstances of the case, to act under this authority than to abandon them entirely, he began to discharge it with his usual fidelity. Yet even then he felt that his hold upon those distant parts was little what it should be, if he were indeed to deem himself their bishop. . . . This authority, shadowy as it was, expired with the life of Bishop Gibson, since the commission under which he acted was granted only to himself personally, and not to his successors.'[1] Gibson appointed commissaries to represent him in the colonies, among whom was Dr. Garden, who lived in Charlestown and was supposed to exercise authority in the Carolinas, which had become Crown colonies. His relation to Georgia, a settlement governed by trustees, cannot be

[1] Wilberforce's *History of the American Church*, 136-39.

ascertained, but it is certain that if the authority of the Bishop of London over the colonies was 'shadowy,' that of his commissaries was the shadow of a shade.

Bent on an almost hopeless quest, Wesley, on April 12, set out for Charlestown, determined to put a stop to the proceedings of the clergyman who had married several of his Georgian parishioners without banns or licence. He interviewed Dr. Garden, who assured him he would take care no such irregularity should be committed for the future, and who also told him that he believed no other clergyman in the province, except the man against whom Wesley brought his complaint, would be guilty of such irregularity. He also promised to caution the clergy against such proceedings when he met them at their general meeting during the following week. Being detained in Charlestown through stress of weather Wesley had an opportunity of meeting the clergy of South Carolina at their annual visitation. He stated his case, and says that they severally assured him they would never interfere with him in anything, nor marry any persons of his province without a letter from him desiring them to do so. With this assurance Wesley had to be content. He returned to Savannah on May 30. His visit to Charlestown had given him the opportunity of again seeing Lewis Timothy, and finally arranging with him for the printing of the *Collection of Psalms and Hymns.*

During his absence from Savannah Delamotte had taken his place, and Wesley found his little flock in a better state than he had expected. He says, ' Those who desired to be followers of Christ had not made my absence an excuse for the neglect of assembling themselves together ; and, by the blessing of God on their endeavours, most of them were more steadfast and zealous of good works than when I left them.' Mr. Hows, who conducted a communicants' class, and Mrs. Burnside, who did the work of a deaconess if she did not bear the name, had contributed to this gratifying result. The employment of Delamotte, a layman, as Wesley's substitute interests us, and we wish that we had more light on the duties he discharged. Wesley, as a student of ecclesiastical history, was aware that in the first ages of Christianity laymen took a prominent part in the worship and work of the Christian Church. In the *Apostolical Constitutions* he must have met with the sentence, ' Let him that teaches, although he be one of the laity, yet, if he be skilful in the word and grave in his manners, teach; for they shall be all taught of God.'[1] He must also have been aware of the state of things existing at that time in Virginia. In the colony, owing to the lack of clergy, lay-readers were generally employed, and Bishop Wilberforce says that ' it frequently happened that a benefice was kept unfilled in order to prolong the more acceptable services of the unordained reader.'[2] There was no lack of ancient and modern precedents on the subject of lay readers, and we are not surprised that at Frederica and Savannah, in special emergencies, Wesley availed himself of their help.

It is significant of Wesley's consciousness of the approaching storm that on May 1 he publicly ' subscribed the prayers.' When he entered on his charge in Savannah he had omitted that formal act. It is possible that, in consultation with Dr. Garden, he had seen it would be wise to take the step lest his right to be considered the minister of Savannah should be challenged. Having satisfied himself on this point, he resumed his work with increased confidence. It is not necessary to dwell on that work; its character has been described. There are some incidents, however, which call for passing remark. It was his custom to preach occasionally on the ' grievous errors ' of the Church of Rome, and to warn his congregation of the great danger of continuing in it. His words sank into the heart of a Romanist, who sent for him and expressed a desire to return to the Church of England. He had previously discovered a man who had become a convert to Deism, and further inquiries showed that others had been affected and were inclined to accept views that were then spreading rapidly in England. Though a strong Protestant, he considered the evil of Deism was much greater than that of Romanism. In his *Journal* and *Diary* he contrasts Popery with infidelity, and says, ' I cannot but observe the surprising infatuation that reigns in England, and especially in London. Advice upon advice did we receive there to beware of the increase of Popery, but not one word do I remember to have heard of the increase of infidelity. Now this overgrown zeal for Protestantism, quite swallowing up zeal for our common Christianity, I cannot term anything better than infatuation.' His work among the

[1] See Clarke's Ante-Nicene Library, xvii., 246, second part of the volume; also Hatch's *Organization of the Early Christian Churches*, Synopsis, xix., and. 116-17.
[2] *History of the American Church*, 141.

Papists in Savannah had been successful ; only an Italian or two, with whom he could not converse in their own language, remained to represent the Roman faith ; but he confesses his failure to win back the Deists to Christian beliefs.

Wesley's work amongst the children prospered. He did not forget the fact that, when he was a child, his father had admitted him to the Holy Communion. Towards the end of May four of the scholars who had been instructed daily for several weeks earnestly and repeatedly requested to be allowed to take the Sacrament, and Wesley permitted them to come to the Lord's Table. It was afterwards alleged that his action was not in accordance with the desire of their parents ; it certainly was not in harmony with the condition laid down in the rubric which requires that communicants must have been confirmed. Wesley's answer to the latter objection would be easily given, inasmuch as there was no bishop of the Church of England in America ; but his action ought to have suggested that even rubrics must sometimes give way to the force of circumstances. It was a lesson he learned slowly. It is interesting to note that, in July, he had reverted to his old position, and was once more standing on what he supposed to be the letter of the law In that month John Martin Bolzius, the chief minister of the Salzburgers, who had settled at Ebenezer, visited Wesley at Savannah, and seems to have stayed with him at the parsonage. He was a man of high Christian character and saintliness. He asked permission to join in the Holy Communion, and Wesley told him that he did not dare to administer the Sacrament to him, because he had not been baptized by a minister in episcopal orders. Bolzius accepted the refusal in a charming spirit, and probably soon dismissed the incident from his mind. But Wesley never forgot it. In 1749 he reproached himself for his conduct in his *Journal*, and so late as 1777 he publicly confessed his fault.[1] His subsequent repentance should be remembered.

Wesley's relations with the Moravians were very friendly during all the time he was in Georgia. He spent much time with them and learned many things from them. Their spirit and temper attracted him, and he closely conversed with them on their system of government and doctrine. In order that his doubts concerning the correctness of some of their

---

[1] See *Journal*, iii., 434 ; *Works*, vii., 422, 8vo ed.

LAST DAYS IN GEORGIA

principles might be removed he drew out a list of questions which he submitted to them. To these questions they appended answers. It is important to note that the first inquiry was, ' What do you mean by conversion ? ' That was the chief subject of interest to Wesley at that time, and he must have been impressed by the answers given. The whole of the replies are illuminating, and cast a revealing light on Wesley's spiritual experiences.[1]

In the midst of much that was disturbing Wesley was looking forward to the publication of his *Collection of Psalms and Hymns*. At last a copy was sent him from Charlestown. He turned over its pages, winced at the printer's errors, but gave the little book an author's welcome. The Charlestown *Collection* disappeared from sight for many years. Its existence was forgotten until a stray copy found its way to England and was discovered by a keen-eyed book-hunter. He allowed it to be reproduced in so-called facsimile, and from this reprint we are able to give some account of its contents. It is divided into three parts, and consists of psalms and hymns for Sunday, Wednesday, or Friday, the fast-days of the Church, and for Saturday. Dr. Osborn, who was a master of Methodist hymnology, points out, in his Introduction to the *Collection*, that the first division includes psalms and hymns suitable for general worship ; the second contains hymns marked by a tone of confession and humiliation ; the third consists of hymns of praise to God, especially considered as the creator of the universe. Hymns by Dr. Watts occupy a large place in the book ; in number they amount to one-third of the *Collection*. Some persons have expressed surprise that Wesley should have used so many hymns composed by a Dissenter, but they do not know that his admiration for the hymns of Dr. Watts was of somewhat long standing ; he had used them in the religious meetings of the Holy Club at Oxford. The critic's astonishment may be increased when he discovers a hymn taken from John Austin's *Devotions in the Ancient Way of Offices*. He was a Roman Catholic, but his ' Hark, my soul, how everything strives to serve the bounteous King ' only needed a few touches from Wesley's hand to make it suitable for the use of Protestants.

In the Charlestown *Collection* we welcome some of those

[1] *Journal*, i., 372-74.

translations of German hymns with which John Wesley has enriched the psalmody of England. He had an exquisite ear for the melody of words; his command of cadence and rhythm was wellnigh perfect; his power to rise to the grandeur of an author's conception was exercised without faltering; his taste, as manifested in selection and rejection, was almost unerring. The fame of Charles Wesley as a hymn-writer has somewhat obscured that of John Wesley, but we may confidently point to the Charlestown *Collection* in vindication of his right to a high place among the religious poets. There we find Lange's great hymn, ' O God, Thou bottomless abyss,' Freylinghausen's ' O Jesu, source of calm repose,' Richter's ' Thou Lamb of God, Thou Prince of Peace '—the firstfruits of a rich harvest gathered by John Wesley from the golden fields of German hymnology. Another aspect of his work is illustrated in the *Collection*. His good taste, and his power to change a poem into a singable hymn, are shown in his treatment of George Herbert. If comparison is made between ' Throw away Thy rod ' and ' Lord, in my silence how do I despise,' as they appear in *The Temple* and in the *Collection*, the obligation of George Herbert to John Wesley will be manifest.

It is interesting to note that Wesley was familiar with *The Spectator*, especially with those Saturday numbers in which Addison tried, for a while, to induce his readers to become devout. In the *Collection* we find three of his *Spectator* hymns —' When all Thy mercies,' ' When rising from the bed of death,' and ' The spacious firmament on high '; also Dr. Watts's *Spectator* hymn ' When Israel, freed from Pharaoh's hand.' The Epworth Rectory contributed to the *Collection*. Wesley's father was represented by ' O Thou, who when I did complain,' ' Behold the Saviour of mankind,' and his poem entitled ' Eupolis's Hymn to the Creator.' The hymns to the Trinity of Samuel Wesley, the younger, also appear in the little book.

In turning over the leaves of the *Collection* one thought is constantly in our mind. In many of the hymns the ' evangelical note ' is insistent. Why did not Wesley hear it more clearly ? In Dr. Watts's hymn ' How sad our state by nature is,' and in his father's ' Behold the Saviour of mankind,' the eyes of the penitent sinner are fixed on the crucified

Christ, the only hope of salvation. Wesley admits that in Georgia he was seeking righteousness 'not by faith, but, as it were, by the works of the law,' and yet he selected a hymn entitled 'Christ our righteousness,' and sang with his people :

> Our guilty spirits dread
> To meet the wrath of heaven ;
> But in Thy righteousness arrayed
> We see our sins forgiven.

He must have felt that his standpoint did not give him such a view of the Cross as enabled him to ' see ' his sins forgiven. A similar experience is not uncommon among those who are not far from the kingdom of God. As he read, sang, and translated these hymns, as he conversed with the Moravians, as he pondered the evangelical words in the *Collection*, he was gradually moving towards the great experience when ' the heavy night was lifted from his eyes.'

As the months passed Wesley's mind was increasingly disturbed on the subject of Mrs. Williamson's fitness for admission to the Sacrament of the Lord's Supper. He spoke to her and wrote her, but conversation and letters produced no effect on her conduct. In July he resolved to consult Mr. Burnside, a man whose judgement he respected. Mr. Burnside told him that, viewing things as he did, he ought not to allow Mrs. Williamson to communicate ; adding, ' The consequences of rejecting her you know, but be they what they will that does not alter your duty.' After the conversation Wesley determined to do what he judged to be his duty, but with the mildness and prudence which God should give him. He wrote to Causton giving him a hint of his intentions. At an interview with him Causton said, ' If you repel me or my wife, I shall require a legal reason. But I shall trouble myself about none else. Let them look to themselves.' At the suggestion of Mrs. Causton he wrote to Mrs. Williamson and told her plainly what he disliked in her conduct. In addition to her neglect of fasting, public worship, and the Sacrament he reminded her of the 'deliberate dissimulation' she had practised respecting her marriage. She had repeatedly informed him that she had no design to marry Williamson even at the time when she intended to do so. Her dissimulation had so imposed on him that Mrs. Causton's request concerning the publication of banns had come on him as a thunderclap. Mrs. Williamson took no notice of his letter, but presented herself at the Sacrament on Sunday, August 7. She had intermitted her attendance for some time, and had given no notice of her design to communicate. Wesley repelled her. In the evening Mrs. Burnside, who had shown herself her friend, talked to her and told her that she was much to blame, after receiving Wesley's letter, to offer herself at the Table before she had cleared herself to him. She advised her to go to Wesley and meet the charge he had brought against her, ' then she would easily put an end to the matter.' But her temper had been roused, and she declared she would not show such meanness of spirit as to speak to him herself, ' but somebody else should do so.'

Mrs. Williamson's threat was not vain. On August 8 the recorder of Savannah issued a warrant for the apprehension of Wesley on the charge of defaming Mrs. Williamson's character, and refusing to administer to her the Sacrament in a public congregation without cause, the damages being laid at one thousand pounds. The next day Wesley was brought by a constable before the bailiff and the recorder. He denied the first charge of defamation, and as to the second, as it referred to a matter that was purely ecclesiastical, he denied the power of the magistrates to interrogate him. He was told to attend the meeting of the next court. Wesley's adversaries now felt that the weapon they needed was in their hands. Causton, the chief magistrate, threw off the mask of friendship, and proved himself a rancorous antagonist. He used all his influence to secure a condemnation. He went about the town getting up evidence, trying to persuade Wesley's friends to appear against him, and acting, as a magistrate, in a fashion that casts a peculiar light on the administration of justice in the backwoods of America.

It is not worth while to describe in detail the proceedings of the court of Savannah in Wesley's case, but there are certain aspects of those proceedings which must be indicated. The trial began on August 22, 1737. The charges were submitted to a ' grand jury.' It consisted of forty-four of the inhabitants, about a fifth part of the adult male population of the town. Tyerman says one was a Frenchman, ignorant of the English language ; one a Roman Catholic ; one a professed

LAST DAYS IN GEORGIA

infidel; three were Baptists; sixteen or seventeen others were Dissenters; and, of the rest, several had personal quarrels against Wesley, and had openly vowed vengeance.[1] The findings of the majority of such a 'grand jury' on questions that involved civil and ecclesiastical law were inevitable. For the credit of the colony it must be said that there was a minority of twelve men who had their wits about them, and who saw clearly the points at issue, and were aware that the charges were 'an artifice of Mr. Causton's, designed rather to blacken the character of Mr. Wesley than to free the colony from religious tyranny.'[2] Causton, as chief magistrate, presided at the proceedings on August 22, and delivered a charge to the grand jury before dismissing them to their labours. He handed to them an affidavit sworn by Mrs. Williamson, and a paper entitled 'A List of Grievances,' which professed to show that Wesley had deviated from the principles and regulations of the Established Church in many particulars. The work of the grand jury took longer than was expected. We do not wonder that special difficulty was found with the list of ecclesiastical 'deviations.' That points which can only be intelligently discussed by experts in Church law should have been submitted to the investigation of a Savannah jury was extraordinary. At last the findings of the majority were ready for presentation, and the court assembled on September to receive them. The grand jury found true bills on ten counts of the indictment. Nine of them referred to Wesley's 'deviations from the principles and regulations of the Established Church,' and one to his correspondence with Mrs. Williamson.

The list of ecclesiastical deviations is interesting. It includes the repelling of Mrs. Williamson from the Sacrament; Wesley's failure to emit any public declaration of his adherence to the principles and regulations of the Church of England since his arrival in Savannah; his division of the order of morning prayer on the Lord's Day; his refusal to baptize Henry Parker's child otherwise than by dipping; his refusal of the Sacrament to William Gough because he heard he was a Dissenter; his refusal to read the Office of the Dead over the body of Nathaniel Polhill only because the deceased was

---
[1] *Life of Wesley*, i., 154.
[2] See the report of the minority to the trustees for Georgia in Tyerman's *Life of Wesley*, i., 157-58.

not of his opinion; his calling himself the 'ordinary' of Savannah; and certain 'deviations' in the matter of godfathers.[1]

On September 2, the day after the findings of the grand jury were presented, Wesley appeared in court, and said, 'As to nine of the ten indictments against me, I know this court can take no cognisance of them, they being matters of an ecclesiastical nature. But that concerning my speaking and writing to Mrs. Williamson is of a secular nature; and this, therefore, I desire may be tried here, where the facts complained of were committed.' In the afternoon he moved the court again for an immediate trial at Savannah, but the request was not granted. From September 1 to the end of November he attended at least six sittings of the court, asking to be tried on the charge of corresponding with Mrs. Williamson, but all to no purpose. It was understood that Mr. and Mrs. Williamson were about to sail for England, and their contemplated absence was made a pretext for not proceeding with the trial.

During this long interval of waiting Wesley's adversaries were not idle. They sent a copy of Mrs. Williamson's affidavit and of the 'presentments' of the grand jury for insertion in the newspapers in different parts of America in order to prejudice the case. One copy arrived in Charlestown, and came into the hands of Mr. S. Garden, who is described by Henry Moore as 'a gentleman of considerable station and learning.' He wrote to Wesley, and put a question which seems to us inevitable. He asked, 'Has our Sovereign Lord the King given the temporal courts in Georgia ecclesiastical jurisdiction? If he has not, then sure I am that, whatever your failings in your office may be, a grand jury's presentments of them, being repugnant to the fundamental laws and constitution of England, is a plain " breach of his peace," and an open insult on " his crown and dignity "; for which they themselves ought to be presented.'[2]

On September 7 Wesley had an interview with Dison, the clergyman whom we have already mentioned. He was armed with the authority of the magistrates to perform ecclesiastical

---

[1] The report of the minority of the grand jury to the trustees should be consulted. In it several of these charges are shown to be without foundation. See Tyerman's *Life of Wesley*, i., 158; cf. *Journal*, i. 393–95.
[2] Henry Moore's *Life of Wesley*, i., 330.

offices at Savannah, and the next day he superseded Wesley and began his work. This invasion of his parish compelled Wesley to face the question of the advisability of his return to England to lay his case before the trustees. Mr. and Mrs. Williamson were said to be sailing by the next ship. Delamotte told him he ought to go, and other trusted counsellors gave him the same advice. But he stayed in Savannah, doing his utmost to hasten his trial before the court. For three months he had no cash in the house, and that fact probably delayed him. At last pecuniary relief came. Then, having informed the chief magistrate of his intention to visit England, and put up a notice in the public square, he prepared to depart. A show of resistance was made by the court of officials, but they were too glad to be rid of him to prevent his departure by physical force. On Friday, December 2, 1737, he left Georgia, after having acted as the minister of Savannah for a year and nearly nine months.

XII

THE GREAT CHANGE

On December 16, 1737, John Wesley said farewell to Delamotte in Charlestown. He had been his faithful companion during his stay in Georgia, and the parting caused Wesley much pain of heart. On December 22 he took his leave of America, hoping some day to see it again. He went on board the *Samuel*; and, two days later, sailed over the bar and put out to sea. His recent experiences had told on him, and for a time his usual cheerful courage failed. As the ship rolled over the waves apprehensions of danger which had oppressed him for several days increased, and he prayed earnestly for help. In a moment peace was restored to his soul. The experience of alternating alarm and peace recurred at a later date, when a hurricane broke on the ship. In the midst of it he had to acknowledge he was afraid to die, and that the secret of perfect peace was hidden from his eyes.

The voyage lasted through the whole of January, 1738. During its course Wesley gave himself up to religious work among the passengers and crew, private prayer, self-examination, reading, and reflection. He finished abridging the *Life* of M. de Renty, that ' burning and shining light ' of the Roman Catholic Church, and he devoted himself to studying the *Works* of Cyprian. In Cyprian's writings he found much that confirmed his own convictions concerning the antiquity and value of the episcopal method of Church government, and also a doctrine of the sacraments which, at several points, coincided with his own views. We think, however, that these questions were subordinate to others which arose during his reading of Cyprian. At the time he was face to face with the question of his own salvation. When a man's supreme passion is to be a Christian matters of mere ecclesiastical controversy become of subsidiary importance. In Cyprian Wesley saw one who could give him light on the problem that perplexed him. On January 9 there is the following interesting entry in his *Journal*: ' I reflected much on that vain desire, which had pursued me for so many years, of being in solitude in order to be a Christian. I have now, thought I, solitude enough. But am I therefore the nearer being a Christian? Not if Jesus Christ be the model of Christianity. I doubt, indeed, I am much nearer that mystery of Satan which some writers affect to call by that name. So near, that I had probably sunk wholly into it, had not the great mercy of God thrown me upon reading St. Cyprian's works. " O my soul, come not thou into their secret! " Stand thou in the good old paths.'[1]

It is unfortunate that Cyprian's name has become a war-cry in the battles of ecclesiastical partisans. He is now hailed as ' the father of modern High Churchmen,' and that term is supposed, by many, to describe him adequately. It leaves unexpressed his most admirable qualities. Archbishop Benson has brought out into distinctness a trait of character which differentiates Cyprian from those who are supposed to be his present representatives. He has revealed the spirit of charity which governed him in the administration of the Church, and which restrained him in days of keen and furious controversy. Dr. Benson declares that Cyprian ' never parted from the very heart of the Communion of Saints in Christendom,' and that the great truth which he enunciated, in word and conduct, was ' that Christian men must be able to differ in opinions without forfeiting or withholding from each other the right of intercommunion.'[2] Such views must have startled Wesley. They cast a glaring light on some of his recent actions. His late repentance was not vain. In after years he became one of the greatest exponents of Christian charity the world has seen.

A man possessing Wesley's temperament, when he is in quest of personal salvation, generally puts aside all other books save the Bible, and gives himself up to self-examination, reflection, and secret prayer. In the wilderness of waters he found an opportunity for thinking over his experiences in Georgia, and for ascertaining their effect on his character. He used his leisure for the highest purposes, constantly judging himself by the Word of God. The results of his self-examination were disappointing. In his *Journal* we can see the

[1] *Journal*, i., 416.   [2] Benson's *Cyprian*, 533.

processes he employed and the conclusions he reached. In after years he somewhat modified the verdicts he records against himself, but they certainly represent his convictions at the time he wrote them.

Keeping before him Jesus Christ as 'the model of Christianity,' Wesley measured himself by Him, and was humbled. He was convinced there was no hope of attaining the likeness of Christ until a radical change was effected in his own character. Summing up the results of his self-examination he says, ' It is now two years and almost four months since I left my native country in order to teach the Georgian Indians the nature of Christianity. But what have I learned myself in the meantime ? Why, what I least of all suspected, that I, who went to America to convert others, was never myself converted to God.' Subsequently he reviewed this judgement on his spiritual condition, and wrote in the margin of the corrected copy of his *Journal*, ' I am not sure of this.' If we had a clear definition of the word ' converted ' as used by Wesley in January, 1738, and an explanation of the sense in which he afterwards employed it, we could understand his original statement and its cautious amendment. It is certain, however, that when he made the first entry in his *Journal* he believed that he had not been ' converted to God.' That fact is placed beyond dispute by the words that follow his statement : ' I speak the words of truth and soberness, if haply some of those who still dream may awake and see that as I am, so are they.'[1]

Pursuing unflinchingly his self-examination, Wesley surveyed his whole life. He investigated the motives of his actions, and traced them to their source. He did not shrink from placing a due value on his self-denials and his sufferings in the service of God. With a frankness which reminds us somewhat of apostolic ' boasting ' he compares himself with those ' who still dream.' He cries, ' Are they read in philosophy ? So was I. In ancient or modern tongues ? So was I also. Are they versed in the science of divinity ? I, too, have studied it for many years. Can they talk fluently upon spiritual things ? The very same could I do. Are they plenteous in alms ? Behold, I gave all my goods to feed the poor. Do they give of their labour as well as of their substance ?

[1] *Journal*, i., 421-22.

THE GREAT CHANGE

I have laboured more abundantly than they all. Are they willing to suffer for their brethren? I have thrown up my friends, reputation, ease, country; I have put my life in my hand, wandering into strange lands; I have given my body to be devoured by the deep, parched up with heat, consumed by toil and weariness, or whatsoever God should please to bring upon me.' Every item in this statement is literally true; but while doing justice to himself there was a thought that 'tore his anxious breast,' and caused him to look with despair on his 'good works.' He proceeds, ' But does all this—be it more or less, it matters not—make me acceptable to God? Does all I ever did or can know, say, give, do, or suffer justify me in His sight? Yea, or the constant use of all the means of grace? (which, nevertheless, is meet, right, and our bounden duty). Or that I know nothing of myself; that I am, as touching outward, moral righteousness, blameless? Or (to come closer yet) the having a rational conviction of all the truths of Christianity? Does all this give me a claim to the holy, heavenly, divine character of a Christian? By no means. If the oracles of God are true, if we are still to abide by " the law and the testimony," all these things, though when ennobled by faith in Christ, they are holy and just and good, yet without it are " dung and dross," meet only to be purged away by " the fire that never shall be quenched." '[1]

The desperate earnestness of Wesley's inquisition is shown in these words. In a calmer mood he afterwards reviewed them, but left them to stand, save that he guarded himself and his readers against the supposition that, at the time when he drew up this indictment, he had no ' faith in Christ.' He says, ' I had even then the faith of a *servant*, though not that of a *son*.' He also withdrew another accusation he made in the passion of his sorrow. Further reflection led him to believe that he was mistaken when he described himself, at that time, as a ' child of wrath.' These revisions are of great importance. But, having made allowance for them, his words accurately describe the result of his self-examination.

Driven from his sources of confidence, and having nothing in or of himself, Wesley confesses that he had no hope but that of being justified freely ' through the redemption that is in Jesus '; no hope but that if he sought he should find Christ, and

[1] *Journal*, i., 422-23.

be found in Him not having his own righteousness, 'but that which is through the faith of Christ, the righteousness which is of God by faith.' As he journeyed on his way the nature of that faith was revealed to him. 'The faith I want,' he says, 'is a "sure trust and confidence in God, that, through the merits of Christ, my sins are forgiven, and I reconciled to the favour of God." I want that faith which St. Paul recommends to all the world, especially in his Epistle to the Romans; that faith which enables every one that hath it to cry out, "I live not; but Christ liveth in me; and the life which I now live, I live by faith in the Son of God, who loved me, and gave Himself for me." I want that faith which none can have without knowing that he hath it (though many imagine that they have it, who have it not); for whosoever hath it is "freed from sin," the whole "body of sin is destroyed" in him; he is freed from fear, "having peace with God through Christ, and rejoicing in hope of the glory of God." And he is freed from doubt, "having the love of God shed abroad in his heart, through the Holy Ghost, which is given unto him"; which "Spirit itself beareth witness with his spirit, that he is a child of God."[1] Who can doubt that, on board the *Samuel*, Wesley's face was turned in the right direction?

On Wednesday, February 1, 1738, John Wesley landed at Deal. To his surprise he found that George Whitefield was on board the *Whitaker* bound for America, and that his ship was sailing that morning. Whitefield had yielded to the appeal of Wesley and other members of the Holy Club, and was going out to Georgia. Wesley sent him a note advising him to abandon his purpose. Whitefield replied by a messenger, but Wesley had started on his journey to London. From the Downs he wrote a letter giving his reasons for persisting in his purpose. One was exceptionally strong. He says, 'Your coming rather confirms (as far as I can see) than disannuls my call. It is not fit the colony should be left without a shepherd. And though they are a stiff-necked and rebellious people, yet as God hath given me the affections of all where I have been, why should I despair of finding His presence in a foreign land?'[2]

Whitefield went out to Georgia, his first visit to the colony lasting for about four months. During that time he won the affections of the people. In many respects he was more

[1] *Journal*, i., 424. [2] Tyerman's *Life of Whitefield*, i., 115.

adapted than Wesley for achieving success in the Mission. He was not embarrassed with his predecessor's convictions concerning the trade in slaves. In that matter he held the opinions common to most Englishmen in the eighteenth century. In addition, he entered into the grievances of the colonists and became their advocate against the government of the trustees. He softened the rigour of canons and rubrics in ecclesiastical affairs. To the consolation of many mothers he sprinkled instead of immersing their babies. He won the love of the people by his good nature and overflowing sympathy. They felt that Wesley's rigorous rule was over; they crowded around him, and came under the spell of his preaching. While relaxing the severities of Wesley's rule, he followed out Wesley's plan as to services, the Society, open-air preaching, schools, catechizing the children, and the visitation of his parishioners. He was much impressed by the value of Wesley's work, and did much to conserve it. His testimony is well known. He says, ' The good which Mr. John Wesley has done in America, under God, is inexpressible. His name is very precious among the people; and he has laid a foundation that I hope neither men nor devils will ever be able to shake.'[1]

On Friday, February 3, 1738, John Wesley came once more to London. His arrival was unexpected, and caused his brother Charles and General Oglethorpe much surprise. His stay lasted about a fortnight. During his visit he resided with his old friends, Mr. and Mrs. Hutton, in Great College Street, Westminster. He found that a change had come over their family circle. Their son, James Hutton, who had been so impressed by Wesley's demeanour, conversation, and preaching during his former visit to the house, had entered into business as a bookseller, and resided at his shop, ' The Bible and Sun,' in Little Wild Street, west of Temple Bar, and not far from Drury Lane. He had become active in the founding of Religious Societies of a more definitely spiritual type than some of those then existing in London. One was in Islington, and another was in the City, in Nettleton Court, off Aldersgate Street.

During the fortnight's delay in London, Wesley had several interviews with the trustees for Georgia. He frankly described to them the condition of the colony, and banished their dreams

[1] Tyerman's *Life of Whitefield*, i., 135-36.

of its prosperous condition. He found that a copy of the charges brought against him in Savannah had been forwarded to the trustees. They strongly condemned the conduct of the Savannah officials in bringing such charges publicly before they had been first submitted to them, but they evidently felt that there were matters which required explanation. During subsequent visits to London he interviewed the Board, being always ready to vindicate himself against the findings of the grand jury and to explain his conduct in the colony. But the affair dragged on its weary length. On Wednesday, April 26, he gave up his position as the minister of Savannah, surrendering the instrument of his appointment, being convinced that he had 'no more place in those parts.' Charles Wesley, who was still acting as Oglethorpe's secretary, and was intending to return to Georgia, acting under medical advice, abandoned his intention.

On Sunday, February 5, 1738, John Wesley preached in the Church of St. John the Evangelist, Millbank, Westminster, and the next Sunday in St. Andrew's, Holborn. After the former service he was told that many of the best in the parish were so offended that he was not to preach there any more, and at St. Andrew's the same notice was given him. The reason for his exclusion from these churches may be easily guessed. We presume that those who invited him to preach expected to hear interesting descriptions of adventures in the American backwoods. But when the bronzed traveller stood in the pulpit, he spoke of the things burdening his heart. He enforced the necessity of the new birth, and proclaimed the supremacy of Christian charity. It was not to listen to such teaching that the Londoners had gone out to hear him. His doctrine was strange and savoured of 'enthusiasm.' It was the doctrine of the articles and homilies of the Church of England, but it may be safely said that few members of either congregation were aware of the fact. The disappointed officials of these churches had their remedy, and they applied it—they closed the pulpits against the intrusion of such a preacher.

The sound of the voices of those dispersing congregations has long since died on the air, but the questions discussed on the way home are with us still, and claim our attention. They concerned the way of salvation. We have seen that Wesley himself had only begun to doubt the correctness of the almost universal belief that righteousness came by the works of the law. He had been blind to the meaning of the teaching of St. Paul, but sight was coming to him by successive touches of the divine hand. On the voyage home he had arrived at certain conclusions that revolutionized his theological position; and, to his surprise, he found that those conclusions were in harmony with the teachings of the men who laid the strong doctrinal foundations of the Church of England at the time of the Reformation. We have read his self-condemnatory words concerning his efforts to attain righteousness by good works, and we have been relieved by the modification of some of the terms he employed, but who can fail to perceive that the verdict he pronounced against himself is justified by the closing sentence of Article XIII., entitled ' Of works before justification.' The article declares concerning such works, ' For that they are not done as God hath commanded and willed them to be done, we doubt not but that they have the nature of sin.' We are not concerned, at the moment, with the correctness of the decision. We emphasize the fact that it is the doctrine of the articles.

There was another doctrine concerning salvation from which the mists were rising at the time when Wesley preached in London. He was intensely interested in the question which concerned ' The Justification of Man.' Turning to Article XI. he read : ' We are accounted righteous before God, only for the merit of our Lord and Saviour Jesus Christ, by faith, and not for our own works or deservings. Wherefore that we are justified by faith only is a most wholesome doctrine, and very full of comfort, as is more largely expressed in the Homily of Justification.' When Wesley, on board the *Samuel*, abandoned his hope that he could be justified by the works of the law, and that justification must come ' by faith only,' he found his way back to the doctrine of Article XI. Instead of ignoring its concluding words, he read the homily, and everyone who has followed his example knows how unhesitatingly it declares that righteousness comes to us by faith. Wesley in his *Journal* record on board the *Samuel*, quotes the definition of justifying faith from the homily, and admits that he has not attained to it. His preaching, which aroused so much resentment, was in accordance with the article and the homily. The ignorance of his hearers prevented them from recognizing an obvious fact.[1]

Wesley was advancing in the right direction. He accepted the declaration that we are justified by faith only; but many difficulties had to be overcome before the intellectual conviction was supplemented by 'the sure trust and confidence in God' of which the homily speaks. He was fighting the battle alone; then on Tuesday, February 7, a day ever to be remembered, a comrade joined him. He called at the house of Mr. Weinantz, a Dutch merchant, and found there a party of four Germans recently arrived in England. One of them was Peter Böhler, the man with whom Spangenberg once had a searching conversation at Jena. He was brought up a Lutheran, but at the University he came under the influence of Pietists. Following Spangenberg's advice, he was led into the joyful experience of salvation through faith in Christ Jesus. Subsequently he joined the Church of the Moravian Brethren, and, when Wesley met him, he was on his way to America as a missionary to Georgia and the negroes of Carolina. Wesley, finding that Böhler and his friends had no acquaintance in England, offered to procure them a lodging, and found rooms for them near Mr. Hutton's house. He lost no opportunity of conversing with them, his more important conversations with Böhler being in Latin.

On Friday, February 17, Wesley left London and set out for Oxford, the pleasant city of his dreams. He was accompanied by Charles Wesley and Böhler. The latter, writing to Zinzendorf, says: 'I travelled with the two brothers from London to Oxford. The elder, John, is a good-natured man he knew that he did not properly believe in the Saviour, and was willing to be taught. His brother . . . is at present very much distressed in his mind, but does not know how he shall begin to be acquainted with the Saviour.'[2] John Wesley's visit to Oxford was brief. He found that nearly all his old friends had left the University, and that the bright visions he had seen in far-off lands were part of the dreams of life But he preached at the castle to a numerous and serious congregation; and, above all, the absence of his old friends gave him opportunities for close and frequent conversations with Böhler. He was willing to be taught. He felt that his

[1] *Homilies*, 31, S.P.C.K. ed.   [2] *Journal*, i., 439 n.

THE GREAT CHANGE

new friend held a theory of salvation which compelled attention, and so he argued with him, and tried to see with the eyes of the mind the truth that is revealed to the spirit of those who are meek and lowly in heart. Böhler listened to him, watching him quietly. Then he said, ' My brother, my brother, that philosophy of yours must be purged away.' Wesley admits that the statement passed his understanding, but its meaning afterwards became plain to him. His father had noticed that, from his childhood, he would never do anything until he had a reason for doing it. This mental characteristic persisted until it dominated him. When he was confronted with the problem of justification by faith only, he admitted that it was a doctrine of the Church, but even that was not sufficient. He treated it as a problem that must be explained and proved. He could not accept any solution of it that was not commended by his reason. He was yet to learn that when a man kneels at the cross, and pleads for pardon, his prayer is not that of a satisfied philosopher; it is the cry of one who has exhausted his expedients, lost his self-confidence, and can only say, ' God be merciful to me, a sinner.'

Returning to London on February 20, the next day Wesley preached in the Church of Great St. Helen's, which stands in a neighbourhood closely connected with the domestic life and the ministry of Dr. Annesley. The following Sunday he preached at six o'clock in the morning at St. Lawrence's, at ten o'clock at St. Katherine Cree's, and in the afternoon at St. John's, Wapping. All his sermons seem to have offended his congregations. To sum up the question of the exclusion of Wesley from the churches of London, after his return from Georgia, we may say his *Journal* shows that such exclusion was almost invariably the result of his preaching. On May 7 he was excluded from St. Lawrence's and St. Katherine Cree's, and two days afterwards from Great St. Helen's. On May 14 St. Ann's, Aldersgate Street, on May 21 St. John's, Wapping and St. Benet's, Paul's Wharf, and on the following Thursday St. Antholin's were closed against him. On May 28 a similar fate befell him at St. George's, Bloomsbury, and the chapel in Long Acre. In one month, therefore, in nine churches he was informed that his services would not be again required, and it became clear to him that his opportunities of preaching in London were coming to an end.

On Monday, February 22, Wesley travelled by coach to Salisbury, and saw his mother there. After visiting her he was about to set out for Tiverton, to stay with his brother Samuel, the head master of Blundell's School, but alarming news reached him concerning the sickness of Charles Wesley, and he returned to Oxford. He found Böhler there, who had been with the invalid during his sudden sickness and had remained with him in his convalescence. Charles Wesley began to teach him English. The two men were brought into closer association with each other, and their acquaintance ripened into friendship.

John Wesley, during his brief absence from Oxford, had thought over Böhler's words concerning faith, and their meaning was gradually being revealed to him. The interrupted conversations were resumed, and on Sunday, March 5, we find this significant entry in his *Journal*: 'I was clearly convinced of unbelief, of the want of that faith whereby alone we are saved.' In after years he added to this sentence the words ' with the full Christian salvation.' The conviction brought with it the temptation to give up preaching, but Böhler gave him the wise counsel, ' Preach faith *till* you have it ; and then, *because* you have it, you will preach faith.' The snare was broken. He went to the castle, saw a prisoner who was under sentence of death, and made him an offer of 'salvation by faith alone.' The good news was strange to the man, but he did not reject the offer. Some days later Wesley and Mr. Kinchin visited him. He was in great heaviness and confusion, having no rest by reason of his sins. His visitors prayed with him, first using several forms of prayer ; then, under the influence of their vehement desire for his salvation, they broke out ' in such words as were given them in that hour.' The condemned prisoner, after a space, rose up and eagerly said, ' I am now ready to die. I know Christ has taken away my sins, and there is no more condemnation for me.' Wesley says, ' The same composed cheerfulness he showed when carried to execution ; and, in his last moments, he was the same, enjoying perfect peace, in confidence that he was " accepted in the Beloved." ' Wesley learned by teaching. The explanations and assertions of Böhler were illuminated. He had for months striven to attain to such a faith in Christ as would deliver him from the fear of death, and he looked into the peaceful face of the condemned man and was convinced that the prisoner had discovered the secret still veiled from his own eyes. Much moved, he brooded over the scene. On the Saturday following the execution he went to a Religious Society held in the house of Mr. Fox, and says, ' My heart was so full that I could not confine myself to the forms of prayer which we were accustomed to use there. Neither do I purpose to be confined to them any more, but to pray indifferently, with a form or without, as I may find suitable to particular occasions.'

The experiences of Wesley at this point are intensely interesting. Light was breaking in upon him. He was essentially a practical man, more deeply impressed by facts than theories. Against theories he could pertinaciously argue; but he had seen the dungeon flaming with light, he had witnessed the liberation of the condemned man from his chains, and the coming of a great peace into the heart of a prisoner standing on the brink of eternity. In the presence of that experience he refrained from many words. ' I see the promise ; but it is afar off.' Believing that it would be better to wait for the accomplishment of that promise in silence and retirement, he left Oxford, and, complying with Mr. Kinchin's desire, went to stay at Dummer, in Hampshire. But his retreat soon came to an end. He was earnestly pressed to come up to London ; and, therefore, he returned there on April 18. Charles Wesley joined him ; and on Saturday, April 22, the two brothers met Peter Böhler, and had ' a right searching conversation with him.' John Wesley, describing this interview, says, ' I had now no objection to what he said of the nature of faith ; namely, that it is (to use the words of our Church) " a sure trust and confidence which a man hath in God, that through the merits of Christ his sins are forgiven and he reconciled to the favour of God." Neither could I deny either the happiness or holiness which he described as fruits of this living faith. " The Spirit itself beareth witness with our spirit that we are the children of God," and " He that believeth hath the witness in himself " fully convinced me of the former ; as " Whatsoever is born of God doth not commit sin," and " Whosoever believeth is born of God " did of the latter. But I could not comprehend what he spoke of an *instantaneous work*. I could not understand how this faith should be given in a moment : how a man could *at once* be thus turned from darkness to light, from sin and misery to righteousness and joy in the Holy Ghost. I searched the Scriptures again touching this very thing, particularly the Acts of the Apostles ; but, to my utter astonishment, found scarce any instances there of other than *instantaneous* conversions ; scarce any so slow as that of St. Paul, who was three days in the pangs of the new birth. I had but one retreat left ; namely, " *Thus*, I grant, God wrought in the *first* ages of Christianity ; but the times are changed. What reason have I to believe He works in the same manner now ? " '

On Sunday, April 23, Wesley was beaten out of his last retreat. Böhler came to him with four of his English brethren. They told, one after another, what had been wrought in them. They testified that God had given them in a moment such a faith in the blood of His Son as translated them out of darkness into light, out of sin and fear into holiness and happiness. Böhler says, ' Wesley and those that were with him were as if thunderstruck at these narratives. I asked John Wesley what he then believed. He said four examples were not enough. I replied I would bring eight more here in London.' A silence fell on the company. John Wesley was thinking of a hymn he had translated from the German, and was feeling that his experience could only be expressed by it. He stood up and asked that ' My soul before Thee prostrate lies ' might be sung. During the singing of the Moravian version tears fell from his eyes. His disputings were over ; all that he could say was, ' Lord, help Thou my unbelief ! ' Afterwards, in a private conversation, he told Böhler that he was satisfied as to what had been said of faith, and he would question no more. Again he asked for advice as to teaching others, and Böhler said to him, ' Do not hide in the earth the talent God hath given to you.' Acting on this advice, he spoke to Mr. Delamotte's family at Blendon on the nature and fruits of faith. Charles Wesley and Thomas Broughton were there. The latter held views that must have been strange among Protestant Churchmen. He strenuously denied that sinners were justified by faith. On one occasion when *The Book of Homilies* was mentioned, he confessed it was a work he had never read. As he subsequently became Secretary of the Society for the Promotion of Christian Knowledge we presume that he formed an acquaintance with this standard of his own Church. Charles Wesley and Broughton were much scandalized at the views which John Wesley expressed in Mr. Delamotte's house, and a sharp dispute arose on the question whether conversion was gradual or instantaneous. John Wesley held the latter view, but stood alone. The next day John Wesley and Broughton returned to London, and Charles Wesley, seeking to edify the Delamotte household, read them the *Life of Mr. Haliburton.* He must have chosen the book without being intimately acquainted with its contents. He had to admit that Haliburton's conversion was instantaneous; but soothed himself with the reflection that it was only one instance of such a change.

On Wednesday, April 26, Wesley set out once more for Oxford. Peter Böhler walked with him a few miles, and exhorted him not to stop short of the grace of God. Reaching Oxford, he was much confirmed in his convictions concerning the faith which brings salvation. He had a close conversation with Mr. John Hutchings, of Pembroke College, a young man who had recently taken his degree, and who had written a letter of welcome to Wesley on his return from Georgia.[1] He also talked with Mrs. Fox, who took a prominent part in the work of the Religious Society meeting in her house. They were both living ' witnesses that God can (at least, if He does not always) give that faith whereof cometh salvation in a moment, as lightning falling from heaven.'

May 1 was a day of exceptional importance in the history of John Wesley. He had hastened to London to see his brother Charles, who was again ill. He was at James Hutton's, and Wesley found him there, better in health than he expected, but strongly averse from what he called ' the new faith.' In the evening of that day a Religious Society was formed at ' The Bible and Sun,' which, after a time, met in Fetter Lane. It will be convenient to postpone further reference to this event. It is necessary, however, to note a fact which had a decisive influence on the relations which existed between John Wesley and the group of High Churchmen living in Manchester. On May 1 Clayton, his old friend, whose influence had done

---

[1] See *W.H.S. Proceedings*, v., 151. The letter was in the collection of the late Mr. George Stampe.

[2] *Journal*, i., 457.

much to mould his ecclesiastical views, wrote him a letter, which has been preserved.¹ In this letter he says:

> I would have writ you before, had I known where a letter might have found you, to express the great uneasiness that myself as well as all your Lancashire friends, labour under on your account. Indeed, we are greatly afraid of you, and doubt that you are running yourself into difficulties beyond your strength to bear. We all see and rejoice at your sincerity and zeal, and pray fervently for your perseverance therein. But we think ourselves likewise obliged to beseech Almighty God to give you a right judgement in all things, that so your zeal may be tempered by prudence, and you may have the light of the gospel as well as the heat. What I feared would be the case is actually come to pass ; few or none were edified by Mr. Wesley's preaching, because they were offended with his manner. And your using no notes, and so very much action, has with the generality established your reputation for self-sufficiency and ostentation. It is to me most piteous, it is a matter of grief, because they fear that such prodigious singularities set you upon such an eminence as makes such behaviour necessary as the spirit of an apostle alone can produce. And who is sufficient for these things? I remember, in the holy *Life of Bernard Gilpin*, preaching extempore is called tempting God ; at least it is certainly a tempting of the world to censoriousness, and yourself to think more highly of yourself than you ought to think. Dr. Byrom says of you that if he were in your place he would constantly preach by book. He would have you cut off your hair, which he thinks contributes much to the distinguishing appearance you make, and to curb your action and vehement emphasis, that so there might not be so remarkable a singularity in your person and behaviour ; and all this he thinks a sacrifice you ought to make of self-will for the sake of your brethren's weakness. And that you would gain more progress in the spiritual life by such a submission upon principle than you can possibly do by any outward thing.

> We feared much that you was the author of the Oxford Methodists prefixed to Mr. Whitfield's (*sic*) sermons, but Mr. Kinchin has relieved us. It is the opinion of Dr. Deacon, Dr. Byrom, and his brother Josiah, as well as myself, that you had better forbear publishing, at least for a time, till your difficulties are blown over. Because it does not appear that you are necessarily called to it, and therefore the doing it would be like running into temptations which you have power to avoid. Dr. Byrom has the same fears about the poems as the Methodists, and doubts you are too sanguine and hasty about them. O my brother ! that you had a director ; one to whom you might submit the conduct of your soul. For I cannot but think, however mean his attainments were, provided he had more age and experience than yourself you would find your spiritual account in abiding by his counsels. Did it serve no other end, it would save you from the danger of self-will, which is not

---
¹ The letter was in Mr. G. Stampe's collection.

to be avoided while you are your own director. And I believe there is nothing where self-will proves stronger, and is attended with more consequences, than where it is engaged upon spiritual matters. God Almighty direct you for the best, and raise up a proper instrument for the promoting of His glory and your welfare.

I still must request you to send me a copy of all your statutes relating to the constitution and power of your visitor and the obedience you are bound to pay him. But this not on your own account; but for the sake of the Fellows of our Collegiate Church, to whom it may possibly prove of the greatest service.

John Wesley was a placable man, and was accustomed to the plain speaking of the members of the Holy Club. We do not think that Clayton's letter would excite his resentment, but it probably exerted a strong unconscious influence. After its reception we watch the spreading of the rift between the two men; it widened until they stood far apart. To Wesley's regret they became strangers. We do not share that regret. If Wesley had placed himself under the control of the Manchester High Churchmen the Methodist Revival would have been impossible.

We must now fix our eyes for a few moments on Charles Wesley. At the beginning of May he was in London, slowly recovering from sickness. The new views of saving faith held by his brother were most repugnant to him; he attacked and denounced them. On May 3, the day before Peter Böhler left London to embark for Carolina, he and Charles Wesley met at James Hutton's and had a quiet talk. The result was that misconceptions were corrected and prejudice gradually disappeared. Charles Wesley's eyes were opened, so that he saw clearly what was the nature of that one true living faith whereby alone ' through grace we are saved.' He confessed to Böhler his unbelief and want of forgiveness, but declared his firm persuasion that he should receive the atonement before he died. The interview was of critical importance. It led to the kindling of a spark of desire for salvation in Charles Wesley's heart. The spark was quickened into a flame. On May 11 he had intended to leave James Hutton's house and remove to his father's in Westminster; but, on that day, Mr. John Bray, who was a brazier living in Little Britain, visited him. He was known to Böhler and the Wesleys. Charles Wesley describes him as ' a poor ignorant mechanic, who knows nothing but Christ; yet by knowing Him, knows and discerns all things.' He saw in him a man who had realized conscious salvation, and who could, in a special sense, supply Peter Böhler's place. They prayed together, and Charles Wesley was quite overpowered and melted into tears. He knew that he had met the man he needed; and so, instead of going to Westminster, he was carried in a chair to Bray's house in Little Britain. In that house he pursued his quest, waiting patiently for the Lord in prayer and reading. His brother came to see him, and found the spirit of the evangelist strong in him. John Wesley was 'exceeding heavy,' but, says Charles, 'I forced him, as he had often forced me, to sing a hymn to Christ, and almost thought He would come while we were singing.' He was assured that Christ would come quickly.[1]

The story of Charles Wesley's experiences, as recorded in his *Journal*, is of surpassing interest; but we must concentrate our attention on two vital facts. On May 17 he was visited by Mr. Holland, who had accidentally alighted on a copy of Luther on the Galatians. They began to read it together. They not only found Luther 'nobly full of faith,' but Charles Wesley discovered to his astonishment that his doctrine was that of the Church of England. He says: 'I marvelled that we were so soon and so entirely removed from him that called us into the grace of Christ, unto another gospel. Who would believe our Church had been founded on this important article of justification by faith alone? I am astonished I should ever think this a new doctrine, especially while our articles and homilies stand unrepealed, and the key of knowledge is not yet taken away. From this time I endeavoured to ground as many of our friends as came in this fundamental truth, salvation by faith alone; not an idle, dead faith, but a faith which works by love, and is necessarily productive of all good works and all holiness.'[2] In the evening he spent some hours in private with Martin Luther. The conclusion of the exposition of the second chapter was greatly blessed to him. He must have read the comments on 'Who loved me and gave Himself for me' with intense interest, studying them as for his life. Luther says:

> Wherefore these words: *Which loved me*, are full of faith. And he that can utter this word *me*, and apply it unto himself with a true and a constant faith, as Paul did, shall be a good disputant with Paul

[1] Charles Wesley's *Journal*, i., 87.   [2] *Ibid*,, i., 88.

THE GREAT CHANGE

against the law. And this manner of applying is the very true force and power of faith. . . . Read, therefore, with great vehemencie these words, *me*, and *for me*, and so inwardly practise with thy selfe, that thou, with a sure faith, maist conceive and print this *me* in thy heart, and apply it unto thyselfe, not doubting but thou art in the number of those to whom this *me* belongeth.[1]

From the time of reading this comment Charles Wesley ' laboured, waited, and prayed ' to feel the truth of the words, ' Who loved *me* and gave Himself for *me*.' He left the pathless wilderness, and walked on the highway leading to the ' sabbath rest ' that remains for the people of God.

On Whit-Sunday, May 21, at nine o'clock, John Wesley and some of his friends came to see Charles Wesley, who had waked in hope and expectation of the coming of Christ. They sang a hymn to the Holy Ghost, by which his comfort and hope were increased. Then they left him. During that day, step by step, he approached the cross. We can imagine how he repeated to himself with increasing emphasis the sentence that had been illuminated by Luther. Gradually the light shone into his mind. He turned to his Bible, and Isaiah's words greeted him : ' Comfort ye, comfort ye, my people, saith your God ; speak ye comfortably to Jerusalem, and cry unto her, that her warfare is accomplished, that her iniquity is pardoned ; for she hath received of the Lord's hand double for all her sins.' Seeing plainly the possibility of a pardon which comforts the man who receives it, by a quiet act of faith he accepted the free gift, and found himself at peace with God ' and rejoiced in hope of loving Christ.' That hope was realized. On Tuesday, May 23, he says, ' I waked under the protection of Christ, and gave myself up, soul and body, to Him.' At nine o'clock, filled with deep emotion, he sat down and commenced to write a hymn on his ' conversion,' but was persuaded ' to break off, for fear of pride.' Mr. Bray came in and encouraged him to proceed. Praying to Christ to stand by him, he finished the hymn. No one can read it, knowing the circumstances under which it was composed, without a glow of heart. It commences ' Where shall my wondering soul begin ? '[2] It is wistful, chastened with humility, confident in its conviction of sins forgiven, radiant with the light of a passionate love for

---
[1] See art. by Rev. T. F. Lockyer, on ' Luther and Wesley,' *W.H.S. Proceedings*, viii., 61–66.
[2] No. 358 in *The Methodist Hymn-Book*.

the 'Great Deliverer,' bold in its outlook on the hosts drawn up in battle-array against 'the Sinner's Friend,' tender in its appeals to the outcast sons of men, triumphant in its closing cry, ' Believe, and all your sin 's forgiven ; only believe, and yours is heaven ! ' Mr. Telford truly describes this hymn as the birth-song of the Evangelical Revival. So far as we know, it stands first in order of time among the hymns with which Charles Wesley enriched the psalmody of the Christian Church.

John Wesley must have watched with much sympathy and some sorrow the spiritual progress of his brother. He saw him going into the Kingdom before him, reading the ' open secret ' that was still a mystery to him. But celestial light was travelling towards him. On May 24, in great heaviness of heart, he went to St. Paul's. He was, as we know, exceptionally sensitive to the beauty and quietness of cathedral worship, and to the power of music. He listened to the great words ' He pardoneth and absolveth all them that truly repent and unfeignedly believe His holy gospel ' ; he stood up and declared that he believed in the forgiveness of sins ; he knelt and heard a voice crying, ' O God, make clean our hearts within us,' and he replied, ' And take not Thy Holy Spirit from us.' Did these familiar sentences begin to vibrate with a new meaning ? We may be sure that to him St. Paul's was not ' a fane of useless prayer.' Much is left to our imagination, but we know that it was during the singing of the anthem that a great impression was made on him. ' Out of the deep have I called unto Thee, O Lord ; Lord hear my voice.' Then there came the triumphant close, ' O Israel, trust in the Lord ; for with the Lord there is mercy, and with Him is plenteous redemption. And He shall deliver Israel from all his sins.' With this music in his heart he left the cathedral, and the busy life of London once more surged around him. He had looked into the deep of his own misery and to the height of God's mercy, and subdued in spirit, he wandered towards home.

In the evening John Wesley went, very unwillingly, to the meeting of a Religious Society in Nettleton Court, Aldersgate Street.[1] He sat among the people. What happened there is best stated in his own words. He says :

> One was reading Luther's preface to the Epistle to the Romans. About a quarter before nine, while he was describing the change which

[1] See art. by Rev. H. J. Foster in *W.H.S. Proceedings*, iii., 246-48.

God works in the heart through faith in Christ, I felt my heart strangely warmed. I felt I did trust in Christ, Christ alone, for salvation; and an assurance was given me that He had taken away *my* sins, even *mine*, and saved *me* from the law of sin and death. I began to pray with all my might for those who had in a more especial manner despitefully used me and persecuted me. I then testified openly to all there what I now first felt in my heart. But it was not long before the enemy suggested, ' This cannot be faith; for where is thy joy ? ' Then was I taught that peace and victory over sin are essential to faith in the Captain of our salvation; but that, as to the transports of joy that usually attend the beginning of it, especially in those who have mourned deeply, God sometimes giveth, sometimes withholdeth them, according to the counsels of His own will.[1]

These words, marked by a noble simplicity, can be fully understood only by those who have passed through his experience. Leaving Nettleton Court, accompanied by a troop of friends, he went to Mr. Bray's to see his brother. Arriving there towards ten o'clock he quietly said to Charles, ' I believe.' The words thrilled the hearts of those who heard them. The new hymn was sung, then there was prayer, and the great day came to a close. Through the fading light John Wesley walked to Westminster, little thinking that the dawn of a great religious reformation was touching the skies.

[1] *Journal*, i., 475-76.

XIII

A NEW RELIGIOUS SOCIETY

In 1738 the number of Religious Societies of the old model was considerable. In London it was still their custom to assemble, once a quarter, in the Church of St. Mary-le-Bow, Cheapside, to hear a sermon from some clergyman friendly to the movement. On Wednesday, September 27, John Wesley was present at such a service, reading prayers, and listening uneasily to an unsatisfactory discourse. It has been suggested that the preacher was a Mr. Harris, who presided over one of the Societies. In the previous month Charles Wesley had been ' dragged out ' by Bray to a meeting of this Society, and after much disputing with those who were present, he ' confuted rather than convinced ' them by reading the homily on justification. If the identification of the clergyman who preached in Bow Church is correct, we can surmise the cause of John Wesley's dissatisfaction with his teaching.

The condition of the Religious Societies at that time in London may be judged by the testimony of those who were acquainted with them, it being always remembered that such testimony may be coloured by the convictions and prejudices of the observer. It is impossible to doubt that into the ' old Societies ' certain evils had crept which were weakening their strength as religious organizations. In Whitefield's *Letter* to the Religious Societies lately set on foot in several parts of England and Wales, he counsels them to be very cautious in the admission of new members. He says that such persons should be examined again and again, ' not barely whether they receive the Sacrament, and go to church, but whether they be in the faith.' He continues, ' Set them upon proving their own selves ; and by no means receive them into your brotherhood unless they can produce sufficient evidences of their having tasted the good word of life, and felt the powers of the world to come. Some may object that this is not a very good

A NEW RELIGIOUS SOCIETY

way to increase and multiply you as to number; but it is the best, the only way, to establish and increase a communion of true saints.' He declares that the only end of their assembling is the renewing of their depraved natures and the promoting of the hidden life of Jesus Christ in their souls. He exhorts them to contend earnestly for the doctrine of justification by faith only, warning them against the advice to the clergy given by a bishop, reputed to be one of the most orthodox prelates in the kingdom: ' So explain the doctrine of justification in the sight of God by faith only as to make good works a necessary condition.' Looking upon the Societies as a means of Christian fellowship, he counsels them as follows:

> Content not yourselves with reading, singing, and praying together; but set some time apart to confess your faults, and to communicate your experience one to another. For want of this, which I take to be one chief design of private meetings, most of the old Societies in London, I fear, are sunk into a dead formality, and have only a name to live. They meet on a Sabbath evening, read a chapter, and sing a psalm, but seldom, if ever, acquaint each other with the operations of God's Spirit upon their souls; notwithstanding this was the great end of those who first began these Societies. Hence it is that they have only the form of godliness left amongst them, and continue utter strangers to the state of one another's hearts. My brethren, let not your coming together be thus altogether in vain, but plainly and freely tell one another what God has done for your souls. To this end you would do well, as others have done, to form yourselves into little companies of four or five each, and meet once a week to tell each other what is in your hearts; that you may then also pray for, and comfort, each other as need shall require. None but those who have experienced it can tell the unspeakable advantages of such a union and communion of souls. I know not a better means in the world to keep hypocrisy out from amongst you. Pharisees and unbelievers will pray, read, and sing psalms; but none, save an Israelite indeed, will endure to have his heart searched out.[1]

From Whitefield's letter, and especially from its closing paragraph, we gain our needed insight into the condition of the old Religious Societies in London. It was written in 1739, after the new Societies had been set on foot, and we must now turn towards those Societies in order that we may see the points of difference between them and those they were destined to supplant.

James Hutton was thoroughly dissatisfied with the condition

[1] Tyerman's *Life of Whitefield*, i., 317-19.

and work of the old Societies, and formed others on a better basis. The Society that prospered most met in his house in Little Wild Street. It was in existence when John Wesley returned from Georgia. The coming of Wesley and Böhler caused a definite change to take place in its constitution. That change was effected at a meeting held at Hutton's house on May 1, 1738, when 'a little Society' was founded. Among those present were John and Charles Wesley, Henry Piers (the vicar of Bexley), and James Hutton. The advice of Peter Böhler had been asked, and his counsels influenced the minds of those who proceeded to draw up the ' Orders ' by which the new Society was to be governed. Those ' Orders ' were not settled at one sitting. Some were accepted at the first meeting, others on May 29, and the remainder on September 25.[1] The new Society grew swiftly, and it was necessary to secure another place of assembly. There was in Fetter Lane an old Nonconformist meeting-house, which had been occupied by a succession of ministers. In 1732 the Independent congregation worshipping in it removed to a new chapel, erected for Mr. Rawlin, on the opposite side of the way, and afterwards the old building, with its house adjoining, numbered 32 Fetter Lane, was taken as the meeting-place of the new Religious Society.[2] The constitution and character of that Society can be best judged from a consideration of its ' Orders.'

ORDERS OF A RELIGIOUS SOCIETY MEETING IN FETTER LANE.

In Obedience to the Command of God by St. James, and by the Advice of Peter Boehler, May 1, 1738, it was agreed,

1. THAT they will meet together once in a Week to confess their Faults one to another, and to pray for one another that they may be healed.

2. That any others, of whose Sincerity they are well assured, may, if they desire it, meet with them for that Purpose. And, May 29, it was agreed,

3. That the Persons desirous to meet together for that Purpose, be divided into several Bands, or little Societies.

4. That none of these consist of fewer than five, or more than ten Persons.

5. That some Person in each Band be desired to interrogate the rest in order, who may be called the Leader of that Band. And on *Monday, September* 26, it was agreed,

[1] Monday was September 25, not 26, as entered in the ' Orders.'
[2] Wilson's *History of Dissenting Churches in London*, iii., 421.

A NEW RELIGIOUS SOCIETY

6. That each Band meet twice in a Week, once on *Monday* Evenings, the second Time when it is most convenient for each Band.

7. That every Person come punctually at the Hour appointed, without some extraordinary Reason.

8. That those that are present begin exactly at the Hours.

9. That every Meeting be begun and ended with Singing and Prayer

10. That every one in order speak as freely, plainly, and concisely as he can, the real State of his Heart, with his several Temptations and Deliverances, since the last Time of meeting.

11. That all Bands have a Conference at eight every *Wednesday* Evening, begun and ended with Singing and Prayer.

12. That Nine of the Clock the Names of the Members be called over, and the Absenters set down.

13. That Notice of any extraordinary Meeting be given on the *Wednesday* Night preceding such Meeting.

14. That exactly at ten, if the Business of the Night be not finished, a short concluding Prayer be used, that those may go who are in haste, but that all depart the Room by half an Hour after ten.

15. That whosoever speaks in this Conference stand up, and that none else speak till he is set down.

16. That nothing which is mentioned in this Conference be by any Means mentioned out of it.

17. That every Member of this Society, who is a Member of any other, prefer the meeting with this, and with his particular Band, before the meeting with any other Society or Company whatsoever.

18. That if any Person absent himself without some extraordinary Reason, either from his Band, or from any Meeting of the whole Society, he be first privately admonished; and if he be absent again, reproved before the whole Society.

19. That any Person who desires or designs to take any Journey, shall first, if it be possible, have the approbation of the Bands.

20. That all our Members who are in Clubs be desired to withdraw their Names, as being Meetings nowise conducing to the Glory of God.

21. That any who desire to be admitted into this Society be asked, What are your Reasons for desiring this? Will you be entirely open, using no kind of Reserve, least of all in the Case of Love or Courtship? Will you strive against the Desire of ruling, of being first in your Company, or having your own Way? Will you submit to be placed in what Band the Leaders shall choose for you? Have you any Objections to any of our Orders? The Orders may then be read to them.

22. That those who answer these Questions in the Affirmative, be proposed every fourth *Wednesday*.

23. That every one then present speak clearly and fully whatever Objection he has to any Person proposed to be a Member.

24. That those against whom any reasonable Objection appears be acquainted with that Objection, and the admitting them upon Trial postponed till that Objection is removed.

25. That those against whom no reasonable Objection appears or

remains, be, in order for their Trial, formed into distinct Bands, and some Person agreed to assist them.

26. That if no new Objection then appear, they be, after two Months' Trial, admitted into the Society.

27. That every fourth *Saturday* be observed as a Day of general Intercession, which may continue from twelve to two, from three to five, and from six to eight.

28. That on Sunday Se'en-night following be a general Love-feast, from seven till ten in the evening.

29. That in order to a continual Intercession every Member of this Society choose some Hour, either of the Day or Night, to spend in Prayer chiefly for his Brethren.

30. That in order to a continual Fast, three of the Members of this Society Fast every Day (as their Health permits), *Sundays* and Holidays excepted, and spend as much as they can of that Day in retirement from Business and Prayer.

31. That each Person give Notice to the Leader of his Band how much he is willing to subscribe towards the general charge of the Bands, and that each Person's Money be paid in to the Leader of his Band once a month at farthest.

32. That no particular Person be allowed to act in any Thing contrary to any Order of this Society, but that every one, without Distinction, submit to the Determination of his Brethren ; and that if any Person or Persons do not, after being thrice admonished, conform to the Society, they be not esteemed any longer as Members.

33. That any Person whom the whole Society shall approve may be accounted a correspondent Member, and as such, may be admitted at our general Meetings, provided he correspond with the Society once in a month at least.[1]

In comparing the ' Orders ' of the Fetter Lane Society with those of the Horneck and Woodward Societies there is one difference which immediately strikes us. There is no rule which confines membership in the new Society to those who belong to the Church of England. Seeking for the reason of this omission we would suggest that, in 1737, Count Zinzendorf, being in London, had united together a few Germans and formed them into a Moravian Society. Peter Böhler, Neisser, and Schulius had been deputed to visit this Society on their way to America. They preached to them, and several of the hearers were deeply affected and became witnesses for the truth. Through Wesley, Hutton became acquainted with Böhler. Hutton urged him and the other two Germans to spend an hour for edification in the Society he had formed, and the

---

[1] Benham's *Memoirs of James Hutton*, 29–32. In Wesley's *Journal* there appears an abbreviated list of the ' Orders.' It contains those he considered ' fundamental,' viz. Nos. 1, 3, 10, 11, 21, 23, 25–28, and 32. *Journal*, i., 458–59.

invitation was accepted. The German preachers also visited other Religious Societies. In this way the small Moravian Society and some of the Religious Societies were brought into association. When the 'Orders' of the Fetter Lane Society were drawn up it would seem reasonable to omit the stringent rule concerning the Church of England test of membership. There was a danger in that omission arising from the Conventicle Act, but it is possible that those who drew up the 'Orders' did not perceive it.

A second fact is revealed by a comparison of the 'Orders' of the old and the new Religious Societies. The latter contained regulations for the establishment of bands and the appointment of their leaders. The value of this arrangement had been tested by Wesley in Savannah. We presume that he borrowed the original idea from the Moravians. He had a quick eye for the practicable, and a firm grasp on methods the value of which had been tested in actual work. In the Fetter Lane 'Orders' we see that little companies, each consisting of from five to ten persons, met at stated times, and that, once a week, these companies assembled in conference, and formed a general meeting of the Society. The bands are the outstanding feature of the new arrangement. Their purpose was spiritual fellowship. In some of the old Societies conversation on personal religious experience had its place, but in others it was discouraged. In Fetter Lane it is of prime importance. It is directed that the conversation must rise above the level of desultory talk. Every one has to speak of his experience as freely, plainly, and concisely as he can ; he has to tell his temptations and deliverances since the last time of meeting. That sounds a new note in the proceedings of the Religious Societies.

In examining these 'Orders' we are impressed by the increased care shown in the admission and exclusion of members. Candidates are to be closely examined as to their reasons for desiring admittance ; the 'Orders' are read to them ; when they are proposed those present have a right to state any reasonable objection to their reception ; they are placed on trial for two months in a band, and are only received into the Society when, at the end of that period, there is no new objection against them. As to exclusion, the 'Orders' are clear. No person is to be allowed to absent himself, either from his band or from any meeting of the Society, without some extraordinary reason. If he does so he is first to be privately admonished; then, if absent again, he is to be reproved before the whole Society. No member is allowed to act in anything contrary to any ' Order '; if he does he is to be admonished; if he should persist in breaking the rules, after being thrice admonished, he is to be no longer esteemed a member of the Society. Regular attendance at his band and at the Society Meeting, and obedience to the ' Orders,' are essential to the continuance of membership. In the admission and exclusion of members the whole Society acts together. It is interesting to note the financial arrangements, and to compare them with those existing in the old Religious Societies.

There is one order of the new Society—No. 29—not marked by Wesley as fundamental, but in which he must have been profoundly interested. It relates to ' the continual intercession.' It reveals Wesley's conviction concerning the influence of constant prayer, and it carries our thoughts away to George Herbert, and his friend Nicholas Ferrar, of Little Gidding. Not only so. It reminds us that such ' continual intercession ' occupied a prominent place in the religious life of the Moravians, as we shall see when we visit the settlement at Herrnhut.

In these ' Orders ' there is no mention of the Sacrament of the Lord's Supper, or of attendance at the worship of the Church. In the old Societies the rules touching these subjects were clear. Those who are continually glancing onward will understand why we indicate this fact. At first the Church of England members constantly attended their parish churches, and assembled there at the Table of the Lord; but days were approaching when the question of the necessity of using ' the means of grace ' was to be raised in an acute form, and the discussion was to determine the destiny of the Society. At its beginning John Wesley was the President of the Fetter Lane Society, James Hutton taking his place when he was absent, and we can understand that so long as Wesley maintained his influence over the members they would attend the Sacrament in the churches. With the gradual diminishing and the final disappearance of that influence we shall have to deal in other pages.

XIV

OXFORD AND GERMANY

On June 11, 1738, John Wesley preached in St. Mary's, Oxford, before the University.[1] The subject of the sermon was 'Salvation by Faith,' the text Eph. ii. 8. It was delivered to a scholarly audience by a scholarly evangelist, who sought, above everything else, to reason, convince, and persuade. The plan of the sermon was clear, its logical sequence unbroken. The definitions of 'the faith through which we are saved' and 'the salvation which is through faith' possessed the grace of simplicity, and were supported by irresistible quotations from the Bible and the standards of the Church of England. Summing up the first part of his discourse, Wesley said: 'Christian faith is, then, not only an assent to the whole gospel of Christ; but also a full reliance on the blood of Christ; a trust in the merits of His life, death, and resurrection; a recumbency upon Him as our atonement and our life, *as given for us*, and *living in us*; and, in consequence hereof, a closing with Him, and cleaving to Him, as our "wisdom, righteousness, sanctification, and redemption," or, in one word, our salvation.' As to the salvation which is through faith, he explained it as follows: 'This, then, is the salvation which is through faith, even in the present world: A salvation from sin, and the consequences of sin, both often expressed in the word *justification*, which, taken in the largest sense, implies a deliverance from guilt and punishment, by the atonement of Christ actually applied to the soul of the sinner now believing on Him, and a deliverance from the power of sin, through Christ *formed in his heart*. So that he who is thus justified, or saved by faith, is indeed *born again of the Spirit* unto a new life, which "is hid with Christ in God." And as a new-born babe he gladly receives the ἄδολον—sincere milk of the Word—and grows thereby; going on in the might

[1] The date on the printed sermon, June 18, is incorrect.

of the Lord his God, from faith to faith, from grace to grace, until, at length, he come unto " a perfect man, unto the measure of the stature of the fullness of Christ." [1]

All who are interested in the development of Wesley's teaching should compare the foregoing definition of faith with that given in his sermon on 'The Circumcision of the Heart,' preached in St. Mary's on January 1, 1733. Five years of thinking and experience had led him into a completer understanding of the meaning of faith. When he published the 1733 sermon in 1748, he enlarged his definition of faith by adding, ' It is likewise the revelation of Christ in our hearts ; a divine evidence or conviction of His love, His free, unmerited love to me, a sinner ; a sure confidence in His pardoning mercy, wrought in us by the Holy Ghost ; a confidence, whereby every true believer is enabled to bear witness, " I know that my Redeemer liveth," that I have " an Advocate with the Father," and that " Jesus Christ the righteous " is my Lord, and " the propitiation for my sins " ; I know He hath " loved me, and given Himself for me," He hath reconciled me, even me, to God ; and I have redemption through His *blood*, even the forgiveness of sins " ' [2] By this revision Wesley not only brings the two University sermons of 1733 and 1738 into harmony, but also expresses more completely his mature view of the great doctrine of salvation by faith.

At the conclusion of his sermon, in 1738, Wesley answered several objections to the doctrine he had preached. We can only glance at two of them. His teaching is now so widely accepted that it is threatened with the perils of the commonplace ; but in his day it was fiercely and disdainfully contested. Amongst other objections it was alleged that when a man taught the doctrine of ' salvation, or justification, by faith only ' he preached against holiness and good works. Wesley's answer was that those who so believe, while they trust in the blood of Christ alone, use all the ordinances which He has appointed, do all the ' good works which He has before prepared that they should walk therein,' and enjoy and manifest all holy and heavenly tempers, even the mind which was in Christ Jesus. Wesley was aware of the grave dangers which accompany the unguarded declaration of the doctrine of justification by faith, and he incessantly taught that they

[1] *Works*, v., 11–12, 8vo ed.   [2] *Ibid.*, v., 205.

which have believed in God must be 'careful to maintain good works.'

Listening to Wesley's voice sounding in St. Mary's, we wait for the note of passion. We do not wonder that it is delayed. The preacher, for the most part, speaks as a cool and self-restrained expositor who is intent on making his meaning unmistakable. But, suddenly, the tone is changed, and the voice of the evangelist rings out the note of the coming mission. He is meeting the objection of those who say that when a preacher declares that the righteousness which is of faith cannot be given to a man while he trusts in that which is of the law, he is proclaiming 'an uncomfortable doctrine.' Musing for a moment on the phrase, the fire kindles:

> But this, it is said, is an uncomfortable doctrine. The devil spake like himself, that is, without either truth or shame, when he dared to suggest to men that it is such. It is the only comfortable one; it is 'very full of comfort' to all self-destroyed, self-condemned sinners, that 'whosoever believeth on Him shall not be ashamed'; that 'the same Lord over all is rich unto all that call upon Him.' Here is comfort, high as heaven, stronger than death! What! Mercy for all? For Zaccheus, a public robber? For Mary Magdalene, a common harlot? Methinks I hear one say, 'Then I, even I, may hope for mercy!' And so thou mayest, thou afflicted one, whom none hath comforted. God will not cast out thy prayer. Nay, He may say the next hour, 'Be of good cheer, thy sins are forgiven thee'; so forgiven that they shall reign over thee no more; yea, and that 'the Holy Spirit shall bear witness with thy spirit that thou art a child of God.' O glad tidings! Tidings of great joy, which are sent unto all people. Whatsoever your sins be, 'though red, like crimson,' though more than the hairs of your head, 'return ye unto the Lord, and He will have mercy upon you; and to our God, for He will abundantly pardon.'

This impassioned appeal would, doubtless, touch some who listened to it, but to most of those present it would seem rank 'enthusiasm,' a mere riot of emotion. In our ears, as it sweeps across the distance, it sounds like a clarion-call ushering in a great religious revolution.

At the close of the sermon Wesley spoke other words which, also, are not only for an age but for all time. Speaking of the doctrine, 'By grace are ye saved through faith,' he said:

> Never was the maintaining of this doctrine more seasonable than it is at this day. Nothing but this can effectually prevent the increase of the Romish delusion among us. It is endless to attack, one by one, all

the errors of that Church. But salvation by faith strikes at the root, and all fall at once where this is established. It was this doctrine, which our Church justly calls *the strong rock and foundation of the Christian religion*, that first drove Popery out of these Kingdoms ; and it is this alone can keep it out. Nothing but this can give a check to that immorality which hath ' overspread the land as a flood.' Can you empty the great deep, drop by drop ? Then you may reform us by dissuasives from particular vices. But let the ' righteousness which is of God by faith ' be brought in, and so shall its proud waves be stayed. Nothing but this can stop the mouths of those who ' glory in their shame, and openly deny the Lord that bought them.' They can talk as sublimely of the law as he that hath it written by God in his heart. To hear them speak on this head might incline one to think they were not far from the kingdom of God. But take them out of the law into the gospel ; begin with the righteousness of faith ; with Christ, ' the end of the law to every one that believeth,' and those who but now appeared almost, if not altogether Christians, stand confessed the sons of perdition ; as far from life and salvation (God be merciful unto them !) as the depth of hell from the height of heaven.

These far-seeing, vehement words, show that Wesley's outlook was widening. He had his eyes fixed on the nation. He saw beyond the narrow confines of a parish or a University. He faced the tremendous problem of the religious condition of England. In his heart there was ' the cry of the sea,' the voice of the storm-vexed ocean of English life. That voice moved him profoundly ; it called him away once more from Oxford, the beloved city in which he longed to live and die.

After a brief visit to London Wesley carried out a cherished project. In company with Benjamin Ingham and others he went to Germany, landing at Rotterdam on June 15, 1738. His visit lasted three months. His principal object in going to Germany was to see the Moravian settlements, and to get into touch with men who could answer questions concerning certain aspects of his spiritual experience which were perplexing him. He had learned much from Spangenberg and Böhler, and from the articles and homilies of the English Church. He had put his new knowledge concerning justification ' by faith only ' to the test of personal experience, and great peace had come to him, but he was in doubt concerning the possibility of attaining to a constant assurance of his salvation. In his sermon before the University he spoke of the deliverance from fear which comes when the love of God is shed abroad in the heart of the believer by the Holy Ghost. In dealing with the subject he said, 'And hereby they are persuaded (though perhaps not at all times, nor with the same fullness of persuasion) that neither death, nor life, nor things present, nor things to come, nor any other creature, shall be able to separate them from the love of God, which is in Christ Jesus our Lord.' The parenthesis is striking. The 'perhaps' indicates wavering of mind. After his experience in Nettleton Court Wesley possessed a peace to which, up to that time, he had been a stranger. But strong temptations assailed him, and his bright new day was darkened by shadows. He had little joy, and his assurance of salvation varied with the passing phases of his experience.

In the course of their journey Wesley and Ingham visited Marienborn, where Count Zinzendorf resided as the head of a 'family' of Moravians, consisting of about ninety persons, gathered out of many nations. The visitors attended the services; and at one of them Ingham, who was drifting towards Moravianism, was admitted to the Lord's Supper. Benham says, ' When the congregation saw Wesley to be *homo perturbatus* and that his head had gained an ascendancy over his heart, and being desirous not to interfere with his plan of effecting good as a clergyman of the English Church, when he should become more settled—for he always claimed to be a zealous English Churchman—they deemed it not prudent to admit him to that sacred service.' We do not know Benham's authority for this statement. Neither in his *Journal* nor in his letters does John Wesley record the incident, and it must be borne in mind that Benham's book was not published until more than a century after the alleged event; but its occurrence is probable. Among the Moravians in Germany the 'fencing of the Table' was exceptionally strict. Before communicants were admitted to the Lord's Supper they had to answer the following questions: ' Is Christ formed in you? Have you a new heart? Is your soul renewed in the image of God? Is the whole body of sin destroyed in you? Are you fully assured, beyond all doubt or fear, that you are a child of God? In what manner, and at what moment, did you receive that full assurance?' Christian David told Wesley, in a conversation at Herrnhut, ' If a man could not answer all these questions, we judged he had no true faith. Nor would we permit any to receive the Lord's Supper amongst us till he could.'[1] It is interesting to note that at Herrnhut, under Christian David's influence, the rigour of the inquiry concerning 'full assurance' was softened.

On August 1 Wesley reached Herrnhut, the principal Moravian settlement, and stayed there nearly a fortnight. He was much impressed by what he saw and heard there, and he gives a full description of his visit in his *Journal*.[2] Longing for light on the mysteries of his new experiences he conversed closely with several of the most prominent Moravians on the subject that was perplexing him. Especially illuminating was his talk with Christian David, a man after his own heart, who was the first 'planter' of the settlement. He found that he had passed through a spiritual experience which, at a crucial point, resembled his own. He listened as the story was told, and either took it down in shorthand or stored it in his well-practised memory. David described to him his experience of peace at the time when he was assured of the forgiveness of his sins; how, afterwards, he was assailed with doubts concerning his salvation, and continued in trouble because he had not learned that 'being justified is widely different from having the full assurance of faith.' After several years, during one of his visits as a missionary to Greenland, light came. Explaining his illumination, he said that he perceived 'full assurance was a distinct gift from justifying faith, and often not given till long after it; and that justification does not imply that sin should not *stir* in us, but only that it should not conquer.' He continued, 'And now first it was that I had that full assurance of my own reconciliation to God through Christ. For many years I had had the forgiveness of my sins and a measure of the peace of God, but I had not till now that witness of His Spirit which shuts out all doubt and fear.' This experience had led him to the conclusion that it was not expedient to insist on the assurance of faith as a necessary qualification for receiving the Lord's Supper. He stated his views on assurance to the Herrnhut authorities, and found it difficult to persuade them to accept them. Gradually they admitted their correctness; and then, in their preaching, they began to lay the chief emphasis on '*Christ given for us*,' being convinced that if that great truth were believed, then 'Christ will surely be *formed in us*'[3]

[1] *Journal*, ii., 35.   [2] ii., 19–56.   [3] ii., 35–36.

In an interview with Michael Linner, the Eldest of the Church, that is, its highest officer, Wesley found that he, also, had passed through a similar experience respecting that full acceptance of Christ which excludes all doubt and fear. But Linner wisely said, ' Indeed, the leading of the Spirit is different in different souls. His more usual method, I believe, is to give, in one and the same moment, the forgiveness of sins and a full assurance of that forgiveness. Yet in many He works as He did in me, giving first the remission of sins, and, after some weeks or months or years, the full assurance of it.'[1] Other conversations with the officers and members of the Moravian Church confirmed Wesley's conviction of the truth of Michael Linner's judicious words concerning ' the leading of the Spirit.' He ascertained that the variety of experience concerning ' assurance ' was fully exemplified in those with whom he conversed. As he listened, and noted, and pondered the things he heard, the tarrying of the vision in his own case was explained ; and, contented with the peace he enjoyed, he waited for the coming of the day when the abiding sense of his own salvation would gladden his soul.

We cannot regret the experience of doubt and uncertainty that followed Wesley's conversion. The doctrine of the assurance of the forgiveness of sins and of personal salvation was to become of surpassing importance in his ministry. It was well that he was forced to examine it in the light of reason, Scripture, and human experience. The examination was thorough, and the conclusions reached were those of a man who was compelled to see things with his mind as well as his heart. The effect of his conversations with Christian David and Michael Linner was abiding. In after years, when he was in the midst of his mission, he allowed that there may be very many degrees of seeing God ; even as many as are between seeing the sun with the eyelids closed, and with the eyes open ; nor do we forget his comforting words to Lady Maxwell : ' It may be, He that does all things well has wise reasons, though not apparent to us, for working more gradually in you than He has done of late years in most others. It may please Him to give you the consciousness of His favour, the conviction that you are accepted through the Beloved, by almost insensible degrees, like the dawning of the day. And it is all one how it began,

[1] *Journal*, ii., 37.

so as you do but walk in the light. Be this given in an instant, or by degrees, hold it fast. Christ is yours. He hath loved you; He hath given Himself for you. Therefore you shall be holy, as He is holy, both in heart, and in all manner of conversation.'[1]

Wesley's visit to Herrnhut was fruitful in suggestions which, after lying hidden in the seed-plot of his mind, came to light in later days. He investigated the organization of the Moravian Church, and writes a most interesting description of its officers, the division of the people, the conferences and lectures, the government of the children, and the order of divine worship. He supplements his own account by printing 'An extract of the constitution of the Church of the Moravian Brethren at Herrnhut, laid before the Theological Order at Würtemberg in the year 1733'; and he gives us materials from which we may judge the condition of the settlement at the time of his visit. His description is important, because it helps us to detect the origin of certain arrangements afterwards adopted when he organized his own Societies. We are chiefly concerned with the hints of which he made practical use.

At the head of the Moravian settlement was an officer styled 'The Eldest of the whole Church.' His work was to assist the Church by his counsel and prayers, and to determine what should be done in matters of importance. Over each particular branch there was an eldest. There were four pastors or teachers. They were overseers of the whole flock and every person therein. Their duty was to baptize the children, to form their minds, and to bring them up in the nurture and admonition of the Lord. When they found in the children a sincere love of the Cross, they received them into the Church. The pastors administered the Sacrament of the Lord's Supper, married those 'who were already married to Christ,' reproved, admonished, quickened, comforted, as need required. They were charged to declare the whole counsel of God, 'taking heed at all times to speak as the oracles of God and agreeably to the analogy of faith.' They also buried those who died in the Lord. It was their duty to keep that safe which had been committed to their charge, 'even the pure doctrine and apostolic discipline which we have received from our forefathers.' In addition to the pastors there were deacons, also called helpers. Their duties

---

[1] *Works*, xii., 324, 8vo ed.

were to instruct in the private assemblies, and to take care that 'outward things were done decently and in order.' They were charged to see that every member of the Church 'grew in grace and walked suitable to his holy calling.' A second class of deacons existed. They had to take care that nothing was wanting to the orphan house, the poor, the sick, and the strangers. Two of them were entrusted with the public stock, and kept accounts of all that was received or expended. There were also deaconesses who discharged similar duties among their own sex. In addition to the officers we have named there were censors and monitors. The work they had to do was difficult, and called for experience, quick-sightedness, wisdom, and modesty. The censors reported what they had observed in the conduct of the members either to the deacons or the monitors. Some of the monitors were secretly appointed; the appointment of others was known. They could admonish the members, and, in cases of need, the rulers of the Church.

Concerning the members of the Church, it is only necessary to state that the husbands, the wives, the widows, the maids, the young men, the boys, the girls, and the little children were arranged in distinct 'classes.' Each class was visited daily by some one appointed for the purpose. The larger classes were divided into nearly ninety smaller classes, or 'bands,' over each of which a person possessing large experience presided. Such persons were called leaders. The leaders met the senior officer every week, and laid open to him and to the Lord 'whatsoever hindered or furthered the work of God in the souls committed to their charge.' The rule as to the exclusion of members was as follows:

> If any man among us, having been often admonished, and long forborne, persists in walking unworthy of his holy calling, he is no longer admitted to the Lord's Supper. If he still continues in his fault, hating to be reformed, the last step is, publicly, and often in the midst of many prayers and tears, to cast him out of our congregation. But great is our joy if he then see the error of his ways, so that we may receive him among us again.[1]

The Sacrament of the Lord's Supper held a high place in the estimation of the Moravians of Herrnhut. Once or twice a month, either at Berthelsdorf or at Herrnhut, all the members

[1] *Journal*, ii., 56.

of the Church received it. The administration at Berthelsdorf is noteworthy. The settlement had been planted within that parish. Berthelsdorf was a Lutheran village about an English mile from Herrnhut, and the service in its church was Lutheran. The living had been purchased by Zinzendorf, and he had presented it to Johann Andreas Rothe, a man in full sympathy with the convictions of the Moravians concerning salvation and the experiences of the spiritual life. The settlers attended their parish church. The meeting of Wesley and Rothe has a special significance in the eyes of Christian hymnologists. The two men have blended their voices in a great song. Rothe was the author of a hymn that has gone round the world in Wesley's translation. That translation was probably made in Georgia, but it was not published until 1740. Since then innumerable singers have joined in its ecstatic cry :

> Now I have found the ground wherein
> Sure my soul's anchor may remain !

Wesley did not lay aside his habit of ' collecting ' during his visit to Germany. When reading a book, as we have shown, he was quick to see the things worth remembering, and in order to fasten them in his mind he wrote them down. He pursued a similar course when he read the book of human life and experience. Visiting a town, he set himself to understand it. He saw its outward aspect, and with a few swift strokes of his pen he noted it in his *Journal*. Then with remarkable keenness of insight he perceived its spirit, and described his impressions of its moral and spiritual condition. He was irresistibly drawn to the study of the German Churches. He ascertained their history, doctrines, constitution, discipline, the manner of life of their ministers and members, and the effect of their work on the surrounding population. His estimates may have been sometimes wrong, but they possess a high average of correctness. It is incontestable that by his investigations and habit of ' collecting ' he stored his mind with a wealth of ideas concerning men, and the forms, methods, and results of Church organization. In after years, either consciously or unconsciously, he adopted or adapted other men's ideas if he saw that they were of practical value. He had no desire to be considered an original inventor in ecclesiastical matters. He possessed the treasure of an open mind, and he attained pre-eminent skill in availing himself of everything which in any way would help him to lead men to God, and assist them to 'grow in the grace and knowledge of our Lord and Saviour Jesus Christ.'

Wesley was an educational enthusiast, and while he was in Germany he had opportunities for examining systems of work from which he gathered hints that were serviceable to him. In the school at Herrnhut he found that the curriculum included reading, writing, arithmetic, Latin, Greek, Hebrew, French, English, history, and geography. The comparison of the time-table of a Moravian and an English school of the same class must have impressed him; it would confirm his conviction that it was possible to 'unite the pair so long disjoined, knowledge and vital piety.' That conviction he never relinquished, and it sustained him in his educational work in England. He learned one thing in Herrnhut of doubtful value. The orphan house time-table, which he gives in his *Journal*, has, in modern eyes, a forbidding aspect. The 'larger children' rose at five o'clock, and, after a day crowded with work, went to bed at ten. The 'smaller children' rose between five and six, and went to bed at eight o'clock. It is clear that the super-child existed in those days. Our compassion for these sufferers is intensified when we note that the only form of recreation during the day was walking. We presume that the Moravian authorities were of the opinion that if a boy played when he was a boy he would play when he was a man. Wesley's good sense and love of vigorous athletics failed to guard him against the fallacy contained in this dangerous maxim.

In addition to the Moravian schools at Herrnhut Wesley came in contact with the German system of education at Halle, where he visited Professor Francke, the second son of Augustus Hermann Francke. He was a professor of divinity, the archdeacon of St. Mary's, and the director of his father's benevolent institutions. In addition, when Wesley reached Jena, on his return journey to England, he visited the schools founded through the influence of Stolte, of whom he gives an interesting account in the *Journal*. These schools were of a different type from those already mentioned. They were for poor children, and bore a strong resemblance to those which were formed by the Holy Club in Oxford and by Wesley in Georgia. After Stolte left Jena, Dr. Johann Franz Buddaeus, who succeeded to his work of preaching ' the real gospel,' hearing that a school which had been set up by a few of the townsmen had been abandoned, mentioned the matter to the students in his house. About ten of them recommenced the school, and devoted themselves to caring for the children. Before long other schools were opened, and filled with children and teachers. Among the students in the house of Buddaeus was Spangenberg, who was one of the volunteers. With a mind stored with new ideas, Wesley turned his face toward England, and on September 16 arrived in London.

XV

CHARLES WESLEY

WHILE John Wesley was in Germany, fighting his doubts and gathering strength for battle, Charles Wesley was beginning his special work as an evangelist in England. He had his own difficulties with the passing phases of his spiritual experience, but his zeal for the salvation of others carried him out of himself. His conversion had heightened all his powers. He possessed in a pre-eminent degree the poet's dower. He was quick to see, to feel, to act. He had the 'love of love.' He was made for friendship and companionship, and the change that had come to him caused him passionately to desire that all whom he knew should enter into an understanding of the love of God as revealed in the death of Jesus Christ. As we turn over the pages of his *Journal* we see abundant evidences of his passion for the salvation of his friends. He hastens to their homes, engages in intimate talk with them, persuades them to accept the Saviour by an act of simple faith, tells them the story of his own conversion, reads to them and prays with them, and uses every means to lead them into the enjoyment of conscious salvation. His charm of manner, fervour of speech, absolute sincerity, transparent goodness, fitted him for work from which many shrink—the work of trying to win their friends for Christ by serious private conversation. As a domestic evangelist, speaking generally, he had much success. In some cases he seemed to fail; but after a time an incident occurred which wrought a change of mind in those who had angrily rejected his teaching and, at last, in deep penitence, they accepted the mercy of God through Jesus Christ. In this class Mrs. Delamotte, of Blendon Hall, was included. At first she indignantly rejected the idea that any assurance of the forgiveness of sins could be given, but one day, in her reading, she alighted on one of Jeremy Taylor's prayers, which opened her eyes. In that prayer he cries, 'Lord, I am as sure Thou didst the great work of redemption for me, and for all mankind, as that I am alive. This is my hope, the strength of my spirit, my joy and my confidence. And do Thou never let the spirit of unbelief enter into me and take me from this rock. Here will I dwell, for I have a delight therein. Here will I live, and here I desire to die.' This prayer made a deep impression on Mrs. Delamotte. She listened with meekness to Charles Wesley's appeals, and shared his experience of conscious salvation.

It would be pleasant to linger over the home-scenes which shine out at this time from the pages of Charles Wesley's *Journal*, but we must turn away to note illustrations of his influence, with its far-reaching effects. On June 9, we see him riding from Blendon to Bexley, in Kent, in company with Henry Piers, the vicar of Bexley, and John Bray. As we watch the three horsemen riding through the leafy lanes of Kent we hear Charles Wesley's voice distinctly. He is telling Mr. Piers his experience ' in simplicity and confidence.' The vicar is listening with calm attention. Later we see the three men walking in the garden of the vicarage. They sing and pray there. Mr. Piers is greatly moved, and testifies his full conviction and desire of finding Christ. He has been prepared for the conversation by reading the homily on justification, and he begins to see the ' open secret ' more clearly. On Saturday, June 10, we hear the voice of importunate prayer in an upper room of the vicarage. And then there is great joy in the hearts of the three men who have been wrestling with God. Mr. Piers can say with his guests, ' I believe.' With him it is no longer morning twilight ; it is ' the day of salvation.'

On May 10 Mr. Stonehouse, the vicar of Islington, ' was convinced of the truth as it is in Jesus.' He was of Pembroke College, Cambridge, taking his Master's degree there in 1736. Two years afterwards he was presented to the family living of Islington, holding it for two years. When John Wesley was in Germany Mr. Stonehouse came into close association with Charles Wesley, and they had serious conversation on the subject of faith. In the case of Mr. Stonehouse the way to the cross was strewn with hindrances. He ' stuck to fitness ' ; then he insisted that a man must be sanctified before he was justified ; and in other ways, perplexed and disappointed his spiritual guide. But Charles Wesley continued his task, and though he made slow progress in it, gradually the two men were drawn together into friendship. On July 24 an arrangement was made between them that Charles Wesley should act in the parish, under Mr. Stonehouse, as his curate.[1] The arrangement was quite informal. Inasmuch as Charles Wesley was not licensed to preach in the diocese of London it was impossible that he could be legally appointed to the position, and no trace of his appointment is to be found in the minutes of the Islington vestry of the time.[2] The arrangement, however, gave him opportunities for preaching in the parish church. It is important to note the beginning of the formation of the little group of friendly clergymen who welcomed the evangelists into their pulpits at the commencement of the great mission.

Charles Wesley, during his brother's absence, was fortunate in receiving invitations to preach in some of the City churches. He did not veil his testimony, but boldly preached salvation by faith. John Wesley's University sermon on that subject had made a deep impression on him. He carefully studied it, and sometimes read it or preached its substance to his congregations. On Sunday, September 3, he tells us that he preached ' salvation by faith ' in Westminster Abbey, assisting afterwards in the administration of the Lord's Supper. The old captain of Westminster School, rejoicing in this service, hurried away and preached in the afternoon at St. Botolph's, and once more at Mr. Sims's, where he expounded Romans ii., a chapter which gave him full opportunity to proclaim the neglected doctrines of the English Church.

Charles Wesley's work in the summer of 1738 was not restricted to the domestic circle and the London churches. On July 10, at the request of Mr. Sparks, who was one of the visiting ministers of Newgate, he went to the prison with Mr. Bray and Mr. Burnham, and preached to ten men who were under sentence of death. He did so with a heavy heart. His old prejudices against the possibility of a death-bed repentance still hung upon him, and he hardly hoped that there could be mercy for those whose time was so short. He says, ' But in the midst of my languid discourse a sudden spirit of faith came upon me, and I promised them all pardon, in the name of Jesus Christ, if they would then, as at the last hour, repent and

[1] C. Wesley's *Journal*, i., 124.   [2] *W.H.S. Proceedings*, v., 238.

believe the gospel. Nay, I did believe they would accept of the proffered mercy, and could not help telling them, " I had no doubt but God would give me every soul of them." [1] The next day he preached with earnestness to the prisoners again, and he saw that one or two of them were deeply affected. From that time he redoubled his efforts to lead the condemned men to Christ, and he did not labour in vain. One of them was a negro, who, under the terrible laws of that time, had been sentenced to death for robbing his master. He was sick, and separated from the other prisoners, being confined in ' the condemned hole.' Charles Wesley was moved by his sorrow and earnest desire of Christ Jesus. On July 15 he had the joy of knowing that his ' poor happy black ' believed that ' the Son of God loved him, and gave Himself for him.' The ' condemned hole ' became the scene of great rejoicing. As the day of execution approached two of the other prisoners came into the place, and Charles Wesley and James Hutton conversed with them, and saw them moving towards the Cross. On the night before the execution Charles Wesley and Bray were locked into a cell with the men who were to suffer on the morrow. A change had come over the little company. When Wesley had administered the Communion to the condemned men, having previously instructed them in the nature of it, one of them had found perfect peace ; others, at intervals, had seen, by faith, the Saviour crucified for them. Joy was visible on all faces. After wrestling in mighty prayer, they sang the hymn written by the father of the Wesleys :

> Behold the Saviour of mankind
> Nailed to the shameful tree !
> How vast the love that Him inclined
> To bleed and die for thee !

Charles Wesley declared that it was one of the most triumphant hours he had ever known.

The next day, Wednesday, July 19, the men were executed at Tyburn. The scene must be depicted in Charles Wesley's own words. He says :

I rose very heavy, and backward to visit them for the last time. At six I prayed and sang with them all together. The ordinary would

---

[1] C. Wesley's *Journal*, i., 117.

have read prayers, and preached most miserably. Mr. Sparks and Mr. Broughton were present. I felt my heart full of tender love to the latter. He administered. All the ten received. Then he prayed; and I after him. At half-hour past nine their irons were knocked off and their hands tied. I went in a coach with Sparks, Washington, and a friend of Newington's (N. himself not being permitted). By half-hour past ten we came to Tyburn, waited till eleven; then were brought the children appointed to die. I got upon the cart with Sparks and Broughton; the ordinary endeavoured to follow, when the poor prisoners begged he might not come; and the mob kept him down. I prayed first, then Sparks and Broughton. We had prayed before that our Lord would show there was a power superior to the fear of death. Newington had quite forgot his pain. They were all cheerful; full of comfort, peace, and triumph; assuredly persuaded Christ had died for them, and waited to receive them into paradise. Greenaway was impatient to be with Christ. The black had spied me coming out of the coach, and saluted me with his looks. As often as his eyes met mine he smiled with the most composed, delightful countenance I ever saw. Read caught hold of my hand in a transport of joy. Newington seemed perfectly pleased. Hudson declared he was never better, or more at ease, in mind and body. None showed any natural terror of death; no fear, or crying, or tears. All expressed their desire of our following them to paradise. I never saw such calm triumph, such incredible indifference to dying. We sang several hymns, particularly :

> Behold the Saviour of mankind
> Nailed to the shameful tree !

and the hymn entitled ' Faith in Christ,' which concludes :

> A guilty, weak, and helpless worm,
> Into Thy hands I fall ;
> Be Thou my life, my righteousness,
> My Jesus, and my all.

We prayed Him, in earnest faith, to receive their spirits. I could do nothing but rejoice; kissed Newington and Hudson; took leave of each in particular. Mr. Broughton bade them not to be surprised when the cart should draw away. They cheerfully replied they should not; expressed some concern how we should get back to our coach. We left them going to meet their Lord, ready for the Bridegroom. When the cart drew off, not one stirred, or struggled for life, but meekly gave up their spirits. Exactly at twelve they were turned off. I spoke a few suitable words to the crowd, and returned, full of peace and confidence in our friends' happiness. That hour under the gallows was the most blessed hour of my life.[1]

It was under such circumstances that Charles Wesley first

[1] C. Wesley's *Journal*, i., 122-23.

met the wild English mob, and commenced his work as a ' field-preacher.' His 'few suitable words' spoken to the crowd prefaced a series of fervent appeals subsequently made by him in the open air in many parts of England. Not only so. The experiences through which he passed, when face to face with men standing on the brink of eternity, awoke in him the passion of the evangelist. Prejudice disappeared, hesitation ended; there was nothing left but to test the truth of the doctrine, which had come to him suffused with new light, that by faith, by faith only, a penitent sinner is reconciled to God. During the opening months of his career as an evangelist at least thirty persons, in his presence, had instantaneously received the witness of their sonship. The scenes of Newgate and Tyburn, however, spoke with exceptional emphasis. Most of the persons whose conversion he had previously witnessed had been standing 'not far from the kingdom of God'; but the experience of the prisoners, who rejoiced with him under the gallows, opened his eyes to the fact that even at their last hour the outcasts of men, Christ's farthest wandered sheep, could be found and folded. The condemned cell occupies a place of honour in the history of the Wesleys. It was in the cell in Oxford Castle that John Wesley learned a lesson that humbled him, and filled him with the hope of his own salvation; it was in Newgate that Charles Wesley found that the late repentance of criminal men is not vain; that 'the heart of the Eternal is most wonderfully kind.'

During these months, when Charles Wesley was doing pioneer work in London and the neighbourhood, his pen was busy. His great gift of song asserted itself. Hymns that are now the heritage of the whole Church whispered in his mind, were written out in seclusion, and then sung by men and women intent on glorifying the God of their salvation. His ' Hymn to Christ ' occupies a conspicuous position. It often helped those who, wavering between hope and fear, hesitated to make the great decision. As they sang,

> Take me now, possess me whole,
> Who for me, for me, hast died!

faith won its victory; they saw the Saviour on the cross. In the stories of conversion belonging to this period these words frequently occur, but the whole hymn is sacred. It is a herald-song of the Methodist Revival. It speaks good tidings of great joy. It tells of One who is the Fountain of Life, the Good Shepherd, the pilgrim's Daily Bread, his Prophet, Priest, and King. It is a guide of the Christian through his earthly journey. From the initial act of faith it accompanies him in all the stages of his spiritual life, ever pointing him to the source of his strength and safety. So long as its words are remembered and accepted as true, no child of God needs to dread the advancing host of difficulties and temptations. He passes through every battle shadowed by the mighty hand of his loving Lord.

Charles Wesley must have found exquisite delight in hymn-writing. The rapture of the music brought its own reward to him. His pen, however, had to be used in a less congenial task. That was an age of journals. He kept one for some years himself, but seems to have had no intention to publish it. At the beginning of August we find him busy correcting George Whitefield's *Journal* for the press. He did the work reluctantly, as he disapproved of its publication. In after years Whitefield regretted the character of some of its contents, and, warned by the attacks made on it, vigorously revised it. If Charles Wesley had used his pruning-knife more ruthlessly he might have prevented much mischief. The publication of the first edition occurred at a supremely critical time, and aggravated the hostility of Churchmen against the new evangelists. It must be remembered that Whitefield was only twenty-three years of age, and the impetuosity of youth was still strong in him. He was a stranger to the bondage of literary prudence, and poured out the secrets of his soul unconscious of the fact that his book would be read by unsympathetic people. His opponents, who prided themselves on their moderation, reticence, and good taste, soon enlightened him; and when he returned to England he found that the popularity which had cheered him before sailing for Georgia had seriously declined.

At the end of August Charles Wesley went by coach to Oxford, and once more rejoiced in the society of some of his old friends. During this visit he waited on the Dean of Christ Church, Dr. John Conybeare. He was a protagonist in the controversy with the Deists, and was especially distinguished by his reply to Tindal's *Christianity as old as the Creation*.

Warburton considered it 'one of the best reasoned books in the world.' He also took a prominent part in the controversy on subscription which raged in 1751. He may be said to have commenced the discussion by declaring, in a sermon preached before the University, that persons who subscribe the articles give their assent to everything contained in them 'in the sense of those who wrote them'; and that they were not 'articles of peace,' but, as their title shows, were compiled 'for the avoiding diversities of opinion, and for establishing consent touching true religion.' These declarations were attacked by Clayton, the Bishop of Clogher, who, in his *Essay on Spirit*, dedicated to the Primate of Ireland, recommended such changes in the law of subscription as would leave Arianism an open question. The bishop frankly declared he had ceased to hold the opinions which he held when he subscribed to the articles, and gave his assent and consent to all and everything in the Book of Common Prayer. He also asserted that he did not agree with the persons who drew up the articles and compiled the Prayer Book. The positions of the two controversialists were in sharp contrast, and the battle they fought is not yet ended.[1]

The conversations that took place between the Dean of Christ Church and Charles Wesley bring out a distinction between the men who contended with the Deists and those who led the crusade against the sin of the nation during the great revival in the eighteenth century. The former had done invaluable work as reasoners with men who were in intellectual doubt concerning the unique authority of Revelation and the truth of Christianity. If the moral and religious reformation of the people could have been effected by arguments against the Deists such men as Dr. Butler and Dr. Conybeare would occupy a high place among reformers. The *Analogy* and the *Defence of Revealed Religion* made a victorious appeal to the intellect of wavering thinkers; they had little effect on the masses. The Wesleys, while fully appreciating the work of the defenders of Revelation, had found a more excellent way of bringing men into close and continuous communion with God. By the preaching of justification by faith and the possibility of the assurance of personal salvation they had discovered the weapons which prevailed in the fight against the worldliness

[1] Hunt's *Religious Thought in England*, iii., 300 *et seq.*

of the Church and the wickedness of the nation. It is to be regretted that those who contended against the Deists sometimes failed to appreciate the position of the new reformers. Had they done so it is possible that their sympathetic counsel might have assisted the Wesleys in their strange and difficult enterprise, and might have saved them from some of the mistakes they committed at the commencement of their campaign. But such co-operation was not realized. The men pursued their high aims by diverging pathways, and a great opportunity was missed.

Charles Wesley called on Dr. Conybeare on August 31, and was received with great friendliness. The subject of their conversation was faith. It was discussed on both sides with candour, and Wesley says, 'We could not quite agree in our notions of faith.' We judge that he mentioned the 'Sermon of Salvation' and claimed that his teaching was in harmony with it. The Dean significantly remarked that 'he wondered we had not hit upon the homilies sooner.' He knew that the homilies, as a whole, were not legally binding on those who signed the articles, but that the 'homily of justification' occupied a distinct position by reason of the reference to it in the eleventh article. The Dean was too fair a controversialist to blink that fact, and he made due allowance for it. He also knew that the thirty-fifth article commended both books of the homilies as containing 'godly and wholesome doctrine' necessary for the times. A man who holds the view that the articles must be read 'in the sense of those who wrote them' perceives, in a moment, the strength of the position occupied by the Wesleys, and we have no doubt that after the close of the interview Dr. Conybeare refreshed his memory by reperusing the eleventh article and the 'Sermon of Salvation.'

Later in the year Charles Wesley, when in Oxford, waited on the Dean once more. Dr. Conybeare complained of John Wesley's 'obscurity' in his sermon on salvation, a charge which can rarely be brought against him. But the mind of the critic was becoming darkened by prejudice. In the conversation the Dean 'expressly denied the assurance of faith, and earnest of the Spirit.' In June and July, 1739, other interviews occurred. By that time his prejudice was confirmed. Charles Wesley says 'he explained away all inward religion and union with God . . . used his utmost address to bring me off from preaching abroad, from expounding in houses, from singing psalms; denied justification by faith only, and all vital religion; promised me, however, to read Law and Pascal.'[1] Notwithstanding their differences in opinion the Dean continued to treat Charles Wesley with civility. If the two men had been able to perceive the mutual relations of their work, if they had seen that in order to bring about a permanent revival of religion in the nation the apologist and the evangelist are both necessary, civility might have passed into appreciative friendship. Canon Overton's verdict recurs to us when closing our description of these interviews. 'The Evangelical Revival could never have been the force it was unless it had been preceded by the work which was done most effectually by those who placed Christianity upon a thoroughly firm intellectual basis. Such men as Butler and Waterland and Conybeare and Law not only paved the way for the Wesleys and Whitefield, for Newton, Venn, and Cecil, but rendered their mission possible; and as the former group could never have done the work of the latter, so neither could the latter have ever done the work of the former. The one set lacked the fire of energy, the other intellectual equipment.'[2]

[1] C. Wesley's *Journal*, i., 137, 156.
[2] *A History of the English Church*, 1714–1800, vii., 4.

XVI

CONFLICTS WITH THE LAW

When John Wesley returned from Germany, in September, 1738, he found a sphere of work in the old Religious Societies. After years of sluggishness they were beginning to feel the impulses of a new life, and he was often asked to expound in them. In the new Religious Society in Fetter Lane there was much work to be done. His long absence had been unfavourable to the increase of his influence; but, on his return, he frequently attended its meetings and visited the bands. The Society consisted of thirty-two persons. James Hutton had taken his place as president while he was away, and other men had become prominent. A tendency towards Moravianism, which afterwards became strongly developed, had begun to declare itself, and we shall see that it so persisted as to result in a decisive change of the spirit and the form of the Society.

On Monday, October 9, John Wesley set out on a walk to Oxford. It was the city of his desire, and we can imagine the delight with which he made his way along the roads and country lanes, and watched the glory of the autumn landscape. It was his custom to read as he walked, and the book in his hands carried his thoughts back to America. Gradually the book absorbed all his attention, and ceasing to dream dreams he saw visions. It contained a description of the wonderful revival in Northampton, New England, under the ministry of Jonathan Edwards. Out of two hundred families in the town scarcely one person remained who was not an earnest seeker of salvation. From Northampton the revival had spread through the colony. Those who are familiar with the story of *The Great Awakening in America* will remember Jonathan Edwards's description of it. He says: 'The work is very glorious if we consider the extent of it, being in this respect vastly beyond any former outpouring of the Spirit that ever was known in New England. There has formerly sometimes been a remarkable awakening and success of the means of grace in some particular congregation, and this used to be much taken notice of and acknowledged to be glorious, though the towns and congregations round about continued dead; but now God has brought to pass a new thing; He has wrought a work of this nature that has extended from one end of the land to the other, besides what has been wrought in other British colonies in America.' As Wesley read this glowing description he must have thought of his own country, and caught a glimpse of work to be done, not only among Religious Societies and friendly Christian congregations, but also among the lost people of England.

During his brief stay in Oxford Wesley was busy in arranging his affairs, but he found time to preach at the castle, to visit the Religious Societies, and to write letters to his friends in Holland and Germany. From the letters we learn facts of considerable importance. Writing to the Church at Herrnhut, he says that though he and his brother were not permitted to preach in most of the Churches in London, yet there were others left wherein they had liberty to speak the truth as it is in Jesus. Likewise every evening, and on set evenings in the week at two several places, they published the word of reconciliation sometimes to twenty or thirty, sometimes to fifty or sixty, sometimes to three or four hundred persons, met together to hear it. He also states that he knows ten ministers in England 'who lay the right foundation, "the blood of Christ cleanseth us from all sin."' In addition, he mentions two or three Baptist and Presbyterian ministers who, to his knowledge, 'teach the way of God in truth.' In his letter to Dr. Koker, of Rotterdam, he declares that the Spirit of God had wrought so powerfully both in London and Oxford that there was a general awakening, and multitudes were crying out, 'What must we do to be saved.' Until more labourers were sent into the harvest all his time was too little for them. It is impossible to read these words without hearing the sound of the wind that was to stir the nation with new life.[1]

During this visit to Oxford John Wesley spent some time in 'correcting proofs.' There can be little doubt that he was then preparing the *Collection of Psalms and Hymns* published

---

[1] Whitehead's *Life of Wesley*, ii., 88, 92.

in 1738. A full account of this rare volume is given in Dr. Osborn's *Outlines of Wesleyan Bibliography*. Only two copies are known to be in existence ; one is in the Archiepiscopal Library at Lambeth, the other in the safe of Didsbury College, Manchester. The book follows the plan of the Charlestown *Collection*. Among the writers of the hymns Dr. Watts occupies the principal place in point of number ; Norris and Herbert are prominent, their contributions being altered by Wesley's hand ; and Bishop Ken's morning, evening, and midnight hymns enrich the little volume. John Wesley's translations from the German are exceptionally valuable. ' Thou, Jesu, art our King,' by an unknown author ; Tersteegen's ' Thou hidden love of God ' ; Zinzendorf's ' O Thou to whose all-searching sight ' ; and Winckler's ' Shall I, for fear of feeble man,' arrest attention. The hymn from the Spanish, ' O God, my God, my all Thou art ' makes its first appearance in its English translation, and carries our thoughts back to the garden of the parsonage in Savannah.[1]

John Wesley left Oxford and returned to London. On October 20 he and his brother Charles waited on Bishop Gibson to answer the complaints made against them for preaching the doctrine of assurance. After they had explained to him their teaching the Bishop said ' If by " assurance " you mean an inward persuasion, whereby a man is conscious in himself, after examining his life by the law of God, and weighing his own sincerity, that he is in a state of salvation, and acceptable to God, I don't see how any good Christian can be without such an assurance.' Being satisfied on this point, the question of preaching ' justification by faith only ' was raised. Dr. Gibson soon dismissed this point with the remark, ' Can any one preach otherwise who agrees to our Church and the Scriptures ? ' Going on to the practice of rebaptizing adults, John Wesley explained that if a person who was dissatisfied with ay baptism should desire episcopal he thought it his duty to administer it, after having acquainted the bishop according to the canon. The Bishop replied, ' Well, I am against it myself, where any one has had the Dissenters' baptism.'

The most interesting, if not the most important, subject debated in this interview concerned the relation of the Conventicle Act to the meetings of the Religious Societies. Dr.

[1] See art. by Mr. C. D. Hardcastle, *W.H.S. Proceedings*, iii., 57-63.

Gibson, the author of the *Codex*, answered John Wesley's questions warily. When he was asked, 'Are the Religious Societies conventicles?' he replied that he thought not, but referred his questioner to the Acts and Laws, and said he would determine nothing. It is clear that the Bishop was not prepared for this searching question, and that, like a prudent jurist, he would not give a decided opinion in the absence of documents. Subsequently he re-examined the statute, and reached conclusions on the subject of conventicles that led him into literary conflicts with Wesley and Whitefield. The subject is so important that we must now consider it.

Archdeacon Hutton, in the volume he contributed to the *History of the English Church*, accurately describes the Conventicle and the Five Mile Acts, passed in the reign of Charles II, as the 'Persecuting Acts,' and declares they were a grave infringement of true liberty of conscience. The modern apologist's only excuse for them is that they were in harmony with the spirit of the age. The religious and political controversies of the seventeenth century were carried on ruthlessly. Episcopalians and Presbyterians, when they were in power, seized the civil sword and struck at their adversaries. Their attacks and counter-attacks may be detected in legislative measures which blotted the English statute-book. The origin of the 'persecutions' may be traced to the attempts made on both sides, to impose uniformity of worship on the nation. Once more it was demonstrated that the preachers of uniformity are often the chief makers of divisions.[1] Blind to the fact that there can be no true unity without diversity it was determined that a standard of worship and Church government should be set up, to which all should conform or be subjected to penalties which included the forfeiture of life.

It will be sufficient for our purpose if we remind our reader that, in the reign of Queen Elizabeth, an Act was passed 'For the Uniformity of Common Prayer and Service in the Church and Administration of the Sacraments.' That Act is still sometimes printed in copies of the Anglican Prayer Book. It bristles with penalties. Passing by those which apply to the clergy, which include imprisonment for life, it will be enough to direct attention to a section relating to attendance

[1] Gwatkin's *Early Church History*, ii., 223.

CONFLICTS WITH THE LAW 227

at public worship. It is as follows : 'All and every person or persons inhabiting within this Realm, or any other the Queen's Majesty's Dominions, shall diligently and faithfully, having no lawful or reasonable excuse to be absent, endeavour themselves to resort to their Parish Church or Chapel accustomed, or upon reasonable let thereof, to some usual place, where Common Prayer, and such service of God, shall be used in such time of let, upon every Sunday, and other days ordained and used to be kept as Holy-days, and then and there to abide orderly and soberly during the time of Common Prayer, Preachings, or other Service of God there to be used, and ministered ; upon pain of Punishment by the Censures of the Church, and also upon pain that every person so offending shall forfeit for every such offence, twelve pence, to be levied by the Churchwardens of the Parish where such offence shall be done, to the use of the Poor of the same Parish, of the Goods, Lands, and Tenements of such offender, by way of distress.' For the due execution of the provisions of the Act full power and authority was given to the archbishops and bishops and their officers exercising ecclesiastical jurisdiction, to reform, correct, and punish by censures of the Church all persons who should offend within their jurisdictions or diocese, and power was also given to Justices of Oyer and determiner or Justices of Assize, in their open and general Sessions, to inquire, hear, and determine all and all manner of offences that should be committed or done contrary to any article contained in the Act.

The money penalty inflicted on absentees from services may seem slight, but the censures of the Church were formidable. It is well known, however, that the Act failed to secure its object, notwithstanding a subsequent increase in the money penalty. It is to be noted that, notwithstanding their objection to some parts of the service, many Puritans continued to frequent the churches in Queen Elizabeth's time. They were strong Protestants, and faithful supporters of the Reformation. In process of time, while still attending their parish churches they began to find a means of relief in small assemblies where a form of worship and fellowship more in accordance with their convictions and feelings could be used and enjoyed. These assemblies gradually became constituted on the Presbyterian model ; but it must be noted that the persons attending these meetings, if called non-conformists, were non-conformists within the Church of England.

During the Civil War the balance of power changed in favour of those who sought to impose the Presbyterian form of worship and government on the Church of England. Using its opportunity, Parliament caused the Book of Common Prayer to be laid aside in the churches, and by an ordinance dated January 3, 1645, ' A Directory of Public Worship ' was substituted for it. The introduction of the new book was opposed ; and so, to quicken the process of its acceptance, another ordinance was passed, dated August 23, 1645, which arranged for the distribution of the ' Directory ' so that a copy of it might be in the hands of each minister in England and Wales. It was further directed that, on the Sunday following the reception of the new book, the several ministers were to read it openly in their respective churches before the morning sermon. The ordinance then forbids the use of the Common Prayer Book in any church, chapel, or place of public worship, or in any private place or family, under a penalty of five pounds for the first, and ten pounds for the second offence ; for the third the punishment of a year's imprisonment was to be inflicted. It was further ordered that such ministers as did not observe the ' Directory ' in all exercises of public worship were to be made liable to a penalty of forty shillings, and those who, with design to bring the book into contempt, or to raise opposition to it, should preach, write, or print anything in derogation of it were to forfeit not less than five and not more than fifty pounds, the money to be given to the poor. All Common Prayer Books remaining in parish churches or chapels were to be removed and disposed of as directed by the ordinance. Neal, after describing the contents of the ordinance, says :

> These were the firstfruits of Presbyterian uniformity, and are equally to be condemned with the severities and oppressions of the late times ; for though it should be admitted that the Parliament or legislature had a right to abrogate the use of the Common Prayer Book in churches, was it not highly unreasonable to forbid the reading of it in private families, or closets ? Surely the devotion of a private family could be no disturbance to the public ; nor is it any excuse to say that very few suffered by it, because the law is still the same, and equally injurious to the natural rights of mankind.[1]

[1] *History of the Puritans*, ii., 277.

CONFLICTS WITH THE LAW

In 1662 the wheel of fortune turned; the Episcopalians once more were in power, and were bent on revenge. After the Book of Common Prayer had been revised by men, some of whom were strongly influenced by the spirit of Laud, the 'Directory' was removed from the churches and the new book was ordered to be read therein. The Houses of Parliament passed the well-known Act of Uniformity, the provisions of which we have stated in our account of John Westley and Dr. Annesley. The penalties of the new Act came into force on August 24, 1662. Those who believe in the inflexibility of justice will be confirmed in their convictions when they note that it was on August 23, 1645, that the ordinance was passed introducing the 'Directory' into the churches.

The Episcopalians, intent on securing uniformity in religious worship, soon found that the Act of Uniformity needed to be supplemented. The Presbyterians who had been accustomed to meet in private assemblies continued their practices. The Parliament determined to make such meetings impossible. In 1664 an Act was passed which made illegal all assemblies, conventicles, or meetings, held ' under colour or pretence of religion,' which were conducted in other manner than was allowed by the liturgy and practice of the Church of England. The first Conventicle Act, the truculence of which may be judged from the fact that it contained a death penalty which was to be inflicted on Nonconformists who, having been banished the country, should escape from the American colonies and return to England, lapsed through efflux of time. In 1670 a second Act was passed which was not repealed until 1812. As this was the Act which Bishop Gibson commended to the perusal of John Wesley it deserves special consideration.

The Conventicle Act of 1670 runs along the main lines of the Act of 1664. The application of the Act is confined to England, Wales, and Berwick-on-Tweed. It enacts that if any person of the age of sixteen or upwards shall be present at any assembly, conventicle, or meeting, under colour or pretence of any exercises of religion in other manner than according to the liturgy and practice of the Church of England, at which there should be five persons or more assembled together, over and beside those of the same household, if it be in a house where there is a family inhabiting, or if it be in a house, field, or place where there is no family inhabiting, then it shall be lawful for any one or more justices of the peace of the county, limit, division, corporation, or liberty, or for the chief magistrate of the place where the offence shall be committed, to proceed according to the directions of the Act and to inflict the penalties therein contained. It is interesting to mark a change made in the later Act in the description of the places in which conventicles were forbidden to assemble. In addition to the houses in which there was ' a family inhabiting,' it was found necessary to guard against the practice of holding secret services in the open air. All who are acquainted with the history of Nonconformity are aware that, during the persecution, such services were often held. At the present day the scenes of these hidden gatherings are still pointed out. Rivington Pike, in Lancashire, is a monument that speaks aloud of the sufferings of harried men and women who were faithful to the commands of conscience in those dark days; the hollows of Durdham Down, Bristol, continue the story; and, though the glades of the King's Wood, near the western city, have vanished, the neighbourhood speaks to some of us of the endurance of the little companies of Broadmead Baptists who sought to worship there in peace. There are few places in England which are without these memories of the reign of the Stuarts. In order to stop the practice the Act of 1664 prohibited assemblies for worship not only in outhouses, barns, or rooms, and yards, but also in ' woods or grounds.' The later Act omits the words ' woods or grounds,' but, by substituting for them ' a house, field, or place where there is no family inhabiting,' it extends its prohibitions. It must also be remembered that the Act contained special provisions for inflicting penalties on persons who should take upon themselves to preach or teach in any meeting, assembly, or conventicle.[1]

Bearing these facts in mind, it will be seen that John Wesley's question concerning the relation of the Conventicle Act to the meetings of the Religious Societies was of exceptional importance. We do not wonder at Dr. Gibson's hesitating reply. He knew that everything depended on the answer to the question, ' Are their proceedings " exercises of religion " in accordance with the liturgy and practice of the Church of England ? ' If not, the Act, with its penalties, applied to them. The

---

[1] For articles on the Acts of Uniformity and the Conventicle Acts see *W.H.S. Proceedings*, xi., 82, 103.

managers of the earlier Religious Societies were aware of the fact, and sometimes were driven to the adoption of questionable expedients to avoid prosecution. It must be borne in mind that the Conventicle Act does not contain any clause exempting members of the Church of England from its penalties. When the Toleration Act was passed in 1689, the rule of the Religious Societies limiting membership to persons who belonged to the Church of England became a source of danger. The Act gave relief, under certain conditions, to Protestants dissenting from the Church of England, and to no one else. Churchmen were still bound by the provisions of the Act of Uniformity. The restricting force of that Act had been greatly strengthened in the reign of Queen Anne. In 1705 the Lord Justices appointed under the provisions of the Succession Act were restrained and disabled from giving the royal assent to any Bill or Bills for the repealing or altering the Act of Uniformity passed in the reign of Charles II, and it was declared that those of them who concurred in giving such assent should be guilty of high treason, and should suffer and forfeit as in case of high treason.[1] In 1706, when the union of England and Scotland took place, it was enacted that the Act of Uniformity, other than such clauses as had been repealed or altered by subsequent Act or Acts of Parliament, 'shall remain and be in force for ever.'[2] The weight of the Act of Uniformity had been greatly lightened in the case of Dissenters, but, without any alleviation, it pressed on the members of the Church of England. This remarkable result of the passing of the Toleration Act is an illustration of the purblindness of the persecutor.

The members of the Religious Societies whose zeal was tempered with some knowledge of English law were conscious of the insecurity of their position. They constantly attended the services and sacraments of the Church, and thereby demonstrated their loyalty, but they were not entirely reassured. In some instances, under the direction of Dr. Woodward, they made an attempt to bring the religious exercises of their meetings into accordance with the liturgy and practice of the Church of England. We have seen that a liturgical service was drawn up and used. But no one who examines it will fail to see that, however admirable it is in spirit and in construction, it is not the liturgy of the English

[1] 4, 5 Anne, cap. 8.   [2] 5, 6 Anne, cap. 5.

Church. Not only so; its use by laymen and its serious divergences from the form legalized by Parliament brought those who used it into conflict with the Act of Uniformity, and exposed them to the penalties of the Conventicle Act. There can be no doubt that, in the eighteenth century, the situation of the Religious Societies that were unprotected by the Toleration Act was grave.

The interview between Dr. Gibson and John and Charles Wesley closed pleasantly, the bishop assuring them that they might have free access to him at all times. The Wesleys went their way to continue their work. On November 7 we find them, in Newgate, pointing the condemned prisoners to the only Saviour of sinners. The following day, at the earnest request of the men, they attended them to Tyburn. In John Wesley's *Journal* and *Diary* we get a glimpse of the little company in the midst of the crowd that pressed around the gallows. We hear the voice of the singers. Glancing at the *Diary*, we note the phrase ' hath died,' and judge that the hymn sung is Charles Wesley's ' Hymn to Christ.' The condemned men were all cheerful. Concerning them John Wesley writes, ' It was the most glorious instance I ever saw of faith triumphing over sin and death.' One of the men, just before his execution, was asked a question, to which he replied, ' I feel a peace which I could not have believed to be possible. And I know it is the peace of God which passeth all understanding.' We are not informed of the crimes for which they suffered the extreme penalty of the law. It may have been the picking of a pocket of twelvepence and a farthing, stealing a horse or a sheep, purloining goods in a shop of the value of five shillings, snatching property from the hands of a man and running away with it, or murder. At that time men and women were liable to be done to death in England for actions that amounted in number to upwards of one hundred and sixty.[1] Offences that would now receive only a slight sentence were enough to send a man to Tyburn, to be hanged there amidst the howlings of a hardened mob. It is no wonder that the kindness of the Wesleys and their companions touched the hearts of the criminals, and that they listened eagerly to the good news of salvation.

On November 8, when the hangman had done his work, the

---

[1] Sydney's *England in the Eighteenth Century*, ii., 268-72.

crowd began to move away; but many lingered, for Charles Wesley, as on a previous occasion, preached to them. He had a very sympathetic listener standing at his side. John Wesley, who was passing through a storm of temptation concerning his own religious experience, heard the words that were spoken to the 'large assembly of publicans and sinners.' We can read his thoughts in the prayer which he afterwards wrote in his *Journal*: 'O Lord God of my fathers, accept even me among them, and cast me not out from among Thy children.' Charles Wesley was not the only preacher on that day. The helpful ministry of the *Diary* reveals the fact that John Wesley also preached to the mob at Tyburn. It was under such extraordinary circumstances that he, in England, recommenced his practice of preaching in the open air.[1]

After the execution at Tyburn Charles Wesley went to Bexley, and on November 10 John Wesley set out once more for Oxford. It is necessary to follow, first, the footsteps of Charles Wesley. We have seen that the churches of London were being closed against the brothers. The doctrines they preached were obnoxious to the mass of London churchmen, and the crowds they attracted inconvenienced the old congregations. It was alleged that the multitudes filling the churches 'left no room for the best of the parish.' Whatever may have been the reason, it was clear that the opportunities of preaching were diminishing, and threatened to disappear. Towards the end of 1738 that danger was imminent. When Charles Wesley went to St. Antholin's the clerk asked him his name, told him that Dr. Venn had forbidden any Methodist to preach, and then inquired, ' Do you call yourself a Methodist ? ' He replied ' I do not; the world may call me what they please.' The clerk rejoined, ' Well, sir, it is a pity the people should go away without preaching. You may preach.' Having received this permission, he preached to the congregation on good works. Among the churches still open to the Wesleys in London and its neighbourhood there were two in which it seemed that their ministry would continue to be welcomed—Bexley and Islington. But clouds were gathering over each of these places. When Charles Wesley arrived in Bexley he expected to join the little Society which had been formed there. He found, however, that Mr. Piers, through dread of the world's

---

[1] *Journal*, ii., 100 n.

threatenings, had left off the meeting on Wednesday night. However, he stayed until Sunday, when he expected to preach. It was then that the pulpit was refused him, ' through fear of man,' Mr. Piers alleging ' tenderness to his flock.' Charles Wesley's temper was touched, and he plainly told his friend that if he so rejected his testimony he would come to see him no more. He then left the house and returned to London, where he expounded in one of the Societies. At Islington the prospect was brighter, but it was soon to be overcast. It is impossible to ignore the fact that the use of the churches by the Wesleys was at the mercy of hostile clergymen and churchwardens, whose legal position was strong. In order to exclude the new preachers it was only necessary that the law should be enforced.

John Wesley's theory concerning his right to preach in a church was simple. It rested, first, on the fact that, when he was ordained priest, the bishop said to him, ' Take thou authority to preach the word of God ! ' and secondly, on the usage of the time. It had been his custom to preach in a church when requested to do so by the incumbent, and he understood that such a request was all that was necessary. When his theory was challenged he was surprised. It must be remembered that, in the eighteenth century, ecclesiastical discipline was in an utterly unsatisfactory condition. Statute law and canon law were, in many places, ignored, and general laxity prevailed. But it was always possible to find bishops, clergymen, and laymen who were less ignorant than their fellow churchmen, and they proved themselves formidable opponents of those who were guilty of ecclesiastical irregularities. Dr. Gibson had a large knowledge of church law, and it was impossible for him to accept Wesley's position. He knew that when a bishop gave a man authority to preach and to administer the sacraments he said more than the words Wesley so often quoted. He added, ' In the congregation where thou shalt be lawfully appointed thereunto.' As to usage, he was aware that it must never be pleaded against the express provisions of statute law. The law was clear. The canons of 1603 state that ' neither the minister, churchwardens, nor any other officers of the church, shall suffer any man to preach within their churches or chapels, but such as, by showing their licence to preach, shall appear unto them to be sufficiently authorized thereunto'; and provision is made for detecting those who presume to preach without licence. It is directed that 'the churchwardens and sidesmen shall see that the names of all preachers, which come to their church from any other place, be noted in a book, which they shall have ready for that purpose; wherein every preacher shall subscribe his name, the day when he preached, and the name of the bishop of whom he had licence to preach.' If the provision concerning the licensing of preachers rested exclusively on canon law it might be said that the chaotic condition of church discipline in Wesley's time justified him in treating the regulations we have quoted as obsolete. It is impossible to admit such a plea. The Act of Uniformity, which had received renewed vitality by the legislation of Parliament in the reign of Queen Anne, provides 'that no person shall be, or be received as a lecturer, or permitted, suffered, or allowed to preach as a lecturer, or to preach or read any sermon, or lecture in any church, chapel, or other place of public worship, within this realm of England, or dominion of Wales, and town of Berwick-upon-Tweed, unless he be first approved and thereunto licensed by the archbishop of the province, or bishop of the diocese, or (in case the see be void) by the guardian of the spiritualities, under his seal.' The licensing of preachers, and especially of strangers, was essential to the realization of the purposes of the Act of Uniformity, and the penalties for preaching without a licence, stated in the Act, were severe.

Charles Wesley soon had an opportunity of gaining a little insight into the condition of the law. On November 14 he waited on the Bishop of London in order to consult him on the subject of the rebaptism of Dissenters. Dr. Gibson maintained his former position. He wholly disapproved of such rebaptisms, and considered them irregular. But he asked his interviewer, 'Who gave you authority to baptize?' As the Bishop had ordained him, Charles Wesley replied, 'Your lordship; and I shall exercise it in any part of the known world.' 'Are you a licenced curate?' was the next question, to which the naïve answer was, 'I have the leave of the proper minister.' 'But,' said Dr. Gibson, 'don't you know, no man can exercise parochial duty in London without my leave?' He reminded Charles Wesley that he had power to inhibit him. 'Do you now inhibit me?' But to the question no decisive reply was given. The conversation turned into other channels, and the Bishop closed the interview. It is impossible to read the description of the interview without admiring the patience of Dr. Gibson. At one point he cried, ' Oh, why will you push things to an extreme ? ' It would have been a relief to him if he could have prevailed by persuasion ; but that course was denied him. As he hesitated to inhibit, Charles Wesley held on his way. He baptized a woman in Islington Church with ' hypothetical baptism,' a curious compromise, seemingly derived from a suggested arrangement concerning the re-ordination of Presbyterian ministers by the bishops of the Established Church.

The discussion between the Bishop of London and Charles Wesley chiefly concerned the question of baptism, but it throws light on other questions which arise when we consider the proceedings of the Wesleys at this critical time. How far the preaching of the brothers at Tyburn may be considered a form of 'field-preaching' we may leave undecided ; but it is necessary to note the fact that, in some private houses, the members of the Religious Societies were receiving the Sacrament of the Lord's Supper. Charles Wesley was present at several of these celebrations, and speaks of the comfort he derived from them. We are especially interested in another departure from strict Church rule. John Wesley says that Joseph Humphreys was the first lay preacher who assisted him in England, and that such assistance was given him in 1738.[1] We judge that the employment of Humphreys was in connexion with Wesley's work in the Religious Societies. It was in harmony with practice. We have noted the employment of laymen in the services held under the Woodward scheme, and we know that James Hutton occasionally preached to the members in Fetter Lane. He did so with some amount of secrecy, lest the news should reach the ears of his father, who was sternly opposed to the preaching of laymen. In reading Wesley's statement concerning Humphreys it is important to emphasize the significant words ' in England,' and to remember the assistance that Charles Delamotte and others gave him in Georgia. The facts cited show that, towards the end of 1738, a number of questions of church order were arising in connexion with the work of the Wesleys which were certain to raise hostile criticism.

[1] *Works*, iv., 493, 8vo ed.

CONFLICTS WITH THE LAW 237

On November 30 George Whitefield landed in England, his arrival having been preceded by that of Charles Delamotte. On December 11 John and Charles Wesley, who were at Oxford, hastened to meet him in London. On the next day Whitefield preached to a vast throng in St. Helen's Church, Charles Wesley being present to hear him. His return was opportune, and his enthusiasm inspired his old companions. On Christmas Day, and during the week following, Islington Church witnessed remarkable scenes. The Wesleys, Whitefield, and Mr. Robson were the preachers. There was a daily administration of the Sacrament. Charles Wesley says, ' The whole week was a festival indeed ; a joyful season, holy unto the Lord.' As we look on this remarkable group of men thought is busy. They met at a grave crisis in the history of religion in England, and we listen to their conversations with profound interest. If we did not hold the key of the future in our hand we should hesitate to predict that these were the men who were destined to bring about the moral and spiritual reformation of England. Everything was against them. So long as they continued true to their convictions there was no room for them in the Church if its rulers inexorably insisted that all its laws and regulations must be scrupulously obeyed. Looking at the men themselves, what hope can we indulge that they will accomplish their superhuman task ? The greatest man in the group is undoubtedly John Wesley. At the close of 1738 the physical weakness that had come to him in Georgia still oppressed him. The anxious eyes of Charles Wesley discerned it ; and he was reluctantly compelled to conclude that, before long, his brother would die. That was not all. John Wesley's mind, at this time, was oppressed by uncertainties concerning his religious state. He was in the Kingdom, but the steady light of the Kingdom was denied him. The temptation to break off his work, and to wait in quietness and stillness for the coming of a perfect assurance, was strong, and he had nearly yielded to it. Oxford allured him, and he longed to rest there in seclusion. His tastes, friendships, inherited instincts, all cried out against the wandering life of a national evangelist. It seemed impossible that he could be God's selected instrument to bring the good news of salvation, not only to England, but also to the world. George Whitefield was a man of another type, but he was ' on the wing.' He had come to England to be ordained priest, to collect money for the contemplated orphanage in Georgia, and, these things being accomplished, he was to take his flight to America. As to Charles Wesley, he was being urged by his brother, George Whitefield, and others, to settle in Oxford. He resisted the pressure, but was on the point of yielding. The living of Cowley became vacant early in 1739; he offered for it, but did not obtain it. As we watch these men, and catch sight of the difficulties that confront them, it seems impossible that they can become the evangelists of the new era. Looking at them, as they sit together in Islington Church, we say: ' If this counsel or this work be of men, it will be overthrown.'

XVII

THE APPROACHING CRISIS

THE year 1739 was of exceptional importance in the life of John Wesley. It began well. The festival week at the old Church of St. Mary's, Islington, was followed by a remarkable love-feast held in Fetter Lane. Sixty members of the Society, and seven clergymen of the Church of England, were present, the latter group including John and Charles Wesley and George Whitefield. In the 'Orders' of the Fetter Lane Religious Society an arrangement was made for the carrying on of 'continual intercession' by day and night. After the love-feast a company lingered that they might continue 'instant in prayer.' About three o'clock, in the darkness of the night, a great experience came to the watchmen. John Wesley says, 'The power of God came mightily upon us, insomuch as many cried out for exceeding joy, and many fell to the ground. As soon as we were recovered a little from that awe and amazement at the presence of His majesty we broke out with one voice, "We praise Thee, O God; we acknowledge Thee to be the Lord."' Some of those who were present must have been reminded of the hour in the 'upper room' in Jerusalem, when Peter and John returned to their own company, and reported all that the chief-priests and the elders had said unto them. 'When they had prayed, the place was shaken wherein they were gathered together; and they were all filled with the Holy Ghost, and they spake the word of God with boldness.' This experience made a deep impression on Wesley, and prepared him for the hard journey that lay before him during the months of a most exacting year.

John Wesley, at this time, had a sentence of death within himself. He did not expect to live long. It was fortunate that, during his visit to London, he had some opportunities of escape from 'the busy ways of men.' We see him in St. Paul's Cathedral, in the little congregation of devout worshippers gathered there for evensong. His sensitive spirit was touched by the music and the noble words of the liturgy, and the memory of the May evening in the year just closed must have spoken to him of the peace that passeth understanding. He had another place of retreat. A friend of his, Mr. Agutter, one of the Gentlemen Pensioners of the Charterhouse, provided a quiet room in which he could hide himself, compose sermons, correct proofs, and write letters. When weary, he walked in the grounds and meditated. We must not forget the thoughtful kindness of this ' brother ' of the Charterhouse !

Wesley was a man possessed of an exceptional capacity for bearing responsibility. He had an active conscience and great boldness; but he was becoming aware of the fact that he was destined to carry, not only his own burdens, but those of other people. He often wondered at his freedom from care, and, in one of those personal confessions which are so suggestive, he admits that he was in danger of ascribing that freedom to his own strength; but, now and again, anxiety threatened him. It is difficult to understand how, as he walked about the Charterhouse grounds, he could preserve his radiant cheerfulness. He had cause for serious thought. The condition of the Fetter Lane Society was not satisfactory. It is necessary once more to emphasize the fact that, at this time, it was a Religious Society in connexion with the Church of England. The presence of the seven clergymen at the love-feast is strong evidence of that fact. No doubt on this subject would have arisen had the historian submitted himself to the tyranny of dates. The members had reason to admire the doctrines taught by the Moravians, and were conscious of their obligations to Peter Böhler and other German teachers; they also valued and adopted some of the disciplinary methods, modes of worship and of service in use at Herrnhut. Up to this time, however, loyalty to the Church of England was a dominant feature in the Society; but influences were beginning to assert themselves that jeopardized that loyalty and led to discord and division.

It must not be supposed that the divisive influences to which we have referred were exclusively or mainly Moravian. The supposition has led to expressions of opinion unjust to the United Brethren. We must take a broader view if we are to arrive at a right conclusion concerning the events which disturbed the peace of the Fetter Lane Society. It is a significant fact that twice in January, 1739, John Wesley came in contact with persons who might justly be deemed 'enthusiasts.' The entry in his *Journal* on January 17 is: ' I was with two persons who, I doubt, are properly enthusiasts. For, first, they think to attain the end without the means; which is enthusiasm, properly so called. Again, they think themselves inspired by God, and are not. But false, imaginary inspiration is enthusiasm. That theirs is only imaginary inspiration appears hence; it contradicts the law and the testimony.' The persons to whom he alludes were Churchmen. The reference to them is useful, as it brings out a feature of their 'enthusiasm' which was reproduced in others who became conspicuous at a later stage. Eleven days later Wesley, yielding to importunity, went, with four or five of his friends, to an interview with a French prophetess. She was a young woman of an agreeable speech and behaviour. Being informed that her visitors had come to 'try the spirits,' she sat down, leaned back in her chair, and soon became the subject of strong convulsive movements. This state of agitation continued for about ten minutes, after which she quoted several texts of Scripture, ' as in the person of God.' They related to the fulfilling of the prophecies, the coming of Christ, which she declared to be at hand, and the spreading of the Gospel over all the earth. ' She added,' says Wesley, ' with many enforcements, that we must watch and pray, and take up our cross, and be still before God.' Her prophetic utterances were commonplace, but her last words ' to be still before God ' were destined, a little later, to acquire special significance. Wesley sums up his impressions of the interview in cautious words : ' Two or three of our company were much affected, and believed she spoke by the Spirit of God. But this was in no wise clear to me. The motion might be either hysterical or artificial. And the same words any person of a good understanding and well versed in the Scriptures might have spoken. But I let the matter alone ; knowing this, that " if it be not of God it will come to nought." '

The ' French prophets ' were well known in England at the beginning of the eighteenth century. They were a kind of by-product of the great immigration of Protestant refugees who left France after the revocation of the Edict of Nantes. To that immigration we owe a debt of gratitude for the inestimable benefits it conferred on the religious and commercial life of this country. Among those benefits we do not number 'the prophets.' Southey's description of them is well known.[1] In Mr. Haycroft's edition of the *Broadmead Records* we get further information concerning them. Writing in 1720, Mr. Foskett, who was then the minister of the Broadmead Baptist Church, Bristol, tells us he was present at a meeting when inquiry was made into the conduct of two of the women members who had been drawn away from association with the Baptist Church 'by a sect of fanatics calling themselves prophets.' He says:

> These men and women pretend to speak by immediate inspiration, having their bodies agitated before they begin to speak. They say they cannot help this agitation, and that they have what they deliver immediately given in to them. Their adherents neglected the stated assemblies of Christians of every denomination, and say there is a new dispensation, in which God pours out His Spirit to enable persons to deliver His mind without study. They, therefore, lightly esteem men that preach what they have premeditated as not being partakers of the Spirit according to the present dispensation. This method and pretence was first set on foot about thirty years since among the Cevennes in France, and about sixteen years since began in London, and spread to other parts of the kingdom. We do not understand that sinners have been converted by their ministrations in any place. The novelty of the thing makes some persons flock to hear them; and some few serious persons are stumbled by them, and prevented from due attendance on the stated means of grace.[2]

Southey declares that the French prophets were the scandal of their own Church, and adds that when they sent deputies to Count Zinzendorf expressing a desire to unite themselves with the Moravian Brethren 'he objected to their neglect of the Sacrament, to their separating themselves from other congregations, and more especially to the hideous circumstances attending their pretended inspirations.'[3] If John Wesley could have foreseen the events which were soon to happen he would have expressed a more hostile opinion on the performances of the French prophetess.

Among the few churches still open to the Wesleys was Sir

---

[1] *Life of Wesley*, 165-68, Bohn's ed.   [2] p. 301.
[3] *Life of Wesley*, 168, Bohn's ed.

George Wheeler's proprietary chapel in Spitalfields. Charles Wesley often preached there during his brother's absence in Germany. But an incident soon occurred which revealed the precariousness of the privilege. John Wesley, having been requested to take the morning and afternoon services at the chapel on Sunday, February 18, promised to do so. He read prayers and preached in the morning, reserving part of his sermon for the afternoon. But when the morning service was over he was forbidden to preach again. In recording the incident he quietly says that it was a reminder that, if possible, he should declare at every time 'the whole counsel of God.' Three days later he and Charles Wesley waited on Dr. Potter, the Archbishop of Canterbury. They were graciously received. Describing the interview, Charles Wesley says: 'He showed us great affection; spoke mildly of Mr. Whitefield; cautioned us to give no more umbrage than was necessary for our own defence; to forbear exceptionable phrases; to keep to the doctrines of the Church. We told him we expected persecution; would abide by the Church till her articles and homilies were repealed. He assured us he knew of no design in the governors of the Church to innovate; and neither should there be any innovation while he lived; avowed justification by faith only; and his joy to see us as often as we pleased.' Dr. Potter knew the Wesleys when he was the Bishop of Oxford; he appreciated their worth, and held them in high esteem. If he had maintained the same spirit he would have been a counsellor whose kindly criticism and sound advice would have been invaluable. After their interview, the Wesleys waited on the Bishop of London. In their conversation Dr. Gibson denied having condemned them, or even having heard much of them. He told them that he had been reading Whitefield's *Journal*, a book of which he made use in his subsequent attacks on Methodism. He described it as being tainted with enthusiasm. As for Whitefield himself, he said that he looked on him as 'a pious, well-meaning youth.' He then warned his visitors against Antinomianism, and dismissed them kindly.[1]

On Sunday, February 25, Charles Wesley had the pleasure of preaching once more in Bexley Church. Mr. Piers had lifted his interdict, and the old friendship was resumed. But

---
[1] C. Wesley's *Journal*, i., 143-44.

there were some who resented his reappearance in the pulpit, and when he began to preach on justification by faith about twenty persons rose and left the church. The visit to Bexley, and the renewal of friendly relations with Mr. Piers, must have enheartened Charles Wesley at a time when he needed encouragement. The condition of the Fetter Lane Society was causing him much concern. In his *Journal* there are several brief entries which give us light on events otherwise obscure. We see the secret working of influences destined to produce decisive results in the near future; and it is possible to note the manner in which he acted in attempting to arrest them. He believed in the wisdom of resisting the beginnings of evil, and swiftly attacked opinions and practices which he believed to be erroneous and dangerous. In glancing over his *Journal* we note two records belonging to this period which possess great significance. Finding that the members of some of the Societies were running into wild notions he read to them Beveridge's sermon on the ministry; and, when meeting the bands at Bray's, he cautioned them against schism. On the latter occasion he tells us he was violently opposed ' by one who should have seconded him.' His admonitions were resented by the people present; they urged him to go to Oxford, hoping thus to get rid of him. ' But,' he says, ' I understood them, and begged to be excused.'[1]

The month of March, 1739, is conspicuous in the annals of Methodism. Its incidents must be carefully observed. On March 3 John Wesley left London for Oxford. He stayed there a few days, and then set out for Dummer, with Mr. Fox, in order to supply Mr. Kinchin's pulpit on the Sunday. The first day's journey brought him to Reading, where he stayed with John Cennick, a young man whom he describes as knowing in some measure the powers of the world to come. For two generations Cennick's family had been Quakers, and endured the persecution which then assailed the members of the Society of Friends. He had joined the Church of England, and through the instrumentality of Mr. Kinchin had come in contact with the Oxford Methodists. A week before John Wesley's visit he had formed a Society in Reading. The minister of the parish determined that this Society should not exist, and had wellnigh overturned it. Several of the members,

[1] C. Wesley's *Journal*, i., 144.

however, spent the evening with Wesley at Cennick's house, and were strengthened and comforted. With Cennick as a companion Wesley set out for Dummer. After preaching there, and also expounding in a room at Basingstoke, on March 12 Wesley and Cennick returned to Reading. It had been intended that the newly formed Society should meet in the evening, but the hostile clergyman had been busy in his parish; he had sent to or seen each of the members, and by arguing or threatening he had utterly confounded them, so that they were all scattered abroad. Among them was Cennick's sister, who was so afraid that, in order to escape an interview with her brother and Wesley, she left her house and avoided them. The policy of the parson was effective; but Wesley hoped that God would once more gather together the dispersed members of the little Society.

From Reading Wesley returned to Oxford, where he spent a few days in pleasant fellowship with the Societies, preaching once to the prisoners in the castle. We note that the 'bands' arrangement had been adopted in some of the Oxford Societies, and that many more people were rejoicing in God their Saviour. The spiritual work was prospering, in spite of opposition. Wesley records an instance of clerical intolerance. Mrs. Compton, who was a leading member of a Religious Society meeting at her house, had been visited by her parish minister, to whom she 'declared the thing as it was.' Relating her spiritual experience, she said that she never had a true faith in Christ until two in the afternoon on the Tuesday preceding. Wesley says, 'After some other warm and sharp expressions he told her, "Upon that word he must repel her from the Holy Communion." Finding that she was not convinced of her error, even by this argument, he left her calmly rejoicing in God her Saviour.'

Wesley left Oxford early on March 15, and in the afternoon reached London. At this point, for a few days, his *Journal* fails us, and we have to depend on glints of light emitted from the jottings in his *Diary*. He was fully occupied. On Sunday he preached at Islington in the morning, was present at evensong in St. Paul's, and closed the day by attending a women's love-feast at Fetter Lane. During this period he was much in request as an expounder in the Religious Societies. Passing by his more public work, it is interesting to mark the use he made of his retreat in the Charterhouse. The noise of London was softened by distance, and in the quietude of his little room he wrote letters to Dr. Doddridge, Whitefield, Clayton, Hervey, Ingham, Kinchin, Cennick, and others. He was also busy with important literary work. A third collection of religious verse was in hand, and that calls for special notice as the book had a determining influence on Wesley and hymnology. On March 19 he enters the following sentence in the *Diary*: ' At Agutter's, writ preface, read Luther.' We think that this entry must have reference to the volume entitled *Hymns and Sacred Poems*, published in 1739 and sold by James Hutton, and at ' Mr. Bray's, a Brazier in Little Britain.' The preface to that book is of exceptional significance. Admitting that some of the verses in the collection were written ' upon the scheme of the mystic divines,' Wesley explains his position in reference to men whom he and his brother once held in great veneration as the best explainers of the gospel of Christ. He shows wherein he had come to differ from them, and why he considered they did not teach the doctrines of Christ. It is easy to see that in defining the position of the mystics he spoke only of those with whose works he was acquainted. He attacked the teaching of 'common writers,' that we are justified for the sake of our outward righteousness, and of ' the mystics,' who teach that we are justified for the sake of our inward righteousness. He declared that neither our inward nor outward righteousness is the ground of our justification, and that the sole cause of our acceptance with God is the righteousness and the death of Christ, who fulfilled God's law, and died in our stead. As to the condition of our justification, he affirmed ' it is not our holiness, either of heart or life, but our faith alone ; faith contradistinguished from holiness as well as from good works.' He guarded himself by the statement that holiness of heart, as well as holiness of life, is not the cause of our justification but the effect of it. With Luther on his table, and the vivid memory of his own experience in his mind, we can understand the meaning of his uncompromising statements.

. After criticizing the manner in which the mystics laid the foundation, Wesley then attacks them for the way in which they built on it. He asserts that they cry ' To the desert, to the desert, and God will build you up,' and says, ' Numberless are the commendations that occur in all their writings, not of retirement intermixed with conversation, but of an entire seclusion from men, perhaps for months or years, in order to purify the soul.' He wrote with special emphasis on this point, for the recollection of the motives that drew him to Georgia was strong within him. As against the mystics who had misled him he asserts, ' According to the judgement of our Lord, and the writings of His apostles, it is only when we are knit together that we have nourishment from Him, and increase with the increase of God.' Whatever may be thought of the justice of his indictment, there can be no doubt that, when he was writing in the room in the Charterhouse, his conviction against the practice of a ' solitary religion ' was confirmed. He was not inclined to condemn the love of quietness that leads a man to seclude himself for a time in order that he may examine himself, and by meditation and prayer become more completely conscious of God. In the hymn-book he was about to publish there is a poem from the Latin, entitled ' Solitude,' and a ' Farewell to the World,' from the French, which seem out of harmony with the assertions of the preface. They reveal the influence of the best ' mystic divines '; but Wesley's own convictions are unmistakable. He says : ' The gospel of Christ knows of no religion but social ; no holiness but social holiness. Faith working by love is the length and breadth and depth and height of Christian perfection. This commandment have we from Christ, that he who loves God loves his brother also ; and that we manifest our love by doing good unto all men, especially to them that are of the household of faith. And, in truth, whosoever loveth his brethren not in word only, but as Christ loved him, cannot but be zealous of good works. He feels in his soul a burning, restless desire of spending and being spent for them. My Father, will he say, worketh hitherto, and I work ; and at all possible opportunities he is, like his Master, going about doing good.'[1]

In studying the contents of this book of *Hymns and Sacred Poems* we find that it differs strikingly from the *Collections* previously published. It is divided into two sections. Part I. shows that John Wesley's loyalty to Herbert continued undiminished, and that he still was allured by the great German hymns he translates with remarkable strength and gracefulness.

[1] *Poetical Works of J. and C. Wesley*, i., **xix.-xxiii.**, Pref.

But it is when we turn over the pages of Part II. that we are conscious of a new spirit moving like the refreshing breeze of a sunny day in spring. Hymns greet the eye that appeal at once to all who have known the sorrows of repentance and the bliss of assured pardon. They are the morning songs of the Renaissance, and Charles Wesley was the author. After his return to England, he suddenly broke into full song. For some months he was content to write out his hymns and sing them in the circle of his friends; but in 1739, in company with his brother, he began to give them to the world. When William Strahan, whose name stands high among English publishers, issued the little volume, he was, probably, unconscious of the effect it would produce; but he was noted for his good taste and keen discernment, and must have admired the literary excellence of its contents. He made his venture, and had the honour of printing a book which has profoundly influenced the worship of the Christian Church. Working quietly in the Charterhouse and among the Religious Societies in London, John Wesley was being prepared for an event which completely changed the whole course of his life.

XVIII

GEORGE WHITEFIELD

WHEN George Whitefield visited London in 1737, on his way to Georgia, he excited much popular enthusiasm. Many churches were open to him and were thronged by crowds of hearers. His preaching stirred the city. London was then a comparatively small place, its population being less than six hundred thousand. The advent of a young preacher of great dramatic power and of thrilling earnestness was an event which quickened the curiosity of many people. For a few weeks he was lionized. This popularity was not gained by any betrayal of his convictions. He did not adapt his denunciations of sin to the tastes of a fashionable audience, nor did he soften his words concerning the necessity of the new birth. He was unflinchingly faithful, and used his popularity as a means of bringing sinners to know themselves and to accept salvation. In not a few cases he had the joy of seeing men and women turning right round from sin to God. When he sailed homeward, on his return from Georgia, the memory of former triumphs must have cheered him; he must have dreamed of enthusiastic welcomes from the clergy and the congregations of the Church of England. But on landing he was disillusioned. He found that the embargo laid on the Wesleys was also placed on him. On December 10, 1738, he writes, 'Five churches have been already denied me, and some of the clergy, if possible, would oblige me to depart out of these coasts.' With the exception of St. Helen's in Bishopsgate, Christ Church in Spitalfields, Wapping Chapel, and the parish church at Islington, nearly all the London churches were closed against him. This was a great disappointment, and would have depressed a less sanguine man. It must be remembered that one of his objects in returning to England was to raise money for an orphanage in Georgia. A scheme for its erection had been under the consideration of the trustees of the colony for some time, and plans of the building had been submitted to them by Charles Wesley. The need was urgent. The epidemics recurring so frequently in the colony swept away scores of men and women, some of whom left children cast on public charity. The fight with disease and death in Savannah and Frederica was incessant. But succour from official sources in England was not easily transmitted. The erection of an orphan-house was imperative. Whitefield's sympathy with the sufferings of little children and their poverty-stricken relatives was acute, and he determined that he would make a personal appeal to the generous English people whom he trusted to help him to lessen the sum of human misery. In his musings on shipboard there was one vision he had not seen—the vision of the closed doors of the churches.

We have explained the reasons of the exclusion of the Wesleys from the churches, and it would have been remarkable if they had not prevailed in the case of Whitefield. It is possible that if he had stood aloof from his old friends, if he had repudiated them, he might have escaped their fate ; but he was incapable of such perfidy. He cast in his lot with them, and bore, in their company, the stress of the storm. His loyalty, without doubt, increased the prejudices of his opponents, and made it easier for them to secure his exclusion from the London churches. We cannot, however, put the whole weight of the opposition to Whitefield on his association with the Wesleys. It cannot be denied that the publication of his *Journal* produced a bad impression. The book was read and criticized, and its faults were unsparingly exposed. We can judge the character of the criticisms when we read *The Bishop of London's Pastoral Letter to the People of his Diocese*, issued on August 1, 1739. It contained nine charges against the Methodists, and all of them were supported exclusively by quotations from Whitefield's *Journal*. The quotations are ninety in number. In Dr. Gibson's *Pastoral Letter* we hear the echoes of conversations which occurred in parsonages and places where clergymen assembled. In addition to the prejudice created by the publication of his *Journal*, Whitefield's attitude towards Dissenters laid him under suspicion. It is often said that he was a Dissenter at heart. Without accepting this assertion in its entirety, it is certain his charity towards those who differed from him in matters of ecclesiastical government was much broader than that of the Churchmen of his time. It contrasted favourably with the spirit of the Wesleys. He had no hesitation in consorting with Dissenters. His Churchmanship was elastic; he was free from the fetters that hindered the progress of John Wesley for many years and hampered Charles Wesley to the end of his life. His broad views were distasteful to the clergy of the period; they irritated them and roused them to strong antagonism.

The prejudice of the London clergy against Whitefield was quickened and confirmed by a regrettable incident which occurred at St Margaret's, Westminster, on Sunday, February 4, 1739. A 'Friendly Society' had arranged that one of its weekly lectures should be delivered in the church on that day, but the lecturer who had been engaged was called away from town. He, however, without intimating the fact to the officers of the Society, secured a substitute. The officers, hearing that he had left London, waited on Whitefield and asked him to preach. He consented, and the two clergymen met in the church, to their mutual surprise. After explanations had been given Whitefield offered to retire, but the officers of the Society insisted on his preaching. He did so, but his action caused an unseemly disturbance in the church, and an angry controversy was at once commenced in the newspapers. The unfortunate incident was much exaggerated by rumour; the news spread into country towns, and served, in some places, to increase the prejudice against Whitefield.

Some days after the St. Margaret's disturbance Whitefield left London. He was a West countryman, having relatives in Gloucester and Bristol. On his way to the latter city he stopped at Bath, and asked permission to preach in the abbey and to make a collection for the orphanage. His request was not granted. Reaching Bristol on February 14, he made his home with his sister, Mrs. Grevil, the wife of a shopkeeper in Wine Street. He found that the *Weekly Miscellany*, containing an account of the St. Margaret's disturbance, had preceded him. Before his voyage to Georgia he had visited Bristol, and had preached in several of the churches to enthusiastic crowds. Bristol, then the second city in the kingdom, had been even more profoundly moved than London, and he was expecting that the friendliness shown him on his former visit would again be manifested. Once more he was disappointed. The morning after his arrival he waited on the Vicar of St. Mary Redcliffe, the Chancellor of the Diocese, and the Dean of Bristol. The vicar told him he could not lend his church without a special order from the Chancellor; the Chancellor declined to issue such an order, but went so far as to say that if any clergyman thought proper to lend his church he would not prohibit it; the Dean, pressed with business, promised to send for him at another time, when he would inform him whether there was any just objection against his preaching in the churches of Bristol. His interviews with the officials of the diocese were not satisfactory. In justice to them we must remember that Whitefield requested to be allowed to preach in St. Mary's in order that he might make a collection for the orphanage, and that such a request complicated the problem submitted to the Dean and Chancellor.

From our 'coign of vantage' we can see things hidden from chancellors and deans, and from Whitefield himself. The latter was, probably, disconcerted by his failure, but we watch him brushing aside the brambles that hid the beginnings of the way into the wilderness in which the lost sheep of England wandered. Great as is our sympathy with the orphanage project, we feel that it was subordinate to the divine design which concerned the salvation of men, not only in this country, but throughout the world. If Whitefield had been able to understand God's plans concerning him, he would have experienced a great elation that morning when he was dismissed from the deanery, and walked home through the narrow streets of Bristol. Watching his movements, it is with a sense of relief that we follow him in the afternoon of the day of his disappointments, and see that he is going to Newgate, the city prison, to see his old friend, Mr. Dagge, the governor. Mr. Dagge has won a niche in the Temple of Fame. He was 'the tender jailor' whose kindness to Savage has been immortalized by Dr. Johnson. He had heard Whitefield preach during his previous visit to Bristol, and had then accepted the joyful news of salvation through faith in Christ. The old friends talked together, and Whitefield asked permission to minister to the prisoners. The request was not complicated by the collection difficulty! In its simple form it was immediately granted. Services were at once commenced and regularly conducted until the mayor and sheriffs stopped them, the municipal authorities being indignant because Whitefield insisted on the necessity of 'the new birth'; such a doctrine being unfit for the ears of debtors and criminals.

Surveying the position, Whitefield found himself encompassed by difficulties. He saw that his chances of preaching in churches were swiftly diminishing, but his determination to preach somewhere was firm. There were several Religious Societies in Bristol, and he knew their members would welcome him into their meetings; Mr. Dagge's friendship also seemed to warrant a hope that his work in the prison would be continued; but, after thinking of these two sources of opportunity for proclaiming the gospel, the prospect was not promising. His time in England was limited; his Georgian parishioners awaited his return. Bristol was an attractive place; but the closing of the churches made it too narrow a sphere for him. At this crisis the evangelist within him asserted its passionate claims. He knew that he had a message from God to deliver to the people. The transforming power of that message, when spoken and accepted, had been illustrated in many instances, and he longed to prove it once more, and to see the light of a new joy shining on the faces of sinners returning to God. So he brooded, prayed, and resolved. The question he faced and answered concerned the opposition of the ecclesiastical authorities to his public ministry in Bristol. Was that opposition to be fatal? We have no desire to undervalue its seriousness, but the Church and the world have reason to be thankful for Whitefield's decision. In that decision we see the spirit of compromise. Whitefield was too high-spirited to thrust himself on unwilling clergymen and congregations, but was there not an ecclesiastical 'No Man's Land' in the neighbourhood into which he might enter, and where he might deliver his message?

When Whitefield visited Bristol in 1737 the citizens who crowded to hear him expressed their surprise that a man who was so much needed in England should be sent on a mission to America. Describing their astonishment, he says, 'All wondered that I would go to Georgia. Some urged that if I had a mind to convert Indians I might go among the Kingswood colliers, and find Indians enough there.' Two years had passed, Georgia had been visited, and it is probable that this criticism recurred to Whitefield when he was thinking over his difficulties. Whatever may have been the provoking cause, it is certain that on Saturday, February 17, 1739, in company with William Seward and another friend, he went out to Kingswood. After dinner, standing on a mount he preached to two hundred people who clustered around him. We have seen John and Charles Wesley preaching in the open air in Georgia and to the Tyburn mob in England, but that little group in Kingswood has a significance that arrests and compels our attention. The preacher was face to face with men who were almost untouched by religious influence. They represented some thousands of colliers who worked in the one hundred and fifty pits of the forest. For these men there was neither church nor school in the area of the wood. They grew up in darkness and ignorance, and their violence and brutality were by-words. They were the terror of Bristol. When work was scarce and bread was dear they sometimes marched into the city, and their coming caused panic among the shopkeepers. So long as they remained among their pits, few wasted a thought on them. There was a part of the old wood that was reserved as a chase, but it lay in the parishes of St. Philip and St. Jacob, Stapleton, Mangotsfield, and Bitton, and the usual fate in the case of such sub-division of responsibility ensued. We have spoken of an ecclesiastical 'No Man's Land,' and we may well say Whitefield found it near Bristol. His heart was moved by the spectacle of the misery of the colliers, and he determined that, without asking the consent of the ecclesiastical authorities, he would preach to them. He did so; and it came to pass that the people that walked in darkness saw a great light, they that dwelt in the land of the shadow of death, upon them the light shined.

In the present day few persons will defend the 'persecuting Acts' by which it was thought uniformity in public worship would be secured. Those who utter a faint apology for them suggest that they had their origin in the zeal of cavalier laymen. That is an imperfect explanation. The inception of the Bills must not be attributed exclusively to laymen. The man who was chiefly responsible for them was Gilbert Sheldon, who, as Bishop of London, and afterwards as Archbishop of Canterbury, used all his influence to suppress Nonconformity. Canon Overton, in attempting to show us

Sheldon's better side, has to confess that 'he was more of a statesman than a divine, that spiritual-mindedness was, to say the least, not a conspicuous trait in his character, that he took a leading part in the persecution of Nonconformists, and that his disgust at hypocrisy led him, like many others in the anti-puritanical reaction of the time, far too much in the opposite direction.' Sheldon was energetically supported by Seth Ward, successively Bishop of Exeter and Salisbury, a lover of sport, 'a manly, free-handed, light-hearted prelate, rather too much of the secular type, but most acceptable, if for no other reason, as affording an agreeable relief to the reign of saints.'[1] He was devoted to the pleasures of the chase, and his passion found a large sphere in his pursuit of Nonconformists. These bishops played a decisive part in the enactment of the persecuting legislation of the period, and they were strongly supported by the clergy.

In our charity we will suppose that the authors of the persecuting Acts did not see the results they would inevitably produce. If they had known 'the soul of the nation' they would have foreseen that their measures would increase the number of Nonconformists. The dislike of injustice and oppression never completely dies out of the hearts of Englishmen. When it asserts itself persecuting legislation either becomes impotent or is destroyed. It may work havoc for long years, but far-sighted men know that its doom is writ. But the ultimate success of Nonconformity was not the only outcome of the Acts which ought to have been perceived. Did no man utter the warning that the attempt to compel attendance at the parish churches might lead to the increase of the number of people who never went to any church? The fines of the Elizabethan Acts were utterly ineffective. Did the Act of Uniformity contain any better suggestion for securing attendance? When we remember that its aim was to exclude a great number of people from the churches in which they had worshipped for many years, we have no difficulty in answering the question. Many of those excluded were ministers beloved of their flocks, who followed them when they went out into the wilderness. If the Act of Uniformity had stood alone these people would have been shepherded in their meeting-houses; but the folly of the persecutors led them to pass the

[1] Overton's *Life in the English Church*, 20, 30.

Conventicle and the Five Mile Acts in the hope that by them Nonconformity would be destroyed. There can be no doubt these Acts arrested the work of some of the most effective ministers the Church of England has ever possessed. The Five Mile Act was especially injurious. It prevented the ministers from working in neighbourhoods in which they were best known, and where their spiritual influence was strong. When they were driven from their homes, fined, and imprisoned, a prejudice was created against the Church which caused the people to forsake its services and to defy its despotism. We know approximately the number of the ministers who were lost to the Church of England on St. Bartholomew's Day, 1662, but there is no reliable record of the number of the people who left the churches as a consequence of the passing of the Act of Uniformity. Many were true to their convictions, and became the nucleus of the great Dissenting Churches which have done invaluable service in the cause of vital religion in this country ; but we fear that not a few drifted away, to increase the ever-growing mass of the irreligious population of England.

Let us fix our eyes on the neglected masses of England at the time when Whitefield responded to the call of his conscience and went out to Kingswood. Since 1662 the number of persons who were outside all the Churches had greatly increased. The problem that still remains with us confronted the earnest Christian men of the eighteenth century and baffled them. Bishops in their pastorals admitted and deplored the evils that abounded. Dr. Gibson confessed that it seemed to him as if the entire nation was on the point of being overwhelmed by profligacy and unbelief, and declared that he was unable to entertain any hope for a generation so evil and rebellious except a diligent endeavour on the part of the parochial clergy to check and resist it by putting fresh incense in their censers, and standing between the dead and the living.[1] In Mr. W. C. Sydney's *England and the English in the Eighteenth Century*, a chapter on ' The Religious World ' is to be found that deserves the close study of every man who wishes to ascertain the condition of this country at the beginning of the Methodist reformation.[2] His testimony coincides with and establishes the truth of the descriptions given by other responsible and credible writers. It shows that there were men in

---

[1] *Charges to the Clergy of London*, 1741, 7–8.   [2] Vol. ii., 322–77.

high ecclesiastical positions who were aware of the dangers threatening the nation, and who were longing for the coming of a new spirit that would energize the Church and bring its spiritual power to bear on the masses of the people. But it also proves that such a man as Bishop Gibson, when he expected the Church of England to arise from its torpor, rush into the plague-stricken multitude, and stand between the living and the dead, was doomed to disappointment. His vision tarried, waiting for the next century for its fulfilment. It must be sorrowfully confessed that at the time when he delivered his charge it was useless to look in the direction of the parochial clergy for the evangelization of England. In Sir Thomas Erskine May's *Constitutional History of England* we find a description of the Church and clergy at the time preceding the accession of George III, which is undistorted by prejudice. He says : ' It was an age of spiritual indifference and lethargy. With many noble exceptions the clergy had been inert and apathetic. A benefice was regarded as an estate, to which was attached the performance of certain ecclesiastical duties. These once performed—the service read, the weekly sermon preached, the child christened, the parishioner buried—and the parson differed little from the squire. He was generally charitable, kindly, moral, and well educated—according to the standard of the age—in all but theology. But his spiritual calling sat lightly upon him. Zealous for Church and king, and honestly hating Dissenters, he was unconscious of a mission to spread the knowledge of the gospel among the people, to solve their doubts, to satisfy their spiritual longings, and to attach their religious sympathies to the Church.'[1] It was in vain to look to such men in the hope that the smoke of fresh incense would rise from their censers. They were content to keep within the limits of their own parishes ; they had a horror of ' enthusiasm ' ; they had no zest for evangelism ; and all the time the flood of profligacy and unbelief crept on and on in England.

Glancing in the direction of the Dissenting Churches the prospect was discouraging. The Toleration Act of 1689 brought great relief to Protestant Dissenters, but that relief was accompanied by disadvantages. The assertion that a people reposes the moment it has gained its rights, and that

[1] ii., 179.

it begins to grow weak as soon as it reposes, found striking illustration in the case of the Dissenters in the opening years of the eighteenth century. Having licensed their meeting-houses, taken the oaths, and made and signed the declaration according to the provisions of the Act, they found themselves in a position of comparative security, and settled down to enjoy the privilege of quiet worship. The change was congenial, but it was not favourable to aggressive evangelistic work. Those who have followed the footsteps of the persecuted Nonconformist ministers who, in despite of opposition, evangelized the villages and small towns of this country in the seventeenth century, honour them for their self-denial and their heroism. They proclaimed the gospel, not only in conventicles assembled in houses, but also in woods, fields, and chasms of wild hills. Oliver Heywood, in Lancashire and Yorkshire, having a clear view of the perishing multitude, went out to it and stood between the living and the dead. He preached Christ and Him crucified to men and women who sorrowed for their sins, and then rejoiced in conscious salvation. The reward he received was to be excommunicated, and thrown, as a prisoner, into York Castle; but he showed the way to the lost people of England, and anticipated, in the northern counties, the work of the evangelists of the next century. The Toleration Act, by protecting the meeting-houses, diverted the Dissenters from their aggressive work among the masses, and hindered them from those well-planned spiritual enterprises which must be undertaken if the nation is to be won for Christ. It did another disservice to the Protestant Dissenters. Being delivered from the fear of persecution, they had time to examine more closely their religious differences. Calamy has described the theological discussions that arose among the Presbyterians, Independents and Baptists. Many in each Church stood firm to the evangelical doctrines, but others wavered. It is well known that a large number of Presbyterians accepted views of the Person of Christ similar to those then rife in the Church of England. They gradually drifted away from the theological position of the other Dissenters, and became the founders of Unitarian Churches. This process of decay of evangelical belief was fatal to aggressive work. Dr. Gwatkin's assertion speaks to us with convincing force as we survey the position of the Presby terians, at one time the most numerous section of the Protestant Dissenters: 'It is historically evident that the power of the gospel is in the cross of Christ. . . . Whenever the wise men of the world were pleased to construct a gospel, they always left out this—and they were quite right in doing so, if there is no sin in the world which needs to be taken away.'[1] Under the conditions then prevailing it was useless to look to the Protestant Dissenters to lead the campaign against the evils which were destroying the neglected masses of the nation. Neither among them nor the parochial clergy were such leaders to be found.

Whitefield's sermon at Kingswood was an event of national importance. He knew the way to the cross and he showed it to others. As he spoke of the compassion of God, manifested in the death of His Son, unwonted tears filled the eyes of colliers and rolled down their faces. He brought to them strange tidings that troubled them and then filled them with exceeding joy. They learned that for them had been born and had died a Saviour, Christ the Lord. Returning to Bristol, Whitefield was surprised to find that, on the next day, he was to have opportunities of preaching in churches. He availed himself of them, and preached in St. Thomas's, and, to his great delight, in St. Mary Redcliffe. On the day following he preached to a great multitude in the parish church of St. Philip and Jacob, and collected £18 for the orphan-house in Georgia. The attendance at these services showed that thousands of people wished to hear him, many being turned away from the doors for lack of room. The city was moved, as on his former visit, and Whitefield's hope was kindled. But the ecclesiastical authorities were watching him. They ascertained the opinions of some of the clergy and laity, consulted together and determined to act. With the exception of Bishop Butler, it is impossible to regard with respect the chief officers of the Church of England in Bristol at that time. The Dean was Samuel Creswicke, who was about to be promoted to the Deanery of Wells. He was a sportsman who had a passion for cock-fighting. At his residence near Wells he ordered a cockpit to be constructed, so that he and his guests might witness the 'sport' from his dining-room, the window of which was enlarged so that a full view of the contests might be obtained.

[1] *Early Church History*, ii., 142.

When Dean of Wells he retained the living of St. James's, Bristol. Latimer says that he seems to have held clerical conventionalities in slight esteem. The Chancellor of the Diocese was ' a worldly cleric ' named Reynell, who afterwards became an Irish bishop.¹ An interview took place between Whitefield and the Chancellor which was of great importance. Tyerman gives a brief but valuable account of it. On Whitefield's appearance the Chancellor informed him that he intended to stop his proceedings, and that the registrar of the court was present to take down his answers. The following conversation then took place :

Chancellor : ' By what authority do you preach in the diocese of Bristol without a licence ? '
Whitefield : ' I thought that custom was grown obsolete. Pray, sir, why did you not ask the Irish clergyman this question who preached for you last Thursday ? '
C. : ' That is nothing to you.' Then, reading part of the Ordination Office, and the canons forbidding ministers to preach in private houses, he asked, ' What do you say to these ? '
W. : ' I apprehend these canons do not belong to professed ministers of the Church of England.'
C. : ' But they do.'
W. : ' There is a canon forbidding all clergymen to frequent taverns, and play at cards. Why is not that put in execution ? '
C. : ' Why does not somebody lodge complaints ? In such a case it would.'
Referring to his printed sermons for his principles, Whitefield asked, ' Why am I singled out ? '
C. : ' You preach false doctrine.'
W. : ' I cannot but speak the things that I know, and am resolved to proceed as usual.'
C. : ' Mr. Registrar, observe his answer.' Then, turning to Whitefield, he said, ' I am resolved, sir, if you preach or expound anywhere in this diocese, till you have a licence, I will first suspend, and then excommunicate, you.'

On taking his leave, the Chancellor waited on Whitefield very civilly to the door, and dismissed him with the words, ' What I do is in the name of the clergy and laity of the city of Bristol.' ²
The conversation between the Chancellor and Whitefield casts a curious light on the condition of discipline in the Church of England in the eighteenth century, especially in respect of

¹ Latimer's *Annals of Bristol in the Eighteenth Century*, 170-202.
² Tyerman's *Life of Whitefield*, i., 181-2.

the observance of the law concerning licences. The requirements of statutes and canons were clear and strict; but it is evident that, in many cases, they were ignored. Still, they were not 'obsolete,' as Whitefield supposed; any unfriendly clergyman or churchwarden could use them effectively, and thereby prevent an unlicensed preacher from ministering in a church. It is rather difficult to follow the Chancellor's argument concerning the canons forbidding ministers to preach in private houses. We presume that the canons read to Whitefield were those numbered from nine to twelve. If so, Whitefield's answer was right; they are directed against schismatics. An ingenious objector might forge the twelfth into a weapon to be used against the Religious Societies, but he would only do so by disregarding the connexion in which it stands. Taken alone, it reads: 'Whosoever shall hereafter affirm that it is lawful for any sort of ministers and lay persons, or of either of them, to join together, and make rules, orders, or constitutions, in causes ecclesiastical, without the king's authority, and shall submit themselves to be ruled and governed by them, let them be excommunicated *ipso facto*, and not be restored until they repent, and publicly revoke those their wicked and baptistical errors.' Inasmuch as the Chancellor contemplated excommunicating Whitefield we think that he must have been relying on the canons; he would have been on firmer ground if he had taken his stand on statute law, and pointed out the provisions of the Conventicle Act.

Whitefield was undaunted by the Chancellor's threat. The clergy of Bristol, however, were affected by it, and closed their churches against him. A few of the clergymen in the neighbourhood refused to follow this example. Whitefield was welcomed by them, but their churches were too small to accommodate the people. In order that all might hear, Whitefield on more than one occasion preached in the churchyard, or in some convenient gathering-place. At four different times he went to Bath and preached in the open air. The services in Kingswood were continued, and thousands flocked from Bristol and joined the colliers in their worship. In Bristol a large bowling-green was lent to him, where he preached twice in the last week in March. It is satisfactory to note that his orphan-house scheme did not suffer from his exclusion from the churches. He made collections at some of his open-air services and among his friends which amounted to about £200. In addition to preaching to great crowds in the open air he 'expounded' in several of the Religious Societies then existing in Bristol. He also made a short excursion into Wales, visiting the Religious Societies there, preaching in Cardiff and Newport, and rejoicing in the great work that was being done by Howell Harris, a young layman, and those who were associated with him. He met Harris, and his heart at once clave to him. He listened to the story of his evangelistic work, and found that his own field-preaching had been anticipated in Wales. Howell Harris had found that services held in the open air were invaluable in the attempt to reach the masses, and Whitefield listened to his descriptions of success with a glowing heart. The meeting of these two men led to results of exceptional importance in the history of the revival in the eighteenth century. It should also be noticed that, at Bath, Whitefield met Griffith Jones, the founder of the famous Circulating Welsh Free Schools. At their founder's death these schools numbered three thousand, in which were one hundred and fifty-eight thousand scholars. When Whitefield was in Wales he heard much about Griffith Jones's work, and a vision of a charity school in Kingswood shone before his eyes.

Whitefield's stay in the west country was coming to an end. His success, notwithstanding all opposition, had been remarkable. His preaching had attracted crowds numbering in some instances ten thousand persons. The fields were white unto harvest. But his work in America was calling him away, and it seemed to him as if the unreaped harvest would perish for lack of labourers. His hope was that the Lord of the Harvest would send some other reaper, so that the calamity which sudden success often brings might be averted. He conversed with his friend and travelling-companion, William Seward, and found that he was in agreement with him as to the choice of a successor in Bristol. The result of their consultation was that each dispatched a letter to John Wesley entreating him, in the most pressing manner, to come to Bristol without delay. Whitefield's letter was written on March 22. It was his intention to leave Bristol on April 2. He took it for granted that his appeal would be successful, and immediately advertised

Wesley's coming in the newspaper. He was conscious, however, that delays might occur, inasmuch as the question of the journey would have to be discussed in the Fetter Lane Society. The ' Orders ' required that any person who desired or designed to take any journey should first, if it be possible, have the approbation of the bands; and that no particular person should be allowed to act in anything contrary to any order of the Society, but that every one without distinction should submit to the determination of his brethren. Whitefield was aware of these ' Orders,' and, in his letter, said, ' If the brethren, after prayer for direction, think proper, I wish you would be here the latter end of next week.' Wesley received the letters, felt the urgency of the matter, but at first was disinclined to go to Bristol. He followed his usual plan of seeking direction from the Bible. It was his ' living oracle,' and it spoke to him with a voice of authority. The texts that met his eye on opening the book seemed applicable to his circumstances, and produced a deep impression on his mind. They spoke of suffering and death. He looked on them as indicating the consequences of his removal to Bristol, and accepted them as trials of his faith. He did not consider his life dear unto himself, but would not determine the case without consulting others. On March 28 the consultation with the Fetter Lane Society took place. Charles Wesley was present, and strongly opposed Whitefield's project. He knew the condition of his brother's health, and was convinced that any attempt to do Whitefield's work in Bristol would endanger his life. Several of those who were present were of the same opinion. The dispute was continued until it was plain that there was no probability of a unanimous conclusion. When John Wesley was at Herrnhut he was told that under such circumstances it was the custom of the Moravians to decide the question by lot. We do not know who proposed this mode of settling the dispute, but those present agreed that it should be adopted. The lot was in favour of his going to Bristol, and all submitted to the decision. The next day he set out from London on his great mission to the west of England.

XIX

BRISTOL IN 1739

BRISTOL in the opening years of the eighteenth century attained the position of the second city in the kingdom. It won ' the pride of place ' from Norwich ; and its other competitors, Exeter and York, were permanently out-distanced. It owed its eminence to the influence of its trade with America and the West Indies. In June, 1497, a year before Columbus reached America, John Cabot, in a Bristol ship manned by a Bristol crew, had landed on the northern coast of Cape Breton and planted the flags of England and of St. Mark on American soil. He discovered Prince Edward's Island, which he named St. John's, and seems to have sailed round the Gulf of St. Lawrence, and then returned to England. It was fitting that Bristol should reap a harvest of honour and prosperity from such an enterprise. Lest its position among the towns of England should mislead us as to its population we may say that Mr. Latimer, in his *Annals of Bristol in the Eighteenth Century,* shows that, exclusive of the dwellers in the suburbs, the population of the city in 1735 was about thirty thousand.

Accepting Mr. Latimer for our guide, we will attempt to see the city when George Whitefield and John Wesley visited it in 1739. The approach to Bristol from the Somerset side was sometimes almost impracticable owing to the condition of the road from Bath. In the winter and spring carriages and carts were frequently bogged in sloughs of mud, and foot travellers had to leave the highway and find paths across the fields. We note that John Wesley entered Bristol from the Gloucester side ; it may be that Whitefield, who came along the Bath road, had given him a word of warning. Defying the difficulties of the way, we will follow Whitefield's example. Our road from Bath runs along the south bank of the Avon. We pass Keynsham, and soon find ourselves at Brislington, where 'the civilized colliers' dwell. Proceeding along the road when it bends to the right we find ourselves among the meadows of the parish of Temple. At that time Bristol was a walled city. It preserved much of the aspect it wore in Plantagenet times, but its spreading suburb on the Somerset side had altered its appearance. Passing through Temple Gate, in the outer wall, we see Temple Church, with its leaning tower. Its slant from the perpendicular was occasioned by the church-building zeal of the men, who in the fifteenth century imposed on the tower its rich upper stage, the weight of which caused the structure to incline. It is impossible to pass Temple Church without thinking of the distant days when the Knights Templars worshipped in it, and of the later times when the parish became the home of the weavers' craft. The weavers' chapel, now a part of the church, was built in 1299, and was dedicated to St. Katharine. We remember that the mayor, sheriff, and council of the city were accustomed to attend the service in Temple Church on St. Katharine's eve, and, in thought, we follow the civic procession as it leaves the church and wends its way to the feast in Weavers' Hall. Passing the hall, we glance towards the red cliff, where houses are clustered round St. Mary's Church that lifts itself above them in stately beauty. We note how the suburbs of the old city are growing, and dream of a day when, perchance, the verdant meads of Temple, Redcliff, and Bedminster will live only in name.

We have reached the bank of the river, and on the other side see the inner walls of the city. We shall have to cross the stone bridge, which for half a century has spanned the Avon. We wonder it has stood so long. Like old London Bridge, it has to carry a row of houses on either side. It is picturesque but over-burdened. When Alexander Pope crossed it, in 1739, it was crowded ' with a strange mixture of seamen, women, children, loaded horses, asses, and sledges with goods, dragging on all together without posts to separate them.' Having crossed, Pope tells us, ' You come to a key along the old wall, with houses on both sides ; and, in the middle of the street as far as you can see, hundreds of ships, their masts as thick as they can stand by one another, which is the oddest and most surprising sight imaginable. This street is fuller of them than the Thames from London Bridge to Deptford.

When the tide is out and the ships ground then a long street full of ships in the middle, with houses on each side, looks like a dream.'

We have now reached the inner wall of the city. Our way lies through St. Nicholas Gate, a narrow entry through which we pass at peril of life. Carriages, carts, sledges, pack-horses, and people thrust against each other, and, in the contest, not a few hapless foot-passengers are thrust against the walls. It is a relief to emerge scatheless beyond the gate and the church, and to find ourselves in High Street. If our journey is on a Saturday, as we climb the hill we find that High Street is blocked by stalls set up for the sale of butchers' meat, butter, fowls, vegetables, and other produce. The roadway is littered with refuse. It is rarely swept. Latimer declares that the neglect of scavenging remained chronic in Bristol throughout the eighteenth century. Numerous pigs forage among the garbage. We make our way into the centre of the city, but in Wine Street and Broad Street the roar of the market resounds and the narrow spaces between the houses are packed with citizens and country-people.

Pausing for a few moments at the top of High Street, we find it is possible to get a clear view of the plan of the city. We see that the enclosure within the walls is divided into sections by four principal streets, which form a cross, High Street and Broad Street making one long limb and Wine Street and Corn Street the other. We turn into Wine Street. On old maps it is called Winch Street, the name indicating that the pillory was set up there. Walking along Wine Street, we come to the old castle, which has been dismantled and turned into Newgate, the city prison. Going beyond the city walls and the old boundaries of the castle, we see, to the right, the Church of St. Philip and Jacob; not far from it a brickyard. We traverse the site of an old Norman village and market which grew up as dependencies of the castle, and reach the town ditch, crossing it at Lawford's Gate, near to which stands the Holy Trinity Hospital. Beyond, the highway stretches to Two Mile Hill and Kingswood.

Returning to Wine Street, we find it is possible to escape the pressure of the crowd by walking a little way from the crest of the hill, and standing on a slope which descends into a green valley. The houses in the Pithay, the hollow to our left, attract our attention. We catch a glimpse of the roof of the old assembly room and can determine the site of the bowling-green. The Pithay is beyond the inner wall of the city, and near the bank of the river Frome. The eye travels across the Frome, over the valley, until it rests on the heights of Kingsdown, at that time a hill beautiful with grass, and yellow furze, and the flowers of spring. It is scarcely touched by the hand of the builder, the Montague Tavern, the first house on it, being erected in 1737. In the valley one object immediately fixes our attention. It is the parish church of St. James, a remnant of the Benedictine Priory. The original church was an interesting example of those double churches which, in their present state, record the zeal of strenuous reformers. The east end, which belonged to the monks, perished; the nave, in which the parishioners worshipped, survived. From our coign of vantage we can read the story of St. James's, and can mark the west front, the arcades, the clerestory of the original church. We think of the crumbling of the old chancel and choir; and then our eye lingers for a moment on the Barton, which still preserves the memory of the Priory farm. There were busy scenes in those distant days in the broad space fronting the church. The monks possessed the right to hold a fair, and long after they had passed from the scene the fair, in one form or another, was continued. In 1739 it was one of the two great Bristol fairs. In 1737 the date for commencing it was altered to September, and then Broadmead was given up to merchandise and merriment. In 1731 the city council ordered that a market for the sale of hay should be established in Broadmead for Gloucestershire produce, and carts loaded with straw and hay stood in the Horsefair, close to the churchyard. The noise of markets and fairs disturbed the quietude of Broadmead for only a few days in the week and year; otherwise it was a peaceful neighbourhood, the stillness being deepened by the drone of the water-wheel of the mill. Those who have discerned the spirit of Bristol in the eighteenth century have detected a characteristic of the townsfolk which still persists. The city streets, as we have seen, were narrow. They were made in an age of pack-horses. The beetle-browed houses on either side leaned towards each other, and reduced the summer sky to a strip of blue. But if we enter one of the houses and pass through it, it is probable that we shall see at the back a long strip of garden filled with fruit-trees and gay with shrubs and flowers. The love of gardens lay deep in the heart of the citizens, and found abundant expression. As we look at Broadmead we see this spirit displayed. The interval between the hillside on which we are standing and Kingsdown has its groups of houses ; but in Broadmead there are avenues of trees, gardens, orchards, and stretches of greensward. In 1739 the country was making a bold defence against the encroachments of the town, and the citizens could still rejoice in scenes of rural loveliness.

Among the buildings in the valley one arrests special attention. It is a Baptist meeting-house. It stands as a memorial of an intensely interesting period of religious history. In 1660 the Baptists, who had been meeting in private rooms, took a ' large Place or Hall towards ye end of Broadmead, called ye Fryars, which formerly had been some Chapell.' Mr. Haycroft suggests that it had once belonged to the Franciscan friars. From this building the Baptists were driven by persecution in 1664. They continued to meet in various places until 1671, when they occupied the meeting-house which had been used by the Quakers. The building consisted of four rooms made into one square room, about sixteen yards long and fifteen broad. In 1695, the church built a new meeting-house fifty feet long by forty feet in the clear, and a vestry room twenty feet square. It is on this building we are looking from the hillside, and as we think of the history of the little church we seem to be listening to whispers prophetic of the experiences of the new reformers whose voices were beginning to quicken the religious life of Bristol. We linger for a few moments to trace the roads that lead from Broadmead. We catch sight of King Street, and follow it as it passes into Stokes Croft, then beautiful with trees. At the end of the Croft there is a diverging road leading to Baptist Mills, a hamlet probably so called because of the public baptisms by immersion that took place there in the river Frome in 1666. The main road, which leads to Cotham and Redland, is beyond our sight. We know, however, that if we had time to follow it we should find ourselves ere long on the far-spreading, lonely heights of Durdham Down.

Leaving the slope of the hill from which we have seen Broadmead, we return to Wine Street. We pass the end of Broad Street and walk the length of Corn Street. Soon we are beyond the inner wall of the city. We pause to admire the tower of St. Stephen's Church, and then find ourselves on the banks of the Frome, the river being crowded with ships. We look across to the houses on St. Augustine's Back, and to St. Michael's Church, standing on its steep hill. No drawbridge then existed for the convenience of travellers, so we are ferried across the harbour, and, following the road, reach College Green and the cathedral, formerly the Abbey of St. Augustine. On the opposite side of the green stands the Mayor's Chapel, the old Church of St. Mark, which had been used for many years by the Huguenot refugees. Roaming round the Green, it seems as if the city, in this direction, had reached its limits. There is no Park Street. It was not until 1740 that a scheme for making a road up the hill began to take shape, and more than twenty years elapsed before a house was built. Climbing up the ascent, we strike a path running towards a hill from the summit of which we gain a view of the city and river. But our eyes look far beyond the horizon of the eighteenth century. We see the monk St. Brendan, in the sixth century, standing on the hill, gazing on the little village on the banks of the Avon. He is an Irishman who has been trained in the famous school of Clonard, where he has been educated by St. Finnian, ' the preceptor of the twelve apostles of Ireland,' among whom he is now numbered. We judge that he has sought the seclusion of Gloucestershire in order that he may give himself up to meditation and prayer. He was unconscious of the important work to which he would soon be called ; so he built his cell on the hillside, and lived the solitary life of an anchorite monk. In the wilderness he is influenced by many things, not least by the landscape and the river that catches the light of the new morning and of the dying day. In the years to come he will write the story of his dream-voyage in search of paradise. As we read the description of his arrival, with his monks, in the Land of Promise, it seems to us strongly reminiscent of sacred personal experiences. In that land all the trees were charged with ripe fruit, and the ' herbes were full of flower.' They come to a river, but they dare not go over it. A fair youth approaches them. He gives them gracious greeting, and tells them that they have gained sight of the land they sought, the earthly paradise, but he sends them away laden with fruits, since ' the water of that river divides the two worlds, and no man in this life may cross to the other side.' The fruits he has brought them from beyond the stream ripen all the year round in that land of eternal day, of eternal spring.[1] In other years he doubtless watched the play of the sunlight on Irish rivers, but he did not forget his early days on Brandon Hill, and his musings as he sat outside his cell. He did a great work in Ireland, and died in 576. In the centuries that followed he was still remembered. Mr. Hunt says, ' His legendary voyage to the islands of the blessed made him a special object of veneration to seamen, and above all to the seamen of Ireland, as they sailed beneath his hill to anchor in Bristol river.'[2] We can picture them lifting up their eyes to the little chapel of St. Brendan that stood on the hill. They recalled his memory and saluted him in their hearts. Those who are familiar with the story of the Irish Missionaries, who preached Christ in this and other countries before St. Augustine came to Kent, will join in that salutation.

We cross a valley, and then climb up to Clifton-on-the-Hill. At the beginning of the eighteenth century the little hamlet consisted of about a dozen dairy-farms, separated from each other by an enclosed common. A church and a few cottages dotted the down. In 1739 there was little change in the place. In 1716 the parish church had been enlarged by the addition of an aisle. We suspect that the reason of the addition is to be found in the presence of a few isolated houses built by wealthy men bent on escaping from the turmoil of the city streets. Those houses are soon counted. So late as 1750 there were only twenty of them, and at one time eleven of them were ' to be let or sold.' Even in 1780, or thereabouts, the ' upper-class ' dwellings scarcely exceeded thirty. Clifton-on-the-Hill, during the eighteenth century, was a small place but what we may call Clifton-under-the-Hill made rapid progress. In 1710 the population of Clifton was estimated at four hundred and fifty, and Latimer thinks that probably about five-sixths of the parishioners resided on the low ground near the Avon. At one point on the river bank lodging-houses clustered round the Hot Well. In the neighbourhood of the spa the builders were busy erecting houses to meet the needs

[1] Miss Margaret Stokes's *Three Months in the Forests of France*, Pref., xliii., xliv
[2] *Bristol*, 9, Historic Towns Series.

BRISTOL IN 1739

of those who were engaged in the rapidly increasing business of the port of Bristol.

Our sketch of the physical aspect of Bristol will enable us to form some idea of its appearance at the time when John Wesley first visited it, but we never see a town as it is until we have seen its inhabitants, and know something of the experiences that have told on the formation of their character. At this point in our researches, more than at any other, we feel our indebtedness to Mr. Latimer, on whose rich stores we have already laid a heavy tribute. He has provided us with abundant material for estimating the character of the Bristol people at the time when John Wesley, riding his tired horse, entered the city on Saturday evening, March 31, 1739. Since then the social, moral, intellectual, and religious condition of Bristol has been transformed, but in order to ascertain the state of the town and its people at the time of which we write we must escape from the present and live for a while in distant years.

We have seen that the advance of Bristol to the position of the second city in the kingdom was determined by the fact that it was a shipping port claiming an exceptionally large share of the American and West Indian trades. As the forest of masts and spars grew in the harbour there were some far-seeing people who noted the moral dangers of maritime prosperity. When men have been cooped up for months on board ship, and are then let loose in town, a 'dark spot' is apt to be created on an English river. The vice of drunkenness, unless the facilities for obtaining intoxicating drink are severely restricted, becomes a curse to the place. In Bristol, in the eighteenth century, such restrictions did not exist. Latimer says that the consumption of beer was 'prodigious.' In 1736 the licensing authority fixed the number of alehouses in the city at 331, exclusive of inns, wine shops, and coffee-houses. There was one alehouse for every sixteen private dwellings. Not content with this liberal allowance, the magistrates, in December, 1742, increased the number of alehouses to 384, nearly double the number existing in 1700. In 1754, when there were 6,250 houses in the city, the number of alehouses was 625. There can be no doubt that this great increase in licensed houses indicates an attempt on the part of the authorities to meet the demands of the seafaring population, and the crowds of sailors swarming in the streets. It must also be remembered that the home brewing of beer was a universal custom. On this point William Cobbett's testimony is illuminating. Speaking of the custom prevailing up to 1780 he says, ' In former times to set about to show to Englishmen that it was good for them to brew beer in their houses would have been as impertinent as gravely to insist that they ought to endeavour not to lose their breath ; for in those times to have a house and not to brew was a rare thing indeed.'[1] If we add the amount of beer brewed in the homes of the people to that sold in the alehouses we shall get some idea of the quantity consumed in a year in Bristol.

The drinking of ale was so familiar a custom in Bristol that it excited little comment. But no one could have visited the inns, wine-shops, and coffee-houses in the city without seeing that other liquors were in strong demand. In the absence of offices merchants and others transacted their business in these places. There were few ' dry ' bargains. Much ' Bristol milk '—that is, Spanish sherry—was consumed. Some slow-moving men who needed a more powerful stimulant were plied with spirits. The English distillers fought hard against the trade in French brandy, but it was not difficult to obtain it in seaports. The distilleries abundantly supplied the kingdom with gin. The year 1724 wears an ominous look in the eyes of English philanthropists. It was then, according to Lecky, that gin-drinking began to spread in England with the rapidity and violence of an epidemic.[2] Bristol was infected. It is only necessary to glance at the bills showing the cost of civic banquets which Mr. Latimer has preserved in the *Annals* to get some idea of the variety and profuseness of the liquors consumed in the city.

In wandering along the wharves of Bristol in 1739, the eye is often arrested by ships which, by their build and rig, show that they are adapted to special business. The commercial prosperity of some of the leading citizens was much increased by the voyages and adventures of these vessels, and their use, so far as we can ascertain, was almost universally approved. That approval, which would now be altogether withheld, reveals a condition of public opinion which must be considered in our attempt to understand the *morale* of Bristol at the

---

[1] *Cottage Economy*, par. 20.   [2] *History of England*, i., 479.

time. In 1709 fifty Bristol ships were engaged in the slave-trade. Four years later the Peace of Utrecht was proclaimed, and one of its provisions filled the citizens with great joy. In present-day opinion the treaty is generally allowed to have been dishonourable, inasmuch as for little or no compensation it gave away the immense vantage-ground the English victories had gained. But the port of Bristol, fixing its attention on one of its clauses, was well pleased with it. It is well known that the English plenipotentiary who represented this country in the discussions on the terms of the treaty was Dr. Robinson, the bishop of Bristol.[1] Through his influence a clause had been introduced into the treaty of Utrecht which secured for England the monopoly of supplying the Spanish colonies with slaves. Bristol seized the golden opportunity and threw itself into the traffic. The slave-ships sailed to the coast of Guinea, where thousands of negroes were caught and carried off to the American plantations; and Bristol became one of the principal, if not the chief, slaving port in this country. The commanders of the slaves were entitled to transport a few negroes in each cargo for their own profit. They were brought to England, sold here, and lived and died in servitude. In spite of the famous judgement of Lord Mansfield in the Somerset case, the selling of slaves in Bristol went on until the close of 1792.

Our stroll along the wharves enables us to catch sight of other special ships which went down the river and out to sea on a different errand. Sometimes their voyages were successful, and increased the wealth of their owners; but not seldom they sailed away and the port of Bristol saw them no more. It must be remembered that for nearly fifty years during the eighteenth century England was at war. There were intervals of peace, but such intervals were filled with preparation for coming battles. Our right arm of attack and defence was the Navy; but, in addition, privateers sailing under licences from the Government were employed. The fighting spirit of Bristol was roused, and armed ships were sent out in considerable numbers, which not only maintained the honour of the country but often brought back rich prizes. In 1738 the story of Spanish atrocities had set England on fire. The 'Fable of Jenkins's ears' was credulously believed. The

[1] As a reward for his diplomatic services he was elevated to the see of London.

passion of the nation was so excited that Walpole's peace policy was swept aside. In October war was declared. The bells of the London churches pealed for joy. Listening to them, Walpole said, 'They are ringing their bells now; they will be wringing their hands soon.' The declaration of war was made known in Bristol on October 29, 1739. The people had been making preparations for the event, and threw themselves with still greater energy into the work of fitting out ships to fight the Spaniard. Some of the merchants met and subscribed large sums of money for the arming of privateers. The war-passion simmered or seethed during the whole of that memorable year.

Turning away from the consideration of the influences that told on the character of the people of Bristol as dwellers in a great seaport, we must now note other facts that influenced them. A stranger visiting Bristol on June 10, 1739, would have found the city in a state of intense excitement. The streets were thronged by crowds of citizens bedecked with flowers. It was the birthday of the Stuart Pretender, and the Jacobites were jubilant. The next day was a general holiday; and then the supporters of the Government marched in procession, celebrating the anniversary of the accession of George II. On these days, for more than fifty years, Bristol was filled with sound and fury as the rival parties trooped and clashed in the narrow streets. Party divisions, deep and wide, were characteristic of the town, and the annual demonstrations often led to disorderly scenes. By long continuance in the practice of rioting Bristol attained pre-eminence in an art that was cultivated in the eighteenth century. The differences of opinion concerning politics were sharp, but the divisions caused by ecclesiastical and religious convictions were sharper. The Civil War had left a strong mark on the city. During its progress the allegiance of the citizens was divided between the king and the Parliament. During the Commonwealth a strong hand was laid on the Church, and a number of clergymen were deprived of their livings. With the Restoration came opportunities of revenge. The Act of Uniformity and the 'persecuting Acts' were relentlessly applied. The Quakers, who formed an important element in the business life of the city in the seventeenth century, were ruthlessly attacked. In 1683 the fines imposed on Bristol

BRISTOL IN 1739

Quakers, under the Acts, amounted to nearly £16,500. One of them was condemned to death for 'incorrigible nonconformity,' but escaped the gallows through the exertions of his wife, who travelled to London and persuaded the higher authorities to revise the local decision. The Dissenters passed through days of darkness. The *Broadmead Records* reveal a story of suffering that makes an irresistible appeal to a lover of religious liberty. The hunted people, driven from their meeting-houses, assembled in private dwellings, and when that became impossible they met in small groups on Durdham Down, and in the depths of the King's Wood. But the informers, whose hunger for their share in the money-penalties was insatiable, tracked them down, and the hand of the law seized them. Notwithstanding years of persecution, Nonconformity persisted in Bristol. The Dissenters in the eighteenth century had conquered for themselves a strong position in its commercial and social life. It is true that the Jacobite mob classed them with Hanoverians as objects of enmity and attack, and that the Church party, in its more charitable moments merely ' tolerated ' them ; but far-seeing men suspected that the future was with them, and regarded them with a prudent favour. The influence of the long and fierce religious controversy, however, remained. It only required some new exciting cause to provoke a manifestation of its existence.

Apart from the special influences we have indicated, the character of the Bristol people was moulded by forces similar to those which existed in other towns. Mr. Latimer, whose careful researches have made him an authority on the subject, says that in 1700 the moral and intellectual condition of the inhabitants more closely resembled that of the Middle Ages than that of our own time. The same can be said of all the provincial towns of England at the opening of the eighteenth century ; but a change was coming. Mediaevalism, strongly entrenched in the villages, was beginning to retreat, with many a backward look, from the larger centres of population. It is difficult to imagine the isolation of most of the English towns. The mail coaches brought letters, and some news of the doings of the outside world filtered through from passengers who had dared the dangers of the roads ; but, generally speaking, the towns were self-contained, and were satisfied with their own daily supplies of local gossip. It is hard to realize that in 1700 Bristol was without a local newspaper. As for London papers, it is not until 1739 that we come on a record showing that two London newspapers were then taken in Bristol 'for the use of the civic body.' Losing sight of other parts of the country, we note that at the commencement of the century Bristol was becoming conscious of her national position. As a great seaport news of the outside world had previously been discussed in coffee houses and wine shops and in the homes of the citizens; but in 1702 a little sheet entitled *The Bristol Post Boy* made its appearance, and was followed, probably in 1713, by the *Bristol Post Man*, published by Samuel Farley 'at the house in St. Nicholas Street, near the church.' The name of Farley soon became conspicuous in the annals of Bristol journalism. In 1725 the *Post Man* was discontinued, its place being taken by *Farley's Bristol Newspaper*, which contained four pages. It was the only newspaper then published in the city. In 1737 its title was altered to *Sam Farley's Bristol Newspaper*, the alteration suggesting to the instructed eye that the well-known Felix Farley had begun his publishing activities.

The publication of newspapers was a sign of the coming of a better time, but those who were able to read them were few in number. Mr. Latimer bluntly and picturesquely declares that, at that time, the vast majority of Bristolians were 'as illiterate as the back of a tombstone.' In plainer words, we may say that, in common with the rest of England, the elementary education of the masses was almost entirely neglected in the city. The diversion of the King Edward Schools throughout the country from their original purpose is notorious. They were intended for the education of the children of the poor. The wrong done to the people was, however, being slightly redressed. The charity schools, commenced by members of the Church of England in London, Oxford, and elsewhere, were beginning their attack on ignorance. In Bristol the name of Edward Colston is still venerated for his care of poor children. The London movement for establishing parochial charity schools extended, about 1709, to Bristol, the first to take action in the city being the Rev. Arthur Bedford, the vicar of Temple. Between that date and 1739 we catch sight of such schools on the Quay, on Redcliff Back, and in Pyle Street. So early as 1722 we also find that the Dissenters belonging to the Lewin's Mead Meeting erected a school-house and almshouse in Stokes Croft, and in this and other ways the dangerous intellectual darkness was beginning to be relieved.

The condition of morals in Bristol may be imagined from our statements concerning the superabundance of public-houses in the city and suburbs. If we search the melancholy records of executions contained in Mr. Latimer's *Annals* we gain some light on the crimes and punishments of the time. The records are imperfect, but enough evidence is furnished to show that the gallows on St. Michael's Hill was kept busy during the eighteenth century. It must be remembered that the criminal law was then lavish in its infliction of the death penalty for offences other than murder, and that innocent men, charged with felony, ran great risks of condemnation, because they were denied the assistance of counsel. The judge was supposed to be on the prisoner's side. This state of things continued into the nineteenth century. In 1824 Mr. George Lamb tried to persuade Parliament to alter it, but failed. Sir Erskine May says, 'In 1836, Mr. Ewart, after a contention of many years, secured to prisoners on trial for felony the just privilege of being heard by counsel, which the cold cruelty of our criminal jurisprudence had hitherto denied them.'[1] It is impossible to glance over Mr. Latimer's lists without asking how many of those whose names are contained in them were unjustly condemned. We think it is fair to say that, in point of morality, the condition of Bristol resembled that of most of the cities and towns in England. It had the special disadvantages of a great seaport, but there were not a few men in it who hated evil and fought hard for moral reform. In 1729 a movement for the suppression of drunkenness and profanity was commenced, which did something to discountenance these evils. Among other mitigating forces it must be remembered that Bristol, for many years, has been remarkable for the spirit of philanthropy which has possessed its citizens. That spirit was working in the eighteenth century, and played its part in improving the tone of the people.

We cannot close our description of Bristol without looking, for a few moments, in the direction of the cathedral and the

[1] *Constitutional History*, vol. ii., 392.

city churches. One of the most poignant facts in English history is the failure of the Church, as a religious and reforming agency, in the eighteenth century. That failure is now acknowledged. The apologist does good service when he softens some of the condemnatory statements made about the clergy of the time. So far as he brings hidden truth to light we welcome it; but although he may modify he cannot expunge the condemnatory verdict written in the pages of history. Confining ourselves to Bristol, the failure of the Church of England, although it cannot be explained away, may be explained. With surprisingly few exceptions the city was unfortunate in its bishops. The see was poor, and it was notorious as a stepping-stone to higher preferment. The stay of a bishop was usually brief. From 1710 to 1738 Bristol had seven bishops. But, in addition to the weakness of administration caused by this swift succession, the poverty of the see produced another serious effect. A man could not maintain his position, if he had not large private property, unless he became a pluralist, and the pluralist is a man of divided interest and evanescent influence. There can be no denying the ability of Thomas Secker, who afterwards became the Archbishop of Canterbury. He was a man whose preaching attracted large congregations, and whose faculty for the dispatch of business made him a great administrator. He was appointed to Bristol in 1734, stayed there until 1737, and during that short period held a prebend at Durham and a rectory in Westminster. His successor, Sir Thomas Gooch, is described by Hayley as a man of extraordinary talent but not much learning, and not the sort of man who should have been a bishop. Latimer says he was granted permission to hold with his bishopric the rectory of St. Clement's, London, a prebend at Canterbury, another at Chichester, the office of residentiary at Chichester, and the mastership of St. Mary's Hospital in that city. He held the see of Bristol for fourteen months, and was translated to Norwich. What hope of religious and spiritual leadership by word and example could be cherished under such circumstances?

In 1738 the prospect became brighter. Sir Thomas Gooch departed, and Joseph Butler reigned in his stead. Among his many distinctions we must include the fact that he held the Bristol see for nearly twelve years. After experiencing its poverty until 1740, he became Dean of St. Paul's. Dean

Spence, in speaking of him, says that, enduring as his literary work has proved to be, he was a toiler for God in the closet and study rather than in the broad field of active practical life. He was not a man who inspired his contemporaries with living, burning zeal in that comparatively dull and lifeless age when the Church of England was without leaders practical and able, without men of high thoughts and tireless purpose, capable, too, of inspiring others with something of their own spirit and power.[1] He seems to have relied on his Commissary for the discharge of much of the administrative details of the diocese, and we have seen an example of the spirit and manner of that official in our description of his interview with Whitefield.

If we turn from the bishops to the clergy expecting to catch sight of a gleam of hope our disappointment is deepened. The statements contained in Dean Spence's courageous chapter entitled 'The Period of Controversy and Spiritual Decay' have special application to Bristol. If a city can be saved by the multitude of its churches the towers and spires of Bristol would have brought consolation to those who longed for the coming of a revival that would profoundly affect the lives of the citizens; but as, in imagination, we wander from church to church, we fail to find a clergyman fitted for the great task of speaking with a voice that would rouse men and women out of the lethargy that afflicted them. And yet we are not without hope. It was high time that the people should wake out of their sleep; and something tells us that a great religious revival is at hand; a revival which is to spring from a strange and unexpected source, and which in a marvellous way is to influence the religious history of England.

[1] *The Church of England*, iv., 232.

XX

JOHN WESLEY'S FIRST VISIT TO BRISTOL

BRISTOL occupies a unique position in the annals of the Methodist Church. For more than fifty years John Wesley regarded it as one of his chief centres; he constantly visited it; he loved its people; it was the stronghold of Methodism in the west of England. The beginning of his mission in the city is therefore of special importance in the eyes of students of the Reformation of the eighteenth century.

Riding slowly from London, John Wesley arrived in Bristol on Saturday, March 31, 1739, at about seven o'clock in the evening. It was market day. The narrow streets were crowded, but he made his way to Wine Street. One of the shopkeepers in that street was Mr. Grevil, who had married Whitefield's sister. Whitefield was staying with the Grevils. After resting for a short time, Wesley went with him to Weavers' Hall, which then stood near Temple Church, but has now disappeared. It was, at the time, a well-known meeting-place of one of the Bristol Religious Societies. Whitefield preached, and then returned to Mrs. Grevil's, the two men conversing with each other until midnight. Wesley had come to Bristol to take up Whitefield's work, and their conversation enabled him to understand the character of that work and the position of affairs in Bristol, Kingswood, the Religious Societies, and the city prison. He ascertained the attitude of the ecclesiastical authorities, and listened with interest to Whitefield's description of his experiences, and soon grasped the situation. There was only one aspect of the work about which he had any hesitation. He was familiar with the care of Religious Societies and visiting prisoners, but when the subject of field-preaching was introduced he hesitated. Preaching in the open air in Georgia differed from preaching in the fields in England. We have seen that he was in doubt concerning the legality of the meetings of the Religious Societies, and

JOHN WESLEY'S FIRST VISIT TO BRISTOL

had attempted to extract an opinion on the subject from Dr. Gibson. The lawfulness of field-preaching was still more questionable, and he determined to suspend his judgement until he had attended the open-air services that were to be held on the next day.

Sunday, April 1, 1739, is a date conspicuous in the history of Methodism. In the morning Wesley and Whitefield went to the bowling-green, in the Pithay, where Whitefield preached to a large assembly with great power. Afterwards they walked to Kingswood, and Whitefield again preached at Hanham Mount and Rose Green. At the latter place there was an immense crowd. Many came out from Bristol, some in coaches and others on horseback. From the wood and the surrounding country people trooped to the service. It was known that Whitefield was leaving Bristol on the following day. His exclusion from the churches, his success among the colliers, his heart-stirring appeals, had made him a most popular preacher, and thousands listened with gladness to the gospel he proclaimed. As Wesley looked on the strange scenes of that day, and saw the success of field-preaching, his prejudices began to yield, and he made up his mind that he would accept the whole burden of Whitefield's work. Returning to Bristol, he visited the Nicholas Street Religious Society, in which he commenced to expound the Sermon on the Mount. In his *Journal* he laconically says of that sermon: 'One pretty remarkable precedent of field-preaching, though I suppose there were churches at that time also.' While he was expounding in Nicholas Street, Whitefield was preaching in the room in which the Baldwin Street Religious Society was accustomed to meet. At the close of his sermon he told his audience that Wesley would preach in the brickyard at the farther end of St. Philip's Plain on the following day.[1]

On Monday, April 2, Whitefield left Bristol amid many signs of popular regret. Notwithstanding the opposition of the clergy, the people had rallied round him and thronged his services held in the open air. When he left the city many accompanied him to Kingswood. Arriving at the wood, a crowd of colliers greeted him. At their request he placed a stone on a spot deemed suitable for the site of a school for the instruction of their children. He knelt on the stone and

[1] See Mr. Foster's art. in *W.H.S. Proceedings*, ii., 5.

prayed. Leaving Kingswood, he journeyed to Thornbury on his way to Wales. At Thornbury he was hoping to preach in the church. He had done so on a previous visit, but the doctrine then preached had offended the minister, and the pulpit was denied him. Nothing daunted, he went into the street and, as he told Wesley, he 'played the madman' on a table.[1]

Wesley was left alone in Bristol. He went to his appointment at the brickyard on Monday, April 2. He says, 'At four in the afternoon I submitted to be more vile, and proclaimed in the highways the glad tidings of salvation, speaking from a little eminence in a ground adjoining to the city to about three thousand people. The Scripture on which I spoke was this . . . "The Spirit of the Lord is upon me, because He hath anointed me to preach the gospel to the poor. He hath sent me to heal the broken-hearted; to preach deliverance to the captives and recovery of sight to the blind; to set at liberty them that are bruised, to proclaim the acceptable year of the Lord."' No more suitable text could have been chosen. It described the ideal to which Wesley was true to the end of his days.

Wesley took up the work in Bristol with characteristic promptness. On May 13 we find an entry which looks like the precursor of the multitude of Methodist 'plans' since issued. 'My ordinary employment, in public, was now as follows: Every morning I read prayers and preached at Newgate. Every evening I expounded a portion of Scripture in one or more of the Societies. On Monday, in the afternoon, I preached abroad, near Bristol; on Tuesday, at Bath and Two Mile Hill alternately; on Wednesday, at Baptist Mills; every other Thursday, near Pensford; every other Friday, in another part of Kingswood; on Saturday in the afternoon and Sunday morning, in the bowling-green (which lies near the middle of the city); on Sunday, at eleven, near Hanham Mount, at two at Clifton, and at five on Rose Green.' When we remember the frailty of his health at this time we rejoice that the record ends with the words, 'And hitherto as my days so my strength hath been.'

The Religious Societies occupied much of Wesley's time. In addition to those in Baldwin Street, Nicholas Street, and Weavers' Hall he mentions Societies in Castle Street, Gloucester

[1] Wesley's *Journal*, ii., 209.

JOHN WESLEY'S FIRST VISIT TO BRISTOL

Lane, and Back Lane, now the Old Market Street end of Jacob Street. The Bristol Societies had been strongly influenced by Whitefield's preaching; their numbers had been increased, but they needed to be better organized. Whitefield had suggested to Wesley that the time had come when the ' band ' system should be introduced. He knew something of Wesley's administrative skill, and highly esteemed it. On April 3 Wesley wrote out ' Orders ' for the bands, and the next day he began to form them. He adopted the Fetter Lane model. The men and women met separately under ' leaders ' chosen by lot, and new members were received into fellowship by the vote of the band. Wesley seems to have met the leaders occasionally.[1] On Sunday e.ening, April 29, the first love-feast was held in the Baldwin Street Society; and we also note that towards the end of May, and at the beginning of June, the London example of administering the Sacrament of the Lord's Supper, in private, to little groups of members was followed. A close inspection of the *Journal* and the *Diary* enables us to gain important information concerning the Bristol bands. It is clear that they exercised a determining influence on Wesley's subsequent modes of management.

Wesley's principal work in the Bristol Religious Societies was the exposition of the Scriptures. He expounded the Sermon on the Mount, the Acts of the Apostles, and the Epistle to the Romans. His selection suggests that he had discovered the topics which were to dominate his life-teaching. In the Epistle to the Romans he had found doctrines which had led him into a full and deep spiritual experience; in the Acts he had discovered the golden age of the Church; and by studying the experiences of the apostles he had become possessed of a passionate desire to witness the signs and wonders that accompanied their preaching; in the Sermon on the Mount he had found an ethical standard which humbled him. He confessed its severity, but it kindled in him the hope that, by the grace of God, it was possible to be perfect even as our heavenly Father is perfect. For many years he had been a constant and exact student of the New Testament, but his recent experience of salvation had made him more than ever ' a man of one book.' He was an insatiable reader, probably one of the best-read men in England; but the Bible, as the book of final appeal

[1] *Journal*, ii., 213.

on all religious and moral questions, now asserted its supremacy. That supremacy, in his estimation, ruled the realm of Church life. Instead of poring over the Fathers he searched the New Testament. He found there descriptions of the Primitive Church which compelled his admiration, and made him long for the return of the simplicity, fervour, and prosperity of the ancient days. The light shining from the New Testament, and from his own personal experience, gradually led him away from his old ecclesiastical standpoint; a wider landscape spread around him; he saw a new vision of the kingdom of God.

Since the days when Wesley studied the text of the Greek Testament with the members of the Holy Club he had passed through a personal experience that had produced a profound change in his method of teaching. He had seen new meanings in the words sin, faith, consciousness of salvation, holiness, and the new light had brought a warmth of feeling to which he had been a stranger. The members of the Religious Societies were arrested by his clear and fervent expositions. As he spoke of sin and sinfulness the consciences of the listeners were roused, and the cry of the publican in the Temple was heard in the Society room. At Baldwin Street, on April 17, four persons 'cried out aloud with the utmost vehemence, even as in the agonies of death.' At previous meetings Wesley had dwelt on the incidents of the Day of Pentecost, when the cry of those who were 'pricked in their heart' broke out after Peter's sermon. Having reached the fourth chapter of the Acts, Wesley spoke of the wonderful scene in the upper room, when Peter and John came to their own company, and reported all that the chief priests and the elders had said unto them. The words of the sublime prayer uttered on that occasion were read with perfect sympathy. 'And now, Lord, behold their threatenings: and grant unto Thy servants that with all boldness they may speak Thy word, by stretching forth Thy hand to heal; and that signs and wonders may be done by the name of Thy holy Child Jesus.' We can imagine Wesley's aspect when he enforced the lessons of this incident, and showed how signs and wonders might still be wrought. The members knelt down and called on God to confirm His word. It was then that the wail of penitent sinners was heard in the Society room. The members continued in prayer, and soon the cry of sorrow was changed into a song of those who praised their Saviour God.

At Weavers' Hall, a few days later, a young man was suddenly seized with a violent trembling, and in a few minutes sank down to the ground. 'But,' says Wesley, 'we ceased not calling upon God till He raised him up full of " peace and joy in the Holy Ghost."' At Baldwin Street, on May 1, Wesley's voice could scarcely be heard amidst the groanings of some and the cries of others who were calling aloud to Him who is 'mighty to save.' Wesley desired all who were sincere of heart to join with him in praying that the captives might be delivered. The prayer was answered, and ten persons passed into light and peace. This May day service is specialized by the fact that a Quaker was present, who, standing by Wesley, manifested his displeasure at 'the dissimulation of those creatures.' He bit his lips and knit his brows; then he suddenly dropped on the floor as thunderstruck. His agony was terrible to behold. Once more the people prayed. After a time he lifted up his head, and, looking at Wesley, cried aloud, 'Now I know thou art a prophet of the Lord.'

Speaking generally, these 'scenes,' as they have been called, occurred in the meetings of the Religious Societies, but they were not exclusively confined to them. In a service held in the city prison on April 26 disturbances arose which excited the strong disapproval of Mr. Dagge, the governor. Wesley was preaching on the words 'He that believeth hath everlasting life.' Without any previous design he was led to declare, strongly and explicitly, that 'God willeth all men to be saved.' The declaration and the prayer that was to close the service moved his audience. Several persons dropped on the ground, and one cried aloud. Assisted by the earnest supplications of some who were present, two of the number found rest in the mercy of God. In the present day the assurance that 'God willeth all men to be saved' produces little excitement in a Christian audience; it is received as a commonplace that is almost a platitude. But in 1739 the statement was astounding. John Wesley was an Arminian in doctrine. He belonged to a select number of thinkers who dared to question the popular view of the extent of the redeeming work of Christ. He was working, however, in association with men who widely differed from him. Before leaving Fetter Lane he had been conjured not to enter into any disputes, least of all concerning predestination, and when he arrived in Bristol Whitefield supported the Fetter Lane appeal. He was inclined to comply and to restrain his testimony; but an extemporaneous speaker is sometimes carried beyond the bounds marked out by cool and cautious policy. In those moments when the depths of the spirit are stirred he often utters his strongest convictions. It was so with Wesley. In the presence of his prison audience there came before him a bright vision of the infinite love of God. He could not be silent; he spoke from his heart and touched the hearts of his hearers. The 'good news' thrilled them. It was strange and scarcely believable; but some, who had been shut up in the dungeon of despair, saw the dawning of a new day. Only those who have lived, helpless and hopeless, under the ban of an 'irreversible decree' can understand the revulsion of feeling that storms through the soul when a man dares to believe that the gates of mercy have not been deliberately closed against him. He is startled by the splendour of the grace of God. It is no wonder that physical strength fails in the presence of such a revelation.

The 'scenes' also occurred in the homes of the people. In one case a man, who is described as 'of a regular life and conversation, one that constantly attended the public prayers and sacraments and was zealous for the Church and against Dissenters of every denomination,' was informed that people fell into strange fits at the Societies. He came to see and judge for himself. He decided that it was a delusion of the devil. He went home and did his best to bring his neighbours round to his opinions. But he had borrowed Wesley's university sermon on 'Salvation by Faith' and had read part of it. Sitting down about dinner-time he determined to finish it. In reading the last page he changed colour, fell off his chair, and began screaming terribly and beating himself against the ground. The neighbours flocked into the house and these paroxysms continued at intervals. Early in the afternoon Wesley called, and witnessed a violent struggle, but he and the people betook themselves to prayer. The convulsed man grew calm, and Wesley says 'both his body and soul were set at liberty.' Calling again in the evening, Wesley found that though weak in body 'his soul was in peace, full of love, and rejoicing in hope of the glory of God.'

These 'scenes,' which belong to the outset of Wesley's evangelistic mission when he was closely associated with the Religious Societies, have excited much controversy. It has been alleged that their occurrence explains the exclusion of Wesley from the churches in London and Bristol. But the critics forget that his exclusion from the London churches preceded his visit to Bristol; and, also, that when he joined Whitefield in the western city he found that the blockade had been declared and was in force. It is interesting to note that it was after the occurrence of the first 'scenes' that the embargo was temporarily suspended. On April 29, at the desire of the minister, who was dangerously ill, Wesley preached in Clifton Church. He visited the secluded hamlet on the hill several times, preaching in the church, discharging clerical functions, and, in a sense, assisting to supply Mr. Hodges's place until that minister died on May 21, 1739. So fatal are dates to theories!

We are more concerned with John Wesley's opinion concerning these remarkable events than with those of the psychologists who have attempted to explain them. His view is set forth in a letter to his brother Samuel at the time of their occurrence. He says:

> The question between us turns chiefly, if not wholly, on matter of fact. You deny that God does now work these effects; at least that He works them in this manner. I affirm both; because I have heard these things with my own ears, and have seen them with my eyes. I have seen (as far as a thing of this kind can be seen) very many persons changed in a moment from the spirit of fear, horror, despair, to the spirit of love, joy, and peace; and from sinful desire, till then reigning over them, to a pure desire of doing the will of God. These are matters of fact, whereof I have been, and almost daily am, an eye or ear-witness. What I have to say touching visions or dreams is this: I know several persons in whom this great change was wrought in a dream, or during a strong representation, to the eye of their mind, of Christ either on the cross, or in glory. This is the fact; let any judge of it as they please. And that such a change was then wrought appears (not from their shedding tears only, or falling into fits, or crying out; these are not the fruits, as you seem to suppose, whereby I judge, but) from the whole tenor of their life, till then many ways wicked; from that time holy, just, and good.
>
> I will show you him that was a lion till then, and is now a lamb; him that was a drunkard, and is now exemplarily sober; the whoremonger that was, who now abhors the very 'garment spotted by the flesh.' These are my living arguments for what I assert, viz. 'That

God does now, as aforetime, give remission of sins, and the gift of the Holy Ghost, even to us and to our children; yea, and that always suddenly, as far as I have known, and often in dreams, or in the visions of God. If it be not so, I am found a false witness before God. For these things I do, and by His grace *will*, testify.[1]

While the 'scenes' were not the primary cause of Wesley's exclusion from the Bristol churches, we think it cannot be doubted that their occurrence strengthened the opposition of the clergy of the city and neighbourhood to Wesley and his work. That work was extending. Among other places he visited Pensford, about five miles from Bristol. He asked the minister's permission to preach in the church, but no answer was returned to his application. He therefore went to the market-place and preached to a crowd of people from the top of a wall. On May 7, having obtained leave to preach in Pensford Church, he was preparing to set out when he received the following note : ' Sir,—Our minister, having been informed you are beside yourself, does not care you should preach in any of his churches.' In spite of this rebuff he went to Pensford, and, on Priestdown, about half-a-mile from the place, he found an admirable open-air station, where he preached. It is reasonable to conclude that the reports concerning his mental condition had some relation to the events which were producing so much excitement in Bristol and Kingswood. It is pleasant to note that at Pensford, notwithstanding the clergyman's opposition, a little Society was formed. Although frequently assailed, it stood like a rock.

The Religious Societies in Nicholas Street and Baldwin Street rapidly increased in numbers; on certain occasions the rooms in which they met were inconveniently crowded. Departing from the rule of the older Societies, persons who were not members were allowed to be present when the Scriptures were expounded. We can follow Wesley as he walks about the city pondering the problem of a more commodious place in which the Societies might assemble. We see him standing on the hill overlooking Broadmead, or wandering among the gardens skirting the Horsefair, seeking a suitable site for the erection of a new room. This choice was soon made. In the long strip of land between the Horsefair and Broadmead, not far from the Baptist meeting-house, there was a garden, with

[1] *Journal*, ii., 202.

'a little tenement or lodge' in it. It was owned by William Lyne, and was in the occupation of a tenant named Fisher. Taking counsel with his advisers, Wesley determined to secure this garden; and, on May 9, he took possession of it. The following Saturday the first stone of the new room was laid, 'with the voice of praise and thanksgiving.' It would be difficult to exaggerate the importance of this step. Wesley himself did not foresee the consequences of his action; he did not know that, so far as the Church of England was concerned, he had reached the 'parting of the ways,' and was advancing on a path that would lead to the formation of one of the greatest Protestant churches in the world.

Wesley found that the building of the new room increased the load of responsibility that pressed on him. It must be remembered that, in a sense, he was only a casual visitor to Bristol. He had no intention of becoming personally responsible for the erection of the room and for its subsequent management. He appointed eleven 'feoffees,' upon whom he supposed the expense and direction of the work would fall. As to the expense, he was soon undeceived. The workmen began to build; but the small sum subscribed by the two Societies was soon exhausted, and he was confronted with the possible failure of the enterprise. Instead of allowing the work to stand still, he took upon himself the payment of the workmen, and before he knew where he was he had contracted a debt of more than a hundred and fifty pounds. He seems to have applied to Whitefield and to his own friends in London. He thus describes the result of his application:

> I presently received from my friends in London, Mr. Whitefield in particular, backed with a message by one just come from thence, that neither he nor they would have anything to do with the building, neither contribute anything towards it, unless I would instantly discharge all feoffees and do everything in my own name. Many reasons they gave for this; but one was enough, viz. 'That such feoffees always would have it in their power to control me, and if I preached not as they liked, to turn me out of the room I had built.' I accordingly yielded to their advice, and, calling all the feoffees together, cancelled (no man opposing) the instrument made before, and took the whole management into my own hands. Money, it is true, I had not, nor any human prospect or probability of procuring it; but I knew 'the earth is the Lord's and the fullness thereof,' and in His name set out, nothing doubting.[1]

[1] *Journal*, ii., 197.

After the deed was cancelled his friends came to his help. From an incidental allusion we judge that Mr. William Seward gave him substantial assistance.

The 'New Room in the Horsefair' was built in troublous times. In Bristol many persons were waiting for an opportunity of showing their hostility to Wesley and his work; disaffection was rising in the Societies; the continuance of the tenancy of the rooms in Baldwin Street and Nicholas Street was in peril. The signs of a coming storm darkened the sky. Before it broke Wesley had a strengthening experience. Ascension Day in 1739 was on May 31. Seeking rest among fields and woods, he went with a few friends to King's Weston Hill, not far from Westbury-on-Trym. He was hoping for an opportunity for calm reflection and quiet converse on the great event celebrated by the Church on that day. In the morning the little company sang hymns, prayed, and talked. As they were sitting on the grass two gentlemen went by and recognized Wesley. They walked on, and made their way through the woods to the little villages which stand in the plain. For a jest they told the country-people that Wesley was on the hill, and many quitted their cottages and climbed the steep. In the afternoon a crowd had gathered, and Wesley preached on the words, 'Thou art ascended up on high, Thou hast led captivity captive; Thou hast received gifts for men, yea, for the rebellious also, that the Lord God might dwell among them.' As in the morning, so in the afternoon, the sound of singing was heard on the hill. It is probable that one of the hymns sung was Charles Wesley's great Ascension hymn, 'Hail the day that sees Him rise.' It appears in *Hymns and Sacred Poems* published in 1739, and we know that James Hutton had sent a supply of this book to Bristol. In those days the hymns were 'lined out,' and the words were easily remembered. No fitter place for the first public singing of the Ascension hymn could have been found. When, on a May morning, the devout traveller crosses King's Weston Hill on his way to the woodlands of Blaize Castle, let him pause and recall the scene. The undying echoes of that triumphant song seem to linger in the air:

> Grant, though parted from our sight,
> High above yon azure height,

Grant our hearts may thither rise,
Following Thee beyond the skies.

Refreshed by his visit to King's Weston Hill Wesley went back to Bristol, to find that the landlord of the Baldwin Street room would not permit the Society to meet there any more. He, therefore, met the members in Weavers' Hall. On Sunday, June 3, after preaching at the Pithay Bowling Green to about six thousand persons, he went to Hanham Mount, and afterwards to Rose Green, where a congregation, estimated by him at nine thousand, assembled and worshipped with him. He then returned to Bristol and found that it was impossible to meet the Society in Nicholas Street. He therefore made his way to the unfinished 'school-room' in the Horsefair. The 'shell' of the new room was soon filled with people, and a crowd surrounded it in the garden. About two thousand persons were present. Wesley, describing the scene, says, ' We had a glorious beginning. The Scripture which came in turn to be read was, " Marvel not if the world hate you." We sang " Arm of the Lord, awake, awake! " And God, even our own God, gave us His blessing.' The hymn then sung appears in the 1739 edition of *Hymns and Sacred Poems*, and its use at the opening service of the new room is an additional proof that Wesley was introducing the book into the meetings of the Religious Societies. The hymn became one of the great battle-songs of the Methodist Reformation.

The unpleasant experiences in Baldwin Street and Nicholas Street must have quickened the desire for the completion of the new room. It was hurriedly finished; and, in 1748, it had to be rebuilt. Although the structure has disappeared, it is possible for us to discern its original aspect. In the policy of insurance, effected with the Bristol Crown Fire Office, dated May 16, 1740, the property is described as 'a dwelling-house, school, and Society room, all under one roof, and another small school-room adjoining thereto, the whole being situated between the Horsefair and Broadmead, in the parish of St. James's, in the city of Bristol.' It seems to have been a long building divided into a preaching-room and a school, with another small school-room built as a 'lean-to' against the end of the principal structure. There was also 'a little room by the school,' where Wesley was accustomed to speak to the persons who came to him, and a garret in which a bed was placed for him. The Society room was plainly furnished. There was a desk with a piece of green cloth nailed to it; and in the middle of the room were two sconces, each holding eight candles.

The original design of the room was to make it a meeting-place for two of the Religious Societies in Bristol, and for such of their acquaintance as might desire to be present when the Scriptures were expounded. But that design was enlarged. In the Nicholas Street room a charity-school had been commenced by Whitefield. When it was begun we catch a glimpse of him standing at the door, hat in hand, taking the 'retiring collection.' Wesley seized the opportunity of providing accommodation for teaching children in the new building. He deemed that work of the utmost importance. He threw himself with vigour into the project. A charity-school was formed, and its numbers so quickly increased that four masters and a mistress had to be employed in their instruction. For a time the building was commonly known as 'The New School-house in the Horsefair.'

In addition to building the school-house in Bristol Wesley was busily engaged in carrying out Whitefield's project of a school for the colliers' children in Kingswood. Whitefield did not forget it. From time to time he solicited subscriptions and made collections for its erection; he also published a sermon which was sold for its benefit. The first site had been hastily chosen, and was changed. On May 15 Wesley preached in the afternoon at Two Mile Hill, and then went, in company with others, to look for a better site. They found one in the middle of the wood, between the London and Bath roads, not far from Two Mile Hill, about three measured miles from Bristol. A little sycamore-tree marked the position. On Monday, May 21, Wesley laid the foundation of the new structure. When erected, it consisted of a large room for the school, with four small rooms at either end, in which the schoolmasters lodged. Wesley also hoped that some poor children might find a home in these smaller rooms. As the school was designed for the benefit of adults as well as children it was intended that the older people, some of whom were grey-headed, should be taught in the inner rooms, either early in the morning or late at night, so that their daily work might not be hindered.

Seeking for the experiences which had a determining influence on Wesley's character and future work, we find not a few of them in the less conspicuous events of his life. Let us follow him in his field-preaching at Bath. We watch his interview with Beau Nash. The rapier-thrust of wit with which he routed the Master of the Revels is apt to divert attention from the more serious aspects of the interview. As to Nash, we must always remember that we have never seen a man aright until we have seen his best side. We do not forget that the Beau had a better side than he showed to Wesley. He was an amateur reformer, and made a resolute attempt to control the profligacy rife in the pump-room assemblies. He drew up a code of rules, rigorously enforced even on members of the royal family. As a man intermittently enthusiastic concerning 'law and order,' he was shocked with Wesley's irregularities as a field-preacher. In the interview he raised the question of the Conventicle Act, and elicited an opinion which shows that Wesley, at that time, was finding refuge in the unsound theory that the conventicles mentioned in the Act were 'seditious meetings,' and that, therefore, the Act did not apply to field-preaching. If his interviewer had kept to this point of law he might have escaped the deadly blow that followed; but, like many other controversialists, he raised a personal question, lost his temper, and was beaten. As he stood silent, a bystander said to Wesley, ' Sir, let an old woman answer him.' Then, turning to Nash, she said, ' Sir, if you ask what we come here for, we come for the food of our souls. You care for your body. We care for our souls.' That voice from the crowd reveals a secret hidden from the eyes of men who find it impossible to explain the mystery of the gathering of the multitudes assembled in the fields to listen to the good news of the Kingdom from the lips of the Wesleys and Whitefield. The words of the old woman were probably unintelligible to Nash. He heard them, turned, and walked away.[1]

When Wesley left the field many of his opponents followed him and hissed him as he passed along the street. Among the crowd were ten or twelve ' fine ladies,' who pursued him into the passage of Richard Merchant's house. He says, ' I turned back to them, and told them I supposed what they wanted was to look at me ; such they were welcome to do. Perceiving

[1] For the interview, see *Journal*, ii., 214.

them to be more serious, I added, " I do not expect the rich of the world to hear me. For I speak plain truth, a thing you know little of, and do not desire to know." A few words more passed between us, and, I hope, not in vain.' His words to the fashionable women of Bath show that he was more clearly discerning the sphere of work to which he was called. He was not disobedient to the heavenly vision. Feeling convinced God had called him to other work, he deliberately turned away from the coteries of fashionable society and devoted himself to the middle classes, the working men, and the poor.

It was about this time that James Hervey, a member of the Holy Club, wrote a letter to Wesley which received a memorable reply.[1] He wanted to know why Wesley assembled Christians, who were none of his charge, to sing psalms, and pray, and hear the Scriptures expounded; and he expressed his opinion that it would be hard ' to justify doing this in other men's parishes, upon catholic principles.' Wesley answered :

> If by catholic principles you mean any other than scriptural, they weigh nothing with me. I allow no other rule, whether of faith or practice, than the Holy Scriptures; but, on scriptural principles, I do not think it hard to justify whatever I do. God in Scripture commands me, according to my power, to instruct the ignorant, reform the wicked, confirm the virtuous. Man forbids me to do this in another's parish—that is, in effect, to do it at all, seeing I have now no parish of my own nor probably ever shall. Whom, then, shall I hear, God or man ? ' Is it be just to obey man rather than God, judge you. A dispensation of the gospel is committed to me; and woe is me if I preach not the gospel.' But where shall I preach it, upon the principles you mention ? . . . Suffer me now to tell you my principles in this matter. I look upon all the world as my parish; thus far I mean that, in whatever part of it I am, I judge it meet, right, and my bounden duty to declare unto all that are willing to hear the glad tidings of salvation. This is the work which I know God has called me to; and sure I am that His blessing attends it.

Hervey's criticism seems to have been directed, primarily against Wesley's habit of meeting Religious Societies in other men's parishes. Wesley's reply has a wider scope. When we place it in its true historical setting we see its value as a revelation of its writer's altered position. He has become ' a man of one book.' He applies the test of the Holy Scriptures to

[1] See *Journal*, ii., 217–18.

matters of faith and practice, and to what Hervey calls
'catholic principles.' His assertion shows that he was no
longer standing at the parting of the ways; he was making
a quick advance towards a new theological and ecclesiastical
position. His declaration, 'I look upon all the world as my
parish,' has been deemed arrogant. He was not the first to
use the term. It was familiar to the members of the Holy Club.
The air of arrogance which it is made to assume arises from
popular misquotation, and from ignoring the context. Wesley's
national and world-wide view was essential to him. Without
it he might have influenced a small circle of men in a college-
room, or individuals in a country or town parish, but he never
would have become a national religious reformer.

Watching the working of Wesley's mind in these first days,
we note that he was thinking out the question of predestination,
and confirming himself in the conviction that God willed that
all men should be saved. In the *Diary* we also find signs that
he was studying the doctrine of Christian perfection. It is
profoundly interesting to learn that, in these early days, he
was reading Neal's *History of the Puritans*, the fourth volume
of which had been published in 1738. He had no little prejudice
against the Puritans. The atmosphere of the Epworth Rectory
was not favourable to the formation of well-balanced views of
the struggles in which his Presbyterian ancestors had borne
so conspicuous a part. But he read Neal's book, and his own
rough experiences began to quicken his sympathy with Puritan
reformers.

It is with some impatience that we notice the interruption
of Wesley's work in Bristol. He reached the city on the last
day in March; on June 11 we see him travelling to London.
He had received letters showing that the Fetter Lane Society
was in a disturbed condition, and his presence was imperatively
required. To his regret he had to leave Bristol, making such
arrangements as he could for carrying on the work in the city.
He was absent for a week; and, when he returned, he found
the Bristol Societies in a state of disorder, having lacked the
control of his strong hand.

XXI

DECISIVE DAYS

DURING John Wesley's absence in Bristol events occurred in London which deeply influenced the development of Methodism. Some are still obscure, but the most important stand out clearly in the light shed upon them from Charles Wesley's *Journal*. That *Journal* remained in manuscript for many years; extracts were made from it, but it was not published in its entirety until 1849. Its entries may be said to cover the period from March 9, 1736, to November 5, 1756, although there are disappointing gaps in it. It is invaluable to all students of the early stages of Methodist history.

When John Wesley went to Bristol at the end of March, 1739, Charles Wesley seems to have supplied his place in the Fetter Lane Religious Society. It is essential to remember that, like the other Religious Societies of the time, it consisted of members of the Church of England, although there were some departures from the long-standing, rigorous rule as to membership. In addition, he continued his work of preaching in such churches as were open to him, and of expounding in the Societies he was asked to visit. At Islington Church he still acted in the equivocal position of Mr. Stonehouse's 'curate'; and, in private as well as in public, he pursued his career as an evangelist. In each of these spheres of work he found his way hedged up with thorns.

In the Fetter Lane Society influences were at work which were gradually changing its character. Some of its members objected to its connexion with the Church of England. They resented the restraints such a connexion imposed on them, and openly advocated separation as the short way out of their difficulties. The spirit of Charles Wesley was roused. Throughout his life he was quick to oppose any movement he thought to be in the direction of 'schism,' and in him the Fetter Lane 'separatists' found a formidable antagonist. He gathered around him those who were loyal to the original design of the Society, led them regularly to St. Paul's to the Sacrament, and in all ways fought the tendency to divide from the Church. At this time he had an opportunity of consulting Count Zinzendorf, who was visiting England. On Sunday, April 15, in company with Bray and James Hutton, he had a pleasant interview with the Count, who delighted them by his descriptions of the success of the Moravian missions. During the week Zinzendorf attended a meeting of the Fetter Lane Society and became acquainted with the questions agitating the members. One of them concerned the right of the laity to baptize and to administer the Lord's Supper. The most persistent upholder of that right was a man named Shaw, who had caused much division of opinion, not only in Fetter Lane but also in the Oxford and other Religious Societies. Charles Wesley considered that such teaching, if carried to a practical issue, would inevitably lead to the separation he dreaded. On one occasion he told Shaw plainly he would oppose him to the utmost, adding that if the controversy continued either Shaw or himself must leave the Society. On April 21, in company with Hutton, he again visited Zinzendorf, who spoke much against the intended separation.[1] On the following Wednesday Whitefield preached at Fetter Lane. After the service he and Howell Harris, the Welsh evangelist, had a conversation with Charles Wesley, in which Whitefield spoke of the 'dismal effects' Shaw's doctrine had produced in Oxford. He and Harris both insisted on his exclusion from the Society.

Shaw's doctrine went beyond the question of the right of laymen to administer the sacraments He was strongly influenced by the teaching and example of the French prophets. He not only believed in the inspiration of the individual Christian, but insisted on the right and duty of persons so inspired to speak out the messages they received at all times and in all places. The practical consequence of the doctrine of inspiration held by Shaw and an associate of his named Bowers was that they interrupted services and meetings under the plea that God had charged them with a message which they must deliver at that moment. These views of divine inspiration and illumination led to much confusion, and

[1] C. Wesley's *Journal*, i., 147.

jeopardized the work being done by the more discreet members of the Societies.

Charles Wesley set himself resolutely against the teaching of Shaw. He was strengthened in his opposition by an interview with Zinzendorf on Easter Day, April 22. The conversation turned on the subject of 'motions, visions, and dreams,' and its result was that Wesley was confirmed in his dislike of them. The discussion continued to excite the members of the Fetter Lane Society, and on June 6 it reached a climax. Shaw then pleaded for his view concerning the spirit of prophecy. Straying from his subject, he proceeded to attack Charles Wesley, charging him with a love of pre-eminence, and with making his proselytes twofold more the children of the devil than they were before. One of Shaw's supporters told Wesley that he looked on him as delivered over to Satan. This man and Shaw then declared themselves no longer members of the Church of England. Charles Wesley's comment on their declaration is: 'Now I am clear of them. By renouncing the Church they have discharged me.'[1] The state of opinion in the Fetter Lane Society on the subject of 'prophesying' was divided. We think that many of the members must have been impressed by a serious incident which occurred during the time when the controversy was raging. On June 7 Charles Wesley went to Bray's house, and found there a famous prophetess who had great influence over Bray, Bowers, and others. A description of the interview is contained in his *Journal*. He had his suspicions as to the moral character of the woman, and, in a few days, incriminating evidence was obtained. Her paramour, who was also a prophet, confessed that he had cohabited with her. It is surprising that, notwithstanding this confession, a man like Bray was vehement in her defence; but the disclosure opened the eyes of others. They saw the perils threatening the Fetter Lane Society, and earnestly desired the return of John Wesley from Bristol. They had confidence in his judgement, and in his calm and conciliatory methods of proceeding, and were convinced that he could steer them through the rising storm.

The disputes agitating the Fetter Lane Society at this time had a most important bearing on future events, but it is necessary that we should now move away from the city and

[1] C. Wesley's *Journal*, i., 152.

fix our attention on Islington parish church. Mr. Stonehouse had shown special friendliness to the Wesleys and Whitefield at a time when almost all the churches of London were closed against them. In character he was not a strong man. He was eccentric and infirm of purpose, but his weaknesses must not cause us to forget the aid he gave the Wesleys and Whitefield at the commencement of their mission. He was now to be subjected to the beating of a heavy tempest, and it is no wonder he bent under its stroke.

On Thursday, April 26, Whitefield assisted in administering the Sacrament of the Lord's Supper in Islington Church, where, as he says in his *Journal*, the vicar, in conformity to the rubric, takes care to observe the octaves of Easter. The next day he went to the church to preach according to the appointment of Mr. Stonehouse. While the prayers were being read a churchwarden came to him and demanded the production of his licence. As Whitefield did not possess a licence its production was not possible, and the churchwarden told him he forbade him to preach in the pulpit. The service went on, and was followed by the Communion. During the time it was being administered the sound of a host of people was heard, gathering in the churchyard, and the sound disturbed the worship of the communicants. After the Communion Service Whitefield went into the churchyard, saw a prodigious concourse of people there, mounted a tombstone, and preached to the multitude. His impassioned appeal wonderfully affected his hearers. He says, ' I believe we could have gone singing of hymns to prison.' The entry in his *Journal* is memorable. ' Let not the adversaries say I have thrust myself out of their synagogues. No, they have thrust me out, and since the self-righteous men of this generation count themselves unworthy, I go out into the highways and hedges, and compel harlots, publicans, and sinners to come in, that my Master's house may be filled.'[1] The next day he preached again in the churchyard ; and on Sunday, April 29, he began his memorable field-preaching mission in Moorfields and on Kennington Common.

Whitefield's second service in the Islington churchyard was marked by disorder. When he had finished his sermon, Bowers, ' the prophet,' got up to speak. Charles Wesley was in the crowd, and immediately tried to persuade him to be

[1] Tyerman's *Life of Whitefield*, i., 205.

silent. But, as he says, Bowers beat him down and 'followed his impulse.' Failing to check the unrestrainable enthusiast, he left the place, and his example was followed by many people. The intrusion of Bowers had a most unfortunate effect. It undoubtedly strengthened the hands of the men who were determined to prevent Whitefield, Charles Wesley, and all other unlicensed preachers from occupying the pulpit in Islington Church.

Sunday, April 29, was a critical day. The main course of its events may be traced in Charles Wesley's *Journal*, but the brevity and order of the entries make it a little difficult to follow their progress. So far as we can judge, before the morning service was held there was a meeting of the Islington vestry at which Charles Wesley was present. The churchwardens forbade his preaching, and demanded the production of his 'local licence.' As he did not possess such a document, all that he could say was that he took notice of the demand. A man then began to abuse him, asserting that he, Whitefield, and Stonehouse had all 'the spirit of the devil.' After this meeting the morning service commenced. The vicar read the prayers, and then made way for Charles Wesley to ascend the pulpit. But two men, one of them a beadle, stopped him, and forcibly held him back. In order to avoid making a disturbance he yielded to pressure, and another clergyman preached. At some point in the service the clerk read the canon which directs that ' neither the minister, churchwardens, nor any other officers of the church, shall suffer any man to preach within their churches or chapels but such as, by showing their licence to preach, shall appear unto them to be sufficiently authorized thereunto, as is aforesaid.'[1] After reading the canon, he announced that a vestry meeting would be held in the afternoon.

The forcible arrest of Charles Wesley on his way to the pulpit was witnessed with great displeasure by two men in the congregation, Justice Elliot and Sir John Ganson, the latter being at the head of the London magistrates. They went into the vestry after the service and spoke strongly to the churchwardens, condemning their proceedings. In the afternoon another meeting of the Islington vestry was held. The minute book contains the following resolutions:

[1] Canon 50.

> Resolved, that it appears to this vestry that the Rev. Mr. Stonehouse is the real occasion of the frequent disturbances in this church and churchyard, by his introducing strangers to preach in this church, particularly Mr. Charles Wesley, Mr. Whitfield, and other unlicensed persons, by encouraging and promising to stand by and indemnify them in their preaching without producing their licences, as the canon directs.
>
> Resolved, that it be referred to the churchwardens and others, or any five of them, to draw up a presentment to be exhibited by the churchwarden to the Bishop of London or his surrogate at the next visitation relative to the aforesaid facts.[1]

The next day, April 30, Mr. Stonehouse waited on the Bishop of London and found him ' close, shut-up, sour.' Dr. Gibson refused to answer save to the written case. From that time the pulpit stairs were guarded against any attempt on the part of Charles Wesley to ascend them. The state of siege speedily terminated. On Sunday, May 6, another meeting of the Islington vestry was held, and the following extract from the minute book shows the important business that was transacted:

> It having been agreed to refer all matters in difference between Mr. Stonehouse and this parish to ten gentlemen of the said parish, five of whom were nominated by Mr. S. and five by the parish, it has been concluded by the said ten gentlemen that the Rev. Mr. Stonehouse shall absolutely refuse the granting of his pulpit to Mr. John Wesley, Mr. Charles Wesley, and Mr. George Whitfield, and that those gentlemen shall not officiate any more for him in the parish church, or churchyard, in any part of the duty whatsoever.

Under this entry Mr. Stonehouse writes: ' I do hereby ratifie and confirm the above agreement.' The surrender of Mr. Stonehouse left the victory in the hands of the churchwardens, who successfully defended their church against the intrusion of ' common field-preachers ' and ' holders of assemblies in private houses in an unlawful manner.'[2]

Charles Wesley bore his defeat cheerfully. He devoted more time to the Fetter Lane Society; he accompanied Whitefield to Moorfields, Kennington Common, and Blackheath, standing by him as he preached to great multitudes; and he became a field-preacher in places outside London. He says that he ' scrupled preaching in another's parish till he had

---
[1] *W.H.S. Proceedings*, v., 238.   [2] *Ibid.*, v., 238-39.

been refused the church'; being refused, he went into the open air and preached to small companies of country-people, who listened eagerly to the good news of salvation.

John Wesley reached London on June 13. His arrival was opportune. In the evening he promptly faced the difficulties that had arisen in the Fetter Lane Society. He met the women at Bray's and warned them 'not to believe every spirit, but to try the spirits, whether they were of God.' At eight o'clock the men met at Fetter Lane, when 'it pleased God to remove many misunderstandings and offences that had crept in among them, and to restore in good measure " the spirit of love and of a sound mind."' An entry in Charles Wesley's *Journal* enables us to read between the lines of these general statements. He says: 'We had over the prophetess's affair before the Society. Bray and Bowers were much humbled. All agreed to disown the prophetess. Brother Hall proposed expelling Shaw and Wolf. We consented, *nem. con.*, that their names should be erased out of the Society-book, because they disowned themselves members of the Church of England.'[1] The expulsion of Shaw and Wolf establishes the fact that the Fetter Lane Society, at that time, considered itself as in connexion with the Church of England, a fact which receives further confirmation from an entry in the *Journal* of George Whitefield. Under the date May 20, 1739, he says, 'Went with our brethren of the Fetter Lane Society to St. Paul's and received the Holy Sacrament, as testimony that we adhered to the Church of England.' Referring to the same service, the entry in Charles Wesley's *Journal* is, 'I received the Sacrament at St. Paul's with the best part of our Society.' The popular theory that, from the first, the Society in Fetter Lane was a Moravian Society is quite untenable.

The proceedings we have just recorded cast light on John Wesley's powers as an administrator. In preceding years we have seen him acting as the moderator of the classes at Oxford, as the president of the Holy Club, and as the minister of Savannah. Looking at him as he sits in the disturbed Society in Fetter Lane, composing disputes and removing misunderstandings, we are conscious of a change in his spirit and manner. While not less firm in his maintenance of

[1] i., 153.

essential principles, he has a pleasanter way of showing that firmness. He has made progress in the art of suspending his judgement until he understands all the facts of a case, an art which restrains a man from indulging in the luxury of rushing to conclusions; he has learned the difficult lesson that in order to convince an opponent that he is wrong it is essential that sympathy should be shown with him in the points in which he is right. In process of time he became a consummate manager of men. As the years passed he developed virtues which, in their beginnings, we see in him at the outset of his mission in England; especially we note the strength of his sympathetic firmness, and wonder at his long-suffering ways with incorrigible people. His patient endurance with inconvincible opponents often irritated Charles Wesley; but, on the whole, time has been his vindicator.

The good effect of John Wesley's interference in the Fetter Lane disputes is shown by the following record in his *Journal* on Saturday, June 16: ' We met at Fetter Lane, to humble ourselves before God, and own He had justly withdrawn His Spirit from us for our manifold unfaithfulness. We acknowledged our having grieved Him by our divisions, " One saying I am of Paul; another, I am of Apollos "; by our leaning again to our own works, and trusting in them, instead of Christ; by our resting in those little beginnings of sanctification which it had pleased Him to work in our souls; and, above all, by blaspheming His work among us, imputing it either to nature, to the force of imagination and animal spirits, or even to the delusion of the devil. In that hour we found God with us as at the first. Some fell prostrate upon the ground; others burst out, as with one consent, into loud praise and thanksgiving. And many openly testified there had been no such day as this since the January first preceding.' During his brief visit to London John Wesley did not expend the whole of his time in settling the disturbances in the Fetter Lane Society. The day after his arrival in London he went to Blackheath, where Whitefield was to have preached. Some twelve or fourteen thousand people had assembled to hear him. Instead of preaching, Whitefield asked John Wesley to take his place, and with some reluctance he complied. On the following Sunday he preached to six or seven thousand people in the Upper Moorfields. In the afternoon he visited a man who had left the Fetter Lane Society and the Church. Instead of entering into disputes, he prayed with him, with the result that he gladly returned to the Church, and in the evening was re-admitted into the Society. At five o'clock Wesley preached to about fifteen thousand people on Kennington Common. It was a busy day, crowded with prophetic work.

In glancing over the records of this eventful week in the *Journals* of John and Charles Wesley, we notice a fact which needs to be emphasized. It relates to the much-controverted question of the outcries and physical effects which, about this time, occasionally accompanied the preaching of John Wesley. It has been alleged that these effects were not seen in Whitefield's and Charles Wesley's audiences. If so, what are we to understand by Charles Wesley's assertion that when Whitefield preached on Blackheath, on June 4, ' the cries of the wounded were heard on every side ' ? If the critics had been familiar with Charles Wesley's *Journal* they would have abstained from their attempt to injure John Wesley by comparing him with his brother, and by suggesting that Charles Wesley strongly disapproved of the ' scenes.' Let us appeal to facts. On April 1, 1739, Charles Wesley attended a meeting of the Fetter Lane Society, and says, ' I prayed at Fetter Lane that the Lord might be in the midst of us ; received a remarkable answer. B. Nowers, in strong pangs, groaned, screamed, roared out. I was not offended by it nor edified. We sang and praised God with all our might. I could not get home till eleven.' In describing a service conducted by John Wesley in a Religious Society at Wapping on June 15, at which cases of physical convulsion took place, he says, ' My brother was wonderfully owned at Wapping last week.' He was preaching against predestination, and several persons were overwhelmed by their emotions. Charles Wesley's record continues : ' To-night I asked in prayer, that if God would have all men to be saved, He would show some token for good upon us. Three were justified in immediate answer to that prayer. We prayed again ; several fell down under the power of God, present to witness His universal love '[1] As to the ' scenes ' which imply the possibility of demoniacal possession, it must be remembered that Charles Wesley, as a sound Churchman, believed in the practice of exorcism, although he failed to

[1] C. Wesley's *Journal*, 155.

DECISIVE DAYS

observe the direction of Canon 72, which provides that no minister or ministers shall attempt upon any pretence whatsoever, either of possession or obsession, to cast out any devil or devils, by fasting and prayer, without the licence and direction of the bishop of the diocese first obtained and had under his hand and seal.

On Tuesday, June 19, the day after John Wesley had set out on his return to Bristol, Charles Wesley and Henry Piers, the Vicar of Bexley, waited on the Archbishop at Lambeth. The week before John and Charles Wesley had conversed with Mr. Stonehouse, and had found that Dr. Gibson had justified the Islington churchwardens in their proceedings. Charles Wesley was, therefore, prepared for the result of his interview with the Archbishop. In describing the conversation he says:

> His grace expressly forbade Mr. Piers to let any of us preach in his church; charged us with breach of the canon. I mentioned the Bishop of London's authorizing my forcible exclusion. He would not hear me; said he did not dispute. He asked me what call I had. I answered, 'A dispensation of the gospel is committed to me.' 'That is to St. Paul; but I do not dispute, and will not proceed to excommunication YET.' 'Your grace has taught me in your book on church government, that a man unjustly excommunicated is not thereby cut off from communion with Christ.' 'Of that I am the judge.' I asked him if Mr. Whitefield's success was not a spiritual sign, and sufficient proof of his call; recommended Gamaliel's advice. He dismissed us, Piers with kind professions, me with all the marks of his displeasure.[1]

Charles Wesley's report of his interview leads us to conclude that the Archbishop and Dr. Gibson had made the proceedings at Islington the subject of discussion, and had come to the conclusion that if the Wesleys and Whitefield persisted in their irregularities they must be excommunicated.

With the threat of excommunication hanging over him Charles Wesley went on with his work in London. On Sunday, June 24, yielding to the urgent request of Whitefield, he preached in the morning to ten thousand people in Moorfields He had a hard battle with himself before, in this conspicuous manner, he took to the fields. The day before he had retired and prayed for particular direction. In that solemn interview with God he made the great surrender, offering up his friends, his liberty, his life, for Christ's sake and the gospel's.

[1] C. Wesley's *Journal*, i., 154.

He says, ' I was somewhat less burdened; yet could not be quite easy till I gave up all.' On Sunday the load was lifted. After the service in Moorfields he went to St. Paul's. The psalms and lessons for the day put fresh life into him. So did the Sacrament. His doubts and scruples vanished; the light of the presence of God shone on his path; he knew he had done the thing which had pleased Him. He went to Newington Church, and the rector, Mr. Motte, desired him to preach. He did so; and then he walked out on the common and ' cried to multitudes on multitudes, " Repent ye, and believe the gospel." ' He closed the day at Fetter Lane ' at a primitive love-feast.' In this way Charles Wesley fought and conquered ' the fear of man,' and entered definitely on his great career as a field-preacher.

John Wesley's journey to Bristol occupied two days. He walked part of the distance, and thereby secured much time for meditation. It is not difficult to surmise the subjects on which he brooded. He must have been conscious that he was entering on a new epoch of his life, and that his work as a minister of Christ would have to be done in strange and unconventional ways. He never lost sight of the goal described in *The Country Parson's Advice to his Parishioners*: ' The restoring our decaying Christianity to its primitive life and vigour, and the supporting of our tottering and sinking Church.' ' The Country Parson ' suggested that the best way to attain the end was the formation of Religious Societies; but as Wesley strode along the roads he must have owned to himself that the Societies with which he was connected were not answering their high purpose. The echoes of disputes sounded in his ears, and the possibilities of coming contentions could not be ignored. He must have seen that until the Societies were changed in spirit, until they adopted new methods of work, it was impossible they could be used as instruments to bring about a national revival of religion. Upon that revival his heart was set.

One of the principal defects of the Religious Societies was the lack of provision for the evangelization of the people outside their narrow enclosures. The Reformation Societies connected with some of them attacked public immorality and, by legal processes, did much to discourage and repress vice. But when we examine the rules of the Societies of the highest type we fail to detect any organization for effecting the conversion of the multitudes that were outside all the Churches. In Bristol and in London Whitefield and the Wesleys were breaking the bonds that prevented the Churches from reaching the masses. Notwithstanding the restrictive laws of Church and State, they had gone out into the fields, looked the multitudes in the face, and had besought them to be reconciled to God. Scores of men and women, who had never heard the good news, paused, listened, believed, and became the followers of Christ. The spiritual and moral results of field-preaching were undeniable. They abounded in Kingswood, in London, in Bristol, in Wales. It was indisputable that a way had been discovered by which sinners might be brought from the far country home to God. As Wesley pondered that fact his life-work was revealed, and the voice of the Spirit, of conscience, and of experience spoke with irresistible authority. His purpose became fixed. By much communion with God he was convinced that, at all hazards of reputation, at the cost of his most cherished friendships, in spite of his own tastes and preferences, the work that had come to him must be done. He might have to cease his connexion with the Religious Societies, even with the Church of England, but he resolved not to shun the task assigned to him as he believed, by the wisdom and the will of God.

XXII

THE WEST OF ENGLAND

JOHN WESLEY was absent from Bristol from June 11 to June 19, and during his absence events occurred of signal importance. We must assign the chief place among them to those connected with John Cennick. We have mentioned him in our description of Wesley's visit to Reading, Cennick's home. On May 14, 1739, he came to London, and was received into the Fetter Lane Society. He heard of 'the awakening' in Bristol and Kingswood, and was filled with a strong desire to see the great work that was being done in the west. He obtained permission from the Society to visit Bristol. Before setting out he had a conversation with Whitefield, who told him of his design to build a school for the colliers' children at Kingswood, and expressed a wish that he would become one of its masters. Whitefield wrote to Wesley, who sent a pressing letter to Cennick urging him to come to Bristol. He returned to Reading, settled his affairs, took leave of his relatives, and set out for Bristol on Whit-Monday, June 11, being unconscious of the fact that Wesley had left the city on the same day.

When he arrived in Bristol, Cennick visited the Society in Baldwin Street. He describes it as a Society of religious young Churchmen who, in a little time afterwards, wholly mingled with the Methodists.'[1] On Thursday, June 14, in company with Mrs. Norman and others, he walked out to Kingswood in the afternoon to see the colliers. One of the chief members of the Baldwin Street Society, Samuel Wathen, an apprentice to a surgeon in Corn Street, had begun to visit the colliers and to read to them. He was to have done so on that afternoon, but, for some reason, he was delayed, and the people gathered near the sycamore-tree were disappointed. Cennick's companions, seeing that the colliers were a little impatient, earnestly entreated him to expound a chapter, or else to speak to the people. When Mr. Wathen arrived he joined in the request,

[1] *W.H.S. Proceedings*, vi., 106.

and Cennick, standing under the sycamore-tree, preached to the big crowd clustered around him. The news was noised abroad, and he could not avoid preaching again in Kingswood, at White's Hill, and in the Nicholas Street Society.

On Wesley's return to Bristol he heard of Cennick's preaching. There were some who objected to it, and urged him to stop it. Instead of attempting to do so, he encouraged him in his work, and Cennick continued to preach in Kingswood and the neighbourhood for the next eighteen months, sometimes supplying Wesley's place in Bristol. It must be remembered that John Wesley's views of lay preaching differed from those of Charles Wesley and Whitefield. In 1739 they were opposed to the preaching of laymen, and were confirmed in their objection by the wild outbursts of Bowers. The views of Whitefield changed under the enlightening influences of experience, but the convictions and prejudices of Charles Wesley were retained with some modification throughout his life. It is difficult to understand their approval of the work of Howell Harris, the Welsh lay preacher. Charles Wesley declared that he was ' a man after his own heart,' and he and Whitefield revelled in the campaigns in Wales, which they fought shoulder to shoulder with him. John Wesley's view of lay preaching was more liberal and sagacious. In London he had been helped in his work by a layman. He says, in his *Journal*, that Joseph Humphreys was the first lay preacher that assisted him in England in the year 1738.[1] The words ' in England ' imply that elsewhere he received similar assistance. We have shown that Charles Delamotte on one occasion, in Georgia, supplied his place, and his work was so efficient that it received his high commendation. It may be said that such assistance as Charles Delamotte and Joseph Humphreys had given by expounding in the Societies differed from Cennick's field-preaching ; but John Wesley was distinguished by his open-mindedness ; he was not afraid of a new departure when it was in the right direction. On the evening of his arrival from London he had a long and intimate conversation with Howell Harris, with whose work he was in perfect sympathy. Their conversation must have convinced him that there were circumstances in which the preaching of laymen was not only expedient, but imperative.

[1] *Journal*, viii., 93.

On his return to Bristol Wesley found the Societies distracted with disputes, and he had to resume the difficult work of explanation and conciliation. It took him several days to still the storm that had suddenly risen. Its stress must have been severe, for he says, 'All our Society was falling in pieces.' We have little light on the cause and subjects of the disputes, but from one hint we judge that Wesley himself had been attacked in his absence and his teaching assailed. When he reached Bristol, after preaching in the bowling-green he had an interview with Howell Harris. Harris frankly told him that he had been much dissuaded from either hearing or seeing him by many, who said all manner of evil against him. 'But,' said Harris, 'as soon as I heard you preach I quickly found what spirit you was of. And before you had done I was so overpowered with joy and love that I had much ado to walk home.' It is probable that the people who had attempted to prejudice Harris were those who had been roused to anger by Wesley's attacks on the extreme doctrine of predestination. The predestinarians were strong in Bristol and London, and the warning sounds of the coming tempest could be distinctly heard in the Societies in both places.

The settlement of disputes in the Societies consumed much of Wesley's time. We presume that he occupied the position of the director, who is a familiar figure in the older Societies. The power of that officer was limited. Owing to the scarcity of clergymen in sympathy with the spiritual objects of the Societies the management of affairs, in many places, fell into the hands of the members, who were apt to resent clerical interference. In cases in which a clergyman still retained the post he found that his power was small. The Societies admitted and excluded members, decided cases of discipline, and transacted all financial matters. In Fetter Lane they exercised a strong control over those who were associated with them. We have seen that Wesley could not undertake a journey of any importance without first obtaining permission. He was a man under authority. He undoubtedly exercised great power in the Fetter Lane and Bristol Societies, but it arose from his personal influence, and was not the result of an official position guarded by well-established rules. An adverse vote could at any time sever his connexion with a Society and end his career as its director. The disputes in London suggested that such severance was within the bounds of possibility. The erection of the new school-house in Bristol gave him a more influential position.

The question of his relation to the Religious Societies occupied Wesley's attention, but there was another subject which caused him still graver concern. In London, Bristol, and elsewhere, the churches, with scarcely an exception, were closed against him as a preacher. Confining our attention to Bristol, we note that, in addition, at the churches, with the exception of All Saints in the city, and Christ Church, Clifton, the members of the Religious Societies were refused admission to the Lord's Table. Clergymen found it inconvenient to administer the Sacrament to the large numbers of people who had been influenced by the preaching of Wesley and Whitefield. This fact throws light on the references in Wesley's *Journal* to the administration of the Sacrament in private houses. The number of those who attended these administrations steadily grew; on some occasions thirty or forty were present. Wesley must have been aware of 'the stream of tendency' that was carrying away the Societies from the Established Church and imperilling his own connexion with it. On his return to Bristol he found that the drift of the tide had strengthened. On July 14 he preached at Newgate, and received a message from the sheriffs that he was to preach there no more. His exclusion from the city prison was carried out with such rigour that he was forbidden to visit criminals under sentence of death, even although one of them earnestly entreated that he might be permitted to see him. The action of the municipal authorities in this case is noteworthy, but Wesley soon found that the clergy of the city were his most formidable opponents. The conflict between them was reaching a critical point, and we must concentrate our attention on some of its incidents.

Charles Wesley had evidently written to his brother telling him that the Archbishop of Canterbury was considering the advisability of excommunication in their case and that of Whitefield. John Wesley, in a letter written on June 23, takes a firm stand on ground from which he was never driven. He says:

> My answer to them which trouble me is this: God commands me to do good unto all men; to instruct the ignorant, reform the wicked,

confirm the virtuous. Man commands me not to do this in another's parish—that is, in effect, not to do it at all. If it be just to obey man rather than God, judge ye. . . . But what if a bishop forbids this ? . . . I say, God being my helper, I will obey Him still, and, if I suffer for it, His will be done.[1]

In these words he reveals his calm determination to continue his work and to bear the consequences. His decision was reached after much deliberation. The scene in the council of Jerusalem, when Peter and John declared, ' Whether it be just in the sight of God to obey you rather than God, judge ye,' made a deep impression on him. In after years he wrote this comment on the declaration in his *Notes on the New Testament*: ' Was it not by the same Spirit that Socrates, when they were condemning him to death for teaching the people, said, " O ye Athenians, I embrace and love you ; but I will obey God rather than you. And if you would spare my life on condition I should cease to teach my fellow citizens, I would die a thousand times rather than accept the proposal." ' Wesley ever acted in the spirit of these words. He desired intensely that his work should be done with the consent of the ecclesiastical authorities ; but, if that were denied, then he made up his mind to accept excommunication, or any other penalty, rather than cease to proclaim to the neglected masses of this country the message of salvation.

In August Wesley had an opportunity of learning the opinion of the Bishop of Bristol concerning his proceedings in the diocese. The meeting between Dr. Joseph Butler and Wesley was of great interest. The two men had much in common. Both had close relations with Nonconformity. Dr. Butler, like Wesley's father, had been brought up as a Presbyterian, and had been trained for the ministry in a Dissenting academy ; but, after examining the principles of Nonconformity, he had become dissatisfied with them and conformed to the Established Church. How far his former connexion with the Dissenters affected his sympathies it is difficult to determine, but it is probable that he did not escape the fate which often overtakes clergymen who have been Nonconformists ; he was certainly a rigid Churchman. It is more pleasant to note that in temperament Wesley and Butler were not unlike each other. Both were in love with a secluded

[1] *Journal*, ii., 237n.

life. If they could have indulged their tastes they would have shunned crowds and given themselves up to the delights of the studious recluse. At the time when their interview took place Wesley had experienced a return of the yearning to hide himself in Oxford.

In 1736, three years before his interview with Wesley, Butler had done a work for religion in England which will never be forgotten. He had emerged from his seclusion, entered the arena of controversy, and joined in the defence of Christianity against the attacks of the Deists. His great book, *The Analogy of Religion*, is still a classic of English literature. It appealed to a special circle of readers. They are described by Butler as ' reasonable men, who, from lack of close consideration, were inclined to think that Christianity was a subject for mirth and ridicule.' He thought it possible that, if they would study the arguments contained in the *Analogy*, they might reach the conclusion that there was something in Christianity, and that their altered view might have a practical effect on their conduct. The primary object of the book was to appeal to the reason of a select class ; but it would be unfair to say that such was its exclusive object. In the fifth chapter Butler speaks of those ' who have corrupted their natures, are fallen from their original rectitude, and whose passions are become excessive by repeated violations of their inward constitution.' Glancing at such persons he says, ' Upright creatures may want to be improved ; depraved creatures want to be renewed. Education and discipline, which may be in all degrees and sorts of gentleness and of severity, are expedient for those ; but must be absolutely necessary for these. For these, discipline of the severer sort too, and in the higher degrees of it, must be necessary, in order to wear out vicious habits ; to recover their primitive strength of self-government, which indulgence must have weakened ; to repair, as well as to raise into a habit, the moral principle, in order to their arriving at a secure state of virtuous happiness.'[1] Butler's method of renewing ' depraved creatures ' by education and discipline excites the wonder of those who most admire him ; but it must always be remembered that he wrote as in the presence of cynics who were waiting for an opportunity for mirth and ridicule. Wesley

[1] *Analogy*, 153-54, Bohn's ed.

suggested other processes of renewal when preaching to Kingswood colliers.

The principal interview with Dr. Butler took place on August 18. Two days before Wesley had called on him, conversed for a quarter of an hour, and arranged to see him again. A fragment of a report of the second interview has been preserved.[1] Dr. Butler and Wesley were not alone. Mr. Sutton, who was probably the Bishop's chaplain, Dr. Josiah Tucker, the Vicar of All Saints, and the Chancellor of the Diocese were present. Their presence had a determining effect on Dr. Butler's attitude. It might have been possible, by a little frank and friendly conversation, to have reached mutual understandings which would have influenced the future of Wesley's work; but, afraid of committing himself, the Bishop adopted a stiff official tone and sharply examined his visitor on his views concerning justifying faith, and the assurance of forgiveness, and on his proceedings in Bristol. The whole interview was an illustration of a missed opportunity. The doctrinal questions were answered by quotations from the articles and the homilies. Dr. Butler seemed surprised by these replies. As to the assurance of forgiveness, however, he admitted that he believed some good men had it, though he qualified his admission by saying 'but not all.' Being dissatisfied with the result of the encounter up to this point, he changed his ground. 'Mr. Wesley,' he said, 'I will deal plainly with you. I once thought you and Mr. Whitefield well-meaning men; but I cannot think so now. For I have heard more of you; matters of fact, sir! And Mr. Whitefield says in his *Journal*: "There are promises still to be fulfilled in me." Sir, the pretending to extraordinary revelations and gifts of the Holy Ghost is a horrid thing—a very horrid thing!' Wesley's reply to this outburst was obvious. 'My lord, for what Mr. Whitefield says Mr. Whitefield, and not I, is accountable. I pretend to no extraordinary revelations, or gifts of the Holy Ghost—none but what every Christian may receive and ought to expect and pray for.' The conversation was then diverted to other subjects—the administration of the sacraments in the Societies and the 'scenes.' As to the latter, the Bishop said, 'I hear that many people fall into fits in your Societies, and that you pray over them.' Wesley replied,

[1] See *Journal*, ii., 256–57.

'I do so, my lord, when any show by strong cries and tears that their soul is in deep anguish. I frequently pray to God to deliver them from it, and our prayer is often heard in that hour.' Yielding to irritation, Dr. Butler exclaimed, 'Very extraordinary indeed! Well, sir, since you ask my advice, I will give it you very freely. You have no business here; you are not commissioned to preach in this diocese. Therefore I advise you to go hence.' Wesley's answer to this brusque sentence of dismissal is noteworthy, as it shows his view concerning his unlicensed preaching, the illegality of which he stoutly denied. He said, ' Your lordship knows, being ordained a priest, by the commission I then received I am a priest of the Church Universal. And being ordained as Fellow of a college, I was not limited to any particular cure, but have an indeterminate commission to preach the Word of God in any part of the Church of England. I do not therefore conceive that, in preaching here by this commission, I break any human law. When I am convinced I do, then it will be time to ask, " Shall I obey God or man ? " But if I should be convinced, in the meanwhile, that I could advance the glory of God and the salvation of souls in any other place more than in Bristol, in that hour, by God's help, I will go hence, which till then I may not do.' The Chancellor, who knew more Church law than the Bishop, would probably be amazed at this statement; but Dr. Butler closed the interview without any attempt to enter into further argument. He must have recognized the strength of conviction with which Wesley had spoken, and that it was useless to prolong the verbal contest.

The interview with Dr. Butler, and other events which occurred about this time in Bristol, assisted Wesley to see more clearly the position in which he stood and the path that stretched before him. He was much encouraged by a visit Whitefield paid to Bristol; it only lasted a week, but in that time he was helped by congenial companionship. Whitefield was much impressed with the work done during his absence. In his *Journal*, after noting that he had preached at Baptist Mills, he says that 'Bristol had great reason to bless God for the ministry of Mr. John Wesley. The congregations I observed to be much more serious and affected than when I left them; and their loud and repeated ' Amens,' which they put up to every petition, as well as the exemplariness of their conversation in common life, plainly show that they have not received the grace of God in vain. That good, great good, is done is evident.' At Kingswood he was delighted to find that the new school-house was ready for the roof. He preached to several thousand people and colliers, and his testimony concerning the latter is : ' A great and visible alteration is made in the behaviour of the colliers. Instead of cursing and swearing they are heard to sing hymns about the woods ; and the rising generation, I hope, will be a generation of Christians. They seem much affected by the Word, and are observed to attend the churches and Societies when Mr. Wesley is absent from them.'[1] Whitefield was aware of the disadvantages of his own fugitive ministry. He saw that Wesley's impressive evangelistic preaching and constant care of the Societies in Bristol and Kingswood were telling on a multitude of people, and that a widespread and ever-deepening moral and religious reformation was gradually affecting the whole neighbourhood. Looking at his own work through Whitefield's eyes, Wesley was enheartened. He saw that the brightness of God's blessing rested on it, and with renewed confidence in the presence and power of the Holy Spirit he determined he would never abandon it.

Whitefield's brief visit to Bristol was of great service to Wesley. They conversed freely together, exchanged experiences, and arranged for the continuance and extension of the work. The new room in the Horsefair was almost ready for permanent occupation ; and on July 11 Wesley and Whitefield united ' the two leading Societies ' together and transferred them to the Horsefair school-house. The threat of the landlord of the Baldwin Street room to close the place against the Society had not been carried out, for the room had continued to be used for the meeting of the bands and other purposes, but the hour was approaching when the principal centre of the work in Bristol was to be changed. The union of the Baldwin Street and Nicholas Street Societies was a sign that the time for such an arrangement had come. Another indication appears in Wesley's *Diary*. Two days before the union he was busy writing out ' Orders,' and thus preparing for the government of the new Society.

Wesley's interview with Dr. Butler did not occur until after

---

[1] Tyerman's *Life of Whitefield*, i., 259–60.

Whitefield left Bristol, but Whitefield had told him that the Bishop of Gloucester had written to him on the subject of unlicensed preaching, and so the matter was discussed. Dr. Martin Benson, by the universal consent of all who knew him, was one of the best bishops of the Church of England in the eighteenth century. He was conspicuous for his character and his work. He knew Whitefield, and had often done him deeds of kindness, but was uneasy concerning the ecclesiastical 'irregularities' of the man he had befriended. In July he wrote a letter to the young evangelist in which he affectionately admonished him 'to exercise the authority he had received at his ordination in the manner it was given him,' that is, he must preach the gospel only in the congregation to which he was lawfully appointed. Dr. Benson does not seem to have been aware of the fact that Whitefield had applied to the Bristol authority for a licence, and had failed to secure it, and that there was little chance of any similar application, in London or elsewhere, being successful. But the spirit in which he dealt with a difficult question was admirable. Under the circumstances it was impossible that Whitefield could act in accordance with the Bishop's opinion ; but he was impressed by the appeal, and delayed his answer for several days. If he had allowed himself a still longer period of reflection his reply might have been more considerate and respectful.

In addition to Dr. Benson's letter another significant incident occurred during Whitefield's visit to Bristol. Whitefield was on the wing for America, and soon would be out of the reach of the Conventicle Act, but Wesley knew that troublous times were coming for himself and the Societies. He would be interested, therefore, in the report that, at the Quarter Sessions, the Town Clerk of Bristol had desired the grand jury to 'present' the meetings which were addressed by Wesley and Whitefield and to have the Riot Act read, so that they might be dispersed. The grand jury would not listen to the proposal, and Whitefield says that a man who had been called to serve on the petty jury offered to submit to any fine 'rather than do anything against us.' The disregard of the grand jury obviated any immediate proceedings, but the opponents of the new preachers continued to mature their plans.

The bitterness of many of the Bristol people against Wesley was intensified about this time by a report that was diligently spread in the neighbourhood. Its origin is obscure, but it persisted for many years, and undoubtedly was a serious hindrance to his work. It was reported in Bristol that he was a Papist, if not a Jesuit. He tried to discover the original inventor of the fiction, and his search convinced him that its authors were either ' bigoted Dissenters ' or clergymen. We venture to suggest that the report may be traced back to Georgia. There was at that time in Bristol a Captain Williams, a seaman whose ship often sailed to Savannah. He became closely acquainted with the Williamsons and Wesley's enemies in the colony. Returning to Bristol, after one of his voyages, he visited a magistrate and swore before him an affidavit containing charges against Wesley, which related especially to the way in which he had performed his duties as a clergyman. The severity of his discipline was described ; and what may be called his High Churchmanship was set out in glaring colours. Any one reading these descriptions would probably exclaim, ' He must be a Papist ! ' The epithet fails in scientific accuracy, but it became a missile in the war soon to be waged against Wesley.

The Williams episode is supposed to have had an effect unforeseen by the assailant. Up to that time Wesley's *Journal* had been circulated in manuscript among his friends ; but at last an *Extract* from it was printed in Bristol by S. and F. Farley, and sold at the new school-house in the Horsefair, and by the booksellers in town and country. The *Extract* is undated, but Mr. Green includes it in Wesley's publications in 1739. It describes the voyage to Georgia and the subsequent events until the return to London.[1] If its publication was provoked by the action of Williams he unwittingly did a great service to English literature.

The threats of his adversaries did not arrest the progress of Wesley's work. Its sphere constantly widened. From the Bristol centre, in addition to Kingswood, Bath, and places in the adjacent country, he made his way to Gloucester, Bradford-on-Avon, and Wells, preaching, and caring for the Societies which he either found or formed in those places. His success in Gloucestershire, Somerset, and Wilts encouraged him, and increased his passion for the salvation of men. It is with regret that we see him leaving the west of England at the end

[1] Green's *Bibliography*, 14–15.

of August and turning his face once more towards London; but that regret is modified when we remember that, before his departure, Charles Wesley had arrived in Bristol to take his place.

Charles Wesley, on his journey from London to Bristol, visited Gloucester. He had become a street- and field-preacher, and was filled with a fine enthusiasm for seeking those who had been abandoned by the churches. When he was going to the field at Gloucester he had an experience which must have tried him. He was suddenly confronted by a lady who stood in his way. She cried, ' What, Mr. Wesley, is it you I see ? Is it possible that you who can preach at Christ Church, St. Mary's, &c., should come hither after a mob ? ' He looked at her and said, ' The work which my Master giveth me, must I not do it ? ' She was his old and intimate friend, Mrs. Kirkham. But he ' went to his mob,' and thousands heard him gladly as he spoke of the Holy Ghost, the Comforter, and exhorted them to come to Christ as poor lost sinners. These meetings with old friends were exceptionally severe tests of the determination of the Wesleys to continue their work. The references in their *Journals* to such interviews are tense with suppressed feeling, and challenge the silent homage of those who can appreciate the pathos of their great sacrifice.

Charles Wesley began his ministry in Bristol on August 31. At once he took over his brother's work, caring for the Societies, and preaching regularly at the places in the area of the growing ' circuit.' He was a successful evangelist, full of fire and passion, aiming at the conversion of sinners, and rejoicing in their experience of salvation. He seems to have instituted meetings in which those who had passed into the light of conscious salvation bore their testimony to the great change wrought in them. These experience meetings were held on a Monday, and he refers to them as his ' hours of conference.' He was much encouraged by his conversation with many people who had been helped by his preaching. He possessed a full share of the poet's melancholy, and the stories told him in the hours of conference lifted the clouds and confirmed his resolution. In following the record of his ministry in Bristol we are struck with the frequency of his references to persons who were physically affected under his preaching, and who fell down overwhelmed by the conviction of sin.

Like his brother he was sometimes inclined to attribute their convulsions and trances to Satanic agency, but he treated all cases with sympathy, following John Wesley's rule of judging each case by the results afterwards shown in the lives of those who had been so affected.

Charles Wesley's personal convictions concerning the Christian sacraments had been intensified by his recent experiences in London. He laid great stress on baptism. As to the manner of its administration, he was guided by the rubrics of the Church of England. He baptized a man at Baptist Mills by immersion in the river, and as several other adults wished to be so baptized he formed them into a small company and instructed them in the meaning of the rite. In the course of such instruction he was led to the conclusion that 'persons may be inward Christians before they are baptized.'[1] Out of respect to authority he gave notice to the Bishop of Bristol of his intention to baptize those whom he had instructed. As to the Lord's Supper, we note that he attended the Communion at St. Nicholas and at St. Philip's Churches, and continued John Wesley's practice of private administration. He seems to have gone beyond his brother in this matter. On Sunday, September 16, he met between thirty and forty colliers, with their wives, at Mr. Willis's, and administered the Sacrament to them. Their case was exceptionally difficult. At Kingswood they had no opportunity of communicating in a parish church and so had to go to Bristol for that purpose. When they visited the churches in the city their presence was strongly resented by the clergy.

It was during Charles Wesley's first visit to Bristol that we note unmistakable signs of the swift growth of hostility to the work of the Wesleys in the city and neighbourhood. The attitude of the clergy was one of rigid opposition; but, apart from them, we see the development of a tendency to interrupt the services held in the open air. When Charles Wesley was preaching, bystanders began to shout against him from the outskirts of the crowd; then organized attacks were made. At the bowling-green one afternoon, when about six thousand people were present, a troop of soldiers and 'polite gentlemen' took possession of a corner of the green, and roared and raged exceedingly. Their disorderly conduct roused the fighting

[1] C. Wesley's *Journal*, i., 180.

spirit of the old captain of Westminster School, and he lifted up his voice against them until they fled the field. Somewhat similar scenes were enacted at the brickfield and Kingswood. The opposition assumed other forms. Charles Wesley was an industrious pastor. One day he was intending to visit a poor woman who was dying, but he was informed that a churchwarden had been with her who had threatened her and declared that ' if ever Charles Wesley came near her again he would turn her into the street, sick or well.' These attempts at public and private intimidation were premonitory of the outburst of a gathering storm.

XXIII

A NEW SOCIETY

WHITEFIELD left England for America on August 18, 1739. He was anxious about the crowds of people to whom he had been accustomed to preach in the Moorfields, on Kennington Common, Blackheath, and elsewhere. Many had been roused to deep concern on the subject of personal religion, but the call to Georgia was so insistent that they had to be abandoned. He made an attempt to secure Charles Wesley as a successor in his ' field ' work in London, but failed. Charles Wesley was passing through one of his frequent moods of depression and was seriously thinking of giving up preaching and hiding himself from the world. But John Wesley stepped into the breach. Having arranged with Charles Wesley to come to Bristol, he set out for London, and once more great multitudes assembled in the open air and listened to the gospel message. His visit lasted only a month, but during it incidents of great importance occurred.

John Wesley arrived in London in the early morning of Sunday, September 2. In the evening he preached on Kennington Common and resumed the interrupted campaign. On the next day he met his mother, whom he had not seen for a long time. She had been troubled by some of his proceedings, and by reports concerning the doctrines he preached. Samuel Wesley, her eldest son, had a great influence over her, and his criticisms of his brother's ' field-preaching ' and teaching were keen. But Mrs. Wesley's eyes had been opened by a great experience, which she related to John Wesley in their interview. She told him that until quite recently she had scarce heard such a thing mentioned as having the forgiveness of sins now, or God's Spirit bearing witness with our spirit ; much less did she imagine that this was the common privilege of all true believers. ' Therefore,' she said, ' I never durst ask for it myself. But two or three weeks ago, while my son Hall was pronouncing those words, in delivering the cup to me, " The blood of our Lord Jesus Christ, which was given for thee," the word struck through my heart, and I knew God for Christ's sake had forgiven *me* all *my* sins.' John Wesley asked her a question concerning her father's experience of assurance of forgiveness. Her answer was that Dr. Annesley had that faith, but she did not remember to have heard him preach explicitly upon it. She supposed he also looked upon it as the peculiar blessing of a few, not promised to all the people of God. She remembered that he had declared, a little before his death, that for more than forty years he had no darkness, no fear, no doubt at all of his being ' accepted in the Beloved.' Her recent experience had brought to her mind much that she had not previously understood. The half-lights that had led to misapprehension were banished by the radiance of a new day. It would be difficult to over-estimate the effect of this conversation on John Wesley. He had a high admiration for his mother. Few women, and not many men in the country, were her equals in theological knowledge, penetrating insight, calm judgement, and the courage that dares to examine and accept unfamiliar truth. But, chiefly, he prized her sympathy with his own deep conviction, and, with his mission. It must have given him inexpressible pleasure when, after preaching in the Moorfields in the early morning, his mother accompanied him to Kennington Common, where he proclaimed to an immense crowd the ' joyful news of sins forgiven.' Samuel Wesley was shocked at the encouragement she had given to ' field-preaching,' but her convictions were unchanged by his appeals.

During his visit to London Wesley went several times to Fetter Lane. We can ascertain his opinion of the condition of the Society from the fact that he felt it necessary to exhort the members ' to keep close to the Church and to all the ordinances of God, and to aim only at living a quiet and peaceable life in all godliness and honesty.' The exhortation was timely, but its practical effect was slight. The tendencies towards division were gathering strength, and his waning influence failed to control them. It has been supposed that the discussions that subsequently rent the Society were originated by Philip Henry Molther. It is enough to say that he had not arrived in London at the time when Wesley uttered his warning concerning the neglect of ' the means of grace.' He was introduced to the Society by James Hutton towards the end of October, 1739, and found many of the members prepared and eager to listen to his teaching.

With many forebodings of coming difficulties Wesley left London on October 1, and rode to Oxford, finding there little encouragement. The Holy Club had done its work and had disappeared; the Religious Societies were in a state of decay. Gazing on the ruin Wesley says:

> I had a little leisure to take a view of the shattered condition of things here. The poor prisoners, both in the castle and in the city prison, had now none that cared for their souls; none to instruct, advise, comfort, and build them up in the knowledge and love of the Lord Jesus. None was left to visit the workhouses, where also we used to meet with the most moving objects of compassion. Our little school where about twenty poor children at a time had been taught for many years, was on the point of being broke up, there being none now either to support or to attend it; and most of those in the town, who were once knit together, and strengthened one another's hands in God, were torn asunder and scattered abroad. 'It is time for Thee, Lord, to lay to Thy hand.'

A small 'remnant' was left, and when he rode away he cherished the hope that the seed which had been sown even in Oxford would 'take root downward and bear fruit upward.' He made his way to Bristol, preaching at several places on his line of journey, and on October 8 he arrived in the city.

On October 15, accepting a pressing invitation from Howel Harris, John Wesley set out for Wales. At Abergavenny a thousand people stood patiently, though the frost was sharp, while he 'simply described the plain, old religion of the Church of England, almost everywhere spoken against, under the new name of Methodism.' He also preached, among other places, at Pontypool, Newport, and Cardiff. He was much cheered by his short tour. He was filled with admiration of the natural beauty of the country; but, above all, he rejoiced in the fact that the inhabitants were indeed 'ripe for the gospel.'

On Thursday, November 1, Wesley once more was on his way to London. He broke his journey at Reading, where a little company met him in the evening; 'at which,' he says, 'the zealous mob was so enraged they were ready to tear the house down.' On the Saturday he came to London, and lodged with Mr. Bray. He soon found that the Fetter Lane

A NEW SOCIETY

Society was in a critical condition. The first of his acquaintances whom he met was a woman who had been strong in faith and zealous of good works. She told him that Mr. Molther had fully convinced her she never had any faith at all; and had advised her, till she received faith, to be 'still,' ceasing from outward works; which she had accordingly done. In conversation with Bray he found that he, also, was under the spell of the Molther teaching; and Wesley had to listen to him as he spoke largely of the great danger attending the doing of outward works, and of the folly of people that kept running about to church and Sacrament. On Sunday evening Wesley met the women of the Fetter Lane Society. Some men who were present strongly intimated that none of the women had any true faith, and declared that until they possessed it they ought to be 'still'; that is, they ought to abstain from the means of grace, as they were called, the Lord's Supper in particular. They also asserted that the ordinances were not means of grace, there being no other means than Christ. The same week he talked with his old friend Spangenberg, who was working with Molther in the Fetter Lane Society. After much discussion he found that they were hopelessly divided on a vital point. Wesley could not accept Spangenberg's opinion ' that none has any faith so long as he is liable to any doubts or fear; or that, till we have it, we ought to abstain from the Lord's Supper or the other ordinances of God.' Wesley must have been reminded of his own experience when he was excluded from the Sacrament in Germany because of his 'doubts and fears,' and must have remembered the sympathetic words of Christian David, who was not in agreement with the stern views that prevailed at Herrnhut. His own convictions on the help to be derived from the Sacrament had been strengthened by his recent conversation with his mother; above all, his own experience spoke to him. He knew the blessedness that comes to the man who approaches the Table of the Lord truly and earnestly repenting of his sins, intending to lead a new life, following the commandments of God and walking in His holy ways. Humbled by the consciousness of sin, he had looked up into the face of Christ and learned, again and again, the lesson of His patient, illimitable love. The memories of these moments of sacred communion with his Lord guarded him against the dangers that were threatening his old companions. He stood firm; but many turned aside. It must have been clear to him that the pleasant days of close association with the Fetter Lane Society were coming to an end.

The condition of the Fetter Lane Society caused John Wesley deep concern. He did his utmost in private conversation with some of the members to bring them back to the 'right way,' but in many cases his success was small. While he was brooding over the matter, a path was being prepared for him leading him towards the supreme work of his life. In reading the record of his November visit to London we look for signs of his continuance of field-preaching. On November 10 his *Diary* ends for a time, and we are denied its invaluable help until April 13, 1740. The *Journal* contains no record of the events which occurred on Sunday, November 11. We have, therefore, to turn to other sources of information. It has been suggested that Dr. Whitehead, a biographer of Wesley and one of the three persons to whom he left all his manuscripts ' to be burned or published as they might think proper,' may have been responsible for the disappearance of the lost *Diary*. One thing is certain; he knew what Wesley did on Sunday, November 11. In his *Life of Wesley* he makes an extract from one of Wesley's documents, and the required information is given us.[1]

On Sunday, November 11, Wesley tells us that he preached, at eight o'clock in the morning, to five or six thousand persons at a place not indicated but which was almost certainly the Upper Moorfields. North-west of the fields there were two thoroughfares, little more than lanes, leading to the open country between Old Street and Islington. One ran in front of the Artillery Ground and Bunhill Fields, opposite to which there was a large space known as the Tenter Ground, filled with machines for stretching cloth.[2] The prescient eye sees many things as it glances at the old Tenter Ground; but, bent on confining ourselves to the events of 1739, we return to the Moorfields and strike the second thoroughfare, which runs in a northerly direction. It was called Windmill Hill. As the traveller quitted the Upper Moorfields and walked northward along this narrow way his attention would be arrested by a

---

[1] Dr. Whitehead's *Life of Wesley*, ii., 125.
[2] See map in *Journal*, ii., 65. This lane is now part of City Road.

A NEW SOCIETY

heap of shattered buildings lying at his right hand in the open country. This uncouth heap of ruins represented the 'Old Foundery,' where the king's cannon used to be cast. The place was wrecked by an explosion that occurred in 1716. In consequence of this accident the royal foundry had been removed to the rabbit-warren at Woolwich. For more than twenty years the 'Old Foundery' had been a scene of desolation, but a change was coming.[1] John Wesley, in his *Earnest Appeal to Men of Reason and Religion*, says, 'In November, 1739, two gentlemen, then unknown to me, Mr. Ball and Mr. Watkins, came and desired me, once and again, to preach in a place called the Foundery, near Moorfields. With much reluctance I at length complied.'[2] From the extract in Dr. Whitehead's *Life* we learn that the service was held at five o'clock in the evening of Sunday, November 11—another notable day in the history of Methodism.

John Wesley left London the day after he had preached amidst the ruins of the 'Old Foundery,' but it is probable that before he left it was suggested to him to take the place into his own hands. Those who were the most earnest in the matter offered to lend him money to purchase the lease, the price of which was £115. Mr. Watkins and Mr. Ball delivered to him the names of several subscribers who were ready to pay, some four or six, some ten shillings a year, towards the repayment of the purchase money and also of the cost of putting the buildings into repair. We cannot ascertain the precise date when this arrangement was accepted by Wesley, but it is probable that only a short time elapsed before the 'Old Foundery' came into his possession. Dr. Whitehead suggests that his decision to acquire the place was influenced by the fact that, as the majority of the members of the Fetter Lane Society were alienated from him, it was necessary to take a preparatory step towards a final separation from them.[3]

When Wesley left London on Monday, November 12, he journeyed to Wycombe, and preached there to a little Society. Dr. Whitehead, again quoting from the Wesley manuscripts, has brought to light another important fact. In the town he met his old friend John Gambold, and another clergyman named Robson. After much prayer and consultation they

---

[1] See Jackson's *Life of C. Wesley*, ii., 534–36.   [2] *Works*, viii., 37, 8vo ed.
[3] *Life of Wesley*, ii., 125.

made the following agreement : ' 1. To meet yearly at London, if God permit, on the Eve of Ascension Day. 2. To fix then the business to be done the ensuing year : where, when, and by whom. 3. To meet quarterly there, as many as can ; viz. on the second Tuesday in July, October, and January. 4. To send a monthly account to one another of what God hath done in each of our stations. 5. To inquire whether Mr. Hall, Sympson, Rogers, Ingham, Hutchins, Kinchin, Stonehouse, Cennick, Oxlee, and Brown will join with us herein. 6. To consider whether there be any others of our spiritual friends who are able and willing so to do.'[1] In these proposals for the holding of a yearly conference it is easy to discern the outlines of an arrangement subsequently adopted by Wesley. The Wycombe scheme was never carried out, but there are several points in it that deserve attention. It is interesting to note the fact that the conference was not to consist exclusively of clergymen; laymen like Cennick, Oxlee, and Brown were to be invited to join the company.

After spending some weeks in the west of England John Wesley returned to London on Wednesday, December 19, and stayed there until Thursday, January 3, 1740. He would be busy with the affairs of the Foundery, but we are chiefly interested in a supremely important event which occurred during this interval. On Monday, December 24, a significant entry appears in the *Journal*. Wesley tells us that, after spending part of the night at Fetter Lane, he went to a smaller company of people. Those who were assembled occupied the time ' in exhorting one another with hymns and spiritual songs, and in prayer.' We have no information as to the place of meeting nor any other particulars, but the reference to this little company gathered together on Christmas Eve warrants the suggestion that, at this point, we catch sight of a new Society which was undoubtedly formed at the close of 1739. Words that are familiar to all Methodists instinctively recur to our mind. Wesley says :

> In the latter end of the year 1739 eight or ten persons came to me in London, who appeared to be deeply convinced of sin, and earnestly groaning for redemption. They desired, as did two or three more the next day, that I would spend some time with them in prayer, and advise them how to flee from the wrath to come, which they saw

[1] *Life of Wesley*, ii., 125.

continually hanging over their heads. That we might have more time for this great work, I appointed a day when they might all come together. . . . This was the rise of the United Society, first in London, and then in other places. Such a Society is no other than ' a company of men, having the form, and seeking the power, of godliness ; united in order to pray together, to receive the word of exhortation, and to watch over one another in love, that they may help each other to work out their salvation.[1]

In an article contributed to the *Proceedings of the Wesley Historical Society*[2] the Rev. Thomas McCullagh expressed an opinion that the first meeting of the new Society was held in the Foundery in the evening of Thursday, December 27, 1739. He was a careful investigator, and his judgement commands respect. He seems, however, to have overlooked the entry in the *Journal* on December 24. As to the place of the first meeting, it can only be conjectured ; but it is indisputable that, in the opening months of 1740, a Society under the control of John Wesley and distinct from the Fetter Lane Society did habitually meet in a room at the Foundery.

The creation of the new Society raises a number of important questions. It was formed on lines differing essentially from those on which the Religious Societies were based. There is no evidence that Wesley, at the time of its foundation, drew up ' Orders ' for its government ; but it is significant that there was only one condition previously required in persons who sought admission into it. It was imperative that they should possess ' a desire to flee from the wrath to come, to be saved from their sins.' If a Churchman or Dissenter, an Arminian or a Calvinist, was moved by that desire, and sought admission, he was welcomed. When the Society in London increased in numbers, and similar Societies were formed elsewhere, it became necessary to regulate them more definitely, but it was not until 1743 that John Wesley drew up specific ' Rules ' for their guidance. The absence of elaborate organization was a sign that the new Society was not a ' Religious Society.' Consciously or unconsciously, Wesley had entered on a new path which diverged from the way in which he had walked with old companions, and led him towards the extraordinary successes of his work as an evangelist.

In tracing the progress of John Wesley we are often reminded

---

[1] See *Rules of the Society of the People called Methodists.*
[2] *Proceedings*, iii., 166-72.

of Cromwell's aphorism : ' We never mount so high as when we know not whither we are going.' It is probable that the consequences of the formation of the new Society in London were not seen by Wesley ; but we who occupy ' a coign of vantage ' in surveying accomplished facts have an unveiled landscape before us. We are intensely interested in the foreground and in the beginning of the new path which Wesley was to travel. We will confine our attention to one aspect of the new departure. It occurred at a time when Wesley was strongly opposing the determination of the majority of the Fetter Lane Society to separate from the Church of England. Those who were in favour of such a separation were working towards a fundamental change in the organization and character of the Society. They wished to sever it from the Church of England and make it an integral part of the Church of the United Brethren. We have seen that Count Zinzendorf did not, at first, approve of this intention ; but, step by step, it was accomplished. When Wesley formed his new Society did it occur to him that he might be initiating a movement that would take its own direction ? Did he see that by his adoption of ' one condition ' of admission to membership he was opening a door by which many people who had no real connexion with the Church of England might come into his Society ? It is impossible to answer these questions ; but there can be no doubt that his action eventually brought him into the presence of serious problems.

About the time of the formation of the new Society Wesley's attention was directed to the question of his relation to the State Church. His position was critical. That Church, in a sense, had broken with him. A threat of excommunication was hanging over his head. The rulers, the clergy, and the mass of English Churchmen were hostile ; with all their power they were seeking to hinder and end his work. In spite of their opposition he pursued his way, and continued to deliver his message. He was firmly attached to the Church, and refused to separate from it. His love for it was ardent, and survived the severest tests ; but it did not make him blind. He saw its defects, and conscience would not allow him to abandon his attempt to remedy them. In the *Journal* we get light on his broodings ; and, by considering his own statements, we get a better understanding of his position. He was an eager student of the New Testament, and was well acquainted with the history of the Christian Church during the first century. He was convinced that in the Apostolic and sub-Apostolic times a standard of belief and of conduct had been set up that ought to be reached by all churches bearing the name of Christ. Applying that standard to the Church of England, its weaknesses and failures were revealed. Two facts made a deep impression on him : First, the neglect of the doctrines of the New Testament and of the formularies of the English Church which concern the vital question of personal salvation ; and secondly, the ignoring of the fact that a man's membership in the Church of Christ must be decided by his moral and spiritual qualifications. He insisted that the Church was a fellowship of saints, a household of God, built upon the foundation of the apostles and prophets, Christ Jesus Himself being the chief corner-stone ; ' in whom each several building, fitly framed together, groweth into a holy temple in the Lord.' As to the members of the Church, he accepted the apostle's description, ' In whom ye also are builded together for a habitation of God in the Spirit.' He had a lofty ideal of the Church, an ideal created by deep communion with its divine Head.

It will assist us to understand Wesley's position at the time of the new departure if we quote two extracts from his *Journal*. On September 13, 1739, he tells us that a serious clergyman desired to know in what points he differed from the Church of England. He answered, ' To the best of my knowledge, in none. The doctrines we preach are the doctrines of the Church of England ; indeed, the fundamental doctrines of the Church, clearly laid down, both in her prayers, articles, and homilies.' A further question was put : ' In what points, then, do you differ from the other clergy of the Church of England ? ' The reply was given at length :

> In none from that part of the clergy who adhere to the doctrines of the Church ; but from that part of the clergy who dissent from the Church (though they own it not) I differ in the points following :
> *First.*—They speak of justification, either as the same thing with sanctification, or as something consequent upon it. I believe justification to be wholly distinct from sanctification, and necessarily antecedent to it.
> *Secondly.*—They speak of our own holiness, or good works, as the cause of our justification ; or that for the sake of which, on account of which, we are justified before God. I believe neither our own holiness

nor good works are any part of the cause of our justification; but that the death and righteousness of Christ are the whole and sole cause of it; or that for the sake of which, on account of which, we are justified before God.

Thirdly.—They speak of good works as a condition of justification, necessarily previous to it. I believe no good work can be previous to justification, nor, consequently, a condition of it; but that we are justified (being till that hour ungodly, and, therefore, incapable of doing any good work) by faith alone, faith without works, faith (though producing all, yet) including no good work.

Fourthly.—They speak of sanctification (or holiness) as if it were an outward thing; as if it consisted chiefly, if not wholly, in those two points: (1) the doing no harm; (2) the doing good (as it is called); that is, the using of the means of grace, and helping our neighbour. I believe it to be an inward thing, namely, the life of God in the soul of man; a participation of the divine nature; the mind that was in Christ; or, the renewal of our heart after the image of Him that created us.

Lastly.—They speak of the new birth as an outward thing, as if it were no more than baptism; or, at most, a change from outward wickedness to outward goodness, from a vicious to (what is called) a virtuous life. I believe it to be an inward thing; a change from inward wickedness to inward goodness; an entire change of our inmost nature from the image of the devil (wherein we are born) to the image of God; a change from the love of the creature to the love of the Creator; from earthly and sensual to heavenly and holy affections—in a word, a change from the tempers of the spirits of darkness to those of the angels of God in heaven.

There is, therefore, a wide, essential, fundamental, irreconcilable difference between us; so that if they speak the truth as it is in Jesus, I am found a false witness before God. But if I teach the way of God in truth, they are blind leaders of the blind.[1]

In February, 1740, John Wesley visited a young man, who was under sentence of death in Newgate, London. One day he met the Ordinary, who, with much vehemence, told him he was sorry that he had 'turned Dissenter from the Church of England.' Wesley replied that if it was so he did not know it. The Ordinary was surprised, said something in the way of proof which needed no reply. After this interview Wesley wrote a paragraph in his *Journal* which contains a reasoned statement concerning Dissent which sheds light on his ideal of the Church. He says:

Our twentieth article defines a true Church, 'a congregation of faithful people, wherein the true word of God is preached and the sacraments duly administered.[2] According to this account the Church

---
[1] *Journal*, ii., 274-76.
[2] Wesley was quoting from memory; the article is the nineteenth.

of England is that body of faithful people (or holy believers) in England among whom the pure word of God is preached and the sacraments duly administered. Who, then, are the worst Dissenters from this Church ? (1) Unholy Men of all kinds ; swearers, Sabbath-breakers, drunkards, fighters, whoremongers, liars, revilers, evil speakers ; the passionate, the gay, the lovers of money, the lovers of dress or of praise, the lovers of pleasure more than lovers of God : all these are Dissenters of the highest sort, continually striking at the root of the Church, and themselves in truth belonging to no Church, but to the synagogue of Satan. (2) Men unsound in the faith ; those who deny the Scriptures of truth, those who deny the Lord that bought them, those who deny justification by faith alone, or the present salvation which is by faith : these also are Dissenters of a very high kind ; for they likewise strike at the foundation, and, were their principles universally to obtain, there could be no true Church upon earth. Lastly, those who unduly administer the sacraments ; who (to instance but in one point) administer the Lord's Supper to such as have neither the power nor the form of godliness. These, too, are gross Dissenters from the Church of England, and should not cast the first stone at others.[1]

These extracts enable us to understand Wesley's position at the time of the new departure. We see that he was a firm believer in the doctrines of the Church of England which relate to the salvation of the individual. Those doctrines were ignored by the clergy and their congregations. They were embedded in articles and homilies, but Wesley awoke them from their slumber, and, in the Religious Societies and in the open-air assemblies, they once more made their great appeals to the conscience of Englishmen. Personal experience had explained the meaning of these doctrines. In Georgia Wesley had placed so strong an emphasis on baptism that we are tempted to think he looked upon it as the supreme effective cause of the new birth, but he had discovered that the new birth meant much more than the blessing that comes to an unconscious child when it is sprinkled at the font. As to holiness, he had discovered that it could not be gained by a series of meritorious 'good works'; it was an inward thing, the life of God in the soul of man, a participation of the divine nature, the mind that was in Christ, the renewal of the heart after the image of God. If we compare the Wesley of the Holy Club and the Wesley of Georgia with the Wesley of 1739 we are almost startled at the contrast. The punctilious 'High Churchman' can scarcely be recognized. His spiritual vision

[1] *Journal*, ii., 335-36.

has been strengthened ; he sees the things once afar off ; he remembers that he has been cleansed from his sins. As Miss Wedgwood so finely says, in his case the birthday of a Christian was shifted from his baptism to his conversion ; and in that change the partition line of two great systems was crossed.[1]

John Wesley's conversion changed his view of the neglected doctrines of the Church and modified his ecclesiastical position. It did more. It made him an evangelist filled with an insatiable desire to save the souls of men. The mercy he had found he showed to others in simple, clear, persuasive words, and in the actions of a high-toned, unpretentious, moral and spiritual life. He became an evangelist of the best type. He preached, won great successes, but was deeply concerned that those who were impressed by his preaching should be gathered into Societies in which they might be safeguarded, and trained in the doctrines, duties, and privileges of the Christian religion. His ideal of the Church may be gathered from the entry in his *Journal* which follows the record of his interview with the Ordinary of Newgate. That ideal was not realized in the Church of England. It was approached in some of the Religious Societies which answered to the descriptions contained in Dr. Woodward's book. In 1739 a few of these could be found, here and there, in the country, but their influence was not important. Wesley never forgot the *Country Parson's Advice to his Parishioners*. He fully approved of the prediction, ' If good men of the Church will unite together in the several parts of the kingdom, disposing themselves into friendly societies, and engaging each other, in their respective combinations, to be helpful to each other in all good Christian ways, it will be the most effectual means for restoring our decaying Christianity to its primitive life and vigour, and the supporting of our tottering and sinking Church.' Since he read those prophetic words he had organized and attended such Societies, but he had come to the conclusion that something was lacking in their aims, their constitution, their management, and in their spirit, which prevented them from accomplishing the purpose set forth by the ' Country Parson.' And so a new beginning had to be made, a Society on a simpler basis had to be formed, a Society whose supreme work was ' to spread Scriptural holiness over the land.'

[1] *John Wesley and the Evangelical Reaction of the Eighteenth Century*, 157.

INDEX

Abergavenny, John Wesley preached at, 324

Abridgement of books, Practice of, by John Wesley, 120, 144, 153n, 174

Absentees from Church of England services, censured, and penalties on, 227

Academy, Dissenters', London, 46; Newington Green, 46–47; Stepney, 55

ACTS, PERSECUTING, 226, 274:
1. Third Act of *Uniformity* (1559), 226
2. Fourth Act of *Uniformity* ('Uniformity of Public Prayers') (1662), 33, 34, 35, 36, 42, 44, 229, 235, 255, 274; its form of Declaration, 35–36; its demand of re-ordination of Presbyterian ministers, 36; Earl of Anglesey's generous action, 39
3. First *Conventicle Act* (1664), 37, 42, 229, 230, 256, 261
4. Second *Conventicle Act* (1670), 42–43, 62, 225–226, 229, 232, 256, 292; indulgence granted by the King (1672), 43; *Act* strengthened in Queen Anne's reign (1705) and in *Act of Union* (1706), 231, 235; repealed (1812), 229
5. *Five Mile Act* (1665), 37, 256

ACTS, other, affecting above:
1. *Succession Act* ('Act of Settlement,' 1701), 231
2. *Toleration Act* (1689), 231

Addison, Joseph (1672–1719), Chief Secretary for Ireland; his *Spectator* hymns:
1. 'The spacious firmament on high' (*M.H.B.* 75), 168
2. 'When all Thy mercies' (*M.H.B.* 92), 168
3. 'When rising from the bed of death,' 168

Administration of Sacrament of the Lord's Supper in private houses to little groups of members of Religious Societies, 283, 311, 320

Admiralty, Lords Commissioners of, 115

Advice to his Parishioners, The Country Parson's (1680, 1701), quoted, 9, 334; read and distributed by 'Holy Club' at Oxford, 9, 92, 137; referred to, 10, 137, 306

Agutter, Mr., pensioner at the Charterhouse, 240, 246

Allington (suburb of Bridport), 31

Altorf, Religious Society at, formed by Dr. Lange, 26

America, Bristol's trade with, 264, 271; Plantations of, and English slave-trade ('middle passage'), 273

Amherst, Nicholas, on Christ Church men (1733), 67

Analogy of Religion (Butler), 220, 313

Andrewes, Dr. Lancelot, Bishop of Chichester, 1605, 51

Anne, Queen, reign of (1702–1714), 14, 18, 25, 50, 53, 231, 235; her Letter to Magistrates, 22.

ANNESLEYS, the (Chapter II), 38–45; the maternal family line of the Wesleys, 38–39, 39n
1. Arthur Annesley, second Baron Mountnorris (1660), afterwards Baron Annesley of Newport Pagnell and Earl of Anglesey (1662), uncle of Dr. Samuel Annesley, 39, 42
2. Elizabeth Annesley, daughter of Dr. Samuel Annesley, married John Dunton, 55; her *Diary*, 79n
3. Sir Francis Annesley, Bart., afterwards first Baron Mountnorris and Viscount Valentia, grandfather of Dr. Samuel Annesley, 39
4. John Annesley, of Kenilworth, father of Dr. Samuel Annesley, 39, 40
5. Judith Annesley, wife of John and mother of Dr. Samuel Annesley, 40
6. Robert Annesley, great grandfather of Dr. Samuel Annesley, 39
7. Dr. Samuel Annesley (1620–1696), pen portrait, 38; various ministries, 40–41; St. Giles', Cripplegate, 41; ejection, 42; Dissenter, 42–45; Assurance, 45, 322
8. Susanna Annesley, daughter of Dr. Samuel Annesley, married to Samuel Wesley. See SUSANNA WESLEY

Anslye, John, the name of Dr. Samuel Annesley's father as entered in baptismal register, 40

Antinomianism, 243

Apology for the People called Methodists (Joseph Benson), quoted, 61, 84, 93

Apostolic Constitutions, The, 102, 103, 164, 165

Apostolic succession of Bishops, 132

336 INDEX

ARCHBISHOPS of Canterbury of the period:
1. William Laud (1633–1645), 51, 70
2. Gilbert Sheldon (1663–1677), 254, 255
3. John Tillotson (1691–1694), 22, 53, 54
4. Thomas Tenison (1694–1715), 21, 22, 35
5. John Potter (1737–1747), 82, 83, 105, 112, 132, 132n, 243, 305
6. Thomas Secker (1758–1768), 278

Archbishop Sharpe of York, 57
Arches, Court of, 116–117n
Arctic regions, 41
Armada, Spanish (1588), 41
Arminian Magazine, 44n, 158
Arminianism of John Wesley, 285–286
Army and Navy Work (S.P.C.K.), 21
Articles of Church of England, thirty-nine agreed upon by Convocation (1563), 82, 243; Article xi. 35, 181; Article xiii. 181; Article xxxv. 221; Subscription to, 86, 220
Ascension Day (1739), 290
Assembly of Divines, Westminster, 33, 56
Assize, Black (1577), 66; Justices of, 227
'Assurance' of Forgiveness, 45, 81, 130, 205–208, 220, 225, 314, 322–3
Athanasian Creed, 82
Athenae Oxonienisis (Anthony Wood), quoted, 29, 70
Atlantic and Gulf coast, 127
Atterbury, Dr., Bishop of Rochester (1713), High Churchman and friend of Samuel Wesley, junior, 54
Augsburg, Religious Society at, 26
Austin, John, Roman Catholic, 122; his *Devotions in the Ancient way of Offices*, 167
Awakening in America, The Great (Jonathan Edwards), 223–224

Badcock, Mr., in *Westminster Magazine*, on John Wesley at Oxford, 77
Baddeley, Sir J., his *Account of the Church and Parish of St. Giles, Cripplegate*, 41
Ball, Mr., of London, at the Old Foundery, 327
Bands, at Bristol, 283; at London (Fetter Lane) 196–7, 199, 244; at Oxford, 245
Baptism: of infants by trine immersion by John Wesley, 131, 171; of adults by immersion by Charles Wesley, 320; Dissenters', and validity of lay-Baptism, 116–117n, 118, 225, 235, 297; Charles Wesley's 'hypothetical Baptism,' 236; John Wesley's changed views on, 333
Baptismal Service: Prayers for Candidates for Baptism, in Deacon's book, 101
Baptists, 171, 258
Basingstoke, John Wesley expounded in a room at, 245
Bateman, Mr., 93

Bates, Dr., 44
Bath, churches closed to George Whitefield, 251; he preached in open air, 261; John Wesley's fieldpreaching, 282, 318
Battle of Senlac, near Hastings (1066), 28
—— Worcester (Sept. 3, 1651), 30
Beau Nash, Master of the Revels at Bath, John Wesley's encounter with, 293
Bedford, Rev. Arthur, Vicar of Temple Church, Bristol, established parochial charity school, 276
Bedminster (Bristol), 265
Bemerton (Wiltshire), rectory home of George Herbert at, 50, 142; later of John Norris, 50
Bengel, Johann Albrecht, his *Greek New Testament*, 91n
Benham's *Memoirs of James Hutton*, 112, 198, 205
Benson, Dr., Archbishop of Canterbury (1883—1896), his *Cyprian*, 175
Benson, Dr. Martin, Bishop of Gloucester, his *Letter* to George Whitefield on 'unlicensed preaching,' 317
Berry, Rev. John, M.A., father-in-law of Samuel Wesley, junior, 84
Berthelsdorf (Germany), Moravian settlement at, 210. See ROTHE
Berwick-on-Tweed, 229, 235
Beveridge, Dr., supported Religious Societies, 5; his *Sermon* on the Ministry, 244
Bexley (Kent), 196, 214, 233–4, 243, 305. See PIERS
Bible and the Sun, The, James Hutton's shop, 179
Bibles, distribution of, 44
Bibliography of the Works of John and Charles Wesley (Rev. Richard Green), 119n
Bicentenary, The Wesley, in Savannah, 128
Bickersteth, Bishop, on Wesley's translation: 'O God, my God, my all Thou art' (*M.H.B.* 429), 149
Bishop, Moravian ordination of a, 131–132; its validity, 132 and 132n
Bishop of London and pastoral care of the Colonies, 163
BISHOPS mentioned:
1. Bristol. See BUTLER, GOOCH, IRONSIDE, ROBINSON, and SECKER
2. Chester. See WILKINS
3. Exeter. See WARD
4. London. See COMPTON and GIBSON
5. Oxford. See POTTER
6. Rochester. See SPRAT
Bitton, parish of Kingswood, 254
Black Assize (Oxford, 1577), 66
Blaize Castle (near Bristol), 290
Blandford jail, 34
Blendon Hall, 186, 213, 214
Blunt, Rev. John Henry, his *Book of Church Law* (revised by Phillimore, 6th ed.), 36, 117n

INDEX

Board of Trade, 152
Böhler, Peter, of Jena University, interviewed Spangenberg, 130; met John Wesley in London, 182; goes with Wesley brothers to Oxford, 182-184; 185-9, 198, 204, 240
Bolzius, John Martin, minister to the Salzburgers at Ebenezer (Georgia), 166
Book of Common Prayer. See PRAYER-BOOK
Book of Homilies, The, 186, 221, 243
Books for Georgia, 119
Bourchier, Elizabeth, daughter of Sir James Bourchier, married to Oliver Cromwell, 41
Bovey, Miss, of Savannah, 154. See BURNSIDE, MRS.
Bowers, 'the prophet,' an associate of Shaw in Fetter Lane Society, 297-8; interrupted George Whitefield's service in Islington churchyard, 299-300; 'much humbled,' 302
Boyce, Mr., of 'Holy Club,' 95
Bradford-on-Avon (Wilts), 318
Bray, Dr., scheme of, 21; prominent supporter of Religious Societies, S.P.C.K., S.P.G., etc., 21; Books for Georgia through his 'Associates,' 119
Bray, Mr. John, a brazier in Little Britain, and Charles Wesley, 189-191, 214-215; Fetter Lane Society and 'Bands' at his house, 244, 297-8, 302, 324; *Hymns and Sacred Poems* sold at his house, 246
Brett, Dr. Thomas, Bishop amongst the Nonjurors, 120-121
Brevint, Dr. Daniel, Dean of Lincoln, 121; his *The Christian Sacrament and Sacrifice* and his *Depth and Mystery of Roman Mass*, 121
Bridgwater, 37
Bridport, 29, 30, 31
Brigden, Rev. Thomas E., 39*n*, 85*n*, 112*n*
Brislington (Bristol), 264-5
BRISTOL :
1. Second city in the Kingdom in 1739—pop. 30,000, 251, 264. See Bristol in 1739 (chap. xix.), 264-279
2. Its two approaches — George Whitefield entered from Somersetshire side, John Wesley from Gloucestershire, 264
3. Bristol Fairs, 267; Gardens, 267-8; increasing business of its Port, 271
4. Drinking facilities for seamen, 271-272
5. Bristol ships (50 in slave trade), 272-3; and warships, 273-4
6. Jacobite and Hanoverian Riots every June, 274-5

BRISTOL—*continued*
7. Philanthropic spirit of its citizens, 277
8. Its unique position in annals of the Methodist Church, 280
9. For George Whitefield's work there, see GEORGE WHITEFIELD
10. For John Wesley's work there, see JOHN WESLEY
All Saints, 311
Avon river, 264, 265, 270
Back Lane Religious Society, 283
Baldwin Street Religious Society, 281, 282, 284-5, 288-291, 308
Baptist Mills, 268, 282, 315
Barton (Benedictine priory farm of St. James'), 267
Bowling Green in the Pithay, 267, 281, 282, 291, 320
Brandon Hill, 270
Brickyard, 266; site of John Wesley's first open-air service, 282
Bridge over Avon, 265
Broad Street, 266, 268
Broadmead, 267, 268, 288, 291; Baptist Meeting-house in, 268, 288; Baptists of, 230, 242
Castle Street Religious Society, 282
Cathedral, formerly Abbey of St. Augustine, 269
Christ Church (Clifton-on-the-Hill), 270, 282, 287, 311
College Green, 269
Corn Street, 268, 308
Cotham, 268
Durdham Down, 268; Conventicles at, 230, 275
Frome river, 267, 269
Gloucester Lane Religious Society, 282-3
High Street, 266
Holy Trinity Hospital, 266
Horsefair, 267, 288, 291; ground purchased in, for the New Room, 288-289. See p. 338
Hot Well, 270
Jacob's Street, 283
Kingsdown, 267
King Street, 268
King's Wood, Conventicles at, 230, 275
Lawford's Gate, 266
Lewin's Mead, 277
Mayor's Chapel (St. Mark's), 269
Montague Tavern (1737), 267
Newgate Prison (the old Castle), 252, 266, 311
Nicholas Street Religious Society, 281-2, 288, 291, 309
Old Market Street, 283
Park Street, 269
Pithay, the, 266-267
Pyle Street, 277
Quarter Sessions, 317
Quay, The, 276
Redcliff Back, 276
Redcliff Meads, 265
Redland, 268

BRISTOL—*continued*
ROOM, THE NEW, described, 291-2; ground in Horsefair purchased for, 288-9; first stone laid, 289; eleven 'feoffees,' 289; these discharged by John Wesley cancelling the Deed; everything done in his name, 289; Wesley undertook debt, 289; preached in shell of, 291; rebuilt (1748), 291; Charity School: 'The new Schoolhouse in the Horsefair,' 292; Wesley and Whitefield united the Baldwin Street and Nicholas Street Societies there, 316
St. Augustine's Back, 269.
St. Brendan's Chapel, 270
St. James's, parish church of, remnant of old Benedictine priory, 260, 267, 291
St. Mark, the Mayor's Chapel, 269
St. Mary Redcliffe, 252, 259
St. Michael's, 269
St. Michael's Hill (Gallows), 277
St. Nicholas, 320
St. Nicholas Gate, 266
St. Philip and Jacob, 254, 259, 266
St. Philip's Plain, 281
St. Stephen's Church, 269
St. Thomas's, 259
Stokes Croft, 268, 277
Temple Church, 265, 276; and Meads, 265; and Gate, 265
Weavers' Hall, 265; well-known meeting-place of one of Bristol Religious Societies, 280, 282, 285, 291
Wine Street (in old maps Winch Street), 251, 266, 268, 280
Bristol, by Hunt, in Historic Town Series, 270
Bristol, Annals of, in the Eighteenth Century, by Latimer, 260, 264, 266, 271, 275, 276, 277
Bristol, Bishops of, 278. See BUTLER, GOOCH, IRONSIDE, ROBINSON, and SECKER. Seven bishops between 1710-1738, 278
Bristol, Chancellor of Diocese of. See REYNELL
Bristol Crown Fire Insurance Office, 291
Bristol, Dean of. See CRESWICKE
Bristol Fairs, 267
Bristol Newspaper, Farley's (1725), 276
Bristol Newspaper, Sam Farley's (1737), 276
Bristol Post Boy, The (1702), 276
Bristol Post Man, The, published by Samuel Farley (*cir.* 1713), 276
Bristol Riots, 274-5
British Slave trade, with Bristol as one of chief slaving ports, 273
Broadley, Mr. A. M., his *The Royal Miracle*, 30*n*; his article on The Dorset Wesleys, 32*n*
Broadmead Records (Haycraft's ed.), 242, 275

Broadway, near Evesham (Gloucestershire), 80
Brougham, Lord, 117*n*
Broughton, Thomas (Oxford Methodist), 95; afterwards curate at Tower of London, 147; afterwards Secretary of S.P.C.K., 95, 186-7; with Charles Wesley at Tyburn, 217
Brown, Dr. John, his *Pilgrim Fathers of New England*, 33*n*
Brown, Mr., a layman suggested in the Wycombe 'yearly conference' scheme, 328
Brownfield, John, a Georgia settler, 128
Buckingham, Duke of, formerly Marquis of Normanby, befriended Samuel Wesley, 56-57; nominated John Wesley to the Charterhouse, 75
Buckland (Gloucestershire), 80
Buddaeus, Dr. Johann Franz, of Jena, encouraged his students (including Spangenberg) to carry on elementary schools, 212
Bunyan, John, 48
Burges, Dr. Cornelius, brother-in-law of Mrs. John Westley, 33, 41
Burke, Edmund, quoted, 70
Burnham, Mr., visited Newgate with Charles Wesley, Mr. Bray, and Mr. Sparks, 215
Burnside, Mr., of Savannah, consulted by John Wesley in the Williamson case, 169
Burnside, Mrs. (née Margaret Bovey), a deaconess of Savannah, 164, 170
Burton, Dr. John (of Corpus Christi College, Oxford), a Georgia Trustee, secures John Wesley for Georgia, 110-112, 156; his estimate of the clergy (1735), 111
Butler, Dr. Joseph (1692-1752), Bishop of Bristol (1738-1750), also Dean of St. Paul's, and afterwards Bishop of Durham, 220; his *Analogy of Religion* answers the Deistic controversy, 313; teaching contrasted with that of John Wesley, 313-4; his father a Presbyterian, 312; trained for the ministry at a Dissenting Academy, 312; his interview with John Wesley (Aug. 18, 1739), 312-315
Butterworth, Rev. Richard, on *Instructions* of S.P.G., 113-114
Byrom, Dr. John, Nonjuror, of Manchester, 96, 111, 188
Byrom, Josiah, brother of above, 188

Cabot, John, sailed from Bristol and reached North American mainland (1497), 264
Calamy, Dr., his *Account of the Ministers ejected after the Restoration*, 30, 54; his *Continuation of the Account*, 31-32, 34, 38, 40, 258; his ordination, 44

INDEX

339

Canons of Church of England (published 1604), 102, 103, 234, 261
Canterbury, Prebend at, held by Bishop Gooch of Bristol, 278
Cape Breton (North America), 264
Capital punishment in 18th century for 160 various actions, 232, 277
Cardiff, visited by George Whitefield (1739), 262; by John Wesley (1739), 324
Cardwell's *History of Conferences connected with the Revision of the Book of Common Prayer*, 35-36; his *The Two Liturgies of Edward VI compared*, 100n
Care for the children, John Wesley's, 154, 166
Caricatures of Puritans and Dissenters in modern novels, 38
Carolina, 108; traders of, 151
Caroline, Queen (consort of George II), Samuel Wesley's *Job* dedicated to, 111
Carthusian, John Wesley a loyal, 75
Castel, an architect and friend of Oglethorpe in the Fleet prison, 106
Catechetical Schools, 21
Catechisms, distribution of, 44
Catechumens, Prayers for, 101
Catherston (Dorset), 29
Catholics, Roman, 72, 73, 148, 165
Causton, Thomas, storekeeper and chief magistrate of Savannah, 155, 160, 169; his wife, Mrs. Causton, 169, 170
Cavaliers, gay, at Oxford, 71
Cave, Dr. William, his *Primitive Christianity*, 102, 152, 153n
Cecil, Richard, 222
CENNICK, JOHN, of Reading, belonged to a Quaker family but joined Church of England and came in contact with the Oxford Methodists through Mr. Kinchin, 244-5, 246; received into Fetter Lane Society, 308; his work in Bristol Societies and as Master at Kingswood School, 308-310; suggested as a member of the Wycombe 'Yearly Conference' Scheme, 328
Century of Scandalous Priests, The (John White, M.P.), 55
Cevennes (France), 242
Chapman, William (student of Pembroke College, Oxford), 147
Charity Schools, 20, 276, 292
Charles I, Reign of King (1625-1649), 39, 70-71
Charles II, Reign of King (1660-1685), 9, 10, 17, 32, 39, 43, 44, 49, 71-72, 163, 231; escape of, to France (1651), 29-30
Charleston Church (America), Charles Morton was pastor of, 47
Charlestown (South Carolina), a port, 108, 152, 164
Charmouth and Catherston (Dorset), 29

Charnock, Stephen, Dissenting minister, 48
Charterhouse, 58, 75, 145, 240, 246, 248
Cherokees, mission to, 127
Chester, Bishop of (Dr. Wilkins), 43
Chichester, Prebend at, held by Bishop Gooch of Bristol, 278; also office of Residentiary at, 278; also the mastership of St. Mary's Hospital at, 278
Chickasaws, mission to, 127
Choctaws, mission to, 127, 148
'Christian,' John Wesley seeks deeper meaning of the name, 84
Christian Monitor, 92
Christian Perfection, doctrine of, 295
Christian Sacrifice and Sacrament, The (Brevint), 121. See LORD'S SUPPER
Christianity, Primitive (Cave), 102, 152, 153n; compared with *Primitive Christianity Revived* (Whitson), 102
Christianity, True Scriptural, 9
Church Government, Episcopal form of, 32, 132; Presbyterian, 32
Church, Greek, and Nonjurors, 103
Church ideals of John Wesley, 157-158
Church Law, 116
Church Parties—high, 42, 48, 49-52, 54, 85; low, 49, 50
Church, Methodist, origin of, 5, 9, 28; impression made upon it by John and Charles Wesley, 28
Church, Moravian, organized in Savannah, 131; ordination of a bishop, 131
Church of England, Oxford loyal to, 73-74; its failure in eighteenth century, 278
Church, Roman, its heavy tribute of Missionary martyrs in Missions to Red Indians, 127
Churches closed against the Wesleys, 180, 183, 224, 233-5, 243, 250
Churches, Dissenting, 43, 44, 256, 257
Churches of Christendom, 101
Churches, Unitarian, 258
'Circuit' system by John Wesley at Bristol, 282, 319
Civil War, The (1642-1655), 32, 33, 70-71, 73, 228, 274
Clarendon, Lord, on *Act of Uniformity*, 36; on Oxford morals, 70
Clarke, Mrs., her *Susanna Wesley* (Eminent Women Series), 38, 55, 58, 59, 61-63
Clarke, Dr. Adam, his *Wesley Family*, 57, 60
Clayton, Rev. John (Oxford Methodist), Tutor of Brasenose College and a High Churchman, 95-96; influence on 'Holy Club,' 96, 104; friend of Dr. Deacon, 100; *Letter* to John Wesley, 187-189
Clayton, Dr., Bishop of Clogher, his *Essays on Spirit*, 220
Cliffe, near Gravesend, 40
Clonard (Ireland), 269

Clubs, Religious Societies as, 24
Cobbett, William, his *Cottage Economy* quoted on the home-brewing of beer before 1780, 272
Cock-fighting, 259
Cockspur Island, 128
'Collecting,' John Wesley's habit of, 144, 210
Collection of Psalms and Hymns (Charlestown, 1737), by John Wesley, 152, 164, 167–169
  Wesley's second Hymnbook (same title), 225
Colley, Sir Henry, of Kildare, 29; daughter of, married Bartholomew Westley, 29
Colley, Richard, grandfather of the Duke of Wellington, 29*n*; assumed arms and name of Wellesley, 29*n*
Colleys, the, 29*n*
Collier, Jeremy, his *Reasons*, 122
Colonies supposed to be under pastoral care of the Bishop of London, 163
Colston, Edward, of Bristol, his care of poor children, 276
Columbus, 264
Commissaries, appointment of, 163
Commonwealth of England (1649–1660), The, 30, 32, 33, 274
——— in Massachusetts, The, 33
COMMUNION SERVICE in Religious Societies, 13, 17; in the University, 82, 86–87; in the 'Holy Club,' 87, 88, 91, 93, 97–8; in Edward VI's first *Prayer-book* (Roman Mass), 99, 100; in Edward VI's second *Prayer-book*, 100; John Wesley's *Sermon* on, 103; on board the *Simmonds*, 116–7; Literature read by John Wesley on, 120–122; Attendance of Children, 166; Savannah case, 169–173; in Fetter Lane Society, 200, 325; among the Moravians ('fencing the Table'), 205, 209–210; question of administration, 283, 297, 311, 320
'Comprehension' scheme of Archbishop Tillotson, 45, 53
Compton, Dr., Bishop of London (1675–1714), 21, 24, 55
Compton, Mrs., of Oxford, 245
Conference, Religious, written by Susanna Wesley to her daughter Emilia (1712), 59–60
CONFERENCE, YEARLY, foreshadowed in the Wycombe scheme of John Wesley and Gambold, 327–328
Constitutional History of England (Sir Thomas Erskine May), 257, 277
Constitutions and Canons Ecclesiastical on the Lord's Supper, 86–87
Constitutions, Apostolical, The, 102–103
Continuation of Rapin (Tindal), quoted from Overton, 24
Contrast between the John Wesley of the 'Holy Club' and of Georgia, and the John Wesley of 1739, 334
Conventicle Acts of 1664 and 1670. See ACTS, PERSECUTING

Conventicles, in Spitalfields (Dr. Samuel Annesley's), 42; in London, 42; in Epworth, 61–63
'Conversion,' defined, 31, 167, 186; of Haliburton, 187; of Charles Wesley, 191–2; of John Wesley, 192–193, and its results in him, 334
Convocation of 1662, revised the *Book of Common Prayer* (ratified by the *Act of Uniformity*), 35
Convocation, Samuel Wesley elected by the Lincolnshire High Churchmen to, for several years, 54, 58, 60
Convocations of Canterbury and York, 1865, framed new *Canon* revising the Declaration of the *Act of Uniformity* (1662) on the *Book of Common Prayer*, 36
Conybeare, Dr. John, Dean of Christ Church, Oxford (1733), his moral reform of Exeter and Christ Church Colleges, 67; interview with Charles Wesley, 219–222
Cottage Economy (William Cobbett), 272
Council of Jerusalem, 311
Court of Savannah in Wesley's case, 170–173
Cowes Church, Charles Wesley preached his first sermon in, 118
Cowes Roads, 118, 124
Cowley, 238
Cowpen (Georgia), 153, 154
Cranford (Kent), 120
Cranmer, Thomas (Archbishop of Canterbury, 1533–1556), in Bishop's Hole, Oxford, 65; burnt at Oxford, 65
Creeks, Missions to, 127, 148
Creswicke, Dr. Samuel, Dean of Bristol, afterwards Dean of Wells, 252, 259, 260
Cromwell, Oliver, 'Lord Protector of the Commonwealth of England' (1653–1658), married Elizabeth Bourchier, 41; his 'Ironsides,' 31
Cromwell, Richard, 'Lord Protector' (1658–1659), 41
Cruso, Timothy, 'the golden preacher,' a fellow student of Daniel Defoe and Samuel Wesley at Stoke Newington Academy, 47
Curnock, Rev. Nehemiah, Editor of the Standard Edition of John Wesley's *Journal*, 5; opinions quoted 76, 77*n*, 79, 80, 119, 149
Cusacks, 29*n*
Cyprian, St., *Works* of, 174–175

Dagge, Abel, Keeper of Newgate Bristol, convert of Whitefield, the 'tender jailor' of the poet Savage 252, 285
Dangan, co. Meath, Ireland, the home of the Wellesleys, 29, 29*n*
David, Christian, first planter of the Moravian settlement at Herrnhut conversation with John Wesley or Full Assurance before admission to the Communion, 205–7, 325

INDEX

Deacon, Dr. Thomas, Nonjuror, of Manchester, 96, 100, 104, 116; his new *Service Book* for 'Separatists' (1734), 100–102, 142, 148, 188
Deaconesses, in Georgia, appointed by John Wesley, 148, 154, 164; in Moravian settlements, 209
Deal, 178
Defoe, Daniel, 47. See CRUSO
Deistic controversy, 67, 85, 165, 219, 220, 313
Deists, 59, 165
Delamotte, Charles (1714–1796), friend of John Wesley, who accompanied him to Georgia as his servant, 115, 131, 146, 154–157, 161, 164, 173–174, 237, 309
Delamotte family at Blendon Hall, addressed by John Wesley, 186
Delamotte, Mrs., her conversation with Charles Wesley, 213; convinced by Jeremy Taylor's prayers, 213–214
Delany, Dr. (Dean of Down, Ireland), married Mrs. Pendarves, 80
Deptford, 265
Depth and Mystery of Roman Mass laid open and explained (Dr. Brevint), 121
De Renty (Roman Catholic), *Life* of Monsieur, read by John Wesley, 120; and abridged by him, 174
Diary of John Wesley at Oxford, begun 5 April, 1725, 77, 79
Didsbury College (Manchester), 135, 225
DIRECTORY OF PUBLIC WORSHIP (1645) substituted for Prayer Book by Parliament, 228; removed (1662), 229
Dison, Rev. Mr., Chaplain of the Independent Company in Georgia, 146, 153, 172–3
Dissent, John Wesley on, 333
Dissenters, 12, 22, 37, 38, 43, 44, 47, 48, 52, 53, 54, 74, 148, 167, 171, 231, 250, 257, 258, 275, 329
Dissenters, Protestant, 257, 258, 259
Dissenters, Re-baptism of, 225, 235
Dissenters' Academy, London, Samuel Wesley at, 46
Dissenting Churches, History of (Wilson), 43, 44
Distinction of High Church and Low Church, The (Norris), 50–52
Döber, Andrew, with John Wesley at Savannah, 131
Doddridge, Dr. Philip, 246
D'Oilly, Robert, began Oxford Castle (1071), 65
Dolling, Henry, of Wadham College, Oxford, translated into Latin *The Whole Duty of Man*, Samuel Wesley's master at Dorchester; Samuel Wesley's first book dedicated to him, 46
'Domestic' Evangelism by Charles Wesley, 213
Doncaster, 41
Dorchester, 32, 33; St. Mary's Church, 33; Jail, 37, 54; Free School, 46
Dover, 108

Downs, The (roadstead), 118, 124, 178
Dress in Church, John Wesley on, 136
Dublin: William Morgan died at, 96; Edward Veal at Trinity College, 46
Dummer (Hampshire), home of the Kinchin family, 185, 244
Dunton, John, 'the eccentric bookseller,' 55; married Elizabeth Annesley, 55; his *Life and Errors* quoted, 79n
Durham, Prebend at, held by Bishop Secker of Bristol, 278

Earnest Appeal to Men of Reason and Religion (John Wesley), 327
Ebenezer (Georgia), 109, 166
Edict of Nantes (1598), revocation of (1685), 242
Edward the Confessor, Reign of (1041–1066), 65
Edward VI, King, Reign of (1547–1553), Communion Service of his first Prayer Book, used by second class of Nonjurors, 99–100. See NONJURORS
Edwards, Jonathan, his *The Great Awakening in America* (Revival in Northampton, New England), 223–4
Eighteenth century Religious Revival, 5
Ejected Ministers, 25, 32
Elementary Schools in Oxford, 92; in Savannah, 154; in Jena (Germany), 211; in Bristol, 292
Eliot, John, Missionary to the Red Indians, 127
Elizabeth, Queen, Reign of (1558–1603), 51, 226–7
Elliott, Justice, at Islington Church, 300
Energumens, Prayers for, 101, 142
England and the English in the Eighteenth Century (W. C. Sydney), 256–257
English Nonconformity (Dr. Robert Vaughan), 34, 35, 36
'Enthusiasm,' at Oxford, 74, 93–94, 203; of John Wesley in London, 180; in Fetter Lane Society, 241; Indifference of Clergy, 257
Episcopal Re-ordination, 36, 45
Episcopalians, 32, 56, 226, 229
Epworth (Lincolnshire), 57, 83, 95, 98; Life in Rectory of, 57, 63; Rectory of, burnt down (1709), 60
Eucharist as 'the Christian Sacrifice,' 100, 103, 121, 142
Evangelical belief, decay of, fatal to aggressive work, 258
Evangelical doctrines of Dissenters retained by Samuel Wesley, 48–49
Ewart, Mr., secured privilege of counsel for prisoners on trial for felony (1836), 277
Examiner, Swift's, 49
Excommunication, threats of, to George Whitefield, 260–1; to the Wesleys, 305, 311
Exeter in 1739, the fourth city in the Kingdom, 264

INDEX

Experience Meetings ('Hours of Conference'), Charles Wesley's in Bristol, 319
Exposition (Dr. Hammond), 18
'Expounder' in Religious Societies, John Wesley in much request as, 245, 282; George Whitefield as such, in Bristol, 262
Extempore preaching, John Wesley's first, 116

Fairfax, Sir Thomas, received surrender of Oxford (1646), 71
Faith, Christian, John Wesley's early views (1733) on, 98; his definition in the *First Standard Sermon* (1738), 201; the two definitions compared, 202; the first (1733) in his *Sermon* 'The Circumcision of the Heart,' revised when the sermon was published (1748), 98, 202. See SALVATION BY FAITH
Family, the Christian, John Wesley's ideal of, 158
Farley, Felix and Samuel, of Bristol, 276, 318
Fasts and Fasting, 13, 82, 91, 94, 96, 97, 98, 104
Fell, influence of, in study of Greek at Oxford, 89
Fellows of Colleges, duties of, 89
Fellowship Meetings, Nonconformist, 25
Fellowship, John Wesley's ideals of, 157-8
Fellowships, University College, disadvantages of, 83
'Fencing of the Table,' Moravian, 205
Feoffees of 'New Room' at Bristol, 289
Ferrar, Nicholas, of Little Gidding, 200
Ferrar, the family of, 158
Festivals and Fasts (Robert Nelson), 102
Fetter Lane. See under LONDON.
'Field Preaching,' its lawfulness, 281; Samuel Wesley, jun., on, 322-3; Susanna Wesley on, 322-3; John Wesley on, 282; John Wesley's, at Bristol, 282; Blackheath, 303; Upper Moorfields, 303, 326; Kennington Common, 304, 322; Charles Wesley at Moorfields, 305; George Whitefield at Kingswood, 254, 259, 261, 281; Bath, 261; Thornbury, 282; Bristol, 261; Islington Churchyard, 299; Moorfields, 299, 301, 322; Kennington Common, 299, 301, 322; Blackheath, 301, 304, 322; John Cennick at Kingswood, 309; spiritual and moral results of, 307
Fire of London, The Great (1666), 41
First five cities in the Kingdom (1739)—London, Bristol, Norwich, Exeter and York, 264
Fisher, tenant of tenement on Horsefair site, Bristol, 289
Fitzgeralds, The, 29n
Five Mile Act (1665), 37
Fleming, Dr. Richard (Bishop of Lincoln), founded Lincoln College, Oxford (1427), 68

Fletcher, John, of Madeley, 120
Fleury, Claude, his *Manners of the Christians* used by John Wesley in Georgia, 144
Florida, 107
Flute, John Wesley practising Moravian Hymn tunes on his, 137
Fog's Journal, 97
Forms of Prayer for every day in the week, Collection of, prepared by John Wesley, aided by John Clayton (1733), 104-105; Wesley's *First Publication*, 105
Fort Pulaski (America), 128
Foskett, Mr., Minister of Broadmead Baptist Church, Bristol, 242
Foster, Rev. Henry J., 192n, 281
Foundery. See under LONDON
Fox, Mr. (of Oxford), 185, 244
Fox, Mrs., 187
Foxe, John, Martyrologist, 41
Francke, August Hermann (died 1727), founded the Lutheran University of Halle (Germany) in 1694, and encouraged Dr. Woodward in the formation of Religious Societies, 26; wrote *Pietas Hallensis* and *Nicodemus, or Treatise on the Fear of Man*, 120
Francke, Professor, of Halle, second son of above, Archdeacon of St. Mary's, and Director of his father's benevolent institutions; visited by John Wesley, 211
Frankfort, Religious Society founded by Dr. Spener at, 26
Frederica (Georgia), 132-133, 139-143, 146-148, 152-153, 155
French, in America, 108; in Canada, 145; brandy, 272; prophets, 241-242; phrophetess, 241, 298, 302; Protestant refugees, 242
Frere's *History of the English Church*, 51
Freylinghausen, Johann Anastasius (1670-1739), his *Gesang-Buch*, 149; his Hymn, 'O Jesu, source of calm repose' (*M.H.B.* 571), translated by John Wesley, 168
Friar, Spanish (Garcina), 65
Friars, Mendicant, 68
Friendly Society, 251
Friends, Society of. See QUAKERS
Frobisher, Sir Martin, 41
Full Assurance, 45, 130, 205-208, 220-1, 314, 322-323
Fuller, Dr. Thomas, married sister of Dr. Cornelius Burges, 33

Gambold, John (Oxford Methodist, later Moravian Bishop); his description of the Wesley brothers at Oxford, 90; and of the 'Holy Club,' 91-92; published a *Greek New Testament*, 91n; met John Wesley at Wycombe, where they formulated the 'Yearly Conference' scheme (1739), 327-328
Ganson, Sir John, 300
Garcina (Spanish friar), 65

INDEX

Garden, Rev. Dr. Alexander, of Charlestown, the Bishop of London's Commissary in the Carolinas, 134, 152, 163, 165
Garden, Mr. S., of Charlestown, on Wesley's case, 172
George I, King, Reign of (1714-1727), 52, 53, 72
George II, King, Reign of (1727-1760), 53, 72
George III, King, Reign of (1760-1820), 80, 257
GEORGIA (Chap. vii.), 106-114; Colony of, opened as (1) Home for debtors and other released prisoners (1732-3) who settled at Savannah, 106-108; (2) Home for persecuted Salzburgers (1734) who built Ebenezer, 108-109; (3) Settlement for Scottish Presbyterian Highlanders (1735), 109; Colony first in hands of Trustees, 107; who decide to secure Missionaries for colonists and Indians, 110; and through Dr. Burton secured the Wesley brothers, 110-113; their voyage and work described in Chapters viii. to xi., 115-173; Wesley opposed Slave-trade in Colony, 151; and trade in spirituous liquors, 128; and 'white slavery,' 151
Gerard, Rev. Mr., Bishop of Oxford's Chaplain, 91
Gibbon, matriculated at age of fourteen at Oxford (1752), 69
Gibson, Rev. Dr. Edmund, Bishop of London (1723-1748), greatest expert in Church Law at that time, 117, 234; his *Codex Juris Ecclesiastici Anglicani*, 117; ordained Charles Wesley as priest (Sept. 29, 1735), 112; searches out question of care of Colonies, 163; interviews with the Wesley brothers respecting complaints against their preaching and holding 'Conventicles,' 225-226, 235, 243; opposed to the re-baptism of Dissenters, 225, 235; his *Pastoral Letter to the people of his diocese*, 250; and *Charges to the Clergy of London* (1741), 256; interviewed by Rev. Mr. Stonehouse (Islington), 301
Gidding Hall, 159, 200
Gilpin, Life of Bernard, 188
Gin distilleries, 272
Globe, Dr. Samuel Annesley, Chaplain of the, under the Earl of Warwick (Lord High Admiral), 40
Gloucester, 251, 264, 318, 319
Gloucestershire, 269, 318
Godley, A. D., on 'Holy Club,' 94-95. See *Oxford in the Eighteenth Century*
'Godly Club,' another name for the 'Holy Club' at Oxford, 93
Gooch, Sir Thomas, Bishop of Bristol (1737-38), afterwards Bishop of Norwich, 278
Gough, William (Savannah), 171

Gould, Rev. George, edited documents relating to settlement of the Church of England by the Act of Uniformity (1662), 39
Government under King Charles II, 44
Gravesend, 115-117
Greek (New Testament), study of, revived at Oxford, 89-90
Greek Testament, Charles Wesley's, 90n
Green, Rev. Richard, his *Bibliography of the Works of John and Charles Wesley*, 119n, 318
Greenaway at Tyburn, 217
Greenland, Christian David's Mission to, 206
Grevil, Mr., married George Whitefield's sister, shopkeeper in Wine Street, Bristol, 251, 280
Guinea Coast, British slave-hunting ground, 273
Gulf of St. Lawrence, 264
Gwatkin, Dr., his *Early Church History*, 226, 258-9

Haliburton, Life of Mr., 187
Hall, Bishop, 142
Hall, Westley, of the 'Holy Club,' married Martha Wesley, hence Susanna's description 'my son Hall,' 322-3, 328
Hallam's *Constitutional History of England*, 49, 52
Halle, German education system at, 211; University, 129
Hamlets of England, 32
Hammond, Dr., his *Exposition*, 18
Hanham Mount, Kingswood (Bristol), 281, 282, 291
Hanoverian Kings, 26, 52, 73, 275
Hardcastle, Mr. C. D., on Hymns, 225n
Harper, Mrs., 59. See WESLEY, EMILIA
Harris, Howell, the Welsh Evangelist, 262, 297, 309-310, 324
Harris, Mr., 194
Harrison, Rev. A. W., 90n
Harvard College, Charles Morton as Vice-President of, 47
Haseley Church, 40
Hatch's *Organization of the Early Christian Church*, 165n
Hawk, H.M. sloop, commander of, 115; fitted out for Georgia Coast survey, 118
Hawkins, Mrs., surgeon's wife, on board the *Simmonds*, 123; at Frederica (Georgia), 132-3, 140, 146, 152
Hawkins-Welch conspiracy against the Wesleys and Oglethorpe, 140, 146
Haycroft, Mr., 268
Hayley, 278
Hayward, Dr., examined John Wesley for priest's orders, and gave his strong views thereon, 95
Headingley College (Leeds), 59
Hearne's 'honest men' (Jacobites), 73
Henry III, King, Reign of (1216-1272), 66

INDEX

Henry VIII, King, Reign of (1509-1547), 67
Herbert, George (1593-1632), Rector of Bemerton, 200, 247; his *The Temple: Sacred Poems and Private Ejaculations*, 149, 168; his *A Priest to the Temple: or The Country Parson, His Character, and Rule of Holy Life*, 142, 154; *Life* of (Izaak Walton), 158-159
Herrnhut (Germany), principal Moravian settlement of which Christian David was 'planter' and Michael Linner the Head, 115, 149, 206-211; visited by John Wesley, 204
Hervey, James (Oxford Methodist), member of the 'Holy Club,' 246; John Wesley's memorable reply to his Letter concerning the services at Bristol: ' I look upon all the world as my parish,' 294
Heywood, Oliver, in Lancashire and Yorkshire, 258
Hickes, Rev. Dr., formerly Dean of Worcester, then Bishop of Nonjurors (1693), 122; his *Reformed Devotions*, 122, 144, 149
'High Churchman,' meaning of term, 48-52
Highlanders, Scottish Presbyterian, in Georgia, 109
Hird, Mark, at Frederica, 146-147
History of the American Church (Bishop S. Wilberforce), 163, 165
History of Dissenting Churches (Wilson), 43, 44, 196
History of England (W. E. H. Lecky), 272
History of England (John Wesley), 54
History of the English Church (Frere), 51
History of Methodism (McTyeire), 127
History of the Nonjurors (Lathbury), 101-103
History of the Puritans (Neal), 43, 228, 295
History of Religion in England (Stoughton), 115-116
Hodges, Rev. John, Vicar of Clifton, Bristol, John Wesley takes pulpit of, during his illness (1739), 287
Holiness of heart and life: the aim of the Religious Societies, 12, 15, 19, 20; the quest of John Wesley, 79-81, 83, 119-124, 126-127, 202, 246, 332-335; his *Sermon* before the Oxford University, ' Circumcision of the Heart,' 98
Holland, Mr., visited Charles Wesley and read to him Luther on *Galatians*, 190
Holt, (Norfolk), visited by William Morgan, 95, 96
'HOLY CLUB,' THE (see Chap. vi., 89-105):
Formation, 9, 87-88, 89-90; rules, reading, and methods, 9, 90, 91, 92, 97, 98; had approval of the ecclesiastical authorities for its pastoral work, 91; styled 'Methodists' by Christ Churchman to Charles Wesley, 87-88; styled 'Holy Club' by Mertonman to Robert Kirkham, 92-93; and the 'Godly Club,' 93; undisturbed by raillery, 87-88, 92-93; or by opposition, 93-95; views of Samuel Wesley, junior, 93-94, of Mr. Hoole, 94, and of Mr. Godley, 94-95; praised by Samuel Wesley, senior, 95; Morgan's death, and his father's correspondence, 96-97, resulting in his brother Richard Morgan being placed under Wesley's care, 97; Attack on Club by *Fog's Journal* answered by William Law, 97-98. The following members of Club mentioned:
1. John Wesley (Fellow of Lincoln), 90; Leader, 104
2. Charles Wesley (Christ Church), 90
3. William Morgan (Christ Church), 90, 91, 94-97
4. Robert Kirkham (Merton), 90, 92, 95
5. John Gambold (Christ Church), 90-92
6. Boyce (or Boyse), 95
7. Thomas Broughton (Exeter), 95, 147
8. Benjamin Ingham (Queen's), 95
9. John Clayton (Tutor of Brasenose), 95, 96
10. Westley Hall (Lincoln), 322-3, 328
11. Richard Morgan (Lincoln), 97, 147
12. James Hervey (Lincoln), 246, 294
13. Charles Kinchin (Corpus Christi), 184, 185, 244, 328
14. Richard Hutchins (Fellow and afterwards Rector of Lincoln), 68, 328
15. George Whitefield (Pembroke), 105
The names cover the years 1729 (Nov.) to 1735
The little ' company ' on *Simmonds* created a section of ' Holy Club,' 118, 123
Homilies, The Book of (S.P.C.K.), 182, 186, 221, 243, 244
Hone's *Lives of Eminent Christians*— Dr. Anthony Horneck, in Vol. ii., 10, 11*n*, 20
Hoole, Rev. Mr., Rector of Haxey (Lincolnshire), on ' Holy Club,' 94
Hopkey, Miss Sophia C., afterwards Mrs. Williamson, 155, 160-161. See WILLIAMSON, MRS.
Hopkins (Sternhold and), 122
Hopton, Mrs. Susannah, 122
Horneck, Dr. Anthony (Prebendary of Westminster and Preacher at the Savoy); his ' Religious Societies ' (*cir.* 1678), 5, 10, 11; Rules for same, 10, 11; *Sermons*, 19-20; Sermon before King and Queen, 20

INDEX 345

Horton, Mr., of Georgia, 146, 147
'Hours of Conference,' Charles Wesley's at Bristol, 319
Howard, John, 20, 66
Howe, John, 'the great Mr.', 44; Rogers' *Life of Howe*, 45
Hows, Mr., of Savannah, 164
Hudson at Tyburn, 217
Huguenot refugees in Bristol, 269
Humphreys, Joseph, 309
Hunt's *Religious Thought in England*, 220
Hussey, Joseph, ordination of, 44
Hutcheson, Mr., 151
Hutchins, Richard (Rector of Lincoln College, Oxford, 1744), member of 'Holy Club,' which he joined when Fellow of Lincoln, 68, 328
Hutchings, Mr. John (Pembroke College, Oxford); his Letter of Welcome to John Wesley on return from Georgia, 187
Hutton, Archdeacon, in *History of English Church*, on the 'Persecuting Acts,' 226
Hutton, James, son of Rev. John Hutton, attended Westminster School, apprenticed to a bookseller, 112; affected by Wesley's sermon, 113; active in founding Religious Societies of best religious type in Islington and City, 179; also in his own house, 187, 196, and afterwards at Fetter Lane, 196, 223; visited Newgate with Charles Wesley, 216; lay preacher, 236; *Hymns and Sacred Poems* (John Wesley) sold at his shop, 246; interview with Zinzendorf, 297; Benham's *Memoirs*, 112, 198, 205
Hutton, Rev. John, Great College Street, Westminster, Nonjuror, interested in Religious Societies and held one in his house, 112; John Wesley stayed with Hutton family on way to Georgia, 112-113
Hymn Singing, 116, 122, 144-5, 193, 216, 290, 299
Hymns of Herrnhut Collection, 149; of Isaac Watts, 149, 168; of French and Spanish writers, 148-149; John Wesley's translations from German (see FREYLINGHAUSEN LANGE, RICHTER, TERSTEEGEN, WINCKLER, ZINZENDORF), 145, 168, 225, 247; Charles Wesley's Hymns, 218, 232, 248, 290, 291. See WESLEY, CHARLES
Hymns and Sacred Poems (1739) by John Wesley, with important Preface, 246-8; Part I. shows loyalty to Herbert and the German Hymns, 247; Part II. introduces Charles Wesley's 'Morning Songs of the Renaissance,' 248; James Hutton sent supply to Bristol, 290; used at opening service of 'New Room' at Bristol, 291

Ilminster, 37
Imitatio Christi (Thomas à Kempis), 79-81, 119
Independents, 258
Indian traders, 133; controversy, 145, 150-151
Indians, friendship of, secured by Oglethorpe, 108-9; true descriptions of, 127-8; Missions to, 110, 127; ultimate success of work amongst, 128
Indies, West, 41
'Indulgence' of King Charles II (1672), 43
Informers, 23
Ingham, Benjamin (1712-1772), Oxford Methodist, of Queen's College, Oxford (1732), 95; Missionary to Indians of Georgia with John Wesley, 112, 115; Minister to pioneers at Frederica, 132; met the Society in Savannah, 138-139; went to Cowpen, near Savannah, to prepare for his Indian mission, 153; visited England, 156, and Germany, 204; Letter from John Wesley, 246; mentioned in Wycombe 'Yearly Conference' scheme, 328
Instructions to Missionaries of S.P.G., 113-114, 117-118, 136, 148
Intolerance, Roman Catholic, on Continent of Europe, 107
Ireland and St. Brendan, 270
Irene (Georgia), 154
Ironside, Dr. Gilbert, Bishop of Bristol, 31, 34, 36
'Ironsides,' Cromwell's, 31
Isham, Dr. Euseby, Rector of Lincoln College, Oxford (1731-1744), 68; became Vice-Chancellor of Oxford University (1744), 68
Ivry, Roger (Oxford), 66

Jacobite clergy, 52
Jacobite mob, 275
Jacobite tendencies, Religious Societies suspected of, 26, 52-53
Jacobites, 56, 73, 84
James I, King, Reign of (1603-1625), 39; his Court at Oxford, 70, 72
James II, King, Reign of (1685-1688), 17, 23, 53, 73
Janeway, Mr., Presbyterian divine; John Westley became member of his 'particular church,' 31
Jeffrey's *Thirteen Colonies*, 107-109
Jena (Germany), 129, 130, 182, 211
Jenkins' ears, the fable of, 273
Jenner, Sir H., 117*n*
Jesuit, John Wesley supposed to be a, 318
Jesuit Mission to Red Indians, 127
Jews, Christian (Lord's Day and Sabbath), 101*n*
Jews, Spanish, in Georgia, 148
Job (Samuel Wesley), published 1735, 111

INDEX

Johnson, Rev. John (Vicar of Cranford, Kent), his *Unbloody Sacrifice and Altar unveiled and supported* (1714), 120–121
Johnson, Dr. Samuel, his *Life of Savage*, 252
Jones, Griffith, successful founder of circulating Welsh Free Schools, interviews George Whitefield, 262
Journal of Charles Wesley (March 9, 1736, to November 5, 1756), 109, 154, 190, 213, 214, 215, 216, 217, 222, 243, 244, 296, 297, 298, 302, 304, 305, 306
Journal of John Wesley (Standard Edition), 5; for editor, see CURNOCK; Annotators, 5; referred to, 32n, 76, 82n, 96, 97, 108, 119, 128n, 132n, 136, 138, 140, 150, 152, 162, 166, 167, 175, 176, 177, 178, 182n, 187, 193, 198, 206–7, 209, 233, 282–3, 288–9, 293n, 294, 309, 312, 314, 318, 326, 331, 332, 333; first extract printed at Bristol (1739) by S. and F. Farley, 318
Journal of George Whitefield, 219, 243, 250
Justification by Faith, 181–187; John Wesley answers objections to, in conclusion of *First* STANDARD SERMON, 202–4; defines his position in Preface of *Hymns and Sacred Poems*, 246–7; John Wesley and Bishop Butler on, 314; extracts from *Journal*, 331–2. See FAITH, CHRISTIAN. SALVATION BY FAITH.

Kempis, Thomas à, his *Imitation of Christ* (or *The Christian Pattern*), 79–81, 119; John Wesley's edition (1735), 119
Ken, Bishop, Nonjuror, surrendered diocese of Bath and Wells, 99; his morning and evening hymns (*M.H.B.* 900, 909), 225
Kenilworth, 40
Keynsham (Bristol), 264
Kinchin, Mr. Charles (Fellow of Corpus Christi College), Oxford Methodist, 184, 185, 244; mentioned in Wycombe 'Yearly Conference' scheme, 328
King 'on the throne,' 52; 'over the water,' 52; in council, 150
King's Weston Hill, near Westbury-on-Trym; John Wesley preached there on Ascension Day, 1739, 290
Kingswood (Bristol), 266; George Whitefield preached at, 254, 259, 261, 281, 316; placed on Wesley's 'Plan' of services, 282, 318; Whitefield's testimony to Wesley's work, 315–316
Kingswood School, Whitefield lays foundation stone of the colliers' school, 281–2; John Wesley changed site and laid foundation stone, 292; Whitefield's collections and published sermon on its behalf, 292; John Cennick appointed Master, 308
Kirkham, Miss Betty, daughter of Rev. Lionel Kirkham, Rector of Stanton (Gloucestershire), and sister of Robert Kirkham, the 'religious friend' of John Wesley, 80–81
Kirkham, Robert (Merton College, Oxford), Oxford Methodist, 90, 95; called in scorn by a Merton man a member of the 'Holy Club,' 92–93. See HOLY CLUB.
Kirkham, Mrs., her encounter with Charles Wesley at Gloucester, 319
Knights Templars, and Temple Church, Bristol, 265
Koker, Dr., of Rotherham, 224

Lamb, Mr. George, tried to persuade Parliament to improve criminal jurisprudence (1824), 277
Lambeth, Rector of (John White), 33
Lampoons, Morton's warning against writing of, 48
Lange, Ernst (1650–1727), judge at Dantzic; his hymn: 'O God, Thou bottomless Abyss' (*M.H.B.* 38), translated by John Wesley, 168
Lange, Dr. Joachim (1670–1744), and Religious Society at Altorf, 26
Langton Matravers, 29
Lathbury, T., his *History of the Nonjurors*, 101–103
Latimer, Hugh, Bishop of Winchester, burnt at Oxford (Oct. 16, 1555), 65
Laud, High Churchman, 51; Chancellor of Oxford University, 70
Law, William, of Putney, Nonjuror and Mystic, 97, 111, 119, 222; his *Christian Perfection*, 84, 147; his *Serious Call to a Devout Life*, 83-84; his pamphlet defending the Oxford Methodists from attack in *Fog's Journal*, 97–98
Lay Preachers: Charles Delamotte (in Georgia), 164, 236, 309; Joseph Humphreys (1738) in England, 236, 309; Howell Harris (in Wales), 309; John Cennick (in Bristol, 1739), 309; in Religious Societies, 236
Lay Preaching, practice of, opposed for a time by George Whitefield; Charles Wesley always prejudiced against; John Wesley more liberal and sagacious, 309
Lay Readers in Churches of England in Colonies, 164–5
Leaders of 'Bands,' 196, 199, 283
Lecky, W. E. H., his *History of England* 272
Lending Libraries in America, 21
LETTERS of:
  1. Bishop Benson to George Whitefield, 317
  2. Böhler to Zinzendorf, 182

INDEX

LETTERS of—*continued*
3. William Law's friend with copy of *Fog's Journal*, 97; in which anonymous letter attacking the Holy Club, 97
4. John Wesley to *London Magazine*, 9; Mrs. Pendarves and her friends, 80; his mother, 81-82, 84; his brother Samuel, 93, 111, 287; Mr. Hoole, 94; Richard Morgan, senior, 97; John Clayton, 104; Bishop Potter, 105; William Law, 111; Mr. Hutcheson, 151; Trustees of Georgia, 156; Causton, 169; Mrs. Williamson, 169; Church at Herrnhut, 224; Dr. Koker (Rotterdam), 224; many friends from Charterhouse, 246; James Hervey, 294; John Cennick, 308; Charles Wesley, 311-12
5. Samuel Wesley, senior, concerning Religious Societies (1699), 25; to his wife, 62, 95; to John Wesley, 79, 105; supporting Georgia scheme, 111
6. Susanna Wesley to John Wesley, 58, 79, 81, 105; her daughter Susanna, 59; her son Samuel, 59; her husband, 62
7. George Whitefield to Religious Societies, 194, 195
8. Dr. Francke of Halle to Dr. Woodward, 26

LETTERS to John Wesley from: Dr. Morley, 89, 111; Samuel Wesley, junior, 93-4, 105; Mr. Hoole, 94; John Clayton, 104, 188-9; Bishop Potter, 105; Richard Morgan, junior, 147; William Chapman, 147; Secretary of Georgia Trust, 156; George Whitefield, 178, 262, 308; William Seward, 262; James Hervey, 294; Fetter Lane members, 295, 298; Charles Wesley, 87, 311

Library, Archiepiscopal (Lambeth), 225; Dr. Williams', 44
Libraries, Lending, in America, 21
Licensing of Preachers, 234-6, 260-261, 300, 315, 317
Life of Howe (Rogers), 45
Life of John Wesley (Henry Moore), 77, 85, 86, 94, 111, 172
Life of Wesley (Southey), 242
Life of Wesley (Dr. Whitehead), 326
Lincoln jail, and Samuel Wesley (1705), 53, 57
Linner, Michael (Herrnhut), 207
Little Gidding (Huntingdonshire), 158-9, 200
Lloyd, Bishop, last of the original Nonjuring Bishops, 99
Lockyer, Rev. T. F., 191*n*
Lollards, 69
LONDON, population of, less than 600,000 (in 1737), 249;
Aldersgate Street (Nettleton Court) and John Wesley's conversion, 179, 192-3, 205

LONDON—*continued*
Artillery Grounds, 326
Bishopsgate, 38, 43
Bunhill Fields, 326
Charterhouse, 58, 75, 240, 246
Cheapside, 194
Christ Church, Spitalfields, 249
City Road, 326*n*
City Wall, 41
Drury Lane, 179
Fetter Lane, the Religious Society at, 187, 196; met in old Nonconformist meeting-house with house adjoining (No. 32), 196; John Wesley, President, 200; James Hutton, Leader in Wesley's absence, 200; in connexion with Church of England, 240; not at first a Moravian Society, 302; 'Orders' of, 196-200, 239; gave consent by 'lot' to John Wesley visiting Bristol, 263; tendencies towards Moravianism, 223; Lovefeast at opening of year 1739, 239; divisive influences at work, 240, 244; John Wesley at women's Love-feast, 245; Charles Wesley in charge of, 295-6; Shaw and Wolf disowned membership of Church of England and were expelled, 302; John Wesley's good influence and his power as an administrator, 302-3; Spread of Moravianism, 325: Remnant formed by John Wesley into 'a new Society' at the Foundery, 328
Fleet Prison, 106
Foundery, The Old, in Windmill Hill, near Moorfields, 326-7; ruins of explosion (1716), 327; John Wesley's first service at (Nov. 11, 1739), 327; purchase, 327; New Society's first meetings at (Dec. 24 and 27, 1739, and 1740), 328-9
Great Fire (1666), 41
Great Plague (1665), 71
Great St. Helen's, 43, 183, 237, 249
Holborn, 55, 180
Islington, 42, 179, 214, 215, 233, 326; Old St. Mary's (parish church of), 215, 233-7, 245, 249, 299-301
Lambeth, 21, 33, 225
Little Britain, 189, 190, 246
Little St. Helen's, 43
Little Wild Street, 179
London Bridge, 265
Long Acre Chapel, 183
Nettleton Court, 179, 192, 205
Newgate Prison, 215, 216, 218, 232, 332, 334
Newington Green, 46, 306
Old Street, 326
Paul's Wharf, 183
Pentonville, 42
St. Andrew's (Holborn), 55, 180
St. Ann's (Aldersgate), 183

LONDON—*continued*
 St. Antholin's, 183, 233
 St. Benet's (Paul's Wharf), 183
 St. Botolph's, 215
 St. Clement Danes (Strand), 24
 St. Clement's Rectory, held by Bishop Gooch of Bristol, 278
 St. George's (Bloomsbury), 183
 St. Giles (Cripplegate), 41, 42, 47
 St. John the Evangelist, Friday Street, 41
 St. John's, Wapping, 183
 St. Katherine Cree's, 183
 St. Lawrence's, 183
 St. Mary-le-Bow (Cheapside), 194
 St. Paul's Cathedral, 41, 42, 53, 192, 239, 245; Churchyard, 112
Shoreditch, 42
Spitalfields, 42, 44; Sir George Wheeler's proprietary chapel in, 242
Spital Yard (Bishopsgate), 38
Stoke Newington Church, 306
Temple Bar, 179
Temple Church, 56
Tenter Ground, 326
Tower, 147
Tyburn, 216-7, 232
Wapping Chapel, 147, 249, 304
Whitehall, 20
Williams' Library, 44
Windmill Hill, 326
London Merchant (emigrant ship), 115
London Magazine, 1760, Letter from John Wesley to, 9
Long Parliament (1640-1660), 21
Lopez, Gregory, *Life of*, 119-120
Lord's Day and Sabbath, 101
LORD'S SUPPER: Constant references to attendance of true members of the Church of England throughout the book ; the following are main divisions of the subject :
 1. In the 'regulated' Religious Societies, 13, 17
 2. John Wesley's views on, 82, 90, 103, 117, 325; his sermon *The Duty of Constant Communion* (1733, 1788), 103
 3. Charles Wesley's decision at University, 86-87, 90
 4. Habit of the 'Holy Club,' 87-88, 91, 93, 97-98
 5. The Nonjurors and, 99-100
 6. John Johnson's view, 120-121
 7. Dr. Brevint's view, 121-122
 8. Charles Wesley's view, 142
 9. John Wesley gave to unconfirmed children, 166
 10. But refused to Bolzius the Moravian minister, 166
 11. The Williamson case in Savannah, 169-173
 12. Refused to John Wesley by Moravians at Marienborn, 205
 13. Strict Moravian 'Fencing of the Table,' 205, 209-10
 14. In Fetter Lane Society, 200, 297
 15. Question of Administration by laymen, 297

LORD'S SUPPER—*continued*
 16. Received by members of the Religious Societies in private houses, 236, 283, 311, 320
'Lot,' used by the Moravians, 263; and by the Fetter Lane Society in determining John Wesley's visit to Bristol, 263
Lovefeasts, at Fetter Lane, 239, 306; at Bristol in Baldwin Street Society, 283
Luther, Martin (1483-1546), on *Galatians*, 190; his *Preface to the Epistle to the Romans*, 192, 246
Lyme Regis, 30
Lyne, William, of Bristol, 289

McCullagh, Rev. Thomas, on 'The *Rules* of Society,' 329
Magdalen College, Oxford; Fellows of, and King James II (1687), 53; Dr. Macray's Register of, 69
Mail coaches, 275
Manchester, John Clayton from, 96; Nonjurors of, 96; John Wesley's visit to, 99; John Wesley preached at the 'old church' (now the Cathedral), Salford, and in St. Anne's, 99; further visit, 111
'Man of one book,' A, John Wesley as a, 294-5
Mangotsfield, parish of, Kingswood (Bristol), 254
Mansfield, Lord Chief Justice, on the Somerset case: 'Any slave brought to England became at once free' (1772), 273
Marienborn, Moravian Settlement, of which Count Zinzendorf was Head, 205; Ingham admitted there to Lord's Table, 205; Benham's reason for exclusion of John Wesley, 205
Marriages, irregular, 153, 161-164
Mary II, Queen, Reign of (1689-1694) with King William III (1689-1702), 57
Maryland, Colony of, Dr. Bray's scheme for, 21, 37
'Mass,' The, at Royal Chapel, 24; the form of Communion Service in First Prayer-Book of King Edward VI condemned, 100; but used by Nonjurors of second class, 100; Dean Brevint's treatise, 121
Massachusetts Historical Society, 108-109; State, 33, 109
Massingberds, lords of manor and patrons of living of South Ormsby, 57
Mastin *v.* Escott in the Court of Arches (1841), 116-117*n*
Maxwell, Lady, John Wesley's comforting words to, on Full Assurance, 207-8
May, Sir Thomas Erskine, his *Constitutional History of England*, 257, 277
'Means of Grace,' 323, 325

INDEX

Mediaevalism, 68, 275
Meeting-house (Little St. Helen's, Bishopsgate), of which Dr. Samuel Annesley was minister for over thirty years, 43-44
Melcombe Regis (Dorset) (now part of Weymouth), 31, 37
Merchant, Richard (of Bath), 293
METHODISM, Chronological development of early :
1729.
Charles Wesley formed a little society at Oxford, 87 ; and he received the title ' Methodist ' in scorn by a Christ Church man, 87-88
November.
John Wesley returned to Oxford, the little company was formally organized under his leadership, 89-90 ; and Richard Kirkham reported that he had been rallied by a Merton man as belonging to the ' Holy Club '; ' the *first rise of Methodism* ' (Wesley's *Works*, Vol. xiii., p. 273)
1736.
A Religious Society formed by John Wesley in Georgia, 137-138 ; ' the *second rise of Methodism* ' (Savannah) (Wesley's *Works*, Vol. xiii., p. 273)
1737.
John Wesley published his first *Collection of Psalms and Hymns*, printed at Charlestown, 167-169
1738.
Peter Böhler instructed Wesley, who began to preach ' faith,' 182-189
May 21.
Charles Wesley's ' conversion,' 191
May 24.
John Wesley's ' conversion,' the birthday of historic Methodism, 192-193
1739, February 17.
Field-preaching by George Whitefield at Kingswood, 254
April 2.
John Wesley's Field-preaching at the Brickyard, Bristol—' I submitted to be more vile,' 282
November.
The ' Old Foundery ' acquired, 327
December.
The Foundery Society formed—' the Rise of the United Society ' (Historical introduction to the *Rules of the Society·of the People called Methodists*), 328-329
' Methodist,' John Wesley's qualified use of term, 88 ; in general use, 96-97
Michaelmas Day, 1662, 34
Middle Ages, 275
Mill, influence of, in the study of Greek at Oxford, 89, 91*n*
Milton, John, 41

Missionaries, Irish (St. Brendan), 270
Missionary Martyrs of Church of Rome, 127
Missions to Red Indians, Jesuit, 127 ; Protestant, 110, 113, 127
Mississippi river, 127
Molinos, Miguel de (the Quietist), *The Spiritual Guide*, 149
Molther, Philip Henry, 323 ; his doctrine of ' stillness ' (Quietism), 325 ; introduced to Fetter Lane Society by James Hutton (Oct., 1739), 324
Monk, General, 39
Moore, Rev. Henry, his *Life of Wesley*, 77, 85, 86, 94, 111, 172
Moravian Brethren, the Church of, in Herrnhut, 182, 211 ; constitution of, 208-209 :
 1. ' The Eldest of the whole Church ' : ' Head ' of Settlement
 2. Pastors or Teachers : ' Overseers ' of whole flock
 3. Deacons or Helpers
 4. Second Class of Deacons and Deaconesses
 5. Censors and Monitors
 6. Members in *Classes* according to age and sex
 7. ' Classes ' divided into *Bands* with *Leaders*
 8. Rule as to exclusion of members, 209
Moravian migration to Georgia, 115-118
Moravian ordination of a Bishop in Savannah (Anton Seifart), 132
Moravian Settlements in Germany. See HERRNHUT and MARIENBORN.
Moravian Society in London, 198
Moravians, John Wesley's friendly relations with, 166
Morgan, Richard, senior, an Irish resident in Dublin, views on his son's death, 96-97 ; John Wesley's *Letter* to, 97 ; his confidence in John Wesley, 97
Morgan, Richard, junior, brother of William and son of above, placed later under Wesley's care at Oxford, and became member of ' Holy Club,' 97, 147
Morgan, William (Christ Church College, Oxford), one of first four Oxford Methodists, 90 ; pioneer in prison work and other social service, 91, 94, 95 ; his death, 96-97
Morley, Dr. John (Rector of Lincoln College, Oxford) (1719-1731), 68, 82, 89
Morton, Charles (Wadham College, Oxford), Principal of Newington Green Dissenters' Academy, where Samuel Wesley attended, 46-47
Motte, Rev. Mr., Rector of Newington, asked Charles Wesley to preach (June 24, 1739), 306
Mountnorris, Baron (Francis Annesley), 39. See ANNESLEYS.

Mystic Divines, John Wesley on, 246-7

Nantes (France), Edict of, revocation of (1685), 242

Navy, Work in Army and (S.P.C.K.), 21

Neal, Dr. Daniel (1678-1743), his *History of the Puritans*, 43, 56, 228, 295

Neisser (Moravian deputation with Böhler and Schulius to a Moravian Society in London), 198

Nelson, Robert, his *Festivals and Fasts*, 120

New Inverness (Georgia), 109

Newington at Tyburn, 217

Newport Pagnell (Bucks), 39

Newport (Mon.), visited by George Whitefield, 262; and John Wesley, 324

Newspapers in 1739 (Bristol), 276

Newton, John, 222

New Room in the Horsefair, Bristol, 289-290

'New Birth,' The, 253, 332-333

Nitschmann, David, Moravian Bishop, fellow voyager with the Wesleys to Georgia, 115, 118; with John Wesley at Savannah, 131; ordains Anton Seifart, 132

Nonconformist Fellowship Meetings, 25

Nonconformist Ministers of Seventeenth Century, 38, 258; of London, 42-43

Nonconformists within Church of England, 63, 227-228, 255

Nonconformity, 275; *English Nonconformity* (Dr. Robert Vaughan), 34-36

NONJURORS divided into three classes (99-100):
 1. Those who refused to take the oath of allegiance to William III (1689), 52, 99; yet High Churchmen, 52; who accepted the *Book of Common Prayer*, 99
 2. Those who separated from State Church and formed own Church with consecrated bishops, and ordained priests and deacons, and had their own service book, which departed from the *Book of Common Prayer* in adopting the Communion Service of Edward VI's first Prayer Book, 99-100
 3. A small number forming a separate church ('Separatists') ostracized by other classes because the consecration of their bishop, Dr. Thomas Deacon, was irregular, 100; known as the Nonjurors of Manchester, 96, 99, 100-103; John Clayton (friend John Wesley at Oxford, and member of the 'Holy Club') and Dr. Byrom, associated with them, 96

Norman, Mrs. (Bristol), 308

Norman Period of Architecture, 65

Normanby, Marquis of, afterwards Duke of Buckingham, 56-57

Norris, John, the Cambridge Platonist, 50, 52, 120, 149; his *Christian Prudence*, 120, 123; John Wesley published extracts from it (1734), 120; his *Distinction of High Church and Low Church*, 50; lived at George Herbert's old Rectory at Bemerton (Wiltshire), 50

Northampton (New England), revival in, 223-4

Norwich, in 1739, the third city in the Kingdom, 264

Novels, modern, on Puritans and Dissenters, 38

Nowers, Mr. B. (Fetter Lane Society), 304

Nuremberg, Religious Society at, 26

OGLETHORPE, General James Edward, M.P. for Haslemere, 106; distinguished himself in European campaigns, 106; Chairman of 'Prison Reform' Committee, 106; Plan of Colony for released prisoners, 106-112; Governor of Georgia, 107; appointed Charles Wesley his Secretary, 112 (after Charles' return to England, John acted as Secretary, 152, 155); John appointed Missionary, 112, 113; scheme supported by Samuel Wesley and his son Samuel, 111; favoured migration of Moravian settlers, 115; defended Wesleys on board the *Simmonds*, 122; work at Frederica and southern frontier, 132-133; Hawkins-Welch conspiracy, 140, 146; Indian trade controversy, 149-151; visit to England, 155-6; Hopkey case, 161; John Wesley returned to England and met him in London, 179

Open-air preaching, by John Wesley on board the *Simmonds*, 116, in Georgia, 128, at Tyburn, 233; by Charles Wesley in Georgia, 141, at Tyburn, 217-8, 233, in country places around London, 301-2; by George Whitefield at Kingswood (Bristol), 254; by Howell Harris in Wales, 262. See FIELD-PREACHING.

Orders, Presbyterian, 44, 45

Orders of Religious Societies: Dr. Horneck's, 10-11; Dr. Woodwards' Poplar Book (specimen orders), 12-15; Fetter Lane Society, 196-200, 263

Ordination, among the Dissenters, First public (1694), 44-5; Moravian, 132; Re-, 36, 45, 236; of Dr. Annesley, 40; of Presbyterian ministers, 44; of Joseph Hussey, 44; of Anton Seifart, 132

Organized 'mob' attacks on work of Wesleys, first at Bristol and Kingswood, on Charles Wesley, 320-321

Ormsby, South (Lincolnshire), 57

INDEX 351

Orphanage proposed in Georgia, 154, 249, 250, 252, 259, 261-2
Osborn, Dr. George, 167, 247; his *Outlines of Wesleyan Bibliography*, 225
Osney Abbey, 67
Overton, Canon, his *Life in the English Church* (1660–1714), 5, 21, 22, 24, 25, 27, 110, 255; his *History of the English Church* (1714–1800), 222
Owen, Dr. John, Vice-Chancellor of Oxford University, 31
OXFORD in the Eighteenth Century (Chap. iv.), 64–74
  Bishop's Hole, 65
  'Bocardo' prison for debtors over North gate (old gate-house), 64–66, 92, 137, 147; destroyed 1771, 66
  Castle begun by Robert D'Oilly, 65; visited by John Howard (1782), 66
  Castle Prison for criminals, 49, 91, 92, 137; county jail, 66; after 1771, also for city prisoners, 66
  Cathedral (Christ Church Collegiate Chapel), 87, 91
  Chancellor of University, 66
  Christ Church meadow, 71
  City Walls, 64
  Coffee Houses, 76
  COLLEGES:
  Balliol, 65, 68
  Christ Church, begun by Cardinal Wolsey, finished by Wren, 67; John Conybeare, Dean (1733), 67; Gay Cavaliers (1665) at, 71; became Hanoverian, 73; its scholars included Edward Veal, 46, the three Wesley brothers, 75, 77, 87, 90
  Corpus Christi, 110, 77
  Exeter, Samuel Wesley, senior, at, 48–49, 77
  Lincoln, John Morley, Rector (1719–1731), 68; Euseby Isham, Rector (1731-1744), 68; Richard Hutcheson, Rector (1744), 68; John Wesley, Fellow (1726), 82; its 'golden age,' 68
  Magdalen, Fellows of, and King James II, 53; Dr. Macnay's Register, 69; Lord Clarendon at (1621–25), 70; Election of President, 73, 77
  Merton, 77, 86, 92; Robert Kirkham at, 90, 92
  New College, 77
  New Inn Hall, John Westley at, 31
  Pembroke, George Whitefield at, 105; William Chapman at, 147
  Queen's, Dr. Samuel Annesley at, 40
  Wadham, Henry Dolling at, 46; Charles Morton at, 46–47, 77

  Cranmer, Archbishop, in Bishop's Hole, burnt at Oxford (1556), 65
  During Civil War, 70–71
  Heights of Cumnor, 75

OXFORD—*continued*
  Honour schools, 72
  Intellectual condition, 72–73
  James I's visit, 70
  Latimer and Ridley, Bishops, burnt at Oxford (1555), 65
  Magdalen Bridge, 71
  Map of, by Hollar (1643), 64; by Agas (1578), 64
  'Morals' of, 67, 70–73, 86
  North Gate, 64–65 gate-house became 'Bocardo' prison for debtors, 64–66
  'Reign of Saints,' 71, 74
  Royalist capital under Charles I, 70–71
  St. Ebbs' parish, 147
  St. George's Church, 66
  St. Mary's Church, 84, 98, 201
  St. Michael's (North Gate), 65
  'Scholars,' 69–70
  Surrendered to Fairfax (1646), 71
  Trinity Grove, 71
  University, 25, 64
  West Gate, 67
Oxford, by Boase (Historic Town Series), 64, 68, 70
Oxford in the Eighteenth Century (1908) (A. D. Godley), 64, 67, 69, 72, 83, 89, 94–95
Oxford Methodists. See HOLY CLUB
Oxford Methodists, The, Being some account of a Society of young gentlemen in that city, so denominated (William Law), published anonymously 1733 (2nd ed., 1737, 3rd ed., 1738) in answer to attack on 'Holy Club' in *Fog's Journal*, 97–98
Oxford Methodists, The (Rev. Luke Tyerman). See TYERMAN
Oxford, Story of (Headlam) (Mediaeval Town Series), 71
Oxlee, a layman suggested for the Wycombe 'Yearly Conference' scheme, 328
Oyer and Terminer, Justices of, 227

Papist, John Wesley reported to be a, 318
Parker, Henry (Savannah), Baptism of his child, 171
Parkman, Francis, his description of first Jesuit Mission to Red Indians, 127; his *The Old Régime in Canada*, 145
Parliament, 39, 42; and Dr. Sacheverell, 53; and John White, 55; and Edward VI's Second Prayer Book, 100; Long (1640–1660), 21
Pascal, (1623–1662), 222
Paul the tentmaker, 132
Pendarves, Mrs. (afterwards Mrs. Delany), 80
Penitents, Prayers for, 101
Penitential Office, 101
Pennsylvania, Spangenberg goes to, 132
Pensford (Bristol), John Wesley preached 'near,' 282, 288; small society formed at, 288

INDEX

Persecution of Nonconformists, 46
Peter the fisherman, 132, 239
Philanthropy of Bristol citizens, 277
Phillimore, Sir Walter G. F., 117*n*
Piers, Henry, Vicar of Bexley (Kent), 196, 214, 233-4, 243, 305
Pilgrim Fathers of New England (Dr. John Brown), 33*n*
Plague of London, Great (1665), 71
'Plans,' Precursor of Methodist 'Circuit,' 282, 319
Platonists, School of Cambridge, 50, 120
Playhouses, 13
Plunketts, the, 29*n*
Pluralists, 278
Poetical Works of John and Charles Wesley (Dr. George Osborn), 247
Polhill, Nathaniel (Savannah), 171
Politics and Religion, 26, 32
Pontypool (Wales), 324
Poole (Dorset), 37 ; jail, 37
Pope, Alexander, friend of Samuel Wesley, junior, 84 ; describes Bristol old bridge, 265
Popery, 24, 103, 165, 204
Poplar Religious Society, Book of, 12 ; Specimen *Orders* of, 12-15
Portraits of John Wesley, 134-136. See WILLIAMS
Potter, Dr. John (Bishop of Oxford, afterwards Archbishop of Canterbury) (1737-1747) ; ordained John Wesley as Deacon, 82, and Priest, 83 ; also Charles Wesley as Deacon, 112 ; advised Wesley, 105 ; on Validity of Moravian 'Orders,' 132, 132*n* ; interview with John and Charles Wesley, 243 ; also with Charles Wesley and Henry Piers, 305 ; hints at Charles Wesley's excommunication, 305
Prayer Book, First of Edward VI (1549) and First Act of Uniformity, 99 ; Second of Edward VI (1552) and Second Act of Uniformity, 100, 228 ; revised (1662) and Fourth Act of Uniformity, 35
Prayer Book, Articles, and Homilies, The (J. T. Tomlinson), 100*n*
Prayers for Candidates for Baptism, 101 ; Catechumens, 101 ; Energumens, 101 ; Penitents, 101
Preachers, Wiclif's Poor, 68
Predestination, Appeal of Whitefield and Fetter Lane Society to John Wesley not to dispute at Bristol upon, 285-6, 295 ; John Wesley preaches against, at Wapping, 304
PRESBYTERIAN forms of worship and government, 228 ; Ministers and Act of Uniformity, 35, 36, 44 ; Ministers in England, 44 ; Orders, 36, 44 ; Uniformity, 228
Presbyterianism, 31, 32, 33, 226, 258
Preston, near Weymouth, 37, 38, 46
Primitive Christianity (Cave), 102, 152, 153*n* ; John Wesley's abridgement of, 153*n*

Primitive Christianity Revived (Whitson), 102
Prince Edward's Island, 264
Prince Rupert's Horse at Dorchester, 33
Prisoners, John Wesley's work amongst at Oxford, 91 ; at Savannah, 137 ; at Newgate, 232 ; Charles Wesley's work amongst, at Oxford, 91 ; at Newgate, 215-217, 232
Privateers, Arming of Bristol (Spanish War, 1739), 274
Privy Council, 117*n*
Proceedings of Wesley Historical Society. See SOCIETY, WESLEY HISTORICAL
Protestantism in England, 41 ; Dissenters, 257, 258, 259 ; Reformers, 100 ; View of the Sacrament, 100 ; help to expatriated Salzburgers, 107 ; 165, 167, 227
Provincial Towns of England, moral and intellectual condition, 275
Psalm-singing, 11, 17, 144-5, 147
Publications of Wesley Historical Society. See SOCIETY, WESLEY HISTORICAL
Public Houses, 13
Puritan practice of Fellowship in Church of England, 25
Puritans, 38, 74, 227, 295
'Puritans and Precisians,' 71
Puritans, History of (Neal), 43, 56, 228, 295
Purrysburg, 161
Putney, William Law at, 97

Quakers (Members of Society of Friends), 244, 274-5
Quarter Sessions, Bristol, 317
Quincy, Rev. Samuel, at Savannah, 109 ; his *Account* of settlement in 1735, 109 ; resigned connexion with Georgia, 113, 131, 133, 137

Ratisbon, Religious Society at, 26
Rawlin, Mr. (Independent Chapel, Fetter Lane), 196
Read at Tyburn, 217
Reading, visited by John Wesley, 244 ; stayed with John Cennick, who had formed Society there, 244-245 ; Cennick leaves for Bristol, 308 ; John Wesley met 'little company' at, 324 ; 'zealous mob' there, 324
Reasons (Jeremy Collier), 122
Reck, Baron von, commissary at Ebenezer (Georgia), 109
Reed, Mr. (Frederica, Georgia), 153
Reformation of Manners. See under SOCIETY
Reformed Devotions (Hickes), 122 ; written by Austin ; revised, reformed, and adapted by Mrs. Susannah Hopton ; preface by Dr. Hickes, 122
Reformers, Protestant, 100
'Reign of the Saints,' at Oxford, 71

INDEX 353

Religion in England under Anne and the Georges (Dr. John Stoughton) (2 vols., 1878), 43, 115–116
Renty, Monsieur de, 120; John Wesley's abridgement of Life, 174
Restoration (1660), The, 30, 33, 39, 71–73, 274
Revival, Religious, in Eighteenth Century, 5, 306
Revolution, 'The Glorious' (1688), 24, 44, 49
Reynell, Chancellor of Bristol diocese, 252, 260, 314
Richards, Major (Frederica), 146
Richter's Hymn: 'Thou Lamb of God' (M.H.B. 475), 168
Ridley, Nicholas (Bishop of London, 1550–1553), burnt at Oxford (1555), 65
Rigg, Dr. James H., his Living Wesley, 80, 83
Right to preach in a church, John Wesley's view, 234–5
Righteousness by Faith, 124, 126, 148, 169, 175–178, 181, 201–204, 246, 404
Rights of people in Georgia, defended by John Wesley, 150
Riot Act, 317
Rivington Pike (Lancashire), Conventicles at, 230
Rivingtons (London publishers), 96, 119
Robinson, Dr. J. (Bishop of Bristol, afterwards Bishop of London) (1714–1723), 273
Robson, Rev. Mr., 237; planned with Wesley and Gambold the Wycombe 'Yearly Conference' scheme, 327–8
Rogers, Mr., in Wycombe scheme, 328
Rogers, Henry, his Life of Howe, 45
Roman Catholic intolerance in Europe, 107
Roman Catholics in disguise, in Georgia, Wesleys suspected of being, 147–8
Romanism, John Wesley preached against, 165
Rose Green (near Kingswood, Bristol), 281–2, 291
Rothe, Johann Andreas (1688–1758), Lutheran pastor at Berthelsdorf; his Hymn: 'Now I have found the ground wherein' (M.H.B. 362), translated by John Wesley; they meet, 210
Rotterdam, 108, 204
Roxbury (New England), 127
Royal Chapel, Mass at, 24
Royal Miracle, The (A. M. Broadley), 30n
Royalists, 33, 55
'Rule' of Society (The 'Holy Club') at Oxford, 97–98
Rules of the Society of the People called Methodists, the Historical Statement introducing the, 328–9
Rupert's Horse, Prince, 33

Sacheverell, Dr. Henry, Chaplain of St. Saviour's, Southwark, grandson of John Sacheverell, 54; his sermon (1709), 53; impeachment by Parliament (1710) and Trial, 53; his Speech (written by Samuel Wesley, senior), 53–54; Riots (1710), 53
Sacheverell, John, of Wincanton, ejected 1662, and in jail, 54
St. Augustine (of Canterbury) (597–604), and Kent, 270
St. Bartholomew's Day (1662), 33, 34, 42, 256
St. Brendan, Irish monk, educated by St. Finian of Clonard, settled in his cell on Brandon Hill, Bristol, 269, 270; died 576, 270
St. Cyprian's Works, 174–175
St. Finian, Head of famous school of Clonard after St. Patrick's death, 269
St. Simon's Island (Georgia), 141
Salisbury, John Wesley visited his mother at, 184
SALVATION BY FAITH—first sermon preached at St. Mary's, Oxford, by John Wesley after his conversion (1738), and first of 44 Standard sermons, 201, 215, 221; Wesley's definition of, 201–2; outline of sermon, 201–204
Salzburg (Bavaria), Persecution of Protestants in, 107
Salzburgers, expatriated, settled in Georgia, 107; at Ebenezer, 108–9
Samuel, S.S., on which Wesley returned from Georgia, 174–178
Savage, Richard (poet), kindness shown to, by Abel Dagge (Dr. Johnson's Life of Savage), 252
Savannah, Town of (Georgia), 108; on river Savannah, 108–128; described, 133; civil government of, 133–134; ecclesiastical government, 134; John Wesley's ministry there, 136–173; George Whitefield's ministry, 178–179, 249–250; his testimony to work of Wesley, 179; The Wesley Bicentenary in, 128
'Scenes' accompanying Methodist preaching, in Bristol, 284–287; in London, 304–305; view of John Wesley in Letter to his brother Samuel, 287–8; Bishop Butler discusses with Wesley, 314–315; Charles Wesley's experience in Bristol, 319–320
Schaffhausen, Religious Society at, 26
Schools: King Edward, diversion of, 276; Catechetical, 21; Charity, 20, 92, 154, 211, 276, 292
Schulius (Moravian), 198
Secker, Thomas, Bishop of Bristol (1734–1737), of Oxford (1737–58), and Archbishop of Canterbury (1758–1768), 278
Seifart, Anton, ordained Moravian bishop at Savannah, 132

Z

354 INDEX

Senlac (near Hastings), Battle (1066) of, 28
'Separatists' (Nonjurors), 100
Service Book of Nonjurors of second class, 100; of Dr. Deacon ('separatists,' 1734), 100–102
Seward, William, a Whitefield Methodist, accompanied him to Kingswood Field Preaching (1739), 254, 262; John Wesley received 'substantial' help for Bristol 'New Room' from, 290
Shaftesbury (Dorset), 54
Sharpe, Dr. J., Archbishop of York (1691-1714), showed great kindness to Susanna Wesley, 57
Shaw, Mr., of London (probably John, a Moravian), member of Fetter Lane Society, influenced by French prophets, claimed right of laity to administer Sacraments; adverse influence over Bray and Bowers for a time; he and Wolf believed in an individual Inspiration, leading them to interrupt services in London and Oxford, 297–8; when they renounced their connexion with Church of England, expelled from Fetter Lane Society, 298
Sheldon, Dr. Gilbert, Bishop of London (1660–1663), later Archbishop of Canterbury (1663–1677), endeavoured to suppress Nonconformity, 254; chief responsible for 'persecuting Acts,' 254; Canon Overton's view, 255
Simmonds (emigrant ship); 115; voyage to Georgia (Chap. viii.), 115-125
Simon, Dr. John S., visit to Georgia (1910) and note on failure of Frederica as a settlement, 155*n*
Sims, Mr. Peter (of the Minories), 215
Skidoway (Georgia), 154
Slave-trade in Georgia, John Wesley opposed introduction of, 151
Slavery, 'White' in Georgia, also opposed by Wesley, 151
Smalridge, Bishop, 54
Smithies (or Smythies), Rev. Mr., lecturer at St. Michael's, Cornhill, aided Dr. Horneck in founding of Religious Societies, 5, 10
'Social' Holiness and 'Social' Religion (John Wesley's view of Gospel of Christ), 247
SOCIETIES, RELIGIOUS:
1. *First* Societies in London under Dr. Horneck (1678), 5–11; *Rules* of, 10–11, 20; — Admission, 11; Aim, 10; Contributions, 11; Director to be minister of Church of England, 10; Discourse on spiritual concerns, 11; Fines, 11; Membership, 10; Poor Fund Book, 11; No controversy on Divinity, Church and State Government, 10–11; Personal rules, 11; Prayers to be confined to those of Anglican Church, 11; Reading in Practical Divinity guided by minister, 11; Psalm singing, 11; Stewards, 11
2. *Regulated* Societies in London and Westminster in Dr. Woodward's time, 10–27; Specimen of the *Orders* of his Societies, as contained in the Poplar Book, 12–15, 20; Sole design (Holiness), 12, 14–15, 19, 20; Weekly Meetings, 12; Course of Proceedings, 15–16; Singing, 17; Devotional service, 16; '*Conversation*' on spiritual experience, 16; Typical subjects for *Conferences* on Christian duty, 16; Discourses on the Lord's Supper, 16, 24; *Exposition* of Scriptures and Catechism, 19; Clerical Director, 15–17, 18; Lay Director (or *Steward*), 15–17; Admission, 13; Removal of names, 12; Membership with Church of England, 12, 15; Poor Fund and Philanthropic work, 12, 20, 22; Weekly Contributions, 12; *Influence* for good on Churches and in formation of other Societies, 20–24; commended by Bishop Compton, 24; Objections answered, 18–19; Dr. Horneck's Sermons quoted to prove aim, 19–20; Time of great prosperity (42 in London and Westminster in 1710), 18, 25; Time of partial collapse, 17
3. *Sermon* preached to one of Societies by Samuel Wesley, senior (1698), 25
4. *Letter* concerning Religious Societies, by Samuel Wesley, senior (1699), 25, 62
5. *Unrelated* Societies in places other than London and Westminster, 25; in English Universities, 25; and on Continent, 26
6. *Decline* of Religious Societies, 26-27; suspected of Jacobite tendencies and of political purposes, 26; confused with other organizations, 27; *need* of a greater spiritual intent and wider aggressive extent, 27, 306
7. *Society* called 'The Holy Club' ('Godly Club') and 'Methodists' at Oxford (1729), 89–105
8. *Society*, section of 'Holy Club' on the *Simmonds*, 118, 123
9. *Society* carrying out John Wesley's *fixed idea* in Savannah (April, 1736), 137–138; Wesley forms meeting of 'inner circle' of Society, 143–144; sectional meetings conducted by laity, 144; Moravian influence of hymn-singing, 144–145; formed

INDEX 355

SOCIETIES, RELIGIOUS—*continued*
    'little Society' in charge of Mark Hird (in absence of minister) at Frederica, 146–147
10. *Other Societies* founded in England by members of the 'Holy Club,' 147
11. *New Religious Societies*, formed by James Hutton, of a more definitely *spiritual type*, at Islington and at Nettleton Court, Aldersgate Street, 179; John Wesley converted at latter, 192; most prosperous met in Hutton's house, 196
12. *A little Society* out of Religious Society already existing at James Hutton's house formed by John Wesley and others, May 1, 1738, 178, 196; this afterwards met in Fetter Lane, 187, 196, and whole of Chap. xiii., 194–200; State of old Societies in 1738, 194; Quarterly sermon in St. Mary-le-Bow Church, Cheapside, 194; Whitefield's *Letter* to the Societies (1739), 194–195; *Orders* of the Fetter Lane Society, 196–200; main differences from old Societies: (1) No rule confining membership to those belonging to Church of England, 198; (2) rules for *Bands* and appointment of *Leaders*, 199; (3) increased care in admission and exclusion of members, 199; (4) 'continual intercession,' 200; (5) no mention of the 'Lord's Supper,' or of attendance at Church of England services; it was a Religious Society in connexion with Church of England, 240; not at first a Moravian Society, 302; Relation to Conventicle Act, Wesleys interview Bishop Gibson, 225–226, 230–232
13. *Religious Societies* in Bristol at Baldwin Street, 281, 282, 284–5, 288, 291, 308; Back Lane, 283; Castle Street, 282; Gloucester Lane, 282–3; Nicholas Street, 281, 282, 288, 291, 309; Weavers' Hall, 280, 282, 285, 291; Baldwin Street and Nicholas Street finally joined and formed the Methodist Society in the 'Room,' Horsefair, 288–316; John Wesley wrote out 'Orders' for the 'Bands' on April 3, 1739, and began to form them, 283; his *Expositions*, 283–4; the 'parting of the ways,' 289; Sacrament administered in private houses, 311, 320
14. *A new Society* (Chap. xxiii., 322–335); Wesley opposed Molther's teaching of 'stillness,' 325;

and abstinence from Lord's Supper and other 'means of grace,' 325–326; difficulties at Fetter Lane culminated in action of John Wesley (December, 1739), in historic introduction to 'Rules' (1743), 328–329; 'one condition,' 329; consequences, 330; Wesley's own relation to State Church, 330–332; reasoned statement on Dissent, 333; final summaries of history of Societies, 324, 334–335
Society for Promoting Christian Knowledge (S.P.C.K.) (1698), 21; 'daughter of Religious Societies,' 21; primary objects, 21; supported by Samuel Wesley, senior, 21n; Thomas Broughton (Oxford Methodist) became Secretary, 186
Society for the Propagation of the Gospel in Foreign Parts (S.P.G.) (1701), 21; Dean Willis states design, 110; aid sought for Georgia (1735), 110; appointment of John Wesley, 113; 'Instructions' to Missionaries, 113–114, 117–118, 136, 148
Society for the Propagation of the Gospel in New England (1649), 21
Society for the Reformation of Manners (1692), 22, 306; differentiated from other Religious Societies by admission of Dissenters, 22; 'informers,' 23; resulting prejudice to other Societies, 23, 27
Society of Friends. See QUAKERS
Society, Wesley Historical: *Proceedings* of, 5, 28, 29n, 30, 32n, 33n, 40, 85n, 91n, 105n, 112, 113n, 114n, 187n, 191, 192, 215, 225, 230, 281, 301, 308, 329; *Publications*, 5; *Religious Conference* (1712) by Susanna Wesley, 59–60
Socrates, 311
'Solitary Religion,' Wesley against practice of, 246–7
Somerset, 264, 318
'Somerset case,' 273
South Ormsby (Lincolnshire), 57
Southey, Robert, his *Life of Wesley*, 242
Spangenberg, August Gottlieb (1704–1792), scholar of Jena and lecturer of Halle University; Moravian Elder and Pastor, 115; interviews with John Wesley at Savannah, 129–132; departure for Pennsylvania, 132, 157; with Molther and Wesley at Fetter Lane, 325
Spaniards and Georgia, 107–8, 132, 146
Spanish Armada (1588), 41; atrocities 273–4; friar (Garcina), 65; Jews in Georgia, 148; sherry ('Bristol milk'), 272; language, 148–9
Sparks, Rev. Mr., visiting minister at Newgate, London, 215; persuaded Charles Wesley to visit felons, 215–216; and executions, 216–217

Spectator, The, Addison's Hymns from, 168. See ADDISON
Spence, Dean, his *The Church of England*, 279
Spener, Dr. P. J. (Frankfort), 26
Spital Yard (Bishopsgate, London), 38
Spithead, 115
Sprat, Dr. Thomas (1635-1713), Bishop of Rochester, 55; friend of Samuel Wesley, junior, 84
Stalbridge, 54
Stampe, Mr. George (Grimsby), 81, 90*n*, 111*n*, 187*n*, 188*n*
Stanton (Gloucestershire), 80
Stapleton parish, Kingswood (Bristol), 254
'Stations' (Fourth and Sixth days' Fasts), observing the, 104
Sternhold and Hopkins, 122
Stillingfleet, Bishop, 22
Stolte of Jena, Schools founded through influence of, 211
Stonehouse, Rev. George James (Pembroke College, Cambridge), became Vicar of Islington (1738), 214; 'converted,' 214; Charles Wesley *informally* appointed as his 'curate,' 215, 295, although not licensed to preach in diocese of London, 215; friendly to Wesleys and Whitefield, 299; his Churchwardens forbade Wesleys and Whitefield to preach in pulpit, 299-301; interview with Bishop Gibson, 301; included in Wycombe 'Yearly Conference' scheme, 328
Stokes, Miss Margaret, her *Three Months in the Forests of France*, 270
Storms on voyage to Georgia, 124
Stoughton, Dr. John, 43, 115-116
Strafford, Earl of (formerly Sir Thomas Wentworth), 39
Strahan, Mr. William, London publisher of Wesley's *Hymns and Sacred Poems*, 248
Stuart claimants, 26
—— cause, 52, 73
—— influence on Oxford University, 70-72
—— Pretender (the old), James Edward, died 1765, 274
Sturminster Newton, 29
Subscription to 'Articles,' Controversy on, 219
'Succession Act' (Act of Settlement, 1701), 231
Surinam (Dutch Guiana), 37
Sutton, Rev. Mr., probably Bishop Butler's chaplain, 314
Swift, Dr. Jonathan, after 1713, Dean of St. Patrick's, Dublin, his *Examiner*, 49
Sydney, W. C., 'The Religious World' in his *England and the English in the Eighteenth Century*, 256-7
Sympson, Rev. Mr., mentioned in Wycombe 'Yearly Conference' scheme, 328

Tackner, Ambrosius, passenger on the *Simmonds*, taught John Wesley German, 116; baptized by Wesley, 116; then admitted at once to Lord's Table, 116
Tauler, Johann (1300-61), 137
Taunton, 37
Taylor, Jeremy, his *Holy Living and Dying*, 79-81, 98, 213-214
Telford, Rev. John, B.A., Bishop Bickersteth quoted from his *Methodist Hymn Book Illustrated*, on 'O God, my God, my all Thou Art' (*M.H.B.* 429) (John Wesley's translation from Spanish), 149, 149*n*
—— on Charles Wesley's *first* Hymn: 'Where shall my wondering soul begin' (*M.H.B.* 358), 192
Temperance Reformer, John Wesley as a, in Georgia, 128
Tenison, Dr., Bishop of Lincoln, afterwards Archbishop of Canterbury (1695-1715), 21, 22, 35
Tersteegen, Gerhard (1697-1769), German mystic teacher and poet; his hymn: 'Thou hidden love of God' (*M.H.B.* 531), translated by John Wesley, 225
Theologia Germanica, 120
Thornbury Church being closed to Whitefield, he preached in open air ('played the madman' on a table), 282
Thunderbolt (Georgia), 154
Tillotson, Archbishop of Canterbury (1691-1695), one of foremost supporters of the Religious Societies, 22, 54; his 'Comprehension' scheme, 45, 53
Timbs' *Abbeys, Castles, and Ancient Halls of England and Wales*, 66
Timothy, Lewis, printer at Charlestown (South Carolina) of John Wesley's *first* Hymn-Book, *Collection of Psalms and Hymns*, 152, 164, 167
Tindal's *Continuation of Rapin*, 24; —— *Christianity as old as the Creation*, 219
Tiverton, Samuel Wesley, junior, Headmaster of Blundell's School at, 84, 112, 184
Toleration Act (1689), 231, 257, 258
Tomo-chachi, a Creek Indian chief, and John Wesley, 131
Torbay, William of Orange landed (1688) at, 44
Trade in spirituous liquors in Georgia opposed by Oglethorpe and John Wesley, 151
Tranquebar, Danish Mission (1704-1705) to, 60
Transubstantiation, 103, 142
Trine immersion of infant by Wesley, 131, 171
Trustees for the Colonization of Georgia, 107, 110, 113, 115, 133, 150, 152, 156, 160, 179-180

INDEX

Tucker, Dr. Joseph, Vicar of A Saints, Bristol, 314
Turner, Richard, and his sons, rebaptized, 148
Two Mile Hill (Kingswood), 266, 282, 292
Tybee Island, 128
Tyburn, 216-217, 232-233
Tyerman, Rev. Luke, *The Life and Times of the Rev. Samuel Wesley, M.A., Rector of Epworth*, 47, 48, 53, 54, 62, 79
—— *The Oxford Methodists*, 90, 92
—— *The Life and Times of John Wesley*, 147, 148, 170, 171, 171n, 172, 172n, 156, 160
—— *The Life of George Whitefield*, 178-179, 195, 260, 299, 316

Uchees, Mission to the, 127
Ulster (Ireland), Arthur Annesley (afterwards second Lord Mountnorris) sent as Commissioner (1645) to, 39
Uniformity, Episcopalian, 229. See ACT OF UNIFORMITY
—— Presbyterian, 228
'Uniformity of Public Prayers,' Bill for (1662), 34; *Act*, 33
Union of England and Scotland (1706), 231
Unitarian Churches, 258
University of Cambridge, 25; Oxford, 25
—— Sermons of John Wesley, 98, 201. See HOLINESS and SALVATION BY FAITH
Usage *versus* Express provision of Statute Law, 234
'Usages' of *Service Book* of Nonjurors, 100; of Edward VI's First *Prayer Book*, 122
Utrecht, Peace of (1713) allowed England to supply Spanish Colonies with slaves—hence bought and sold in Bristol (until 1792), 273

Valentia, Viscount (formerly Sir Francis Annesley, Bart.), 39
Vaughan, Dr. Robert, his *English Nonconformity*, 34, 35, 36
Veal, Edward, Principal of Dissenters' College, London, 46
Venn, Dr., 222, 233
VESSELS—*Globe*, 40; H.M.S. *Hawk*, 115, 118; *London Merchant* (Emigrant ship), 115; *Samuel*, 174-8; *Simmonds* (emigrant ship), 115-125; *Whitaker*, 178
Vigilance Committees of Society for Reformation of Manners, 23
Villains, outbreak of (1381), 68
Virginian Company, 163

Wales, 229, 235; George Whitefield in, 262; John Wesley, 324
Walker, Dr., Master of the Charterhouse, 75
Walpole, Sir Robert, 155, 274

Walton, influence of, in study of Greek at Oxford, 89
Walton, Izaak, his *Life of George Herbert*, 158-159
War with Spain (1739-1748), 273-4
Warburton, Dr. William, Bishop of Gloucester, 220
Ward, Dr. Seth, successively Bishop of Exeter and Salisbury, 44-45, 255
Warwick, Earl of, Lord High Admiral, 40
Washington at Tyburn, 217
Waterland, Dr. Daniel, 50, 121, 222
Wathen, Samuel, surgeon's apprentice in Bristol, member of Baldwin Street Religious Society, 308
Watkins, Mr. Samuel, with Mr. Ball invited John Wesley *first* to preach at the Foundery (Nov. 11, 1739), 327
Watts, Dr. Isaac, Hymns of, 149, 167, 168, 225; his Hymn: 'How sad our state by nature is' (*M.H.B.* 269), 168; *Spectator* Hymn, 168
Wedgwood, Miss, her *John Wesley and the Evangelical Reaction of the Eighteenth Century*, 334
Weekly Miscellany, 251
Weinantz, Mr., a Dutch merchant, at whose house John Wesley met Peter Böhler, 182
Welch, Mrs., a *Simmonds* passenger, 140; shared with Mrs. Hawkins in the Frederica controversy, 146
WELLESLEIGH, Elizabeth de, only child and heiress of Sir Philip de Wellesleigh, married in 1420; and the estates passed to another family, 28
——, Sir Philip de, 28; his brother founder of Epworth branch of family, 29
WELLESLEY became name of the Irish branch of the family by decision of the Duke of Wellington (1805), 29
——, Elizabeth de, of Dangan (Ireland), married Sir Herbert Wesley, 29; their son known as BARTHOLOMEW WESTLEY, 29
——, Walter, Prior of the mitred Abbey and Bishop of Kildare, used and signed his name as Walter WESLEY (1539), 29
Wellesleys, the, 29n
Wellington, Duke of, not a Wesley, 29n. See COLLEY, RICHARD.
Wells (Somerset), 259, 318
Wells, Dean of. See CRESWICKE
WELSLEGH (Somerset) (or Welswe) after the tragedy of Seniac (1066) the home of widow and young children of the WESLEY family, 28
WELSLY, early spelling, which soon passed into WESLEY, 29
WELSWE (Somerset) (or Welslegh), 28
Wentworth, Sir Thomas, afterwards Earl of Strafford, 39

INDEX

WESLEYS, the (Chap. ii., 28-38 for Westleys, and 38-45 for Annesleys): their characteristic spirit, ancestry, home, training and education, 28; their rich inheritance, 28; Englishmen, whose original settlement was in Sussex in Saxon times, 28; adult male members of family perished at Battle of Senlac (1066), 28; widow and young children fled to Somersetshire, 28; settled at WELSWE or Welslegh, 28; Epworth branch sprang from brother of Sir Philip de Wellesleigh, 29; name spelt WELSLY, WESLY, WESLEY, and WESTLEY, 29; Irish branch took form of WELLESLEY, 29; we find immediate ancestors among the Dorset Wesleys, 29.

1. WESLEY, CHARLES, A.M. (1707-1788), third son of Samuel Wesley (Rector of Epworth) and his wife Susanna (Annesley); prepared by his mother for Westminster School, 58; declined honour of adoption by Irish branch of Wellesleighs, 29; SCHOLAR OF WESTMINSTER (1716-1726), 84; lived with his brother Samuel there (1716-1721), 84; elected King's Scholar with free board and education (1721-1726), 84; captain of School (1725), 84; elected to Christ Church, Oxford (1726), 84; influenced by his brother Samuel—'a scholar, poet, and Christian,' 84-85; a political and ecclesiastical Churchman all his life, 85; his 'artistic' temperament, 85; Life at Oxford (Chap. vi.), 84-88; first year of 'diversions,' 85; a 'change' to serious thought and steady application to work (1728), 85; sought his brother John's advice as to keeping a *Diary* and its cipher, 85; state of faith and morals in University at the time, 85-86; Vice-Chancellor's *programma*, 86; attendance at Lord's Supper, 86-87; he and his friends called METHODISTS, 87-88; 'The Holy Club' (Chap. vi.), 89-105; work at Castle, 91; he and John walked to Epworth and back (1731), 95; went to GEORGIA (Chaps. vii. to x.), 106-152; as Oglethorpe's private secretary and Secretary for Indian affairs, 112; ordained Deacon (Sept. 21, 1735) by Bishop Potter of Oxford, 112; and Priest (Sept. 29, 1735) by Bishop Gibson of London, 112; preached his *first* sermon in Cowes Church, 118; voyage (Dec. 10, 1735, to Feb. 6, 1736), 119-125; with Ogle-

WESLEY, CHARLES—*continued*
thorpe mainly at Frederica, 132, 139; Hawkins-Welch case, 140; unhappy life in Georgia, 140-141; comfort in his work as a clergyman, 141-142; open-air preacher, 141; work in Savannah, 145; returned to England, 145-146; set sail (1736), 152; abandoned work in Georgia (1738), 180; illness at Oxford and London, 184-189; last talk with Peter Böhler, 189; met John Bray and removed to his house, 189-190; met Mr. Holland and read Luther on *Galatians*, 190; CONVERTED (Whit Sunday, May 21, 1738), 191; wrote his *first* hymn: 'Where shall my wondering soul begin' (*M.H.B.* 358), 191-192; *Pioneer* work of an EVANGELIST (Chap. xv.), 213-222; heightened powers through conversion, passion for souls of his friends, and gifts as a *domestic* Evangelist, 213; conversions of Henry Piers and George James Stonehouse, 214; became informally curate to latter, and preached in his (Islington) and other churches, 215; work amongst felons at Newgate jail and Tyburn, 215-217; addressed mob and began work of Field-preaching, 217-218; his *Hymn to Christ* (*M.H.B.* 115), 218-219, 232; corrected Whitefield's *Journal*, 219; interviewed Dr. Conybeare at Oxford, 219-222; and Dr. Gibson, with his brother John, 225-232; gradually the Wesley brothers excluded from churches, 233-234; interviewed Dr. Gibson again, 235-236; Christmas week 'festival' at Islington, 237; brothers interviewed Archbishop Potter, 243; concerned about state of Fetter Lane Society, 244, 296, 299; his *Hymns* 'the morning songs of the Renaissance,' 248; his great Ascension hymn: 'Hail the day that sees Him rise' (*M.H.B.* 181) also 'Arm of the Lord, awake, awake!' (*M.H.B.* 219), 290-291; his *Journal*, 296; Islington church closed to the Evangelists, 300-301; became a Field-preacher in places outside London, 301; 'scenes' in his services, 304-305; Archbishop Potter's hints at excommunication, 305; Field-preaching at Moorfields, 305; WORK AT BRISTOL (Chap. xxii.), 319-321; organized attacks of 'mob,' 320-321; Jackson's *Life* of, 327

2. WESLEY, EMILIA (Mrs. Harper), daughter of Samuel and Susanna

INDEX 359

WESLEY, EMILIA—*continued*
Wesley; *Religious Conference* written by her mother, 59; read to her mother the story of the Danish mission to Tranquebar, 60; which led Susanna Wesley to great devotion for Christ, 60–61

3. WESLEY, GARRETT (of Dangan, Ireland) proposed to adopt Charles Wesley, 29*n*; but Charles declined, and he adopted Richard Colley, his maternal cousin, 29*n*

4. WESLEY, SIR HERBERT, married Elizabeth de Wellesley of Dangan (Ireland), 29; their son known as Bartholomew Wes*t*ley, 29

5. WESLEY, JOHN, A.M. (1703–1791), second son of Samuel and Susanna Wesley, Founder of Methodism: Influence on Religious Societies, 5; permanent impression made upon Methodist Church, 28; life in EPWORTH RECTORY, 57–58; prepared by his mother for the Charterhouse, 58; inherited his mother's zest for reading, 58; his mother's *Letter* to him on her 'way of education,' 58–59; Epworth Rectory burnt down (Feb. 9, 1709), and John rescued, 60–61; had his mother's special attention on Thursday evenings and became a communicant when eight, 60–61; admitted as foundation scholar to the CHARTERHOUSE (1714), 75; received exhibition of £40, and entered at Christ Church (June 14, 1720), 75; LIFE AT OXFORD (Chap. v.), 75–88; captured by charm of Oxford, 75, 78; undergraduate life, 76–77; his Oxford *Diary*, 77, 77*n*, 79; a 'change' (1721) when he took a more serious view of life, resulting in life-long economy of time and method of work, 77; decides to ente.' into holy orders (1724), 78; his father's advice: 'critical learning,' his mother's: 'practical divinity,' 79; read Kempis and Jeremy Taylor, 79–81; his pursuit of 'holiness,' 79–81; his 'religious friend,' Miss Betty Kirkham, 79–81; *Letter* to his mother (June 18, 1725) with his criticism of Taylor's teaching and her inserted note, 81–82; his preparation for holy orders, 82; ordained Deacon (Sept. 19, 1725) by Bishop Potter, 82; elected FELLOW OF LINCOLN COLLEGE (March 17, 1726), 82; his financial economy and benefaction to his family, 83; obtained

WESLEY, JOHN—*continued*
permission to absent himself from University and become his father's CURATE (April–Sept., 1726), 83; returned to Oxford and elected Greek Lecturer and Moderator of the Classes, 83; also a Tutor of Lincoln College; ordained PRIEST by Bishop Potter (Sept., 1728), 83; returned to Epworth until Nov., 1729, 83; read Law's *Serious Call* and *Christian Perfection*, 83–84; his qualified use of the term METHODIST, 88; returned to Oxford to take up duties of Fellowship at request of Dr. Morley, 89; Leader (Nov., 1729) of THE HOLY CLUB (Chap. vi.), 89–106; cared for religious condition of his pupils, 90; prison and other philanthropic work, 91–92; undeterred by raillery or sharper opposition in the 'enthusiasm' of their life and work, 93; opinions of his brother Samuel, his friend Rev. Mr. Hoole (Haxey), Mr. Godley, and his father (who wrote to their mother of 'the shining piety' of their two sons), 93–95; introduced to John Clayton, 95–96; *Letter* to Mr. Morgan, senior, on death of his son William, and received younger son Richard into his care, 96–97; William Law's defence of attack in *Fog's Journal*, 97–98; preached before University on Holiness, 98; anxieties about his father's health and his own future sphere, 98–99, 105; visited Manchester and introduced by his friend Clayton to the Nonjurors, 99–104; with aid of Clayton, published a *Collection of Forms of Prayer* for every day in the week (1733)—his first publication, 104–105; his father died (April 25, 1735), and question of succession closed, 105; his WORK IN GEORGIA (Chaps. vii. to xi.), 106–173; appointed through his Oxford friend, Dr. Burton, one of Georgia trustees, 110–113; under S.P.G. with Benjamin Ingham as 'Missionaries to the Indians,' 112–113; stayed in London with the Huttons, 112–113; studied 'Instructions' of S.P.G., 113–114; voyage on *Simmonds*, 115–125; with Moravians under Bishop Nitschmann, 115; learnt German under Tackner, 116; his services, 116, 118, 123; his reading, 119–122; Moravian influence on him during storms,

INDEX

WESLEY, JOHN—*continued*
124–125; on Cockspur island, 128; open-air services, 128; interview with Spangenberg, 129–131; at Savannah, 131–134, 136–139, 143–145, 148–152, 153–173; portraits of, 134–136; formed Religious Society at Savannah, 137–139; at Frederica, 140–142, 145–148, 152–153; Love of music and singing, 137, 144, 145; translation of German hymns, 145, 168; and of Spanish hymn: 'O God, my God, my all Thou Art' (*M.H.B.* 429), 148–149; formed a little Society at Frederica, 146–147; prepared Charlestown *Collection of Psalms and Hymns*, 149, 152, 164, 167–169; defended rights of people, 149–150; opposed with Oglethorpe invasion of Carolina traders, 150–1; and introduction of slave trade and ordinary drink traffic into colony, 151–152; at Charlestown, 152, 164; Hawkins episode, 123, 140, 152; Hopkey (Williamson) case, 155–173; RETURN FROM GEORGIA: On *Samuel*, 173–178; reading of Cyprian, 174–175; his self-examination, 175–178; visited Huttons in London, 179; abandoned work in Georgia (April, 1738), 180; some London pulpits closed to him, 180, 183; his growing light: Righteousness by Faith, 181–184; interviewed Peter Böhler, 182–184, 185–187; CONVERSION (May 24, 1738), 192–193; at Mr. Bray's company sang his brother's *first* Hymn (*M.H.B.* 358), 193; formation of new Religious Society at FETTER LANE (May 1, 1738) (Chap. xiii.), 194–200; Sermon before University on 'Salvation by Faith' (June 11, 1738), 201–204; visited Moravian settlements, Germany, with Benjamin Ingham (Chap. xiv.), 204–212; on return found his work in Religious Societies, 223–225; published second *Collection of Psalms and Hymns*, 224–225; interviewed Bishop Gibson with his brother Charles respecting their preaching, and the relation of the Conventicle Act to the meetings of the Religious Societies, 225–226, 230–232; at Tyburn, 232–233; Christmas 'Festival' week at Islington, 237; Lovefeast at Fetter Lane, 239; *Retreat* Room at Charterhouse, 240, 246; French prophets and prophetess, 241–242; Inter-

WESLEY, JOHN—*continued*
viewed Drs. Potter and Gibson with his brother Charles, 243; published *Hymns and Sacred Poems*, 246–248; FIRST VISIT TO BRISTOL (Chap. xx.), 280–295; invitation, 262–263; arrived March 31, 1739, 280; began exposition of 'Sermon on the Mount'—'one pretty remarkable precedent of Field-preaching,' 281; next day began FIELD-PREACHING in Brickyard: 'I submitted to be more vile' (April 2, 1739), 281–2; first weekly 'Plan' of Services, 282; organized 'Bands,' 283; expounded topics that were to dominate his life-teaching: *Sermon on Mount*, *Acts* of the Apostles, Epistle to the *Romans*, 283–284; 'scenes' of Conversion, 284–288; 'New Room' in Horsefair: FIRST METHODIST PREACHING-HOUSE *built*, 289–292; School at Kingswood, 292; encounter with Beau Nash at Bath, 293–294; Letter to Hervey: 'I look upon all the world as my parish,' 294–295; return to London respecting Fetter Lane Society, 295, 302–303; his powers as an administrator, 302–303; returned to WEST OF ENGLAND (Chap. xxii.), 308–321; assisted by John Cennick, 308–310; most churches closed against him and against Sacrament to his followers, 311; administration in private houses, 311; interviewed Bishop Butler, 312–315; testimony of Whitefield to his Bristol ministry, 315–317; 'unlicensed' preaching, 317; suspected of being a Papist and Jesuit, 317–318; published first extract of *Journal*, 318 (also see references and quotations: 32*n*, 82*n*, 96, 97, 108, 119, 128*n*, 132*n*, 136, 138, 150, 152, 162, 166, 167, 175, 176, 177, 178, 182*n*, 187, 193, 198, 206–207, 209, 233, 282–283, 288–289, 293*n*, 294, 309, 312, 314, 326, 331, 332, 333; see JOURNAL and CURNOCK); widening sphere of work, 318–319; visited London, 322, 324, 328; Oxford, 324; Bristol, 324, 328; Wales, 324; conversation with his mother, 322–23; concerned about condition of Fetter Lane Society, 324–326; begins work at the FOUNDERY (first *acquired* Methodist preaching-house), 326–327; Wycombe 'Yearly Conference' scheme with Gambold 327–328; founded a

INDEX

WESLEY, JOHN—*continued*
NEW SOCIETY (Dec., 1739), at the Foundery (Chap. xxiii.), 328-335; Historical introduction to the *Rules of Society*, 328-329; wider view and wider sphere of his life's work, with contrast of the Wesley of the 'Holy Club' and Georgia with the Wesley of 1739, 311-312, 334-335

6. WESLEY, MARTHA, daughter of Samuel and Susanna Wesley, married Westley Hall (Oxford Methodist), whom Susanna calls ' my son Hall,' 322-323

7. WESLEY, SAMUEL, A.M. (1662-1735), son of John Westley, and father of John and Charles Wesley; born and baptized at Winterbourne Whitchurch (Chap. iii.), 46-63; educated at Dorchester Free School and at Dissenting Academies in London and Stoke Newington, 46-47; servitor at Exeter College, Oxford, 48-49; abandoned Nonconformity and became enthusiastic Churchman and antagonist of Dissent, 48, 49-52; retained Evangelical doctrines, 48-49; wrote Dr. Sacheverell's Trial speech, 53-54; ordained Deacon (1688) by Bishop Sprat, and Priest (1689) by Bishop Compton, 55; married SUSANNA ANNESLEY (Chap. iii.), 55-63; great poverty, 56-57; Rector of South Ormsby (1691-1697), 57; Rector of Epworth (1697-1735), 57; imprisoned for debt in Lincoln jail (1705), 53, 57; supporter of RELIGIOUS SOCIETIES, preached *Sermon* to one of them (1698), and published *Letter* (1699) concerning them, 25, 62; supported S.P.C.K., 21n; and Georgia scheme, 111; his volume on *Job*, 111; Convocation man, 54, 58, 60; his *Hymn* ' Behold the Saviour of mankind' (*M.H.B.* 168), 216; objected to his wife's ' Conventicle ' in the Rectory, and her reply, 62-63; his notebook, 77n; visited his sons at Oxford and wrote to his wife of their ' shining piety,' 95; closing days, 98, 99, 105

8. WESLEY, SAMUEL, A.M. (1690-1739), brother of John and Charles Wesley; his mother and, 59; at Christ Church, Oxford, 75; head usher at Westminster school, 84; married Ursula, daughter of Rev. John Berry, M.A., 84; provided home and education at Westminster for his brother Charles (1716-1721), 84; High Churchman, 84;

WESLEY, SAMUEL—*continued*
consulted by his brother John on ' Holy Club,' 93-94; friendship with and defence of Bishop Atterbury—the Jacobite—prejudiced his position and prevented promotion, 84; friend of Bishop Sprat and acquaintance of Alexander Pope, 84; became Headmaster of Blundell's school, Tiverton, 84; eulogized Oglethorpe's work, 111; his *Hymns to the Trinity* appeared in John Wesley's Charlestown *Collection*, 168

9. WESLEY, SUSANNA (1669-1742), daughter of Dr. Samuel Annesley, born in London (Chap. iii.), 55-63; friendship with Samuel Wesley, 56; studied Episcopalianism and accepted Church of England position, 56; a Jacobite, 56; married Rev. Samuel Wesley (1688), 56; mother of Samuel, John, and Charles Wesley, 58-59; received much kindness from Archbishop Sharpe, of York, 57; care for her children's education and salvation, 58, 61; her ' way of education ' explained in her *Letter* to John (1732), 58; her *Religious Conference* with her daughter Emilia (1712), 59-60; her *Religious Society* in Epworth Rectory with its effects on both church and people, 61-62; her successful defence of her action in holding the so-called ' Conventicle,' 62-63; her *Letters* to her husband, 62-63; her son Samuel, 59, her daughter Susanna, 59, and her son John at Oxford, 79; approved of Georgian scheme for her sons: ' Had I twenty sons I should rejoice that they were all so employed,' 111; approved of ' Field-preaching,' 323; spoke of her father's ' Assurance ' of acceptance in Christ, 323; her winsome charm and cultured mind, 55, 56, 58, 63, 322; John Wesley's indebtedness to his mother, 60, 61, 85; references to her in Mrs. Clarke's *Susanna Wesley* (Eminent Women Series), 38, 55, 58, 59, 61-63; her watchful love over her daughters, 63

10. WESLEY, SUSANNA (Mrs. Ellison), daughter of Samuel and Susanna Wesley, stayed with her uncle Annesley in London after the Rectory fire, 59; her mother's *Letter* to her quoted, 59

Wesleyan Conference Office Safe contains certificates of Charles Wesley's ordination, 112

Wesley Bicentenary in Savannah, 128
Wesley Family (Dr. Adam Clarke), 57, 60
Wesley Historical Society. See SOCIETY, WESLEY HISTORICAL
Wesley's *Short History of Methodism*, 88
Wesley's *Works*, 8vo ed. quoted, 9, 88, 103, 119, 122, 151, 158, 166, 202, 208, 236, 327
WESLY, JOHN, the signature of John Westley, 32n
West Indies, 41 ; Bristol's trade with the, 264, 271
Westbury-on-Trym, 290
WESTLEY, BARTHOLOMEW (cir. 1600–1671), head of the Epworth branch of the Wesleys and great-grandfather of the Founder of Methodism, son of Sir Herbert Wesley, of Westleigh, Devon, and of Elizabeth de Wellesley, of Dangan, Ireland (Chap. ii.), 28–38 ; early life in Bridport, 29 ; at Oxford, 29 ; married daughter of Sir Henry Colley, of Kildare, 29 ; Vicar of Charmouth and Catherstan (Dorset) (1645–1662), 29–30 ; a Nonconformist and loyal to the Commonwealth, 30 ; ejected from living, 30 ; employed as a physician, 30 ; attempted to frustrate escape of Charles II to France, 29–30 ; died at Lyme Regis, 30
WESTLEY, JAMES, a Bailiff of Bridport (1681), 29
WESTLEY, JASPER, of Weymouth (1655), 29
WESTLEY, JOHN (Prebendary and Vicar of Sturminster Newton), 29
WESTLEY, JOHN (Rector of Langton Matravers), 29
WESTLEY, JOHN, A.M. (1636–1670), son of Bartholomew and grandfather of John Wesley (Chap. ii.), 30–38 ; born at Bridport or its suburb Allington, 30 ; student of New Inn Hall, Oxford, 31 ; a Nonconformist lay preacher, 31, 37 ; Vicar of Winterbourne Whitchurch (Dorset) (1658), 32 ; married daughter of John White, ' the patriarch of Dorchester' and niece of Dr. Thomas Fuller, ' the church historian,' 33 ; his *Diary* used by Dr. Calamy in his work, 30 ; his note-book, 77n ; his portrait, 30 ; explained ' conversion ' to Bishop Ironside, 31 ; before Bishop of Bristol, 34, 36 ; in Blandford jail, 34 ; ejected from living (1662), 34–36, 229 ; removed to Melcombe Regis, other temporary resting-places, and Preston (near Weymouth), 37 ; pastor at Poole (Dorset), 37 ; early death, and burial (probably at Preston), 37–38
WESTMINSTER, Religious Societies at, 10, 112 ; brother Samuel's ' boarding-house ' for Westminster boys, 84 ; School, and Samuel and Charles Wesley at, 58, 84 ; John at Mr. Hutton's home at Great College Street, 112, 179, 193 ; John Wesley preached at St. John the Evangelist's Church, Millbank, 180 ; Charles Wesley preached ' salvation by Faith ' in the Abbey, 215 ; scene in Whitefield's service at St. Margaret's Church at, 251 ; Bishop Secker of Bristol held a Rectory at, 278
Westminster Magazine, Mr. Badcock's estimate of John Wesley at Oxford in, 77
Weymouth, 31, 37
Wheeler, Sir George, proprietary chapel of, in Spitalfields, 242–243
Whitaker, ship which took George Whitefield to Georgia, 178
WHITE, JOHN (1575–1648), Rector of Holy Trinity (1606) and the ' patriarch of Dorchester,' 33 ; married sister of Dr. Cornelius Burges, 33 ; father of Mrs. John Westley, 33 ; Rector of Lambeth during Civil War, 33 ; Member of Westminster Assembly of Divines, 33
WHITE, JOHN, father of Dr. Annesley's second wife, and grandfather of Mrs. Susanna Wesley, 55 ; a grave lawyer and M.P. for Southwark, 55 ; defends action of the House of Commons respecting clergy, 55 ; Chairman of Grand Committee of House, 55 ; his *Century of Scandalous Priests*, 55 ; appointed a lay-assessor of the Westminster Assembly of Divines, 56 ; buried in Temple Church, London, 56
White's Hill, near Bradford (Wilts), 309
Whitechapel Rocks, 30
WHITEFIELD, GEORGE (1714–1770) (Oxford Methodist), of Pembroke College, member of the ' Holy Club,' 105 ; took Wesley's place in GEORGIA, 178–179 ; *Letter* to John Wesley from the Downs, 179 ; four months' successful work, 178 ; testimony to Wesley's work, 179 ; his *Letter* to the Religious Societies, 194–195 ; return from Georgia (1738), 237 ; Christmas ' Festival week ' in Islington, 237 ; at Fetter Lane Lovefeast, 239 ; ' on the wing,' having returned to England only to be ordained priest and to collect money for proposed Georgia orphanage, 237–238, 249 ; his work in LONDON and BRISTOL (Chap. xviii.), 249–263 ; his former popularity before going to Georgia gone, 249 ; under same embargo as the brothers Wesley, 249 ; bad impression produced by his published *Journal*, 243, 250 ; criticisms of, in Bishop of London's

INDEX 363

WHITEFIELD, GEORGE—continued
Pastoral Letter (August 1, 1739), 250; friendly attitude to Dissenters, 250–251; disturbance at 'Friendly Society' service at St. Margaret's, Westminster, 251; his 'elastic' Churchmanship, 251; visited BRISTOL, and stayed with his sister, Mrs. Grevil, 251; churches close against him, 252; preached in Newgate jail, Bristol, 252–253; found ecclesiastical 'No Man's Land,' and preached to Kingswood colliers in open air (Feb. 17, 1739), and continued services, 253–254, 259, 261; preached in three Bristol churches, 259; interview with Chancellor Reynell, 260–261; preached in open air at Bath and Bristol bowling-green, 261; met Griffith Jones, 262; excursion into Wales, visiting Societies there, 262; interview with Howell Harris, 262; invited John Wesley to Bristol to take up his work on his return to Georgia, 262–263; their conversation on the work, 280; his last Sunday at Bristol (April 1, 1739), 281; his exclusion in London with the Wesleys from Islington Church, 299–301; preached to crowds in Moorfields, Kennington Common, and Blackheath, 301; week's return visit to Bristol, 315; his testimony to Wesley's work there, 315

Whitehead, Dr. John, executor of John Wesley's will, and wrote *Life of Wesley*, 84, 224, 326, 327n, 328

Whitson's *Primitive Christianity Revived*, 102

Wiclif, Dr. John (1324–1384), Master of Balliol Hall, Oxford (1361), 68; his 'Poor preachers,' 68

Wilberforce, Bishop Samuel, his *History of the Protestant Episcopal Church in America*, 163, 165

Wilkins, Dr., Bishop of Chester, opposed the new Conventicle Act (1670), 43

William of Orange, landed at Torbay (Nov. 5, 1688), 54, 52

William III, King, Reign of (1689–1702) and Mary II, Queen, Reign of (1689–1694), 9, 14, 18, 20, 25, 44, 50, 52, 53, 73

Williams, Captain (Savannah), reported in Bristol that John Wesley was a Papist, 318

Williams, Dr. Daniel, founder of Library, 44; preached Dr. Annesley's funeral sermon, 44; assisted in public ordination of Dissenters, 44

Williams, John Michael, R.A., the portrait of John Wesley (1743) by, in Didsbury College, Manchester, 135; its description by Rev. Richard Green, 135; its effect on Dr. Alexander McLaren, 135

Williamson, William, and his wife (née Miss Sophia C. Hopkey, 161–162, 169–173

Willis, Dean, on design of the S.P.G., 110

Willis, Mr., house of, where Charles Wesley gave the sacrament to the Kingswood colliers, 320

Wilson, Walter, on *History of Dissenting Churches*, 43, 44, 196

Wiltshire, 318

Wincanton, 54

Winckler's Hymn: 'Shall I for fear of feeble man' (*M.H.B.* 459), translated by John Wesley, and published in his second *Collection of Psalms and Hymns*, 225

Winterbourne Whitchurch (Dorset), 32, 33, 34, 36, 48

Wolsey, Cardinal (died 1530), 67

Wood, Anthony à, his *Athenae Oxoniensis* quoted, 29; quoted from Boase, 70

Woodward, Dr. Josiah (Minister of Poplar), wrote an *Account of the Rise and Progress of the Religious Societies* (1698–1701, 4th ed. 1712, 6th ed. 1744), 10–16, 18–20, 22–24, 25, 334; *Account* translated into German, 26; and gave impetus to the movement on the Continent as well as within the Church of England, 26

Woolwich, 327

Worcester, Battle of (Sept. 3, 1651), 30

Wordsworth, Christopher, on Oxford, 69

Wren, Sir Christopher, 67

Wroot (Lincolnshire), parish of, associated with parish of Epworth, under Samuel Wesley, senior, Rector of Epworth; John Wesley his father's curate there, 83

Wycombe, John Wesley met Religious Society and preached there; also met his friend John Gambold, and they drew up a 'Yearly Conference' scheme, never carried out, 327–328

Xavier, Francis, Jesuit Missionary from Portugal to the East Indies (1541), and to Japan (1549), died 1552; John Wesley on board the *Simmonds* read his *Life*, 119

York, in 1739, the fifth city in the Kingdom, 264
—— Castle, Oliver Heywood in, 258

Zinzendorf, Count von (1700–1760), Moravian Bishop (1737), 115, 198, 205, 210, 242, 297; his Hymn: 'O Thou to whose all-searching sight' (*M.H.B.* 476) translated by John Wesley and published in his second *Collection of Psalms and Hymns*, 225

www.ingramcontent.com/pod-product-compliance
Lightning Source LLC
Chambersburg PA
CBHW071150300426
44113CB00009B/1152